REVOLUTIONARY A
1750–1815

Sources and Interpretation

Cynthia A. Kierner
University of North Carolina at Charlotte

Prentice
Hall

Upper Saddle River, New Jersey 07458

Library of Congress Cataloging-in-Publication Data

Revolutionary America, 1750–1815: sources and interpretation/[edited by] Cynthia A. Kierner.
  p. cm.
  Includes bibliographical references (p.).
  ISBN 0-13-089867-8
  1. United States—History—Revolution, 1775–1783—Sources, 2. United
  States—History—Revolution, 1775–1783. I. Kierner, Cynthia A. (date)

E203 R47 2002
973.3—dc21   2002075259

Senior Acquisitions Editor: Charles Cavaliere
Editorial Assistant: Adrienne Paul
Production Editor: Jean Lapidus
Copy Editor: Stephen C. Hopkins
Prepress & Manufacturing Buyer: Sherry Lewis
Photo Researcher: Elaine Soares
Image Permission Coordinator: Charles Morris
Formatting and Art Manager: Guy Ruggiero
Artist: Mirella Signoretto
Cover Image Specialist: Karen Sanatar
Cover Design: Maureen Eide
Cover Art: "Raising the Liberty Pole."
Courtesy of The Library of Congress

This book was set in 10.5/12 Palatino by Interactive Composition Corporation
was printed and bound by Courier Companies, Inc. The cover was printed by
The Lehigh Press, Inc.

 © 2003 by Pearson Education, Inc.
Upper Saddle River, New Jersey 07458

Printed in the United States of America
10 9 8 7 6 5 4 3 2 1

ISBN 0-13-089867-8

PEARSON EDUCATION LTD., London
PEARSON EDUCATION AUSTRALIA PTY, Limited, Sydney
PEARSON EDUCATION SINGAPORE, Pte. Ltd.
PEARSON EDUCATION NORTH ASIA LTD., Hong Kong
PEARSON EDUCATION CANADA, LTD., Toronto
PEARSON EDUCACIÓN DE MEXICO, S.A. de C.V.
PEARSON EDUCATION–Japan, Tokyo
PEARSON EDUCATION MALAYSIA, Pte. Ltd.
PEARSON EDUCATION, Upper Saddle River, New Jersey

CONTENTS

Chapter 2
Languages of Liberty 29

Chapter 3
Reform and Resistance 54

Chapter 4
The Road to Rebellion   *85*

Chapter 5
Asserting Independence   *114*

Chapter 6
Times That Tried Men's Souls   *141*

Chapter 7
A World Turned Upside Down   *170*

Chapter 10

Federalists and Antifederalists   *255*

Chapter 11

The Federalist Era   *286*

Chapter 12
Forging a National Culture

DOCUMENTS

Chapter 13
Securing the Revolution

DOCUMENTS

Chapter 14

Remembering the Revolution

DOCUMENTS

PREFACE

The American Revolution is the single most important event in the history of the United States. It occasioned the world's first colonial war of liberation and resulted in the creation of its most stable and enduring republic. The Revolution transformed American politics, uniting thirteen disparate colonies, first in war and then in peace, and leading loyal subjects of George III to reject first their king and then monarchy itself. Revolutionary notions of liberty and equality informed a wide range of political and social reforms, from the liberalization of suffrage requirements to the abolition of slavery in the northern states. The ideals and achievements of the Revolution also justified the westward expansion of the United States and encouraged Americans to undertake a second war against Britain in 1812.

Revolutionary Americans engaged in a process of nation-building in both the institutional and cultural senses. They established political institutions that represented and empowered a republican union of states—a process that culminated with the ratification of the U.S. Constitution. Although most Americans today regard the drafting and adoption of the Constitution as the logical, even inevitable, result of American independence, many contemporaries opposed ratification because they saw the document's strongly national orientation as antithetical to the ideals of revolutionary republicanism. Members of the revolutionary generation also attempted to construct and define an American national identity. Seeking to promote national self-consciousness among citizens of the republic, they encouraged those citizens to imagine themselves as a purposefully united political and cultural community. A protracted and far from conclusive project, defining what it meant to be an American was nonetheless a central part of the revolutionary phenomenon for both contemporaries and subsequent generations.

Although fighting and winning the War of Independence was an essential aspect of Americans' revolutionary experience, the Revolution proved to be much more than a military conflict. Because the Revolution was also a political event, this book examines the ideas, interests, and actions that contributed to changes in how people thought about politics. In turn, these changes in political thought brought about the destruction of the old colonial order and the creation of new state and national governments. Because the Revolution was a social and cultural phenomenon, this book also explores how social rank, religion, gender, and race affected and were affected by the revolutionary experience, and how Americans used education, civic ritual, and material culture to respond to the challenges of their times.

A broad understanding of the Revolution as both a war for independence and an occasion for political, social, and cultural conflict and transformation requires an equally expansive chronology. Even if the War of Independence ended officially in 1783, and the implementation of the Constitution in 1789 formally resolved the most pressing political problems arising from independence, it took years—sometimes even decades—for Americans to sort out some of the most important ramifications of the Revolution. At the same time, while the Declaration of Independence marked the formal beginning of the Revolution—at least from the perspective of its supporters—the causes of that declaration reach back to the imperial crisis of the mid-1760s and sometimes even farther. In order to examine the sources of both instability and strength in the British Empire, my narrative begins in the mid-eighteenth century; it ends with the more or less successful conclusion of the War of 1812, which secured the ideals and objectives of the Revolution in the minds of many Americans.

This book includes both contemporary documents and an interpretive narrative. Although the latter can tell students what historians have said about the revolutionary era and supply background and context for the uninitiated, my main purpose in writing this book was to allow a representative cross section of people from the revolutionary era to speak for themselves.

I have benefited from the assistance and insights of many individuals and institutions in the course of preparing this text. The Interlibrary Loan staff at the University of North Carolina at Charlotte flawlessly processed my countless requests for obscure books and documents. The Graduate School at UNC-Charlotte provided funding for some of this book's illustrations. Students in my seminar on Revolutionary America tested documents for the final chapter on historical memory. Professor Jean B. Lee, University of Wisconsin, Madison, offered valuable input. At the New-York Historical Society, Mariam Touba reproduced a particularly rare newspaper that was not available on microfilm, for which I am most grateful. At Prentice Hall, Charles Cavaliere was patient, knowledgeable, and supportive—in short, an ideal editor. Jean Lapidus ably saw the project through production, and Stephen C. Hopkins was an excellent copyeditor. At home, Tom, Zachary, and Anders let me work, and then went to the beach with me when I was done.

The author also thanks the following reviewers for their valuable input: Professor Sheila Skemp, University of Mississippi; Professor Scott Casper, University of Nevada, Reno; Professor Stanley Harrold, South Carolina State University; Professor Joseph C. Morton, Northeastern Illinois University; and Professor Virginia DeJohn Anderson, University of Colorado.

Cynthia A. Kierner

Charlotte, North Carolina

CHAPTER ONE

THE BONDS OF EMPIRE

The story of the American Revolution is in large part that of the creation of a distinct American identity. A first and essential step came when colonists sensed that they were in some fundamental ways different from the inhabitants of the British Isles, with whom they shared a venerable constitutional tradition, a self-conscious Protestantism, and a network of commercial relationships that were for many both convenient and profitable. As late as a decade or so before independence, most white inhabitants of British colonial America considered themselves European and for the most part British. When they identified themselves with the New World, they saw themselves as part of a local community or as Virginians, Pennsylvanians, New Englanders, or inhabitants of other colonies.

For colonists, the bonds of empire were both empowering and somewhat debilitating, both reassuring and unsettling. Politically, American inhabitants of the British Empire celebrated their good fortune in possessing the rights of Englishmen and benefited from British military protection, but some also resented London's occasional interference in their own colonial governments. Religion, which united Britons and colonists in their Protestant antipathy toward Roman Catholicism, also became a source of contention as some non-Anglicans came to resent the privileges of the Church of England in the colonies. Efforts to centralize the authority of the Church of England also angered many of its American members. Trade also became a source of both unity and discontent, promoting prosperity and greater access to consumer goods

1

throughout the Empire, even as imperial trade regulations sometimes benefited Great Britain at the colonists' expense.

In 1750, Britain's North American Empire embraced the thirteen mainland colonies that spanned the continent from New England to Georgia, along with smaller settlements in Newfoundland and Nova Scotia and on eight Caribbean islands. The oldest of those colonies, Virginia, had been founded in 1607; the newest, Georgia, had received its royal charter in 1732. While most of Britain's America colonies were established and first settled by emigrants from the British Isles, others had been founded by—and later seized from—England's European rivals. In 1655, for instance, the English took possession of the Spanish colony of Jamaica, and the colony of New Netherland became the English provinces of New York and New Jersey in 1664, when England defeated the Dutch in the second of three major seventeenth-century wars. In the eighteenth century, the British colonies stretched contiguously along the Atlantic seaboard and their inhabitants spread increasingly inland. Active or potential enemies surrounded the British provinces: the French in Canada and the Great Lakes region, the Spanish in Florida, and native Americans to the west.

At midcentury, the population of British colonial America was diverse and growing, both in numbers and in terms of the territory it covered. The thirteen mainland provinces had a combined population of roughly 1.5 million, of whom about 230,000 were enslaved Africans; by 1775, the colonial population would increase to 2.6 million, including some 540,000 slaves. By the 1750s, settlers had moved westward to the Appalachian Mountains, filling the backcountry of Pennsylvania, Maryland, Virginia, and the Carolinas in subsequent decades. The ethnic composition of the New England colonies—Massachusetts, Connecticut, Rhode Island, and New Hampshire—was overwhelmingly English, but elsewhere the inhabitants were far more diverse. The Dutch presence was significant in New York and New Jersey, and German colonists were numerous in Pennsylvania and throughout the southern backcountry. Ulster Scots—more commonly known as Scots-Irish—accounted for the majority of backcountry settlers and were strongly represented in every colony south of New England. People of African origin or descent resided in every province, although the vast majority labored on the tobacco and rice plantations of the southern colonies.

The economy of British colonial America, like its population, was varied and expanding during the eighteenth century, though it remained overwhelmingly agricultural. Grain, much of which was exported to the sugar-producing West Indies, was the staple crop of the Middle Colonies of Pennsylvania, New York, and New Jersey. Chesapeake tobacco and

Carolina rice and indigo were valuable agricultural staples that planters typically exported to Britain.

Throughout the colonies, population growth and territorial expansion made for an increasingly productive economy, as well as a growing market for consumer goods, most of which the colonists imported from Great Britain. Colonial trade—both imports and exports—increased dramatically during the eighteenth century. Conversely, trade with America was the fastest growing segment of British commerce after 1700. As officials in London came to recognize the commercial value of the colonies, they took steps to augment imperial authority.

Those steps, it would turn out, gradually undermined the colonists' conception of the imperial bond as a source of political liberty. Many colonists professed pride in their membership in the British Empire, in part because, like the king's subjects in Britain itself, they supposed themselves endowed with an array of legal and constitutional rights without parallel in the world as they saw it. Like Britons at home, they also understood what they called the "rights of Englishmen" as the product of both the historical evolution of British political institutions and the resulting achievement of a uniquely mixed, or balanced, constitution.

For colonists and Britons alike, the Norman Conquest of England in 1066 and the Glorious Revolution of 1688 represented key turning points in the story of the creation of a nation whose identity was based in large part on the self-conscious possession of political and legal rights, the most important of which entitled them to representative government, trial by jury, and other customary safeguards against the potential tyranny of the monarch. According to this narrative, the Anglo-Saxons—who were the ancestors of modern Englishmen—enjoyed an ancient constitution that recognized the rights of citizens and afforded them representation in their government. The successful invasion of the French duke William of Normandy in 1066, which ended this happy state of affairs, established a royal tyranny in England.

The standard account of England's subsequent history was a narrative of the long struggle to regain the lost rights of Anglo-Saxons, particularly the right of representative government. Although Magna Carta had established an embryonic Parliament in 1215, for more than four centuries afterwards, Englishmen had fought to expand and to safeguard the legitimate authority of the legislature by shielding it from predatory royal prerogative. In 1649, the English Civil War culminated in the beheading of King Charles I, who had curtailed the rights of Englishmen and attempted to govern without Parliament. In 1688, the Glorious Revolution ousted a similarly authoritarian King James II in favor of William and Mary, who accepted both the supremacy of Parliament and the Bill of Rights of 1689.

In both Britain and America, the Glorious Revolution was widely regarded as the ultimate triumph of the ancient Anglo-Saxon constitution and the rights of Englishmen. At the root of this achievement was the replacement of a monarch who claimed extensive or even unbounded power by divine right with one who would be subject to man-made constitutional limits on his authority. Under this new arrangement, the Crown shared power with the two houses of Parliament, the hereditary Lords and the elected Commons. In practice, however, the Commons' exclusive power to tax gave them the upper hand. Parliament emerged supreme and in so doing forever had secured the rights of Englishmen.

When people praised the British "constitution," they were not referring to a written document but rather to the combination of institutions, laws, customs, and principles that constituted the existing government. Most eighteenth-century commentators described the British constitution as "balanced" or "mixed," by which they meant that power was divided among the king, Lords, and Commons. This arrangement, admirers of the British constitution believed, ideally allowed all orders of society political representation and prevented any single one from getting too much power. Like many enlightened Europeans, British colonists regarded a balanced constitution as uniquely suited to the preservation of liberty.

Besides admiring the constitution as it ideally functioned in Britain, colonial political leaders imagined it as the model for their own provincial governments. As a result of their diverse origins, the thirteen mainland colonies had three different types of governments. By the mid-eighteenth century, most were royal colonies, which meant that they were the property of the king. Maryland, which Charles I gave to Cecilius Calvert, the second Lord Baltimore, in 1634, and Pennsylvania and Delaware, which Charles II gave to William Penn in 1681, remained the properties of the heirs of their respective proprietors. Two colonies, Connecticut and Rhode Island, retained their seventeenth-century royal charters, which afforded them significant autonomy so long as they made no laws contrary to those of England. All of the colonies, however, had a governor and two legislative houses, and many colonists saw this tripartite institutional arrangement analogous to that of the British constitution. Colonial leaders especially regarded their own elective lower houses of assembly as comparable to the House of Commons, Parliament's elected lower house.

Like inhabitants of Great Britain, the king's colonial subjects constructed their political identity in opposition to their image of Britain's traditional enemies, France and Spain, both of which lacked strong traditions of representative government. Because France and Spain were also Roman Catholic kingdoms, Britons identified absolute monarchy and the absence of representative institutions with allegiance to the Church of Rome—a perspective that also shaped their understanding of English history. It was no coincidence, the average Briton would have maintained, that James II, whom the Glorious Revolution deposed, was not only a Roman Catholic but also a tyrant who took subsidies from the king of France in the hope of governing without the advice and consent of Parliament. The overthrow of James II and subsequent accession of the Protestant William and Mary, according to this view, saved England from the twin evils of tyranny and popery. The overwhelming majority of Britons both in Europe and America not only regarded Protestantism as the only true religion but also as a bulwark of political liberty.

The colonists' sense of themselves as people uniquely blessed with both religious probity and political rights also shaped their views of and relations with native Americans and enslaved Africans. White inhabitants of the British colonies regarded native Americans as uncivilized both because they refused to accept Protestant Christianity and because their cultures typically had no concept of private property. Colonists and their governments interpreted these cultural differences as evidence of the Indians' barbarism—which, in turn, served as justification for seizing Indian lands, often in defiance of duly executed treaties. European colonists also used cultural difference to rationalize the occasional enslavement of native Americans and the much more common practice of African chattel slavery. Historians now recognize that the presence of so many thousands of enslaved people profoundly affected the world view of white colonists, making them more acutely conscious of the vulnerability of their own fundamental rights. White colonists often used the term "slavery" to describe what would befall them if they did not vigorously oppose attempts to abridge their liberties or rights.

At mid-century, most white inhabitants of British colonial America valued the imperial bond as a source of liberty. They saw themselves as loyal subjects of the king, professors of the true religion, and beneficiaries of the world's most enlightened constitution. When comparing themselves to the residents of the British Isles, they were far more likely to see similarities than differences. They saw themselves as the equals of the people of London or Glasgow or the rural villages of Britain.

By contrast, imperial authorities in London envisioned the Empire more in economic and strategic terms, valuing the colonies mainly as commercial assets and as potential resources in the ongoing Anglo-French wars. Beginning in 1689, England and France waged more than a century of intermittent warfare that would end only with the defeat of Napoleon in 1815. Between 1689 and 1763, these two powers fought a series of four wars in Europe and North America. The white inhabitants of British colonial America had a vital interest in the defeat of the French and their Indian allies, who threatened their frontiers and impeded the further territorial expansion of their growing population. As a result, they supported the British war effort in spirit, though not always with as much men and money as the home government may have wanted. Indeed, British attempts to assert control over the colonies to facilitate their defense accentuated the differences between colonial and British understandings of the imperial bond and its significance.

With the conclusion of the third Anglo-French war in 1748, British imperial authorities began to focus increased attention on imperial governance. Before then imperial administration was sporadic and decentralized, despite the establishment in 1696 of the Board of Trade as a central clearing house for all matters pertaining to the colonies. Now, however, authorities in London sought to reform imperial governance both because they recognized the colonies' economic and strategic value and because they worried that the American provinces were becoming too autonomous.

After 1748, the home government tried to circumscribe the powers of the colonial assemblies, which, following the example of the House of Commons, had used their control of the purse-strings to increase their powers at the expense of those of the governor. The Board of Trade now reviewed colonial statutes, prevailing on the Crown to disallow those that seemed to overstep the assemblies' legitimate jurisdiction, and it sought to prevent the implementation of colonial laws that had not received express approval from London. In addition, imperial authorities increasingly required colonial statutes to include a clause suspending enforcement pending approval from London—a process that generally took a year or longer because of slow communications between the colonies and Britain and the heavy workload of the imperial administration. Far from viewing the colonial assemblies as comparable to the House of Commons, most imperial officials believed that the colonial legislatures existed solely by the king's leave and possessed no real constitutional authority.

After 1748, imperial authorities also took up two more specific concerns: the systematic regulation of colonial courts and the curtailment of paper currency. British merchants supported the latter measure because paper money, while facilitating trade and economic development in cash-poor colonial societies, also enabled the colonists to satisfy their commercial debts with inflated paper money. In 1751, Parliament passed the Currency Act, which prohibited additional emissions of paper money in the four New England colonies. After piecemeal efforts to force the other colonies to comply with this law, Parliament passed a new Currency Act in 1764 that applied to all the colonies. Beginning in the 1750s, imperial authorities also sought to reorganize colonial courts, in part by standardizing the prevailing practice of appointing colonial judges to serve at the king's pleasure rather than during good behavior, which guaranteed that a judge whose decisions undermined imperial interests could be summarily dismissed. In 1759, the Pennsylvania assembly challenged this policy in a law declaring that judges would serve during good behavior—or, in effect, for life—as did their English counterparts. Other colonies followed suit, arguing that an independent judiciary was an important guarantor of the rights of Englishmen.

These initial efforts to reform imperial governance had little discernable impact on the lives of colonists, but they signaled important differences in how political leaders in London and America interpreted constitutional relationships within the empire. In the decade or so after 1748, imperial authorities had revealed a desire to enforce the political subordination that was the essence of colonial status. The colonists' understanding of their constitutional rights bound them to Britain while simultaneously informing their opposition to certain imperial policies.

So, too, did the strident Protestantism of most white colonists contribute to both the construction and erosion of the bonds of empire. On the one hand, a sense of shared Protestant identity clearly united colonists and Britons in their hostility toward France and other Catholic powers. Protestantism was overwhelmingly the religion of choice for the white inhabitants of British America, where Catholics and Jews together accounted for less than 1 percent of the white population. On the other hand, in part because of their diverse ethnic origins, most colonists were not members of the Church of England. Indeed, roughly two-thirds belonged to the so-called dissenting Protestant denominations— Presbyterian, Congregationalist, Lutheran, Dutch Reformed, Quaker, Baptist, and others—whose numbers grew, both proportionately and in absolute terms, during the eighteenth century. In the southern colonies and in parts of New York, the Church of England was a tax-supported religious establishment; Anglicans elsewhere received financial support from the Church's London-based missionary arm, the Society for the Propagation of the Gospel in Foreign Parts. Like Protestant dissenters in Britain who saw connections between the pretensions of bishops and the tyranny of kings, non-Anglicans in America came to see the objectives of the Church of England in America as both religious and political. In the 1760s, the prospect of sending an Anglican bishop to reside in the colonies concerned even some colonial members of the Church, who worried that the presence of a bishop would undermine their local autonomy.

Unlike their constitutional and ecclesiastical bonds, the commercial relationship between Britain and the colonies had never been ambiguous. Mercantilist precepts inspired the enterprises of European colonizers, including those who established the English colonies. European adventurers—and the kings who supported them—saw the potential value of colonies as both suppliers of raw materials and as markets for

English Delftware Plate, 1715.   Manufactured in Lambeth, England, this plate celebrated the defeat of rebels who sought to overthrow George I in favor of the son of James II, who had himself been deposed by the Glorious Revolution. What does the presence of such a plate in colonial households reveal about the economy and culture of eighteenth-century British America? Source: Artist unknown, "Delftware Plate," 1715. Collection of the Museum of Early Southern Decorative Arts. Courtesy of the Museum of Early Southern Decorative Arts. Earthenware, diameter 9 in., Winston-Salem, N.C. Accession No.: 1109.6. Old Salem, Inc./MESDA. Neg. No. S-24032.

their nations' products. Unlike the Spanish, the English found no gold or silver when they came to America, but they eventually saw that their colonies could produce lumber, fish, iron, and an array of valuable agricultural staples, all of which could be consumed in England or sold elsewhere by English merchants. In 1651, Parliament recognized the value of these commodities by enacting the first of many statutes regulating colonial trade.

Between 1651 and 1696, Parliament passed a series of five trade laws, known collectively as the Navigation Acts. These laws aimed to promote English and colonial shipping and to ensure English access to valuable colonial products. The first Navigation Acts required colonial goods to be transported on English- or colonial-owned ships and stipulated that the most lucrative colonial products—such as sugar, tobacco, cotton, and dye woods—be shipped only to English ports. In 1663, another law mandated that non-English exports to the colonies be sent first to England to be transferred to English vessels. New laws in 1673 and

1696 closed loopholes in the existing legislation and created and then expanded a resident customs service in the colonies. The Navigation Act of 1696 also established the Board of Trade as a central clearinghouse for all administrative work pertaining to the colonies.

Historians have long debated the effects of the Navigation Acts on colonial economic development. Although colonists, especially the New Englanders, resented and frequently evaded certain provisions of the trade laws, most historians now agree that the colonial economy benefited overall from the Navigation Acts, at least up to the 1760s. By requiring that colonial products be shipped on English or colonial vessels, the Navigation Acts encouraged the development of a colonial ship-building industry. In exchange for requiring the colonists to send their most valuable commodities to England, colonial producers received monopolies for their staples in the British market. In addition, colonial merchants and producers benefited from British naval protection of their maritime trade. Their connection with Britain also afforded them easy access to credit and cheap manufactures. All in all, despite occasional complaints from America about the imperial navigation system, the colonial economy was remarkably prosperous and expansive by the standards of the time.

By the middle of the eighteenth century, Great Britain had entered into an unprecedented era of economic expansion, spurred in large part by consumer demand in a prosperous and growing colonial market. Colonial participation in the eighteenth-century commercial revolution showed yet again how the imperial bond could be a source of both pride and anxiety to provincial Americans. From textiles to teapots, colonists were avid consumers of British goods; from 1720 to 1770, colonial per capita imports from Britain increased by some 50 percent. Newspaper advertisements placed by colonial merchants and shopkeepers attest to the variety of British imports available to colonial consumers and to the perceived desirability of London fashions in America. At the same time, however, for some—most notably for the tobacco planters of the Chesapeake—extravagant consumption of imported English goods engendered dependence and resentment, as their debts to British merchants escalated at an alarming rate in bad economic times.

What did it mean to be a Virginian or a New Yorker, a New Englander or a Carolinian, in 1750? Those who pondered the thorny issues of identity and culture would have derived a large part of both from their membership in the British Empire. As subjects of the king and as claimants to a noble constitutional tradition, they all professed allegiance to the king and Parliament and asserted the rights of Englishmen—including the right to representative government. As Protestants, they identified with Britain as the chief foe of Catholic Europe without affording, in many cases, religious or political preference to the Protestant

Church of England. Colonial involvement in a mercantilist economy could be profitable and convenient, but it was also involuntary and sometimes troublesome. At mid-century, then, those who celebrated the bonds of empire had barely begun to explore the ambiguity of the imperial relationship and its potential liabilities.

DOCUMENT 1

"The Revolution Ode" (1760)

This poem celebrated the coronation of King George III in 1760.[1] The poet portrayed the new monarch as the worthy successor of William and Mary, who most Britons believed saved them from the twin evils of tyranny and "popery" by displacing the Catholic Stuart King James II in the Glorious Revolution. American colonists also celebrated the Glorious Revolution as a turning point in the history of British liberty.

Questions to consider:

1. How did the author of the "Ode" describe James II? How did this poet envision the king's ideal relationship to his subjects?
2. Why was anti-French and anti-Catholic rhetoric so appealing to the colonists in 1760?

When James, assuming Right from God,
enslaved this free-born Nation
His Scepter was an Iron Rod,
His Reign a Visitation.
High-Churchmen cried, Obey, Obey,
Let none resist a crowned Head,
He who gainsays what Tyrants say
Is a rebellious Round-Head.

Then let us sing whilst Echoes ring
The glorious Revolution;
Your Voices raise to William's Praise
Who saved our Constitution. . . .

Our State and Church shook off the Yoke,
And lawless Power was banished

The Snares of Priest-Craft too were broke,
And Superstition vanished:
The Tyrant with his Black-guard fled,
By Flight his Guilt confessing,
To beg of France his daily Bread—
Of Rome a worthless Blessing.

From all who dare to tyrannize
May Heaven still defend us,
And should another James arise,
Another William send us—
May Kings like George for ever reign,
With highest Worth distinguished,
But Stuarts who our Annals stain
May they be quite extinguished.

DOCUMENT 2

"Of the Constitution of England" (1748)

Montesquieu

Charles de Secondat, Baron de Montesquieu, was a leading political philosopher of the French Enlightenment and a well-known admirer of the British constitution. Montesquieu believed that government should protect the liberties of its citizenry. In this passage from his most famous work, The Spirit of Laws, *he contended that best means of preventing government from becoming tyrannous was to divide its power among its three constituent parts.[2] Montesquieu celebrated the British constitution while at the same time foreshadowing the American notion of the separation of powers.*

Questions to consider:

1. How did Montesquieu define liberty?
2. What did he believe was the best form of government?
3. What sorts of people, in his opinion, should be included in the legislature? What did he believe to be the legislature's most essential powers?
4. What was his opinion of republican government? On what grounds did he defend the existence of a hereditary aristocracy?

In every government there are three sorts of power: the legislative; the executive in respect to things dependent on the law of nations; and the executive in regard to matters that depend on the civil law.

By virtue of the first, the prince or magistrate enacts temporary or perpetual laws, and amends or abrogates those that have been already enacted. By the second, he makes peace or war, sends or receives embassies, establishes the public security, and provides against invasions. By the third, he punishes criminals, or determines the disputes that arise between individuals. The latter we shall call the judiciary power, and the other simply the executive power of the state.

The political liberty of the subject is a tranquillity of mind arising from the opinion each person has of his safety. In order to have this liberty, it is requisite the government be so constituted as one man need not be afraid of another.

When the legislative and executive powers are united in the same person, or in the same body of magistrates, there can be no liberty; because apprehensions may arise, lest the same monarch or senate should enact tyrannical laws, to execute them in a tyrannical manner.

Again, there is no liberty, if the judiciary power be not separated from the legislative and executive. Were it joined with the legislative, the life and liberty of the subject would be exposed to arbitrary control; for the judge would be then the legislator. Were it joined to the executive power, the judge might behave with violence and oppression.

There would be an end of everything, were the same man or the same body, whether of the nobles or of the people, to exercise those three powers, that of enacting laws, that of executing the public resolutions, and of trying the causes of individuals.

Most kingdoms in Europe enjoy a moderate government because the prince who is invested with the two first powers leaves the third to his subjects. In Turkey, where these three powers are united in the Sultan's person, the subjects groan under the most dreadful oppression.

In the republics of Italy, where these three powers are united, there is less liberty than in our monarchies. Hence their government is obliged to have recourse to as violent methods for its support as even that of the Turks; witness the state inquisitors, and the lion's mouth into which every informer may at all hours throw his written accusations.

In what a situation must the poor subject be in those republics! The same body of magistrates are possessed, as executors of the laws, of the whole power they have given themselves in quality of legislators. They may plunder the state by their general determinations; and as they have likewise the judiciary power in their hands, every private citizen may be ruined by their particular decisions. The whole power is here united in one body; and though there is no external pomp that indicates a despotic sway, yet the people feel the effects of it every moment. Hence it is that many of the princes of Europe, whose aim has been leveled at arbitrary power, have constantly set out with uniting in their own persons all the branches of magistracy, and all the great offices of state. . . .

The legislative power [should be] therefore committed to the body of the nobles, and to that which represents the people, each having their assemblies and deliberations apart, each their separate views and interests . . . The body of the nobility ought to be hereditary. In the first place it is so in its own nature; and in the next there must be a considerable interest to preserve its privileges—privileges that in themselves are obnoxious to popular envy, and of course in a free state are always in danger. But as a hereditary power might be tempted to pursue its own particular interests, and forget those of the people, it is proper that where a singular advantage may be gained by corrupting the nobility, as in the laws relating to the supplies, they should have no other share in the legislation than the power of rejecting, and not that of resolving. . . .

The executive power ought to be in the hands of a monarch, because this branch of government, having need of despatch, is better administered by one than by many. On the other hand, whatever depends on the legislative power is oftentimes better regulated by many than by a single person. . . .

The executive power . . . ought to have a share in the legislature by the power of rejecting, otherwise it would soon be stripped of its prerogative. But should the legislative power usurp a share of the executive, the latter would be equally undone.

If the prince were to have a part in the legislature by the power of resolving, liberty would be lost. But as it is necessary he should have a share in the legislature for the support of his own prerogative, this share must consist in the power of rejecting. . . .

Here then is the fundamental constitution of the government we are treating of. The legislative body being composed of two parts, they check one another by the mutual privilege of rejecting. They are both restrained by the executive power, as the executive is by the legislative.

These three powers should naturally form a state of repose or inaction. But as there is a necessity for movement in the course of human affairs, they are forced to move, but still in concert. . . .

Were the executive power to determine the raising of public money, otherwise than by giving its consent, liberty would be at an end, because it would become legislative in the most important point of legislation. If the legislative power was to settle the subsidies, not from year to year, but for ever, it would run the risk of losing its liberty, because the executive power would be no longer dependent; and when once it was possessed of such a perpetual right, it would be a matter of indifference whether it held it of itself or of another. The same may be said if it should come to a resolution of entrusting, not an annual, but a perpetual command of the fleets and armies to the executive power. . . .

It is not my business to examine whether the English actually enjoy this liberty or not. Sufficient it is for my purpose to observe that it is established by their laws; and I inquire no further.

Britain's Commercial Interest Explained and Improved (1757)

Mercantilism was the economic orthodoxy of the West in the eighteenth century, as it had been since the dawn of the era of exploration and colonization. Imperial commercial regulations, collectively known as the Navigation Acts, envisioned the colonies as suppliers of raw materials and as markets for English manufactures. The desired result, as the English economist Malachy Postlethwayt affirmed in this passage, was to enhance the prosperity and security of both Britain and its colonies.[3]

Questions to consider:

1. Why did Postlethwayt warmly endorse the extensive regulation of trade within the empire?
2. To whom did he chiefly attribute Britain's current commercial problems?
3. What, in his opinion, were the motives of those who violated the Navigation Acts, and what did he believe would be the consequences of those violations?

Though [colonial] commerce is so very considerable . . . the whole advantage thereof does not center in England. But if the commerce of these colonies was directed in the right channel, it might prove of far higher concernment to the nation than it has ever yet been; it would promote the consumption of much greater quantities of British and Irish manufactures, than our traffic to any other part of the world. . . .

Whatever practices amongst the British traders have any tendency to promote and advance the prosperity of our foreign American rivals in trade, ought to be put a stop to. The British northern colonies in America carrying on a commerce with the French and the Dutch islands there, have proved very detrimental to the kingdom. This has been the charge of our West India merchants against those of the northern colonies; and this charge may be supported with no little weight of reason and argument . . . from hence our enemies the French have derived a new mine of profit, unknown to them before, and transferred to themselves the benefit of a trade, which it was the design of those laws to preserve to England.

This being made to appear to our parliament, a further provision was made for putting a stop to this manifest subversion of the fundamental maxims of the British policy, for preserving her commercial interests, by [the Molasses Act of 1733] . . . whereby such high duties were laid on all foreign sugars, rum, and molasses, to be imported into any of his majesty's colonies in America, as it was thought were equal to, and would answer all the ends of a prohibition.

But experience has shewn, that all these laws are too weak to answer the purposes for which they were designed, and that some more effectual remedies should be found to keep the British traders in North America within bounds, if Great Britain resolves to preserve her rights of controlling the trade of her own subjects in that part of the world, and turning the same into such channels only as her wisdom shall direct, and think most conducive to the interests of the whole community. . . .

It may be taken for granted as an undoubted truth, that, as the enlarging the vent of any commodity is one of the best means that can be used to encourage its growth, so the lessening of it is the certain way to discourage it; whence it necessarily follows, that, as we may have rivals in this commerce, nothing could be more detrimental to the British sugar colonies, than to suffer foreign sugars to be consumed in any of its dominions; it being obvious, that this must check the growth of sugar in our own islands, and increase it in those of France; and, therefore, has manifestly tended to strengthen the colonies of our ancient enemies, and to weaken our own.

This trade, as it has long been carried on, has raised the price of lumber to the British planters; and, as the northern traders often refuse to take anything from them but ready money, this has drained so much of their gold and silver, that they have been often in distress for want of specie.

A great part of the money, which our northern colony traders have received from our British planters, has been carried to the foreign sugar colonies, and there laid out either in the purchase of foreign sugars, rum, molasses, or of foreign European and East India commodities; which are carried to the British northern colonies, and there have supplied the place of British manufactures, and British sugars, rum, and molasses; and consequently have robbed this nation, not only of the consumption of so much of its own commodities, but of so much gold and silver too: whereas, if the foreign colonies (who cannot be supplied with lumber but from the English) had been constrained to have purchased the same with ready money only, and had never been allowed to give their sugars, rum, and molasses, in exchange for it, this would have turned the tables upon them, and have made the balance of the lumber-trade as much in our favour as it has been many years against us . . . This point, therefore, had it been strictly attended, and invariably adhered to, would have inevitably damped the prosperity of the French sugar colonies, and increased that of our own; and might, very probably, have long before now, proved the means of enabling the English to have beat the French out of all the foreign markets in Europe for sugar, and have confined them solely to their own consumption. But, have we not, to our eternal ignominy, acted a contrary part? Have we not studied to enrich the French in America, and strengthen their power at the expense of our own, and do we not now experience the fatal effects of such a system of policy?

DOCUMENT 4

Letter to the People of Pennsylvania (1760)

In 1759, Pennsylvania's assembly passed a law providing that judges would serve during good behavior rather than at the king's pleasure. Imperial authorities in London quickly disallowed the law, but thereafter the tenure of judges became a recurring and controversial issue in Pennsylvania and several other colonies. Arguing in favor of an independent judiciary, the anonymous author of this pamphlet invoked the British constitution to dispute the legitimacy of the London ruling, showing how the imperial tie could both limit and legitimate colonial political rights.[4]

Questions to consider:

1. Why did imperial authorities refuse to grant judges tenure during good behavior?
2. How did the author view the political status of the colonies within the empire?
3. What specific "rights of Englishmen" did he identify?
4. What did he see as the constitutional and social roles of the judiciary?

Whoever has made himself acquainted with ancient history and looked into the original design of government will find that one of its chief and principal ends was to secure the persons and properties of mankind from private injuries and domestic oppression.

In forming a plan of government completely to answer these excellent purposes, the fundamental laws and rules of the constitution, which ought never to be infringed, should be made alike distributive of justice and equity, and equally calculated to preserve the sovereign's prerogative and the people's liberties. But power and liberty ever being opponents, should the work stop here the constitution would bear a near analogy of a ship without rudder, rigging, or sails, utterly incapable of answering the end of its construction. For though the wisest and best laws were enacted to fix the bounds of power and liberty, yet without a due care in constituting persons impartially to execute them, the former by its influence and encroachments on liberty would soon become tyranny, and the latter by the like extent of its limits might possibly degenerate into licentiousness. In both cases, the condition of mankind would be little mended, scarcely better than in their original state of nature and confusion, before any civil polity was agreed upon.

The men therefore who are to settle the contests between prerogative and liberty, who are to ascertain the bounds of sovereign power and to determine the rights of the subject, ought certainly to be perfectly free from the influence of either. But more especially of the former, as history plainly evinces that it is but too apt to prevail over the ministers of justice by its natural weight and authority, notwithstanding the wisest precautions have been used to prevent it.

The necessity of this independent state of justice is rendered apparent by the slightest consideration of human frailty. Consider men as they really are, attended with innumerable foibles and imperfections, ever liable to err, and you will find but very few who are so obstinately just as to be proof against the enticing baits of honor and interest. The love of promotion and private advantage are passions almost universal, and admit of the most dangerous extremes. The one in excess generally produces the most servile obedience, the other, intolerable avarice and a base dereliction of virtue. That which we love and engages our attention we are ever ready to purchase at any price. Thus an inordinate lover of promotion, sooner than part with it, would surrender up his regard for justice, his duty to his country and to his God for its preservation. And the avaricious man, sooner than lose his pelf, would part with his honor, his reputation, I had almost said his life. . . .

Whoever has read the form of a commission during pleasure and considered its limitations must certainly be surprised that a generous mind would accept of a tenure so servile and so incompatible with the very nature of justice. He can be but a tenant at will of a g[overnor]r at best . . . The terms of tenure are until our further will and pleasure shall be made known, which by a natural construction, if we may call reason and experience to our aid, is no longer than you gratify us, our favorites and creatures, in your determinations, let our will and pleasure therein be ever so illegal, ever so partial and unjust. That some men of independent circumstances, happy in the possession of virtue, have accepted of those commissions and acted uprightly I will not pretend to dispute. They are remarkable instances of public integrity, and merit the highest commendation. They are among mankind as a comet among the stars, rarely to be seen. But generally to look for strict impartiality and a pure administration of justice, to expect that power should be confined within its legal limits and right and justice done to the subject by men who are dependent, is to ridicule all laws against bribery and corruption, and to say that human nature is insensible of the love or above the lure of honor, interest, or promotion. . . .

Having shown you that a security of your rights and properties was the chief end of your entering into society, and that that security cannot be obtained without an independent and uninfluenced judicature, it becomes an indispensable duty to take some pains to convince you that this security is your undoubted privilege as Englishmen, of which you cannot be divested without violence to your ancient rights and the principles of an English government.

To trace this important privilege to its original source, it will be necessary to follow me back to the first dawn of the present constitution of England, there to learn the precarious situation of property and the wise remedy that was framed to give it a permanent security.

Before the time of the great [King] Alfred, that wise founder of the English government, . . . the nation . . . had property, but no safety in the enjoyment. They had some degree of liberty, but held it as tenants at will of the crown, of the nobility, or their favorites; they had laws, but no protection from the hostile hand of the domestic oppressor. In this unfortunate and desponding situation did the great father of public virtue find liberty and property—the two principal objects of all good laws. A generous compassion for the distressed state of the nation induced him to alter the constitution wherever he found it inconsistent with the welfare and happiness of his people. The security of property, without which private felicity is a mere chimera, engrossed his chief attention. He was the author of the excellent institution of trials by jurors, that solid pillar of English liberty. He altered the former dependent state of justice by appointing and commissionating judges as independent of the crown that they might ever after remain free from its influence and deaf to every solicitation but the convictions of truth. . . .

Agreeable to this excellent policy of the common law, ever since the latter end of the eighth century the judges have held their commissions during their good behavior, a few instances to the contrary made by the encroachments of power excepted: even in the most arbitrary reigns of Charles [I] and James II, the judges were commissionated in this legal and constitutional form, reigns in which power had so great an ascendancy that had it not been consistent with the ancient common law and the usage and custom of ages, the rights of the nation had not met with so great a favor. . . .

The next thing worthy of your attention is how far this invaluable policy, so often suspended by arbitrary power, was restored and confirmed by your predecessors, the first settlers of this province. They had drank the bitter cup of despotic authority; they had suffered the mischiefs of perverted law;

they had seen their liberties both civil and religious bend under its weight; they resolved therefore to seek a more hospitable country, but would not venture their lives and estates in this desert land without some security against any encroachment in this inestimable part of the mother constitution. . . .

If your ancestors here were not wanting in their endeavours to secure you from the mischiefs of perverted law and to transmit to you an upright administration of justice, the Parliament of your mother country have not been less careful in this respect. At the time of the happy Revolution [of 1688], that famous opportunity of overcoming the usurpations of former reigns and restoring the constitution to its ancient freedom, many of the national rights were revived and confirmed by the Bill of Rights. . . .

If these things be so, can the least spark of reason be offered why a British subject in America shall not enjoy the . . . same protection against domestic oppression? Is it because you have left your native land at the risk of your lives and fortunes to toil for your mother country, to load her with wealth, that you are to be rewarded with a loss of your privileges? Are you not of the same stock? Was the blood of your ancestors polluted by a change of soil? Were they freemen in England and did they become slaves by a six-weeks' voyage to America? . . . Is not our honor and virtue as pure, our liberty as valuable, our property as dear, our lives as precious here as in England? Are we not subjects of the same King, and bound by the same laws, and have we not the same God for our protector?

DOCUMENT 5

Observations on the Charter and Conduct of the Society for the Propagation of the Gospel in Foreign Parts (1763)

Jonathan Mayhew

For both Britons and American colonists, Protestantism was an important source of collective and individual identity. Yet many colonists bitterly resented the privileged status of the Church of England and opposed efforts to augment its influence. The Reverend Jonathan Mayhew of Massachusetts specifically condemned the activities of the Church's missionary arm, the Society for the Propagation of the Gospel, which he believed sought to undermine his colony's Congregational establishment.[5]

Questions to consider:

1. What nonreligious motives, in Mayhew's opinion, may have contributed to the founding and support of the Society for the Propagation of the Gospel in Foreign Parts?
2. Why did the ministers of the Society seek to establish themselves in communities that already had churches and ministers?
3. Why did Mayhew fear competition from the Church of England?
4. What does this passage reveal about how New Englanders construed their identity and their relationship to Britain?

The author of the following pages supposes the subject of them to be of real importance, not only to the general interest of religion in America, but particularly in New England. In which respect he is very far from being singular in his opinion. Indeed, none besides those who think that our forefathers separated from the Church of England without just grounds, and that the differences subsisting betwixt the people of that communion and ours, are quite immaterial, can suppose this a needless controversy. The prosperity, if not the very being of our New England churches, is essentially concerned in it. . . .

The author of the following pages desires to have what he disputes about, relative to the . . . Society [for the Propagation of the Gospel in Foreign Parts] and their missionaries, clearly understood in the first place. He apprehends there is no ground for controversy as to religious liberty, or the natural and legal right which protestants of all denominations have, in any part of his Majesty's dominions, to worship God in their own way respectively, without molestation.

Nor is the question, whether any person or persons in Great Britain have a right, considered in their private capacity, if they think it expedient, to encourage and propagate episcopacy in America, by transmitting money to build churches here, to support missions and schools, or the like. Whatever our sentiments may be about the church of England, we are not so vain as to assume a right of dictating to them the manner in which they shall, or shall not bestow their charity; or in any sort to control them herein. . . . Though as this is a matter of public concernment, in which the civil as well as religious interest of the King's subjects in America is nearly concerned, other people have a right to give their opinion about the manner in which that charitable fund is employed. . . .

It is supposed by many persons, that there are some . . . American colonies, whose religious state is such, as renders them improper objects of this charity; and consequently, that whatever has been done by the Society in supporting episcopal missions in them, is a misapplication of that part of their fund, which has been employed in this way; to the neglect, prejudice and injury of other colonies, the Negroes and Indians, who were unquestionably proper objects of their charity.

This therefore, is the main question now proposed for a free and candid discussion: Whether the planting episcopal churches, supporting missions and schools, &c. in certain parts of America, particularly in New England, in the manner, and under the circumstances in which this has been, and still is done by the Society, is conformable to the true design of their institution, according to their charter; or a deviation therefrom, and consequently a misapplication of their fund? . . .

The first thing requisite in order to a right determination of this question . . . is to . . . appeal . . . to their charter, granted by King William III in . . . 1701 . . . the whole preamble of which clearly is therefore here subjoined, without the omission or addition of a single word; only such clauses as are especially necessary to a right understanding of its design, are printed in a different character. . . .

I.   "Whereas we are credibly informed, that in many of our plantations, colonies and factories beyond seas, belonging to our kingdom of England, the provision for ministers is very mean; and many others of our said plantations, colonies and factories, are wholly destitute and unprovided of a maintenance for ministers and the public worship of God; and for lack of support and maintenance for such, many of our loving subjects do want the administration of God's word and sacraments, and seem to be abandoned to atheism and infidelity; and also for want of learned and orthodox ministers to instruct our said loving subjects in the principles of the TRUE RELIGION, divers Romish priests and jesuits are the more encouraged to pervert and draw over our said loving subjects to Popish superstition and idolatry.

II.   And whereas we think it our duty, as much as in us lies, to promote the glory of God, by the instruction of our people in the CHRISTIAN RELIGION; and that it will be highly conducive for accomplishing those ends, that a sufficient maintenance be provided for an orthodox clergy to live amongst them, and that such other provision be made, as may be necessary for the propagation of the GOSPEL in those parts.

III.   And whereas we have been well assured, that if we would be graciously pleased to erect and settle a corporation for the receiving, managing and disposing of the charity of our loving subjects, divers persons would be induced to extend charity to the uses and purposes aforesaid. . . .

The following observations are submitted to the candid reader's judgment.

1.   Nothing is to be supposed the object, or any part of the object of this charitable and royal institution, but what plainly appears to be really so, from the very

words of the charter. . . . It was only for those purposes that are particularly expressed, not any private or secret ones, which they might possibly have had in their own minds, that they were incorporated.

2. It appears that the British plantations . . . were really the primary, more immediate object of this institution, or the King's subjects . . . But it also appears that the grand, or ultimate design of the institution was, the propagation of the Gospel in those parts; which necessarily includes the design of christianizing the Indians bordering on the colonies, as a principle part of the general design.

3. This charitable foundation was not intended for all the plantations, colonies and factories indiscriminately; but for such of them only as really stood in great need of relief and help in this way, and whose religious state corresponded to the description in the charter. . . .

4. Even amongst those plantations . . . which were truly the objects of this charity, there is some difference; for they are differently described, and come under two distinct headings in the charter . . . first, those in which the "provision for ministers is very mean" . . . [and] secondly, such plantations as are "wholly destitute, and unprovided". . . .

5. It is evident that by "ministers," or as they are afterwards called, "learned and orthodox ministers," and "an orthodox clergy," were not intended ministers of any one denomination amongst protestants, exclusively of others. . . . Orthodox ministers, in the charter, stand in direct opposition to romish priests and jesuits. . . . there is not the most remote hint in the charter, at any controversies subsisting among protestants; but only at those which subsisted betwixt them and Roman Catholics. . . . King William himself was bred up in the Calvinistic principles and discipline, quite opposite in some respects to the episcopal. . . . Can it be reasonably supposed then, that in this charter, by orthodox ministers, he intended those of the English church in distinction from those of all other churches in the world; and consequently to brand all the rest as heterodox! . . .

It will now be proper to come to some facts relative to the conduct of the Society in planting churches, and supporting missions in America. And as the principal objection lies against their conduct in New England, it will be necessary . . . to make some remarks on the state of religion here, before the society sent any missionaries into these parts, and since. . . .

1. It is well known, that the first settlers of New England were such as came hither chiefly on account of their sufferings for non-conformity to the church of England. They fled hither as to an asylum from episcopal persecution, seconded by royal power; which often condescended to be subservient to the views of domineering prelates, before the glorious revolution [of 1688]. . . .

2. It is no less certain that these refugees were very far from being persons of a loose irreligious character. Had they been void of conscience toward God, they would not have suffered so much for non-conformity, and fled their dear native country, for the sake of serving him without fear in a wilderness. . . .

3. It is well known that they very early made provision for the public worship of God, and founded a seminary of learning, which has been increasing and flourishing to the present time. The zeal which they shewed both for learning and religion, from the first, was indeed very uncommon; and greatly to their honor. The public worship of God, and the administration of his word and sacraments, have all along been provided for in New England. . . .

4.   Divers acts, relating to the settlement and support of the gospel ministry here, having received the royal sanction, our churches seem to have a proper legal establishment. And it ought to be particularly remembered, that the aforesaid act was passed about nine years before the Society's charter was granted. . . . Churches and schools have from time to time been founded, and are continually multiplying in New England, in conformity both to the pious inclinations of the inhabitants, and to the legal provision made for those purposes.

5.   The people of New England . . . are all in general professed Christians. There is no such monster as an Atheist known amongst us; hardly any such person as a Deist. And as to the superstitions and idolatries of the church of Rome, there neither is, nor has been the least danger of their gaining ground in New England. The Congregationalists and Presbyterians are known to hold them at least in as great abhorrence as the Episcopalians do. . . . How much better then, in all these respects, is the state of religion amongst us, than it is even in England, under the immediate eye . . . of the venerable bishops? Where, notwithstanding all their pious endeavours, there are so many Roman-catholics, Infidels and Sceptics, if not downright Atheists! . . .

6.   As to practical religion . . . we have no cause for blushing on a comparison of our morals with those of the people in England, in the communion of that church. And many vices that are common there, are almost . . . unknown here. . . .

7.   From the foregoing faithful, though brief representation of religion in New England . . . it appears that there neither is nor has been any occasion for the Society to support missions and schools here; and that they had not even a warrant for doing so, by their charter. . . . So that if they send missionaries into these colonies, it cannot be so much to propagate christianity, as to propagate . . . the peculiarities of the church of England. . . .

It is hardly possible to account for the Society's conduct, without supposing them to have had . . . a formal design to dissolve and root out all our New England churches; or, in other words, to reduce them all to the episcopal form. . . . This fully and clearly accounts for their being ready to encourage small episcopal parties all over New England, by sending them missionaries, . . . although the people had the means for religion already, in other protestant communions. For these handfuls of people, scattered here and there, it is supposed, or at least hoped, will in time, by some means or other, become considerable for numbers; and at length eat out, or absorb all our churches.

But supposing them finally to carry this favourite point, at a vast expence, . . . one would think it impossible even for themselves to imagine, that the interest of religion in the colonies would be a quarter part served hereby, as if they had employed this money in those ways which are plainly pointed out in the charter, and from which they have alienated it. Is the effecting an exact uniformity among us in discipline, modes of worship, ceremonies, &c. an object worthy of any attention or expence, in comparison with that of maintaining a public worship in places destitute thereof, or the conversion of the heathen! Can wise men, free from bigotry and the spirit of party, possibly think it is, though they are themselves episcopalians in sentiment?

DOCUMENT 6

John Adams on the British Constitution (1766)

In this letter, addressed to a British correspondent and published in a Boston news-paper, John Adams praised the British constitution as both the protector of colonial liberties and a source of colonial identity.[6] Comparing civil society to the human body—a common analogy of the times—Adams argued that a dispersal of power among institutions tempered by popular influence was essential to the preservation of liberty, just as certain "fundamentals of the human constitution" were necessary to sustain life.

Questions to consider:

1. Since Great Britain had no written constitution, what did Adams mean when he referred to the "British constitution"?
2. According to Adams, what specifically was the role of "the people" in maintaining liberty?

You are pleased to charge the colonists with ignorance of the British constitution; but let me tell you . . . they know the true constitution and all the resources of liberty in it, as well as in the law of nature, which is one principal foundation of it, and in the temper and character of the people. . . . The people in America have discovered the most accurate judgment about the real constitution, I say, by their whole behavior . . . though there has been great inquiry and some apparent puzzle among them about a formal, logical, technical definition of it. Some have defined it to be the practice of parliament; others, the judgments and precedents of the king's courts; but either of these definitions would make it a constitution of wind and weather, because the parliaments have sometimes voted the king absolute, and the judges have sometimes adjudged him to be so. Some have called it custom, but this is as fluctuating and variable as the other. Some have called it the most perfect combination of human powers in society which finite wisdom has yet contrived and reduced to practice for the preservation of liberty and the production of happiness. This is rather a character of the constitution and a just observation concerning it, than a regular definition of it, and leaves us still to dispute what it is. Some have said that the whole body of the laws, others that kings, lords, and commons, make the constitution. There has also been much inquiry and dispute about the essentials and fundamentals of the constitution, and many definitions and descriptions have been attempted; but there seems to be nothing satisfactory to a rational mind in any of these definitions; yet I cannot say that I am at a loss about any man's meaning when he speaks of the British constitution or the essentials and fundamentals of it.

What do we mean when we talk of the constitution of the human body? . . . We can never judge of any constitution without considering the end of it; and no judgment can be formed of the human constitution without considering it as productive or life or health or strength. . . . There are certain . . . parts of the body . . . without which, life itself cannot be preserved a moment. Annihilate the heart, lungs, brain, animal spirits, blood, any one of these, and life will depart at once. These may be strictly called fundamentals of the human constitution. . . . Similar observations may be made, with equal propriety, concerning every kind of machinery. A clock has also a constitution, that is a certain combination of weights, wheels, and levers. . . . But yet there are certain parts of a clock, without which it will not go at all, and you can have from it no better account of the time of day than from the ore of gold, silver, brass, and iron, out of which it was wrought. These parts, therefore, are the essentials and fundamentals of a clock. Let us now inquire whether the same reasoning is not applicable in all its parts to government. For government is a frame, a scheme, a system, a combination of powers, for a certain end, namely, the good of the whole community. The public good, the *salus populi*, is the professed end of all government, the most despotic as well as the most free. . . . I shall take for granted, what I am sure no Briton will controvert, namely, that liberty is essential to the public good, the *salus populi*. And herein lies the difference between the British constitution and other forms of government, namely, that liberty is its end, its use, its designation, drift, and scope, as much as grinding corn is the use of a mill, the transportation of burdens the end of a ship, the mensuration of time the scope of a watch, or life and health the designation of the human body.

Were I to define the British constitution, therefore, I should say, it is a limited monarchy, or a mixture of the three forms of government commonly known in the schools, reserving as much of the monarchical splendor, the aristocratic independency, and the democratical freedom, as are necessary that each of these powers may have a control, both in legislation and execution, over the other two, for the preservation of the subject's liberty. . . .

This is the constitution which has prevailed in Britain from an immense antiquity . . . That constitution which has been for so long a time the envy and admiration of surrounding nations; which has been no less than five and fifty times since the Norman conquest, attacked in parliament, and attempted to be altered, but without success; which has been so often defended by the people of England, at the expense of oceans of their blood;

and which, cooperating with the invincible spirit of liberty inspired by it into the people, has never failed to work the ruin of the authors of all settled attempts to destroy it.

DOCUMENT 7

The Supremacy of Parliament (1766)

While colonists interpreted the Glorious Revolution as a victory for representative government, Britons saw it more specifically as the triumph of Parliament over an encroaching royal prerogative. Eighteenth-century Britons believed their rights and liberties depended on the supremacy of Parliament, which they believed extended throughout the king's dominions. In this speech in the House of Lords in 1766, Lord Lyttelton summarized this doctrine of Parliamentary supremacy as it applied to the colonies in America.[7]

Questions to consider:

1. Why did Lyttelton believe Parliament's authority was virtually unlimited in the colonies?
2. How did he interpret the status of the colonial legislatures?

The first foundation of civil government is, that a civil society was formed by men entering into society on what may properly be called an original compact, and entrusting government with a power over their persons, liberties, and estates, for the safety of the whole. In what form or manner this power is to be exercised depends on the laws and constitutions of different countries.

There cannot be two rights existing in government at the same time, which would destroy each other; a right in government to make laws, and a right in the people, or any part, to oppose or disobey such laws. Another great principle of policy is, that in all states, democratical, aristocratical, or monarchical, or in mixed states, as Great Britain, the government must rest somewhere, and that must be fixed, or otherwise there is an end of all government. . . .

But these great maxims which imply a subjection to the supreme government or legislature, do not exclude the existence of inferior legislatures with restrained powers, subject to the superior legislature. That the colonies are of this kind the many statutes made here to bind them since their first settlement plainly evince.

They went out subjects of Great Britain, and unless they can shew a new compact made between them and the parliament of Great Britain (for the king alone could not make a new compact with them) they are still subjects to all intents and purposes whatsoever . . . If the colonies are subjects of Great Britain, they are represented and consent to all statutes. . . . The only question before your lordships is, whether the American colonies are a part of the dominions of the crown of Great Britain? If not, parliament has no jurisdiction; if they are, as many statutes have declared them to be, they must be proper objects of our legislature. And by declaring them exempt from one statute or law, you declare them no longer subjects of Great Britain, and make them small independent communities not entitled to your protection.

SUGGESTED READING FOR CHAPTER 1

ANDERSON, FRED. *A People's Army: Massachusetts Soldiers and Society in the Seven Years' War* (1984).

BAILYN, BERNARD. *The Origins of American Politics* (1968).

BONOMI, PATRICIA U. *Under the Cope of Heaven: Religion, Society, and Politics in Colonial America* (1986).

BREWER, JOHN. *The Sinews of Power: War, Money, and the English State, 1688–1783* (1985).

BRIDENBAUGH, CARL. *Mitre and Sceptre: Transatlantic Faiths, Ideas, Personalities, and Politics, 1689–1775* (1962).

BUSHMAN, RICHARD L. *King and People in Provincial Massachusetts* (1985).

BUTLER, JON. *Awash in a Sea of Faith: Christianizing the American People* (1990).

———. *Becoming America: The Revolution Before 1776* (2000).

CARSON, CARY; HOFFMAN, RONALD; and ALBERT, PETER J., eds. *Of Consuming Interests: The Style of Life in the Eighteenth Century* (1994).

GREENE, JACK P. *The Quest for Power: The Lower Houses of Assembly in the Southern Royal Colonies, 1689–1776* (1963).

———. *Negotiated Authorities: Essays in Colonial Political and Constitutional History* (1994).

HOFSTADTER, RICHARD. *America at 1750: A Social Portrait* (1971).

KAMMEN, MICHAEL. *Empire and Interest: The American Colonies and the Politics of Mercantilism* (1970).

MCCUSKER, JOHN J.; and MENARD, RUSSELL R. *The Economy of British America, 1607–1789*, rev. ed. (1991).

MORGAN, EDMUND S. *American Slavery, American Freedom: The Ordeal of Colonial Virginia* (1975).

OLSON, ALISON GILBERT. *Anglo-American Politics, 1660–1775: The Relationship Between Parties in England and Colonial America* (1973).

STEELE, I. K. *Politics of Colonial Policy: The Board of Trade in Colonial Administration, 1696–1720* (1968).

NOTES

[1]*Boston Gazette,* 21 Jan. 1760.

[2]Charles Secondat, Baron de Montesquieu, *The Spirit of Laws,* trans. Thomas Nugent (1752; London, 1914), bk. XI, chap. 6.

[3]Malachy Postlethwayt, *Britain's Commercial Interest Explained and Improved,* 2 vols. (London, 1757), 1: 482–92.

[4]*Letter to the People of Pennsylvania* (Philadelphia, 1760), 3–5, 8–9, 15–26, 35–39.

[5]Jonathan Mayhew, *Observations on the Charter and Conduct of the Society for the Propagation of the Gospel in Foreign Parts* (Boston, 1763), 6–7, 11–14, 16–23, 39–46, 50, 103–8.

[6]Charles Francis Adams, ed., *The Works of John Adams,* 10 vols. (Boston, 1850–56), 3: 477–82.

[7]C. T. Hansard, comp., *The Parliamentary History of England, from the Earliest Period to the Year 1803,* 36 vols. (London, 1813), 16: 166–67.

CHAPTER TWO

LANGUAGES OF LIBERTY

Celebrations of liberty and concern for its preservation peppered colonial discourse. Liberty, however, was an expansive concept that might signify anything from the colonists' collective political representation to an individual's unfettered pursuit of economic opportunity. By the middle decades of the eighteenth century, inhabitants of British America used different but sometimes overlapping languages to explain and to defend their notions of political, economic, and religious liberty. One described liberty as the fruit of historic constitutional rights. Another envisioned it as a gift from God. A third defined liberty as a natural right. All three languages were antiauthoritarian, at least implicitly. Each defined liberty as a positive good and justified resistance to authority that jeopardized legitimate liberties and rights.

Colonial discussions of liberty presupposed the existence of a rigid and acknowledged social hierarchy. Like their English contemporaries, colonial Americans inhabited a world of gentry and common folk, patrons and clients, bound together by webs of authority and dependence. In these traditional societies, gentlemen—whose wealth, education, connections, and refined manners distinguished them in their respective communities—had both power over and responsibilities toward their less privileged neighbors. Colonial gentlemen provided credit and other forms of patronage to their dependents; they represented their communities in the colonial legislatures and dispensed local justice in their county courts. Although middling men could meet the property qualifications for voting in many colonies, most nonetheless deferred to the leadership of the gentry during the colonial era.

Colonial Americans typically envisioned liberty as an attribute of white male propertyowners. Independence, attained chiefly through property ownership, was a prerequisite for liberty and hence for the attainment of full political and civil rights. In the colonies, as in England, men with little or no property therefore lacked the right to vote; those who became indentured servants, waged laborers, or apprentices, lost or compromised other rights. While poverty could undermine the liberty of white men, contemporaries deemed white women dependent by nature; when a woman married, the common law doctrine of coverture legitimated and enforced this cultural bias by depriving her of a legal identity apart from that of her husband. By preventing wives from controlling property, signing contracts, and filing lawsuits, coverture—also known as civil death—enforced their economic and legal dependence. Still more debased was the status of free people of color, who suffered de facto disabilities, and of enslaved Africans, who lost liberty in perpetuity and were subject to laws that stripped them of their most fundamental human rights.

The pervasiveness of slavery and dependence may have heightened the appeal of rights and liberties as topics of discussion among politically aware inhabitants of British colonial America. Colonial newspapers and pamphlets, as well as the private correspondence of some prominent provincials, reveal that educated colonists often applauded and dissected the merits of both the English common law tradition and the balanced constitution. They did so in part because, as we have seen, they took pride in their legal and constitutional heritage as Britons but nonetheless sometimes worried about the contested nature of their own liberties and rights. White inhabitants of British colonial America were governed in large part by their elected representatives; they also possessed the customary or common law rights of Englishmen—such as the presumption of innocence, the right to due process and trial by jury, and representative government. Nevertheless, neither the king nor his imperial administrators had ever explicitly recognized these colonial practices as genuine legal rights. Colonists' continual discussion of their rights and liberties at least in part, then, reflected their desire to convince themselves and others of the validity of their claims.

As early as the 1670s, colonial assemblies unsuccessfully pressed imperial authorities to recognize the extension of English law—and thus of English rights and liberties—to the white inhabitants of the colonies in America. The legal status of the king's colonial subjects was a matter of some debate. The first English attempt to colonize an alien territory had resulted in the imposition of martial law in parts of northern Ireland in the 1570s. In 1607, in a case concerning the Irish situation, an English court held that conquered countries, such as Ireland, could be governed directly by the king, who might or might not do so according to the laws of England. Did this ruling, delivered in the year of the founding of England's first successful American colony at Jamestown, apply equally to Virginia and to the other provinces in America? In 1670, England's chief justice implied that it might not, when he distinguished between territory seized by conquest and that acquired by colonization.

On several later occasions, English judges and lawyers addressed the issue directly, maintaining that when Englishmen engaged in colonization, they carried their rights and liberties as a birthright to the new dominions they established. Others disagreed, however, and no one in England pressed for firm and binding clarification from imperial authorities. In sum, there was no consensus in London as to whether the American provinces resulted from conquest or settlement and whether their white inhabitants had the legal status of conquered people or of rights-bearing Englishmen.

Because English jurisprudence made the historical origins of the colonies the central question determining their full access to English law, colonists repeatedly asserted that the first settlers were loyal subjects of the king who expected to retain their rights as Englishmen when they ventured to America. This narrative of colonial history ignored or downplayed for strategic reasons the fact that conquered territories—land previously claimed by either native Americans or other European powers—accounted for most of British America. It also belied the fact that some early settlers—most notably New England's Puritan founders who had left the England of Charles I—were dangerously estranged from the king and his government. Nevertheless, the notion that emigration extended both the king's domain and the rights of his subjects remained a staple of colonial political discourse well into the 1760s.

This language of English liberty was so central to early American political culture that it was even accessible to many outside the political elite. For instance, in 1769 a group of men from Anson County in western North Carolina petitioned their colonial legislature for redress of grievances ranging from the corruption of officials and high taxes to the insecurity of their land titles and the unfair privileges of the established Church of England. The North Carolina Regulators, as they were commonly known, repeatedly appealed to English custom and precedent—and especially to the authority of the king—to justify their right to petition and to criticize what they saw as their own assembly's negligence in defending what they regarded as their historic rights.

Another issue over which colonists sought to secure their rights and liberties involved the powers of their assemblies or, more generally, the status of colonial political institutions relative to the king and Parliament. Just as they sought to secure their access to English law, colonists insisted that they should enjoy the singular benefits of the British constitution, by which they meant chiefly the right to representative government. As we have seen, colonists viewed their provincial assemblies as analogous to the House of Commons, an idea that became more and more plausible as the assemblies significantly increased their powers during the eighteenth century. Although King James II had abolished several colonial legislatures before 1688, William and Mary reinstated them after the Glorious Revolution, seemingly ensuring the existence of representative government in America. Yet no one in England ever expressly granted any rights or powers to the colonial assemblies nor did anyone there ever liken them to Parliament's lower house. In fact, imperial authorities consistently maintained that the colonial assemblies existed at the discretion of the king, who could alter them at any time. Most colonists rejected this view, which, by making their constitutional rights contingent on royal assent, potentially deprived them of all rights, including the right to representation. Citing customs and precedents from both England and America, they repeatedly argued that their assemblies enjoyed powers similar to those of the House of Commons.

At least in its early stages, the defense of the colonial assemblies and of colonial access to English law therefore was a backward-looking enterprise: colonial gentlemen appealed to historical precedent to justify the preservation of an idealized political order. In so doing, they followed the example of England's Radical Whigs, political (and often religious) dissenters who cherished the balanced constitution and the rights of Englishmen but believed that self-aggrandizing power and corruption were imminent threats to both. Radical Whigs saw power—defined as the ability to coerce—as an aggressive and insatiable force, and they saw liberty as its natural prey. Influenced by Radical Whig writings, colonists who wrote of liberty also often envisioned it as a cherished but threatened attribute, one whose survival depended on the vigilance of those who claimed it.

As unabashed admirers of British constitutional and legal traditions, colonial commentators were at a loss to explain British intransigence on the legal and constitutional questions that were of utmost importance to them. For colonial leaders who competed with the governor and other royal appointees for political influence, Radical Whig concerns about self-seeking courtiers who subverted English liberties and corrupted the constitution by manipulating Parliament struck a responsive chord. Colonists' complaints about patronage and corruption in imperial politics, though sometimes justified, were also informed by their own ambitions and interests. As British authorities sought to centralize imperial governance, many colonists concluded that governors and judges, the Board of Trade, and even Parliament sought to enhance their powers at liberty's expense by compromising the colonists' rights as Englishmen and circumscribing the activities of the their representatives in the colonial lower houses.

Both in England and America, the Radical Whig perspective was essentially conservative in that it drew on historical evidence to assert the superiority of British legal and constitutional forms and warn of their impending extinction. Some Americans coupled this strategy of using history to defend their rights and liberties with a more radical—and seemingly contradictory—approach as the conflict with Britain escalated in the 1760s. Drawing on the writings of John Locke and other liberal political theorists of the Enlightenment, they contended that rights derived not from historically constructed laws or charters, but from the laws of nature. All men—by which they meant white males—possessed certain natural rights by virtue of their humanity. Locke listed "liberty" as one of three natural rights of man; "life" and "property" were the others.

Enlightenment theorists believed that natural laws, not the inscrutable acts of a capricious God, determined the workings of the universe. Because the universe was law-governed, they asserted, human reason could understand the mysteries of the universe by discovering the laws of nature. Above all, the philosophers of the Enlightenment celebrated the power of rational men to use their understanding of natural law to effect the progressive improvement of society. This world view stood in marked contrast to the dominant religious culture of the time, which regarded humanity as wretched, depraved, and utterly dependent on divine Providence.

Although most Enlightenment philosophers believed in God, they compared the Supreme Being to a clockmaker who created a complex mechanism—in God's case, the universe—and then left it to run itself. Just as springs and pendulums propelled the movement of a clock, forces known as natural laws guided the regular and predictable workings of the universe. In seventeenth-century England, the scientist Isaac Newton discovered the natural laws of gravity and motion, which went a long way toward explaining how the physical world worked. Other Enlightenment theorists sought to discern the natural laws that governed the social and political universe. For educated provincials, the writings of the Englishman John Locke were among the most influential.

In the 1680s, Locke belonged to a group of Whig politicians who opposed the attempts of the Stuart kings Charles II and James II to expand their prerogatives at Parliament's expense. In 1689, Locke published his *Two Treatises on Civil Government,* in which he advanced a philosophical justification for the recent overthrow of James II and Parliament's elevation of William and Mary to the throne. As a seventeenth-century Englishman, Locke clearly accepted the validity of monarchy as a form of government, but he made the legitimacy of monarchy and, indeed, of all governments, dependent on their adherence to natural law. Locke's interpretation of the applicability of natural law to civil society was deceptively simple: government, he contended, existed solely to protect the natural rights of its constituents, who, in turn, could rebel against any regime that did not protect those rights.

In Locke's political theory, rights were inherent in human nature and thus depended on neither royal charters nor legal precedents for their defense. Men, he argued, were born in a perfectly free state of nature, but they agreed to surrender part of their freedom to band together as a civil society, creating a government to protect their natural rights of life, liberty, and property. Unlike the Stuarts and their partisans, who still contended that kings and governments received their authority from God and thus ruled by divine right, Locke argued that political authority originated in a social compact among men. Government, in other words, was the creation of the people, who alone conferred legitimacy on it. While governments were transient and man-made, rights were inalienable.

Like other Enlightenment theorists, Locke believed that social progress would result from men's rational enjoyment of their natural rights. Most Enlightenment theorists envisioned natural rights as both collective and individual. The concept of a divinely sanctioned law of nature, in particular, coupled social obligation with individual rights. Like the eighteenth-century philosophers of the Scottish Enlightenment—such as Francis Hutcheson and Adam Smith—whose writings also were influential in the colonies, Locke believed that the individual pursuit and enjoyment of property, for instance, could and should promote the general welfare.

By embedding rights in human nature rather than in a specific catalog of shared customs and traditions, natural rights theory appealed powerfully not only to those who resisted imperial authority but also to those who did not see themselves as possessing traditionally recognized liberties and rights. For example, backcountry dissidents in Pennsylvania used the language of natural rights to state their grievances to the eastern gentry who controlled their provincial government. In 1764, the so-called Paxton Boys petitioned the Pennsylvania legislature to give them more representation, for at this time the province's western counties had far fewer representatives than their population warranted. Without a trace of irony, the petitioners invoked natural rights theory—along with constitutional precedent—to justify their desire for both political representation and a more aggressive military effort against the western Indians, whose land they coveted. Typically lacking both a voice in and the protection of the government, such men were likely to express their grievances in the language of natural rights.

After 1765, the idiom of natural rights, employed alone or alongside other languages of liberty, was increasingly attractive to many defenders of colonial liberties and rights. As imperial officials set out to centralize colonial governance, colonists who had long used historic or constitutional arguments to assert the rights of Englishmen in America found that those arguments carried little weight in London. Although some colonial leaders continued to insist on the historic and constitutional basis of their rights and liberties, others buttressed their challenge with assertions of universal natural rights.

Religion provided yet another arena in which colonial Americans could experiment with concepts of liberty, as well as additional impetus for them to question established authority. In most colonies, as in Europe, an established church enjoyed official sanction and financial support from all taxpayers, whatever their beliefs. While Pennsylvania and Rhode Island guaranteed the religious freedom of their inhabitants, the governments of most other colonies merely tolerated religious dissenters, who were nonetheless required to pay taxes to support the established church. The Congregational Church was established in New England; the Church of England enjoyed this privileged status in parts of New York and in the southern colonies. But resentment of the privileges of ecclesiastical establishments and their clergy helped fuel a series of religious revivals known as the Great Awakening.

These revivals and the new emotion-laden spirituality they promoted transformed the form and content of American religion in the decades before the Revolution. Although revivalist clergy represented various Protestant denominations, they all preached that people attained salvation through faith alone and that individuals could obtain faith only by establishing a personal relationship with God. Ministers encouraged each of their listeners to cultivate such a relationship, a process that culminated in a heartfelt conversion experience. Revivalist or evangelical religion, then, privileged individual introspection over the judgment of worldly authorities—some of whom, not surprisingly, criticized the revivals as harbingers of disorder.

Revivals occurred throughout British colonial America in the middle decades of the eighteenth century. In the 1720s, New Jersey's Dutch Reformed congregations experienced a spiritual awakening. William and Gilbert Tennent led revivals among the Scots-Irish Presbyterians of New Jersey and Pennsylvania in the 1730s and 1740s. Meanwhile, Jonathan Edwards led New England's first revival in Northampton, Massachusetts, in 1734, and for the next decade he and other New England ministers eased anxiety born of land scarcity, local conflicts, and economic stagnation by encouraging people to recommit their lives to God. By the 1750s, Presbyterian evangelicals were challenging what amounted to an Anglican monopoly of religion in Virginia. A decade later, the Separate Baptists, who rejected worldly hierarchies and pretensions and admitted slaves and women as equal members of their congregations, challenged the religious and cultural authority of the Church of England and the elite men who ran it in most southern colonial communities.

The impact of the revivals on colonial religion was both invigorating and divisive. On the one hand, the revivals clearly strengthened many existing churches and led to the creation of others, in both previously unchurched areas and more established colonial communities. On the other hand, they also resulted in increased denominationalism and ended in most places, once and for all, the ability of any one church to bring together an entire community. Instead, religion divided people as new denominations appeared and schisms erupted in many existing congregations, causing supporters and opponents of the revivals—known as New Lights and Old Lights, respectively—to go their separate ways. Fearing disorder and the subversion of established social hierarchies, some opponents of the revivals went so far as to support the passage of laws enforcing orthodoxy and silencing particularly incendiary preachers.

Supporters of the revivals, in turn, employed two languages of liberty in their defense. Like those who defended political rights and liberties, those who championed religious liberty appealed to law—which in their case could be God's or the king's—and to a theory of natural rights. Some revivalists claimed Christian liberty, which they defined as the liberty to pursue godliness, thereby implying that there was one true religion that people should be free to seek. Other friends of the revivals, by contrast, articulated the more radical notion of liberty of conscience as a natural right. Both lines of argument, however, had important political implications because they aimed to limit the power of political and ecclesiastical authorities to control the religious observance of ordinary people. Religious awakening therefore indirectly politicized its adherents by encouraging them to question the authorities who criticized or impeded the revivals.

Indeed, when colonists pursued their religious beliefs to their logical conclusions, they sometimes challenged the most deeply entrenched social hierarchies. Take, for instance, the case of the Society of Friends—better known as the Quakers—an English pietist sect whose members founded Pennsylvania and settled there and in western New Jersey, where they remained influential throughout the colonial era. Because the Quakers believed that the spirit of God—which they called the Inner Light—lived in each individual, they regarded all people as equal in the eyes of God. The Society of Friends had no ecclesiastical hierarchy and no ordained clergy: men and women of all social ranks could lead prayers and preach at Quaker meetings. Quaker belief in the equality and shared godliness of all people led them to reject earthly social distinctions and oppose all violence, including war. Condemnation of man-made hierarchies and violence, in turn, made some Friends early and impassioned critics of the institution of slavery. Quaker criticism of slavery, which began in earnest in the 1750s, asserted the humanity of enslaved people, who could claim liberty under the laws of God as an inherent right.

In the decades preceding the imperial crisis, colonists deployed libertarian ideals and rhetoric in an array of antiauthoritarian causes. Their experience in championing some of these causes—such as the powers of their lower houses of assembly—would directly inform their response to changes in imperial policy in the 1760s and 1770s. The issues surrounding the religious ferment of the Great Awakening, by contrast, pertained only indirectly to imperial governance but nonetheless impelled people to question authority and articulate a libertarian worldview in defense of the revivals. Political traditions, economic aspirations, and religious fervor, together, shaped the languages of liberty in which a diverse colonial population would protest imperial transgressions against their liberties and rights.

DOCUMENT 1

The Dangers of an Unconverted Ministry (1740)

Gilbert Tennent

In the middle decades of the eighteenth century, religious revivals swept through the American colonies. Revivalist clergy preached salvation through faith, not works, and emphasized the responsibility of the faithful to seek and support a godly ministry. In this 1740 sermon, Gilbert Tennent, a New Jersey Presbyterian, bluntly urged his listeners to reject "ungodly" clergy. Tennent's controversial views resulted in his being barred from preaching in some localities.[1]

Questions to consider:

1. How did Tennent define "Christian liberty"?
2. On what grounds did he deem it both "lawful and expedient" to abandon a "dead" minister?
3. What sorts of people were most likely to find Tennent's message dangerously controversial?

As a faithful ministry is a great ornament, blessing, and comfort, to the Church of God, even the feet of such messengers are beautiful. So on the contrary, an ungodly ministry is a great curse and judgment. These caterpillars labour to devour every green thing. . . . Such who are contented under a dead ministry, have not in them the temper of that Saviour they profess. It's an awful sign, that they are as blind as moles, and as dead as stones, without any spiritual taste and relish. And alas! isn't this the case of the multitudes? If they can get one, that has the name of a minister, with a band, and a black coat or gown to carry on a Sabbath-days among them . . . if he is free from gross crimes in practice, and takes good care to keep at a due distance from their consciences, and is never troubled about his insuccessfulness . . . Poor silly souls! . . . [But] it is both lawful and expedient to go from them to hear godly persons; yea, it's so far from being sinful to do this, that one who lives under a pious minister of lesser gifts, after having honestly endeavoured to get benefit by his ministry, and yet gets little or none, but doth find real benefit and more benefit elsewhere; I say, he may lawfully go, and that frequently, where he gets most good to his precious soul. . . .

If God's people have a right to the gifts of all God's ministers, pray why mayn't they use them, as they have opportunity? And if they should go a few miles farther than ordinary, to enjoy those, which they profit most by, who do they wrong? . . . To bind men to a particular minister, against their judgment and inclinations, when they are more edified elsewhere, is carnal with a witness; a cruel oppression against tender consciences, a compelling of men to sin . . . Besides it is an unscriptural infringement on Christian Liberty . . . It's a yoke worse than that of Rome itself.

DOCUMENT 2

The Essential Rights and Liberties of Protestants (1744)

Elisha Williams

In May 1742, the government of Connecticut outlawed deviations from the colony's established Congregational Church. Designed to prevent itinerancy, schisms, and the removal of orthodox ministers by congregations that were sympathetic to the revivals, these laws aroused opposition on both religious and political grounds. One political objection was that the Connecticut laws violated the English Toleration Act of 1689, which decriminalized Protestant dissent in England—a law that many assumed applied equally to the colonies. In 1744, Elisha Williams, former rector of Yale College and a member of New England's leading clerical family, penned the most powerful critique of the Connecticut legislation.[2]

Questions to consider:

1. How did Williams define "Christian liberty"?
2. From which intellectual traditions did Williams draw evidence in support of his assertion of the rights of Protestants?
3. When Williams wrote of "our Nation," to whom was he referring?

[Because] the end of civil government . . . [is] the greater security of . . . the natural and unalienable right[s] of every man, . . . it is but a just consequence, that [men] are to be protected in the enjoyment of this [religious] right as well as any other. A worshipping assembly of Christians have surely as much right to be protected from molestation in their worship, as the inhabitants of a town assembled to consult their civil interests from disturbance. This right I am speaking of, is the most valuable right, of which every one ought to be most tender, of universal and equal concernment to all; and security and protection in the enjoyment of it the just expectation of every individual . . . .

If there be any rights and liberties of men that challenge protection and security therein from the civil magistrate, it is this natural right of private judgment in matters of religion, that the sacred Scriptures only may become the rule to all men in all religious matters, as they ought to be. In a word, this is the surest way for the ease and quiet of the rulers, as well as peace of the state, the surest way to love and obedience of all the subjects. And if there be diverse religious sects in the state, and the one attempts to offend the other, and the magistrate interposes only to keep the peace, it is but a natural consequence to suppose that in such case they all finding themselves equally safe, and protected in their rights by the civil power, they will all be equally obedient. . . . And should the clergy closely adhere to these principles, instead of their being reproached for pride and ambition, as the sowers of strife and contention and disturbance of the peace of the Church of God, they would be honoured for their work's sake, esteemed for their character, loved as blessings to the world, heard with pleasure, and become successful in their endeavours to recommend the knowledge and practice of Christianity.

It also follows from the preceding principles, that every Christian has the right to determine for himself what church to join himself to; and every church has the right to judge in what manner God is to be worshipped by them, and what form of discipline ought to be observed by them, and the right also of electing their own officers . . . From this right of private judgment in matters of religion . . . it follows, that no Christian is obliged to join himself to this or the other church, because any man or order of men command him to do so, or because they tell him the worship and discipline thereof is most consonant to the sacred Scriptures. For no man has the right to judge him. . . .

'Tis a scandal to Christians, to contend and quarrel with their neighbours for enjoying [the rights of conscience in matters of religion], and inexcusable in a Protestant state to make any infringement upon them. And it was on these very principles, . . . that our first reformers acted, and on which all reformations must be built. And though our nation in times past under the influence of a bigoted clergy, and arbitrary weak or popish princes, have made laws founded on principles contrary to these I have been pleading for; yet they seem in a great measure rooted out of the nation: and these principles of truth have taken root, and been growing ever since the happy Revolution [of 1688], and Act of Toleration; and 'tis to be hoped, will prevail & spread more and more, until all spiritual tyranny, and lording it over the consciences of men, be banished out of the world. . . .

It has commonly been the case, that Christian Liberty, as well as civil, has been lost by little and little; and experience has taught, that it is not easy to recover it, when once lost. So precious a jewel is always to be watched with a careful eye: for no people are likely to enjoy liberty long, that are not zealous to preserve it.

DOCUMENT 3

Some Considerations on Keeping Negroes (1762)

John Woolman

John Woolman of New Jersey was one of the first Americans to write extensively on the topic of slavery. His opposition to slavery stemmed in part from his Quaker beliefs but also from his observations while traveling in the southern colonies, where he often lodged with slaveowning Quaker families. Woolman's antislavery tracts, published in 1754 and 1762, helped to convince the Philadelphia Yearly Meeting to urge all Quakers to emancipate their bondpeople and work in other ways to undermine slavery and the Atlantic slave trade. Woolman and other Quakers pioneered the enlistment of religious ideals and rhetoric in the early fight against slavery.[3]

Questions to consider:

1. How did Woolman explain the origins and spread of slavery in the New World?
2. Why did he believe that slavery was "detrimental to the real prosperity of America"?
3. On what grounds did Woolman assert that the "colour of a man avails nothing in matters of right and equity"? Would most of his contemporaries have agreed?

As some in most religious societies amongst the English are concerned in importing or purchasing the inhabitants of Africa as slaves, and as the professors of Christianity of several other nations do the like, these circumstances tend to make people less apt to examine the practice so closely as they would if such a thing had not been, but was now proposed to be entered upon. It is, however, our duty and what concerns us individually, as creatures accountable to our Creator, to employ rightly the understanding which he hath given us, in humbly endeavouring to be acquainted with his will concerning us and with the nature and tendency of those things which we practice. For as justice remains to be justice, so many people of reputation in the world joining with wrong things, do not excuse others in joining with them nor make the consequences of their proceedings less dreadful in the final issue than it would be otherwise. . . .

Under an apprehension of duty, I offer some further considerations on this subject [of slavery], having endeavoured some years to consider it candidly. I have observed people of our own colour whose abilities have been inferior of the affairs which relate to their convenient subsistence, who have been taken care of by others, and the profit of such work as they could do applied toward their support. I believe there are such amongst Negroes and that some people in whose hands they are keep them with no view of outward profit, do not consider them as black men who, as such, ought to serve white men, but account them persons who have need of guardians, and as such take care of them. Yet where equal care is taken in all parts of education, I do not apprehend cases of this sort are likely to occur more frequently amongst one sort of people than another.

It looks to me that the slave trade was founded and hath generally been carried on in a wrong spirit, that the effects of it are detrimental to the real prosperity of our country, and will be more so except we cease from the common motives of keeping them and treat them in future agreeable to truth and pure justice. . . .

Some who keep slaves have doubted as to the equity of the practice; but as they knew men noted for their piety who were in it, this, they say, has made their minds easy. To lean on the example of men in doubtful cases is difficult. For only admit that those men were not faithful and upright to the highest degree, but that in some particular case they erred, and it may follow that this one case was the same about which we are in doubt; and to quiet our minds by their example may be dangerous to ourselves, and continuing in it prove a stumbling block to tender-minded people who succeed us, in like manner as their examples are to us.

But supposing charity was their only motive and they, not foreseeing the tendency of paying robbers for their booty, were not justly under the imputation of being partners with a thief (Prov. 29:24), but were really innocent in what they did, are we assured that we keep [slaves] with the same views they kept them? If we keep them from no other motive than a real sense of duty, and true charity governs us in all our proceedings toward them, we are so far safe. But if another spirit which inclines our minds to the ways of this world prevail upon us, and we are concerned for our own outward gain more than for their real happiness, it will avail us nothing that some good men have had the care and management of Negroes.

Since mankind spread upon the earth, many have been the revolutions attending the several families, and their customs and ways of life different from each other. This diversity of manners, though some are preferable to others, operates not in favour of any so far as to justify them to do violence to innocent men, to bring them from their own to another way of life. The mind, when moved by a principle of true love, may feel a warmth of gratitude to the universal Father and a lively sympathy with those nations where divine light has been less manifest.

This desire for their real good may beget a willingness to undergo hardships for their sakes, that the true knowledge of God may be spread amongst them. But to take them from their own land with views of profit to ourselves by means inconsistent with pure justice is foreign to that principle which seeks the happiness of the whole creation. Forced subjection, on innocent persons of full age, is inconsistent with right reason: on one side, the human mind is not naturally fortified with that firmness in wisdom and goodness necessary to an independent ruler; on the other side, to be subject to the uncontrollable will of a man liable to err, is most painful and afflicting to a conscientious creature.

It is our happiness faithfully to serve the Divine Being who made us. His perfection makes our service reasonable; but so long as men are biased by narrow self-love, so long an absolute power over other men is unfit for them. Men, taking on them the government of others, may intend to govern reasonably and make their subjects more happy than they would be otherwise. But as absolute command belongs only to him who is perfect, where frail men in their own wills assume such command it hath a direct tendency to vitiate their minds and make them more unfit for government.

Placing on men the ignominious title SLAVE, dressing them in uncomely garments, keeping them to servile labour in which they are so often dirty, tends gradually to fix a notion in the mind that they are a sort of people below us in nature, and leads us to consider them as such in all our conclusions about them. And, moreover, a person which in our esteem is mean and contemptible, if their language or behaviour toward us is unseemly or disrespectful, it excites wrath more powerfully than the like conduct in one we accounted our equal or superior, and where this happens to be the case it disqualifies for candid judgment; for it is unfit for a person to sit as judge in a case where his own personal resentments are stirred up, and as members of society in a well-framed government we are mutually dependent. Present interest incites to duty and makes each man attentive to the convenience of others; but he whose will is a law to others can enforce obedience by punishment, he whose wants are supplied without feeling any obligation to make equal returns to his benefactor, his irregular appetites find an open field for motion, and he is in danger of growing hard and inattentive to their convenience who labour for his support, and so loses that disposition in which alone men are fit to govern.

The English government hath been commended by candid foreigners for the disuse of racks and tortures, so much practiced in some states; but this multiplying slaves now leads to it. For where people exact hard labour of others without a suitable reward and are resolved to continue in that way, severity to such who oppose them becomes the consequence; and several Negro criminals among the English in America have been executed in a lingering, painful way, very terrifying to others. . . .

There is superiority of men over brute creatures, and some of them so manifestly dependent on men for a living, that for them to serve us in moderation so far as relates to the right use of things looks consonant to the design of our Creator. There is nothing in their frame, nothing relative to the propagating their species, which argues the contrary; but in men there is. The frame of men's bodies and the disposition of their minds is different. Some who are tough and strong and their minds active choose ways of life requiring much labour to support them. Others are soon weary, and though use makes labour more tolerable, yet some are less apt for toil than others and their minds less sprightly. These latter, labouring for their subsistence, commonly choose a life easy to support, being content with a little. When they are weary they may rest, take the most advantageous part of the day for labour, and in all cases proportion one thing to another that their bodies be not oppressed.

Now while each is at liberty the latter may be as happy and live as comfortably as the former; but where men of the first sort have the latter under absolute command, not considering the odds in strength and firmness, do sometimes in their eager pursuit lay on burdens grievous to be borne, by degrees grow rigorous, and aspiring to greatness they increase oppression; and the true order of kind Providence is subverted. There are weaknesses sometimes attending us which make little or no alteration in our countenances, nor much lessen our appetite for food, and yet so effect us as to make labour very uneasy. In such cases masters intent on putting forward business and jealous of the sincerity of their slaves may disbelieve what they say and grievously afflict them. . . .

Seed sown with tears of a confined oppressed people, harvest cut down by an overborne discontented reaper, makes bread less sweet to the taste of an honest man, than that which is the produce or just reward of such voluntary action which is one proper part of the business of human creatures.

Again, the weak state of the human species in bearing and bringing forth their young, and the helpless condition of their young beyond that of other creatures, clearly show that Perfect Goodness designs a tender care and regard should be exercised toward them, and that no imperfect, arbitrary power should prevent the cordial effects of that sympathy which is in the minds of well-met pairs to each other and toward their offspring.

In our species the mutual ties of affection are more rational and durable than in others below us, the care and labour of raising our offspring much greater. The satisfaction arising to us in their innocent company and in their advances from one rational improvement to another is considerable when two are thus joined and their affections sincere. It however happens among slaves that they are often situated in different places, and their seeing each other depends on the will of men liable to human passions and a bias in judgment, who with views of self-interest may keep them apart more than is right. Being absent from each other and often with other company, there is a danger of their affections being alienated, jealousies arising, the happiness otherwise resulting from their offspring frustrated, and the comforts of marriage destroyed. These things being considered closely as happening to a near friend will appear to be hard and painful.

He who reverently observes that goodness manifested by our gracious Creator toward the various species of beings in this world, will see that in our frame and constitution is clearly shown that innocent men capable to manage for themselves were not intended to be slaves. . . .

The colour of a man avails nothing in matters of right and equity. Consider colour in relation to treaties; by such, disputes betwixt nations are sometimes settled. And should the Father of us all so dispose things that treaties with black men should sometimes be necessary, how then would it appear amongst princes and ambassadors to insist on the prerogative of the white colour? Whence is it that men who believe in a righteous Omnipotent Being, to whom all nations stand equally related and are equally accountable, remain so easy in it, but for that the ideas of Negroes and slaves are so interwoven in the mind that they do not discuss this matter with that candour and freedom of thought which the case justly calls for?

To come at a right feeling of their condition requires humble serious thinking, for in their present situation they have but little to engage our natural affection in their favour . . . But such who live in the spirit of true charity, to sympathize with the afflicted in the lowest stations of life is a thing familiar to them.

DOCUMENT 4

The Paxton Boys' Remonstrance (1764)

Westerners in many colonies resented both the difficulty of obtaining land and their lack of political representation—both of which they saw as abridgements of their liberties and rights. In Pennsylvania, a group of westerners known as the Paxton Boys opposed the conciliatory Indian policies of their Quaker-dominated government, waging war against the Conestoga Indians and pursuing other peaceful Indians to Philadelphia, where the Indians sought the protection of the colonial government. Some 1,500 westerners marched on Philadelphia in 1763. Returning home at the urging of a sympathetic Benjamin Franklin, they nonetheless stated their grievances in this February 1764 petition to the governor and assembly.[4]

Questions to consider:

1. Who did the petitioners blame for their suffering?
2. What did they regard as the chief liberties of "British Subjects"?
3. Why might the governor and assembly be reluctant to accede to their demands?

We, Matthew Smith and James Gibson, in behalf of ourselves and His Majesty's faithful and loyal subjects, the inhabitants of the frontier counties . . . humbly beg leave to remonstrate and to lay before you the following grievances, which we submit to your wisdom for redress.

First. We apprehend that as freemen and English subjects, we have an indispensable title to the same privileges and immunities with His Majesty's other subjects who reside in the [eastern] counties . . . and therefore ought not to be excluded from an equal share with them in the very important privilege of legislation; nevertheless, contrary to the Proprietor's Charter and the acknowledged principles of common justice & equity, our five counties are restrained from electing more than ten representatives . . . while the three [eastern] counties and the city of Philadelphia . . . elect twenty-six. This we humbly conceive is oppressive, unequal, and unjust, the cause of many of our grievances, and an infringement of our natural privileges of freedom & equality; wherefore we humbly pray that we may no longer be deprived of an equal number . . . to represent us in the assembly.

Secondly. We understand that a bill is now before the house of assembly, wherein it is provided that such persons as shall be charged with killing any Indians . . . shall not be tried in the county where the fact was committed . . . This is manifestly to deprive British subjects of their known privileges, to cast an eternal reproach upon whole counties, as if they were unfit to serve their country in the quality of jurymen, and to contradict the well-known laws of the British nation in a point whereupon life, liberty, and security essentially depend, namely, that of being tried by their equals in the neighbourhood where their own, their accusers', and the witnesses' character and credit, with the circumstances of the fact, are best known. . . .

Thirdly. During the late and present Indian war, the frontiers of this province have been repeatedly attacked and ravaged by skulking parties of the Indians, who have with the most savage cruelty murdered men, women, and children without distinction, and have reduced near a thousand families to the most extreme distress. It grieves us to the very heart to see such of our frontier inhabitants as have escaped savage fury with the loss of their parents, their children, their wives or relatives, left destitute by the public, and exposed to the most cruel poverty and wretchedness while upwards of an hundred and twenty of these savages, who are with great reason suspected of being guilty of these horrid barbarities under the mask of friendship, have procured themselves to be taken under the protection of the government, with a view to elude the fury of the brave relatives of the murdered, and are now maintained at the public expence. . . .

Fourthly. We humbly conceive that it is contrary to the maxims of good policy, and extremely dangerous to our frontiers, to suffer any Indians of what tribe soever to live within the inhabited parts of the province while we are engaged in an Indian war. . . .

Seventhly. We daily lament that numbers of our nearest & dearest relatives are still in captivity among the savage heathen, to be trained up in all their ignorance & barbarity, or to be tortured to death with all the contrivances of Indian cruelty, for attempting to make their escape from bondage. We see they pay no regard to the many solemn promises which they have made to restore our friends who are in bondage amongst them. We therefore earnestly pray that no trade may hereafter be carried on with them, until our brethren and relatives are brought home to us.

Eighthly. We complain that [the] Society of [Friends] in this province, in the late Indian war, & at several treaties held by the King's representatives, openly loaded the Indians with presents, and that . . . a leader of the said Society, in defiance of all government, not only abetted our Indian enemies, but kept up a private intelligence with them, and publicly received from them a belt of wampum, as if he had been our governor or authorized by the King to treat with his enemies. By this means the Indians have been taught to despise us as a weak and disunited people, and from this fatal source have arose many of our calamities under which we groan. . . .

Ninthly. We cannot but observe with sorrow that Fort Augusta, which has been very expensive to this province, has afforded us but little assistance during this or the last war. The men that were stationed at that place neither helped our distressed inhabitants to save their crops, nor did they attack our enemies in their towns, or patrol on our frontiers. We humbly request that proper measures be taken to make that garrison more serviceable to us in our distress, if it can be done. . . .

DOCUMENT 5

The Colonel Dismounted . . . Containing A Dissertation upon the Constitution of the Colony (1764)

Richard Bland

In 1758, the Virginia assembly passed the Two-Penny Act, which fixed the price of tobacco used to pay debts at roughly half its market value at that time. This measure was designed to alleviate the problems of indebted planters at a time of inflation due to crop failure. Imperial authorities disallowed the act, however, partly in response to pressure from Virginia's Anglican clergy, whose tax-funded salaries it adversely affected. Virginians protested both the ruling from London and the clergy's attempts to sue for compensation. Addressed to the Reverend John Camm, a leading ministerial spokesman, Richard Bland's contribution to the debate introduced what would become an important issue in colonial political discourse: the distinction between internal and external government.[5]

Questions to consider:

1. How did Bland define the "constitution" of Virginia?
2. Why—and on what grounds—did he continue to acknowledge the colonies' "dependence upon the mother kingdom"?
3. How did Bland differentiate the rights and obligations of "internal" and "external" government?

I do not suppose, Sir, that you look upon the present inhabitants of Virginia as a people conquered by British arms. If indeed we are to be considered only as the savage aborigines of this part of America, we cannot pretend to the rights of English subjects; but if we are the descendants of Englishmen, who by their own consent and at the expense of their own blood and treasure undertook to settle this new region for the benefit and aggrandizement of the parent kingdom, the native privileges our progenitors enjoyed must be derived to us from them, as they could not be forfeited by their migration to America. . . .

Under an English government all men are born free, are only subject to laws made with their own consent, and cannot be deprived of the benefit of these laws without a transgression of them. To assert this is sufficient; to demonstrate it to an Englishman is useless. He not only knows, but, if I may use the expression, feels it as a vital principle in the constitution, which places him in the situation without the reach of the highest executive power in the state, if he lives in an obedience to its laws.

If the people of this colony are freeborn and have a right to the liberties and privileges of English subjects, they must necessarily have a legal constitution, that is, a legislature composed in part of the representatives of the people who may enact laws for the internal government of the colony and suitable to its various circumstances and occasions; and without such a representative, I am bold enough to say, no law can be made.

By the term internal government it may be easily perceived that I exclude from the legislature of the colony all power derogatory to their dependence upon the mother kingdom; for as we cannot lose the rights of Englishmen by our removal to this continent, so neither can we withdraw our dependence without destroying the constitution. In every instance, therefore, of our external government we are and must be subject to the authority of the British Parliament, but in no others; for if the Parliament should impose laws upon us merely relative to our internal government, it deprives us, as far as those laws extend, of the most valuable part of our birthright as Englishmen, of being governed by laws made with our own consent. As all power, therefore, is excluded from the colony of withdrawing its dependence from the mother kingdom, so is all power over the colony excluded from the mother kingdom but such as respects its external government. . . .

But it may be objected that this general position excludes all laws of England, so as that none of them are obligatory upon us in our internal government. The answer to this objection is obvious: the common law, being the common consent of the people from time immemorial, and the "birthright of every Englishman, does follow him wherever he goes," and consequently must be the general law by which the colony is to be governed. So also the statutes of England in force at the time of our separation, having every essential in their institution to make them obligatory upon our ancestors, that is, by their consent by their representatives, and having the same sanction with the common law, must have the same extensive force, and bind us in the same manner the common law does; if it was otherwise it would involve this contradiction, that of the two laws made by the same power, one is coercive upon us when the other is not so, which is plainly absurd.

DOCUMENT 6

The Rights of the Colonies Examined (1765)

Stephen Hopkins

The author of this pamphlet was the governor of Rhode Island, a chartered colony, one of five British provinces not under direct royal control during the prerevolutionary era. Stephen Hopkins wrote both to defend Rhode Island's charter against efforts to make it a royal colony and to protest the increasing trend toward centralization in British imperial policies.[6] Appealing to historical precedent and to the writings of English libertarians like Algernon Sidney, he attempted to reconcile the colonists' avowed dependence on Britain with the "rights and privileges of freeborn Englishmen."

Questions to consider:

1. How did Hopkins define liberty?
2. How did he define slavery?
3. Why, according to Hopkins, did the English who settled in America remain subjects of the King? Why did they retain their rights as Englishmen?

Liberty is the greatest blessing that men can enjoy, and slavery the heaviest curse that human nature is capable of. This being so makes it a matter of the utmost importance to men which of the two shall be their portion. Absolute liberty is, perhaps, incompatible with any kind of government. The safety resulting from society, and the advantage of just and equal laws, hath caused men to forego some part of their natural liberty, and submit to government. This appears to be the most rational account of its beginning, although, it must be confessed, mankind have by no means been agreed about it. Some have found its origin in divine appointment; others have thought it took rise from power; enthusiasts have dreamed that dominion was founded in grace. . . .

This glorious [British] constitution, the best that ever existed among men, will be confessed by all to be founded by compact and established by consent of the people. By this most beneficent compact British subjects are to be governed only agreeable to laws to which they themselves have some way consented, and are not to be compelled to part with their property but as it is called for by the authority of such laws. The former is truly liberty; the latter is really to be possessed of property and to have something that may be called one's own.

On the contrary, those who are governed at the will of another, or of others, and whose property may be taken from them by taxes or otherwise without their own consent and against their will, are in the miserable condition of slaves. "For liberty solely consists in an independency upon the will of another; and by the name of slave we understand a man who can neither dispose of his person or goods, but enjoys all at the will of his master," says Sidney on government. These things premised, whether the British American colonies on the continent [of North America] are justly entitled to like privileges and freedom as their fellow subjects in Great Britain are, shall be the chief point examined. In discussing this question we shall make the colonies of New England, with whose rights we are best acquainted, the rule of our reasoning, not in the least doubting but all others are justly entitled to like rights with them.

New England was first planted by adventurers who left England, their native country, by permission of King Charles I, and at their own expense transported themselves to America, with great risk and difficulty settled among savages, and in a very surprising manner formed new colonies in the wilderness. Before their departure the terms of their freedom and the relation they should stand in to the mother country in their emigrant state were fully settled: they were to remain subject to the King and dependent on the kingdom of Great Britain. In return they were to receive protection and enjoy all the rights and privileges of freeborn Englishmen. . . .

Colonies in general, both ancient and modern, have always enjoyed as much freedom as the mother state from which they went out. And will anyone suppose the British colonies in America are an exception to this general rule? Colonies that came out from a kingdom renowned for liberty, from a constitution founded on compact, from a people of all the sons of men the most tenacious of freedom; who left the delights of their native country, parted from their homes and all their conveniences, searched out and subdued a foreign country with the most amazing travail and fortitude, to the infinite advantage and emolument of the mother state; that removed on a firm reliance of a solemn compact and royal promise and grant that they and their successors forever should be free, should be partakers and sharers in all the privileges and advantages of the then English, now British, constitution.

DOCUMENT 7

A Vindication of the British Colonies (1765)

James Otis

Judge Martin Howard, Jr., of Rhode Island responded to Stephen Hopkins's Rights of the Colonies Examined *(Document 6, above) by asserting the supremacy of Parliament, which he regarded as a fundamental part of the common law tradition from which Britons derived their liberties and rights. The prominent Massachusetts lawyer James Otis, in turn, answered Howard in this pamphlet in which he drew heavily on the works of Sir William Blackstone, the leading interpreter of the common law, to argue against encroaching imperial authority and the resulting abridgement of colonial rights.[7]*

Questions to consider:

1. What, in Otis's view, was the difference between natural and civil rights, and why did he stress that distinction?
2. Why did Otis insist that colonial rights derived from the common law, and not—as his opponent argued—from royal charters?

The rights of men are *natural* or *civil*. Both these are divisible into *absolute* and *relative*. The natural absolute personal rights of individuals are so far from being opposed to political or civil rights that they are the very basis of all municipal laws of any great value. "The absolute rights of individuals regarded by the municipal laws compose what is called *political* or *civil liberty*." "The absolute liberties of Englishmen, as frequently declared in Parliament, are principally three: the right of personal security, personal liberty, and private property." "Besides these three primary rights, there are others which are secondary and subordinate (to preserve the former from unlawful attacks): (1) The constitution or power of Parliament; (2) The limitation of the King's prerogative (and to vindicate them when actually violated); (3) The regular administration of justice; (4) The right of petitioning for redress of grievances; (5) The right of having and using arms for self-defense." See Mr. Blackstone's accurate and elegant analysis of the laws of England. [Judge Howard] seems to have taken this and some other of his distinctions from that excellent treatise very ill understood. The analysis had given this general view of the *objects* of the laws of England: I. Rights of persons; II. Rights of things; III. Private wrongs; IV. Public wrongs. Rights of persons are divided into these: (1) of natural persons; (2) of bodies politic or corporate, i.e., artificial persons or subordinate societies. The rights of these are by [Howard] strangely confounded with the political and civil rights of natural persons. And because corporate rights so far as they depend upon charter are matters of the mere favour and grace of the donor or founder, he thence infers that "the colonies have no rights independent of their charters," and that "they can claim no greater than those give them." This is a contradiction to what he admitted in the preceding page . . . that "by the common law every colonist hath a right to his life, liberty, and property." And he was so vulgar as to call these the "subject's birthright." But what is this birthright worth if it depends merely upon a colony charter that, as he says rightly enough, may be taken away by the Parliament? I wish the gentleman would answer these questions. Would he think an estate worth much that might be taken from him at the pleasure of another? Are charters from the crown usually given for enlarging the liberties and privileges of the grantees in consideration of some special merit and services done the state, or would he have his readers consider them like the ordinances of a French monarch, for limiting and curtailing those rights which all Britons and all British subjects are entitled to by the laws of God and nature, as well as by the common law and the constitution of their country so admirably built on the principles of the former? By which of these laws in contradistinction to the other are the rights of life, liberty, and estate, personal? . . .

We want no foreign codes nor canons here. The common law is our birthright, and the rights and privileges confirmed and secured to us by the British constitution and by act of Parliament are our best inheritance. Condes, pandects, novels, decretals of popes, and the inventions of the devil may suit the cold, bleak regions [of] Brandenburg and Prussia or the scorching heats of Jamaica or Gambia; but we live in a more temperate climate, and shall rest content with the laws, customs, and usages of our ancestors, bravely supported and defended with the monarchy, and from age to age handed down. These have and ever will finally triumph over the whims of political and religious enthusiasts, the extremes of which are libertinism and despotism, anarchy and tyranny, spiritual and temporal, from all which may God preserve us.

SUGGESTED READING FOR CHAPTER 2

APPLEBY, JOYCE. *Liberalism and Republicanism in the American Historical Imagination* (1992).

BAILYN, BERNARD. *The Ideological Origins of the American Revolution* (1967).

CLARK, J. C. D. *The Language of Liberty, 1660–1832: Political Discourse and Social Dynamics in the Anglo-American World* (1994).

GREENE, JACK P. *Peripheries and Center: Constitutional Development in the Extended Polities of the British Empire and the United States, 1607–1788* (1986).

———. *Pursuits of Happiness: The Social Development of Early Modern British Colonies and the Formation of American Culture* (1988).

HEIMERT, ALAN. *Religion and the American Mind: From the Great Awakening to the Revolution* (1966).

ISAAC, RHYS. *The Transformation of Virginia, 1740–1790* (1982).

JORDAN, WINTHROP D. *White over Black: American Attitudes toward the Negro, 1550–1812* (1968).

KARS, MARJOLEINE. *Breaking Loose Together: The Regulator Rebellion in Pre-Revolutionary North Carolina* (2002).

KLOPPENBERG, JAMES T. "The Virtues of Liberalism: Christianity, Republicanism, and the Ethics of Early American Political Discourse." *Journal of American History*, 74 (1987): 9–33.

LAMBERT, FRANK. *Pedlar in Divinity: George Whitefield and the Transatlantic Revivals, 1737–1770* (1994).

MAY, HENRY. *The Enlightenment in America* (1976).

SODERLUND, JEAN R. *Quakers and Slavery: A Divided Spirit* (1985).

NOTES

[1] Gilbert Tennent, *The Dangers of an Unconverted Ministry* (Philadelphia, 1740), 3, 18–21.

[2] Elisha Williams, *The Essential Rights and Liberties of Protestants* (Boston, 1744), 44, 46, 64–65.

[3] John Woolman, *Some Considerations on Keeping Negroes, Part Second* (Philadelphia, 1762), 7, 9, 21–28, 30–32.

[4] *Minutes of the Provincial Council of Pennsylvania*, 10 vols. (Philadelphia, 1852), 9: 138–42.

[5] [Richard Bland], *The Colonel Dismounted: or the Rector Vindicated, In a Letter addressed to His Reverence: Containing A Dissertation upon the Constitution of the Colony* (Williamsburg, Va., 1764), 20–23.

[6] [Stephen Hopkins], *The Rights of the Colonies Examined* (Providence, R.I., 1765), 3–5, 8.

[7] James Otis, *A Vindication of the British Colonies, against the Aspersions of the Halifax Gentleman, in His Letter to a Rhode Island Friend* (Boston, 1765), 8–9, 32.

CHAPTER THREE

REFORM AND RESISTANCE

Before the 1760s, conflicts had emerged between London and the colonies from time to time, but none had been sufficiently serious or enduring to jeopardize the colonists' loyalty to the king and to Britain's much heralded constitution. After the successful conclusion of the latest war with France in 1763, however, British authorities launched a sustained effort to reorganize the imperial administration and to assert control over the colonies. In the process, they articulated a view of the colonies' constitutional status within the empire that differed significantly from that espoused by most of the king's colonial subjects.

After 1763, colonial leaders repeatedly declared their loyalty to the king and to the British Empire while simultaneously contesting attempts to centralize imperial authority and defining what they saw as their constitutional and civil rights. As they did so, many took three steps that ultimately would be essential preconditions for the emergence of a popular revolutionary movement in the next decade. First, the imperial crisis that began in earnest with the Stamp Act of 1765 forced opponents of British policies to articulate in a more systematic fashion their understanding of fundamental constitutional issues—for example, the allocation of authority within the empire and the nature of representation. Second, because changes in imperial administration affected all the colonies, some leaders looked beyond their borders to facilitate intercolonial cooperation in opposing British policies. Third, some colonial leaders also cautiously encouraged popular involvement in protests, boycotts, and other forms of resistance to imperial measures. They formed extralegal committees to promote such efforts, thereby beginning the process of organizing a mass rebellion.

From the perspective of British authorities and from that of more conservative provincials, opponents of the new imperial policies were selfish and opportunistic, as well as erroneous in their interpretation of the imperial constitution. Since the Glorious Revolution, after all, Britons had celebrated the supremacy of Parliament as the fountainhead of all rights and liberties. By denying Parliament's authority to tax them, colonial dissidents seemed, therefore, to challenge the legacy of 1688. They also appeared to refuse to pay their fair share of the costs of the recent war, from which they had greatly benefited.

The fourth in a series of wars with France for mastery in both Europe and North America, the French and Indian War, as it was known in the colonies, was a decisive victory for the British against their long-time rivals. When the war began in 1754, France controlled Canada and much of the Great Lakes region, along with some Caribbean sugar islands. When it was over in 1763, the French retained only their island colonies, having been driven from the mainland of North America; their Indian allies were left weakened and without support against the westward-moving inhabitants the British colonies. The French and Indian War was the first in which North America was a major military theater, as well as the first in which colonists contributed significantly to the British war effort. Imperial officials expected the colonial assemblies to raise both funds and troops. Although the assemblies' efforts often fell short of London's demands, more than 70,000 colonists performed military service, in either provincial or British units. Colonists joined with Britons in 1763 to celebrate their great triumph.

The French and Indian War was a turning point in the history of the British Empire. On the one hand, the benefits of victory were significant. Total defeat of the French in North America, as well as in India, vastly expanded Britain's colonial possessions. From the colonists' perspective, moreover, the defeat of the French cleared the way for westward expansion, which in turn would increase the prosperity of individuals and the productivity of the colonial economy generally. On the other hand, Britain incurred staggering debts as a result of the war, which was fought on many fronts on both land and sea. British military and civilian authorities had noted the independence of the colonial assemblies when they solicited support for the war. Imperial officials worried that the assemblies had too much autonomy, while Britons generally grumbled that the colonists, who reaped the chief benefits of victory, did little to help defray its costs.

The related problems of paying this war debt and governing an expanded empire preoccupied British authorities in the postwar years. In 1763, George Grenville, Britain's new prime minister, addressed these concerns in a legislative agenda that sought both to strengthen imperial

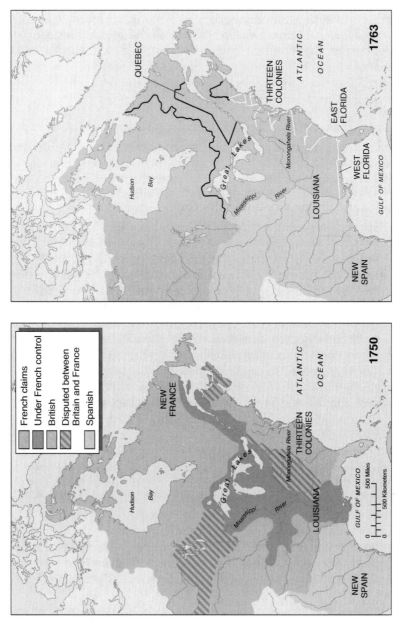

Europe's North American Empires, 1750–1763. In 1750, hostile French, Spanish, and native American settlements surrounded Britain's thirteen mainland colonies. Great Britain's triumph in the French and Indian War transformed the map of North America, while creating new administrative and fiscal problems for imperial authorities in London.

authority in America and raise much-needed revenue for the home government. In the next two years, Parliament enacted four laws pertaining to the colonies: the Sugar Act (1764), the Currency Act (1764), the Stamp Act (1765), and the Quartering Act (1765). All four laws elicited colonial protest, but widespread opposition to the Stamp Act began the first phase of a more general imperial crisis.

In 1764, colonial response to the Sugar Act and the Currency Act was ambivalent or understated. The latter law, which prohibited further colonial emissions of paper currency, attracted little criticism initially, though the colonists would come to condemn it in later years as its economic impact was more widely felt. The Sugar Act was more controversial. It actually lowered the import duties on foreign molasses in the hope of curtailing colonial smuggling. At the same time, however, Parliament made a concerted effort to catch and punish colonists who sought to evade the Navigation Acts by increasing the powers of customs officials and giving vice-admiralty courts—military tribunals without juries—jurisdiction over cases arising from alleged violations of the law. Although the preamble of the Sugar Act clearly stated the intent to raise revenue, many colonists regarded it, like the Navigation Acts, as another attempt to regulate colonial trade. For that reason and because the law only directly affected merchants who imported large quantities of molasses and sugar, few colonists protested the Sugar Act and most who did complained mainly of its economic consequences. Only the legislatures of New York and North Carolina explicitly recognized the Sugar Act as a revenue-raising measure, and only they protested it on constitutional grounds.

The Stamp Act of 1765, by contrast, unambiguously aimed to raise revenue in America by levying taxes on newspapers, pamphlets, almanacs, and other sorts of printed matter, as well as on legal documents such as leases, land titles, and licenses. The law compelled those who acquired these items to purchase stamps to be affixed to them to signify payment of the tax. The Stamp Act was scheduled to go into effect in all the colonies on 1 November 1765. As in the case of the Sugar Act, Parliament made the vice-admiralty courts responsible for handling cases arising from alleged violations of this law.

Many colonial leaders roundly condemned the Stamp Act as an unprecedented violation of their right to be taxed only by their own representatives. For more than a century, of course, the colonists had grudgingly accepted the legitimacy of the Navigation Acts, but the main purpose of those laws was to regulate trade, not to raise revenue. In 1765–66, as they attempted to explain their objections to the Stamp Act, colonial commentators distinguished between trade laws—which imposed duties, or external taxes—and revenue laws, such as the Stamp Act, which imposed internal taxes. In a torrent of pamphlets, speeches, and resolutions, colonial spokesmen repeatedly characterized the latter as unconstitutional, asserting that they would suffer "no taxation without representation."

The Stamp Act crisis began a persistent debate between colonial leaders and imperial authorities—and among the colonists themselves—over the nature of representation. To justify the statute, imperial authorities invoked the theory of virtual representation, whereby each member of Parliament was alleged to represent the interests of all of Britain and the empire, not just those of his constituents. In 1765 and after, many colonists rejected this notion, at least as it applied to propertied white men who resided in North America. They demanded actual representation—in other words, the sort of direct representation that their own assemblies afforded to those who met the race, gender, and property qualifications for voting in their respective provinces. Critics of the Stamp Act asserted that only legislators whom the voters elected—and those they accordingly could turn out of office—had the power to tax them. Because the colonists elected no members of Parliament, they maintained, Parliamentary taxation deprived them of their property without their consent.

Both individually and collectively, colonial leaders spoke out against the Stamp Act. In May 1765, Virginia's House of Burgesses, led by Patrick Henry, adopted an official statement of protest, and in the coming months leaders in other colonies followed the Burgesses' example by drafting their own versions of the Virginia Resolves. Colonial leaders also penned pamphlets, broadsides, and newspaper essays to explain what they saw as the dangers of the Stamp Act and to promote resistance to it. Inexpensive and quickly produced, pamphlets were the eighteenth-century equivalent of cheap paperback books; between 1765 and 1776, colonial authors published some 400 of them on topics related to the imperial crisis. During the Stamp Act crisis, the most influential pamphlet came from the pen of Daniel Dulany of Maryland. Dulany utterly rejected Parliamentary taxation and ridiculed the logic of virtual representation, at least as Grenville's ministry sought to apply it to the distant colonies in America.

In 1765–66, opponents of the Stamp Act also experimented with three tactics that would become characteristic of the colonial resistance movement in the coming years: popular mobilization, intercolonial cooperation, and commercial boycotts. During the Stamp Act crisis, in nearly every major seaport, crowds—typically countenanced or even led by prominent men—targeted stamp distributors and other imperial officials, wrecking their houses or symbolically hanging and burning them in effigy. A new organization, the Sons of Liberty, encouraged popular mobilization, especially in urban areas, where crowds thwarted the enforcement of the Stamp Act by forcing the stamp distributors to resign their commissions. To persuade Parliament to repeal the law, representatives from nine colonies gathered in October at the Stamp Act Congress in New York to draft a series of fourteen resolutions and address petitions for redress of colonial grievances to the king and Parliament. Far more effective, however, were the actions of many merchants in the northern seaports, who decided to boycott British imports to pressure London to repeal the law. Economic sanctions, which in 1765–66 mobilized British merchants in favor of repeal of the Stamp Act, would be the weapon of choice among colonial dissidents in the coming decade.

Many in America condemned colonial resistance to the Stamp Act, especially when it turned violent. Colonial officials, such as lieutenant governors Thomas Hutchinson of Massachusetts and Cadwallader Colden of New York, who became victims of violence and intimidation at the hands of angry crowds, denounced their assailants as lawless rabble. Many conservative men of property shared their concerns, fearing they would be next. At the same time, others criticized opposition to the Stamp Act on constitutional grounds. Some colonial leaders—even many who disliked the Stamp Act—believed that Parliament was, indeed, the supreme political authority in America, as in Britain. Some would cling steadfastly to the view throughout the constitutional crises of the ensuing decade.

In London, radical politicians and some members of Parliament spoke out against the Stamp Act, but political and constitutional considerations precluded compromise on the principle of Parliamentary supremacy. The 1760s were a decade of political instability in Britain, as a succession of prime ministers struggled to maintain the support of the king and a coalition of factions in the House of Commons. George Grenville, who became prime minister in 1763, had lost the support of George III by July 1765, when the king called on the marquis of Rockingham to form a government. While Rockingham and his supporters sympathized with the colonists, they knew that most members of Parliament would support the repeal of the Stamp Act only if it were coupled with a strong affirmation of the principle of Parliamentary supremacy. Britons, whose ancestors had struggled to establish the sovereignty of Parliament, considered it the fundamental basis of their constitutional rights. Imperial authorities therefore rejected a colonial proposal to have their own legislatures raise revenue for the Crown on the grounds that the king's access to an independent revenue would undermine his dependence on and subordination to the Parliament of Great Britain.

In March 1766, Parliament therefore enacted two important pieces of legislation. One repealed the Stamp Act. The other, known as the Declaratory Act, sought to clarify the relationship between Parliament and the colonies in America. The Declaratory Act asserted the authority

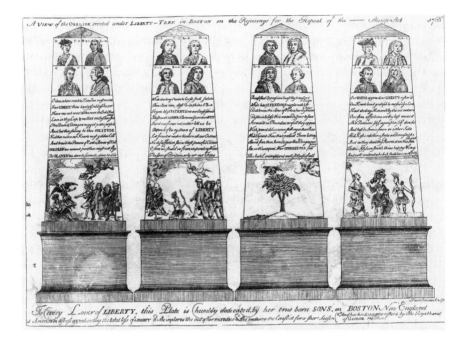

A View of the Obelisk erected under the Liberty-Tree in Boston on the Rejoicings for the Repeal of the—Stamp Act 1766. The pictorial panels of the obelisk told the story of the Stamp Act crisis in four parts: America in distress over the loss of her liberty, seeks the aid of her patrons, endures oppression, and ultimately regains her liberty through the efforts of her "darling Monarch." The obelisk also featured portraits of sixteen Britons—ranging from the king and queen to the radical politician John Wilkes—whom Bostonians regarded as friends to American liberty. What does this obelisk, erected by outspoken opponents of the Stamp Act, reveal about colonial attitudes toward Great Britain and its government in 1766? Source: Etching with watercolor, on laid paper; 23.9 × 33.4 cm (border). Courtesy of The Library of Congress, Washington, D.C.

of Parliament to legislate for the colonies "in all cases whatsoever." Although the law did not mention taxation specifically, clearly imperial authorities believed that Parliament's authority in America extended to taxation. They supported repeal of the Stamp Act because enforcing it would be difficult and inconvenient, not because they came to accept the colonists' view that the law was unconstitutional.

The Declaratory Act elicited no significant protest on the part of the colonists. Opponents of the Stamp Act gleefully celebrated the news of its repeal. In 1766, both sides may have claimed victory, but the issues that ignited the Stamp Act crisis remained unresolved and volatile.

The Stamp Act crisis sowed seeds of mutual suspicion that shaped subsequent imperial agendas as well as colonial responses to new imperial policies. The next major conflict between the colonies and the home government arose in 1767, when yet another new ministry renewed the attempt to raise revenue in America, thereby testing the powers Parliament claimed in the Declaratory Act of 1766. To that end, Charles Townshend, chancellor of the Exchequer, devised a program that included a new revenue law and improvements in the enforcement and collection of colonial customs duties. In addition, Townshend set out to punish the province of New York for its failure to comply fully with the Quartering Act of 1765.

Enacted just two days after the Stamp Act, the Quartering Act required colonial assemblies to provide barracks and supplies for British troops that remained in America after the French and Indian War. New York's assembly initially refused to do so, in part because most of its members resented Parliament's attempt to dictate policy to them and in part because New York, as the American headquarters of British forces, would bear the brunt of the burden for their support. In July 1766, the assembly passed a quartering bill that construed support for the troops as evidence of New Yorkers' loyalty to the king—and, indeed, as a direct gift to him—rather than as humble submission to the will of Parliament. In response, in June 1767, Townshend prevailed on Parliament to pass the New York Restraining Act, which suspended the provincial legislature, pending full compliance with the Quartering Act. By then, however, New York leaders were contemplating the use of military force to suppress an uprising of tenant farmers in the Hudson River Valley. The assembly therefore complied with the law but at the same time petitioned Parliament for its repeal.

Townshend's overriding concerns were to raise revenue and to oblige the colonists to accept the general principle of Parliamentary sovereignty. Accordingly, in May and June 1767, he sponsored the Revenue Act of 1767, which imposed customs duties on imported lead, paper, paint, glass, and tea, which the home government would use to pay the salaries of some colonial governors and judges, thereby rendering them independent of the colonial assemblies. A second law established a Boston-based colonial Board of Customs Commissioners. Imperial authorities selected Boston as headquarters for the customs board because New Englanders were notorious for evading the Navigation Acts. Finally, another law created three new vice-admiralty courts in Boston, Philadelphia, and Charleston to improve enforcement of the tax and trade laws. Known collectively as the Townshend Acts, these measures were in many ways similar to the Sugar Act of 1764. Both imposed customs duties—or external taxes—for the express purpose of raising revenue in the colonies, and both used military courts to enforce compliance. While the colonial response to the Sugar Act had been muted, however, resistance to the Townshend Acts was widespread and vigorous.

Employing the literary, organizational, and economic strategies they pioneered in the Stamp Act crisis, colonists mobilized to oppose the Townshend Acts.

Of the many pamphlets and newspaper essays the Townshend Acts elicited, none was more influential than John Dickinson's *Letters from a Farmer in Pennsylvania*. In a series of twelve essays or "letters," Dickinson alerted his readers to the dangers of the New York Restraining Act, the presence of British troops in the colonies, the proliferation of imperial officials in America, and, of course, the Townshend duties. Dickinson's first letter made its debut in November 1767 in Philadelphia, and this essay and its successors soon appeared in nineteen of the twenty-three English-language newspapers in America, besides being republished at least seven times in pamphlet form. Although he firmly emphasized his loyalty to the king and empire, Dickinson was determined to arouse his readers to resist what he saw as a steadily widening assault on colonial rights and liberties.

Crowds in Charleston, South Carolina, and in Norfolk, Virginia, protested the Townshend Acts in May and September 1767, respectively, but by 1768, Boston was emerging as the center of colonial resistance to the new imperial policies. Boston's radicals, fueled in part by their resentment toward their neighbor-turned-lieutenant-governor Thomas Hutchinson, urged a general boycott of British imports, in response to which at least 24 towns adopted nonimportation agreements by mid-January. In the Massachusetts assembly, radical leader Samuel Adams and lawyer James Otis presented the Massachusetts Circular Letter, which the legislators adopted and sent to their counterparts in other colonies. The letter declared Parliamentary taxation unconstitutional, warned of an ever-widening offensive against colonial liberties, and called for intercolonial cooperation in their defense.

In London, Lord Hillsborough, who had assumed the new post of secretary of state for the southern department, which included the colonies, interpreted the action of the Massachusetts assembly as a dangerous affront to imperial authority. Hillsborough therefore ordered the assembly to rescind the Circular Letter. On 21 April 1768, the assembly refused to do so, and the governor dissolved the legislature on orders from London. In June, Bostonians rioted when the newly established Customs Commissioners seized a ship belonging to merchant John Hancock, an associate of Samuel Adams. Imperial authorities soon took the novel step of sending regiments to Boston to protect the customs men and restore order.

The dissolution of the assembly and the decision to send troops to Boston impelled radicals to action. Like most Britons, the king's American subjects feared standing armies as minions of tyranny. While imperial authorities previously justified the presence of troops in America as necessary for defense against the hostile French and Indians—and many colonists gratefully accepted such protection—the four regiments dispatched to Boston were explicitly charged with policing the populace, maintaining order, and enforcing imperial authority. Capitalizing on the widespread fear and distrust of standing armies, in September Boston radicals organized a convention of delegates from Massachusetts towns to discuss their growing list of grievances.

Radical leaders urged commercial reprisals against Great Britain to protest the Townshend duties, hoping that British merchants would clamor for repeal as they had done during the Stamp Act crisis. In March 1768, Boston merchants resolved to stop importing nonessential British goods for one year, and they urged their counterparts elsewhere to follow suit. In April, New York merchants, still protesting the New York Restraining Act, agreed to cease trade with Britain in August. Although Philadelphia's merchants remained aloof, those in Charleston strongly supported nonimportation. In Virginia and North Carolina, where many tobacco planters traded directly with merchants in England or Scottish merchants who resided in the colonies, leaders solicited broadly based popular support for nonimportation. As early as 1767, contributors to the *Virginia Gazette* were urging men and women alike to show their patriotism by forgoing imported luxury items. In 1769 and 1770, the Sons of Liberty reorganized throughout the colonies to protest the Townshend Acts and enforce nonimportation.

Although colonists implemented nonimportation too late and violated it too often for it to be effective, resistance to the Townshend Acts represented a transitional phase in the imperial crisis. Colonial elites had dominated resistance efforts during the Stamp Act crisis, even to the point of directing or leading riotous urban crowds. Nonelite men and even women were more prominent participants in colonial resistance to the Townshend Acts. Middling men turned out for extralegal committees and local meetings, and women and men, as consumers, spurned imported goods and sometimes even replaced them with domestic manufactures. Newly politicized artisans and mechanics were increasingly assertive, especially in the cities, where gentlemen lamented their inability to control the people out-of-doors. In both Boston and New York, violence erupted, as political differences and antagonism between gentry and common folk led to riots, tarring and feathering, and other ritual acts to force recalcitrant merchants to forgo their trade.

By 1770, nonetheless, nonimportation was crumbling, despite the best efforts of radicals to sustain it. Merchants, some of whom were among the earliest supporters of the boycotts, complained that they suffered disproportionately because of them. Indebted tobacco planters, who initially supported the boycotts in part to curtail the escalation of their debts to British merchants, now wanted to market their crops and thus resume their trade. Colonial consumers, long accustomed to having access to an array of British imports, found it inconvenient to do without the plain and fancy products of the Atlantic trade.

In the short term, however, the boycotts hurt the business of British merchants, who for economic reasons once again pressed the ministry to make peace with colonial dissidents. In 1770, the home government, now headed by Lord North, prevailed on Parliament to repeal all the Townshend duties except the tax on tea. North was not capitulating to colonial demands. The tea tax was the most lucrative of the duties; retaining it would generate funds to pay the salaries of some colonial officials and maintain the all-important principle of Parliament's authority to impose taxes in America. The new Board of Customs Commissioners and expanded vice-admiralty courts also remained intact. The regiments remained in Boston, where their presence was a continual source of discontent.

The years between 1763 and 1770 had brought major changes in the relationship between Britain and its colonies in America. From the British perspective, efforts to restore hierarchy, order, and discipline within the empire were resisted at every turn by colonists who fundamentally misunderstood constitutional relationships among the institutions and entities that together composed the British Empire. Colonists, of course, believed that their understanding of the imperial constitution was thoroughly grounded in both law and historical precedent. They regarded the Stamp Act as a dangerous innovation. Caught off guard in 1765, thereafter many were increasingly suspicious of Britain—or at least of Parliament and the king's ministers—with each ensuing crisis. By 1770, after years of intermittent conflict, many colonists were more attuned to imperial politics and less certain of the security of their rights and interests within the British Empire.

DOCUMENT 1

A French Traveler Visits Virginia's House of Burgesses (1765)

In May 1765, the House of Burgesses, Virginia's lower house, debated how best to respond to the Stamp Act. Patrick Henry, a newly elected burgess who recently had won fame as legal counsel for Virginians in the Two-Penny Act controversy, insisted that the legislators take a hard line against the law and state their position to the king in a series of resolutions. Some Burgesses opposed Henry and some withdrew from the house rather than vote on his resolutions. A French visitor to Williamsburg recorded his impressions of one of Henry's famous early speeches and the remaining Burgesses' eventual adoption of what became known as the Virginia Resolves.[1]

Questions to consider:

1. Why did the Speaker of the House of Burgesses interrupt Henry's speech?
2. How could Henry reject the Stamp Act while simultaneously asserting his loyalty to the king?
3. In 1765, what were the sources of factional divisions in Virginia's House of Burgesses?

May the 30th. . . . arrived at Williamsburg at 12, where I saw three Negroes hanging at the gallows for having robbed Mr. Waltho . . . I went immediately to the assembly which was sitting, where I was entertained with very strong debates concerning duties that the parliament wants to lay on the American colonies, which they call or style stamp duties. Shortly after I came in one of the members stood up and said he had read that in former times Tarquin and Julius had their Brutus, Charles had his Cromwell, and he did not doubt but some good American would stand up, in favour of his country, but (says he) in a more moderate manner, and was going to continue, when the speaker of the house rose and said, he . . . had spoke treason, and was sorry to see that not one of the members of the house was loyal enough to stop him, before he had gone so far. Upon which the same member stood up again (his name is Henry) and said that if he had affronted the speaker, or the house, he was ready to ask pardon, and he would shew his loyalty to his majesty King George the third, at the expence of the last drop of his blood, but what he had said must be attributed to the interest of his country's dying liberty which he had at heart, and the heat of passion might have led him to have said something more than he intended . . . Some other members stood up and backed him, on which the affair was dropped.

May the 31st. I returned to the assembly today, and heard very hot debates still about the stamp duties, the whole house was for entering resolves in the records but they differed much with regard to the contents or purport thereof. Some were for shewing their resentment to the highest. One of the resolves that these proposed, was that any person that would offer to sustain that the parliament of England had a right to impose or lay any tax or duties whatsoever on the American colonies, without the consent of the inhabitants thereof, should be looked upon as a traitor, and deemed an enemy to his country. There were some others to the same purpose, and the majority were for entering these resolves, upon which the governor dissolved the assembly, which hindered their proceeding.

The King's Birth Night [celebration] which was on the Tuesday following, was given by the lieutenant governor . . . I went there in expectation of seeing a great deal of company, but was disappointed for there were not above a dozen people. I came away before supper.

DOCUMENT 2

Considerations on the Propriety of Imposing Taxes in the British Colonies (1765)

Daniel Dulany

The Stamp Act elicited a barrage of pamphlets from its colonial critics, of which Daniel Dulany's August 1765 contribution was by far the most influential.[2] A wealthy Marylander who had been educated at Cambridge University and the Inns of Court, Dulany denounced the Stamp Act on constitutional grounds. He rejected the idea that the colonies could have virtual representation in Parliament, arguing that the colonists' right to be taxed only by their own representatives was compatible with their dependence on and subordination to the king's government. In 1776, Dulany remained loyal to the Crown, unwilling to accept American independence.

Questions to consider:

1. Why did Dulany reject both the Stamp Act and the Grenville minstry's justification for it?
2. How did he distinguish between colonial "dependence and inferiority" and "absolute vassalage and slavery"?
3. Why did Dulany accept the colonies' dependence on and subordination to Great Britain?

In the constitution of England the three principal forms of government, monarchy, aristocracy, and democracy, are blended together in certain proportions; but each of these orders, in the exercise of the legislative authority, hath its peculiar department from which the others are excluded. In this division the granting of supplies or laying taxes is deemed to be the province of the House of Commons, as the representative of the people. All supplies are supposed to flow from their gift; and the other orders are permitted only to assent or reject generally, not to propose any modification, amendment, or partial alteration of it. This observation being considered, it will undeniably appear that in framing the late Stamp Act the Commons acted in the character of representative of the colonies. They assumed it as the principle of that measure, and the propriety of it must therefore stand or fall as the principle is true or false, for the preamble sets forth that the Commons of Great Britain had resolved to give and grant the several rates and duties imposed by the act. But what right had the Commons of Great Britain to be thus munificent at the expense of the commons of America? To give property not belonging to the giver and without the consent of the owner is such evident and flagrant injustice in ordinary cases that few are hardy enough to avow it; and therefore when it really happens, the fact is disguised and varnished over by the most plausible pretenses the ingenuity of the giver can suggest. But it is alleged that there is a virtual or implied representation of the colonies springing out of the constitution of the British government; and it must be confessed on all hands that as the representation is not actual it is virtual or it doth not exist at all, for no third kind of representation can be imagined. The colonies claim the privilege, which is common to all British subjects, of being taxed only with their own consent given by their representatives, and all the advocates for the Stamp Act admit this claim. Whether, therefore, upon the whole matter the imposition of the stamp duties is a proper exercise of constitutional authority or not depends upon the single question, whether the Commons of Great Britain are virtually the representatives of the commons of America or not.

The advocates for the Stamp Act admit, in express terms, that "the colonies do not choose members of Parliament," but they assert that "the colonies are *virtually* represented in the same manner with the nonelectors resident in Great Britain."

How have they proved this position? Where have they defined or precisely explained what they mean by the expression *virtual representation?* . . . They argue that "the right of election being annexed to certain species of property, to franchises, and inhabitancy in some particular places, a very small part of the land, the property, and the people of England are comprehended in those descriptions. All landed property not freehold and all monied property are excluded. The merchants of London, the proprietors of the public funds, the inhabitants of Leeds, Halifax, Birmingham, and Manchester, and that great corporation of the East India Company, none of them choose their representatives, and yet they are all represented in Parliament, and the colonies being exactly in their situation are represented in the same manner."

Now this argument, which is all that their invention hath been able to supply, is totally defective, for it consists of facts not true and of conclusions inadmissible. . . .

Lessees for years, copyholders, proprietors of the public funds, inhabitants of Birmingham, Leeds, Halifax, and Manchester, merchants of the city of London, or members of the corporation of the East India Company are as such under no personal incapacity to be electors, for they may acquire the right of election; and there are actually not only a considerable number of electors in each of the classes of lessees for years, etc., but in many of them, if not all, even members of Parliament. The interests therefore of the nonelectors, the electors, and the representatives are individually the same, to say nothing of the connection among neighbors, friends, and relations. The security of the nonelectors against oppression is that their oppression will fall also upon the electors and the representatives. The one can't be injured and the other indemnified.

Further, if the nonelectors should not be taxed by the British Parliament they would not be taxed at all; and it would be iniquitous as well as a solecism in the political system that they should partake of all the benefits resulting from the imposition and application of taxes and derive an immunity from the circumstance of not being qualified to vote. Under this constitution, then, a double or virtual representation may be reasonably supposed. The electors, who are inseparably connected in their interests with the nonelectors, may be justly deemed to be the representatives of the nonelectors at the same time they exercise their personal privilege in their right of election, and the members chosen, therefore, the representatives of both. This is the only rational explanation of the expression *virtual representation.* None has been advanced by the asserters of it, and their meaning can only be inferred from the instances by which they endeavor to elucidate it, and no other meaning can be stated to which the instances apply. . . .

There is not that intimate and inseparable relation between the electors of Great Britain and the inhabitants of the colonies which must inevitably involve both in the same taxation; on the contrary, not a single *actual* elector in Great Britain might be immediately affected by a taxation in America imposed by a statute which would have a general operation and effect upon the properties and inhabitants of the colonies. The latter might be oppressed in a thousand shapes without any sympathy or exciting any alarm in the former. Moreover, even acts oppressive and injurious to the colonies in an extreme degree might become popular in England from the promise or expectation that the very measures which depressed the colonies would give ease to the inhabitants of Great Britain. . . .

The colonies are dependent upon Great Britain, and the supreme authority vested in the King, Lords, and Commons may justly be exercised to secure or preserve their dependence whenever necessary for that purpose. This authority results from and is implied in the idea of the relation subsisting between England and her colonies; for considering the nature of human affections, the inferior is not to be trusted with providing regulations to prevent his rising to an equality with his superior. But though the right of the superior to use the proper means for preserving the subordination of his inferior is admitted, yet it does not necessarily follow that he has a right to seize the property of his inferior when he pleases or to command him in everything since, in the degrees of it, there may very well exist a dependence and inferiority without absolute vassalage and slavery. In what the superior may rightfully control or compel, and in what the inferior ought to be at liberty to act without control or compulsion, depends upon the nature of the dependence and the degree of the subordination; and these being ascertained, the measure of obedience and submission and the extent of the authority and superintendence will be settled. When powers compatible with the relation between the superior and inferior have by express compact been granted to and accepted by the latter, and have been, after that compact, repeatedly recognized by the former—when they may be exercised effectually upon every occasion without any injury to that relation—the authority of the superior can't properly interpose, for by the powers vested in the inferior is the superior limited.

By their constitutions of government the colonies are empowered to impose internal taxes. This power is compatible with their dependence and hath been expressly recognized by British ministers and the British Parliament upon many occasions; and it may be exercised effectually without striking at or impeaching in any respect the superintendence of the British Parliament. May not then the line be distinctly and justly drawn between such acts as are necessary or proper for preserving or securing the dependence of the colonies and such as are not necessary or proper for that very important purpose?

DOCUMENT 3

Destruction of the Home of Thomas Hutchinson (1765)

In 1765, Thomas Hutchinson, a Massachusetts native and descendant of the colony's Puritan founders, was its lieutenant governor. Although he questioned the wisdom of the Stamp Act, Hutchinson's royal commission charged him with enforcing all acts of Parliament, so he vowed to oversee the law's implementation. On 14 August 1765, crowds in Boston rioted to protest the Stamp Act and force the resignation of the stamp distributor, without whose services the law would not be viable. Twelve days later, as Hutchinson reported in this letter to an English friend, the rioters targeted his home and those of other royal officials who still sought to enforce the unpopular legislation.[3]

Questions to consider:

1. Why did the rioters attack Hutchinson and his family so viciously?
2. Who did Hutchinson blame for the crisis in Boston?
3. What "terrible consequences" did he anticipate as a result of the Stamp Act riots?

I came from my house [to Boston] with my family on the 26th in the morning. After dinner it was whispered in town there would be a mob that night and that . . . the customs-house and admiralty officers houses would be attacked . . . In evening whilst I was at supper and my children round me somebody ran in and said the mob were coming. I directed my children to fly to a secure place and shut up my house as I had done before, intending not to quit it but my eldest daughter . . . hastened back and protested she would not quit the house unless I did. I could not stand against this and withdrew with her to a neighbouring house where I had been but a few minutes before the hellish crew fell upon my house with the rage of devils and in a moment with axes split down the doors and entered. My son being in the great entry heard them cry damn him he is upstairs we'll have him. Some ran immediately as high as the top of the house; others filled the rooms below and cellars and others remained without the house to be employed there. Messages soon came one after another to the house where I was to inform me the mob were coming in pursuit of me and I was obliged to retire through yards and gardens to a house more remote . . . where I remained until 4 o'clock, by which time one of the best finished houses in the province had nothing remaining but the bare walls and floors. Not contented with tearing off all the wainscot and hangings and splitting the doors to pieces they beat down the partition walls and although that alone cost them nearly two hours they cut down the cupola or lantern and they began to take the slate and boards from the roof and were prevented only by the approaching daylight from a total demolition of the building. The garden fence was laid flat and all my trees . . . broke down to the ground. Such ruins were never seen in America. Besides my plate and family pictures, household furniture of every kind, my own children's and servants' apparel, they carried off about £900 sterling in money and emptied the house of every thing whatsoever except a part of the kitchen furniture not leaving a single book or paper in it and have scattered or destroyed all the manuscripts and other papers I had been collecting for 30 years together besides a great number of public papers in my custody . . . Many articles of clothing and good part of my plate have since been picked up in different quarters of the town but the furniture in general was cut to pieces before it was thrown out of the house and most of the beds cut open and the feathers thrown out of the windows. . . .

The encouragers of the first mob never intended matters should go to this length and the people in general express the utmost detestation of this unparalleled outrage and I wish they could be convinced what infinite hazard there is of the most terrible consequences from such demons when they are let loose in a government where there is not constant authority at hand sufficient to suppress them.

I am told the government here will make me a compensation for my own and my family's loss which I think cannot be much less than £3,000 sterling. I am not sure that they will. If they should not it will be too heavy for me and I must humbly apply to his Majesty in whose service I am a sufferer but this and a much greater sum would be an insufficient compensation for the constant distress and anxiety of mind I have felt for some time past and must feel for months to come. You cannot conceive the wretched state we are in. Such is the resentment of the people against the stamp duty that there can be no dependence upon the [lower house] to take any steps to enforce or rather advise the payment of it. On the other hand, such will be the effects of not submitting to it that all trade must cease, all courts fall and all authority be at an end. Must not the ministry be extremely embarrassed? On the one hand it will be said if concessions be made the Parliament endanger the loss of their authority over the colonies; on the other hand if external force should be used there seems to be danger of a total lasting alienation of affection. Is there no alternative?

DOCUMENT 4

Proceedings of the Stamp Act Congress (1765)

Although most of the colonial assemblies had followed the Virginians' example by adopting their own resolutions to protest the Stamp Act, on 7 October 1765 twenty-seven delegates from nine colonies also gathered in New York to draft an intercolonial declaration of rights and grievances. The delegates spent twelve days hammering out fourteen basic principles, which became the basis for the petitions they sent to the king and both houses of Parliament.[4]

Questions to consider:

1. Which of the fourteen declarations are statements of general principles, and which specifically concern the Stamp Act crisis?
2. Did the position of the Stamp Act Congress go beyond that taken by Virginia's House of Burgesses five months earlier?
3. Why was the assertion that the colonies "are not, and from their local circumstances cannot be, represented in the House of Commons of Great Britain" both essential to the colonial position and utterly unacceptable to British members of Parliament?

The members of this Congress, sincerely devoted, with the warmest sentiments of affection and duty to His Majesty's person and government, inviolably attached to the present happy establishment of the Protestant succession [to the throne], and with minds deeply impressed by a sense of the present and impending misfortunes of the British colonies on this continent; having considered as maturely as time will permit the circumstances of the said colonies, esteem it our indispensable duty to make the following declarations of our humble opinion, respecting the most essential rights and liberties of the colonists, and of the grievances under which they labour, by reason of several late Acts of Parliament.

I.   That His Majesty's subjects in these colonies, owe the same allegiance to the Crown of Great Britain, that is owing from his subjects born within the realm, and all due subordination to that august body the Parliament of Great Britain.

II.   That His Majesty's liege subjects in these colonies, are entitled to all the inherent rights and liberties of his natural born subjects within the Kingdom of Great Britain.

III.   That it is inseparably essential to the freedom of a people, and the undoubted right of Englishmen, that no taxes be imposed on them, but with their own consent, given personally, or by their representatives.

IV. That the people of these colonies are not, and from their local circumstances cannot be, represented in the House of Commons in Great Britain.

V. That the only representatives of the people of these colonies, are persons chosen therein by themselves, and that no taxes ever have been, or can be constitutionally imposed on them, but by their respective legislatures.

VI. That all supplies to the Crown, being free gifts of the people, it is unreasonable and inconsistent with the principles and spirit of the British Constitution, for the people of Great Britain to grant to His Majesty the property of the colonists.

VII. That trial by jury is the inherent and invaluable right of every British subject in these colonies.

VIII. That the late act of Parliament, entitled, An Act for granting and applying certain Stamp Duties . . . in America . . . by imposing taxes on the Inhabitants of these colonies, and the said Act, and several other acts, by extending the jurisdiction of the Courts of Admiralty beyond its ancient limits, have a manifest tendency to subvert the rights and liberties of the colonists.

IX. That the duties imposed by several late acts of Parliament, from the peculiar circumstances of these colonies, will be extremely burthensome and grievous; and from the scarcity of specie, the payment of them absolutely impracticable.

X. That as the profits of the trade of these colonies ultimately center in Great Britain, to pay for the manufactures which they are obliged to take from thence, they eventually contribute very largely to all supplies granted there to the Crown.

XI. That the restrictions imposed by several late acts of Parliament, on the trade of these colonies, will render them unable to purchase the manufactures of Great Britain.

XII. That the increase, prosperity, and happiness of these colonies, depend on the full and free enjoyment of their rights and liberties, and an intercourse with Great Britain mutually affectionate and advantageous.

XIII. That it is the right of the British subjects in these colonies, to petition the King, or either house of Parliament.

Lastly, that it is the indispensable duty of these colonies, to the best of sovereigns, to the mother country, and to themselves, to endeavour by a loyal and dutiful address to his Majesty, and humble applications to both houses of Parliament, to procure the repeal of the Act for granting and applying certain Stamp Duties, of all clauses of any other acts of Parliament, whereby the jurisdiction of the Admiralty is extended as aforesaid, and of the other late acts for the restriction of American commerce.

The New York Stamp Act Riot (1765)

In New York City, the resignation of the local stamp distributor in August 1765 averted violence, at least until 1 November, the date on which the Stamp Act was to go into effect. Then, an angry crowd mobilized against Lieutenant Governor Cadwallader Colden, a staunch defender of imperial authority who they believed would enforce the offensive legislation. New York's leaders, unlike those in most other colonies, had taken no official action against the Stamp Act beyond sending delegates to the Stamp Act Congress. In New York, middling men—soon to be known as the Sons of Liberty—and sea captains led the attack on Colden, who described the episode in this letter to his superiors in London.[5]

Questions to consider:

1. How did the methods of the New York rioters differ from those of their Boston counterparts?
2. Why did the rioters particularly target Colden's chariot and carriages?
3. Why might the "gentlemen" of New York, as Colden claimed, have "stood around to observe the outrage on their King's governor"?
4. Why might the royal garrison have failed to defend Colden?

Sir,

In a day or two after the date of my letter of the 26th of last month . . . the packages of stamped papers were landed from His Majesty's ship *Garland* at noonday without a guard or the least appearance of discontent among the people . . . But on the evening of the first day of this month the mob began to collect together, and after it became dark they came up to the Fort Gate with a great number of torches, and a scaffold on which two images were placed, one to represent the governor in his grey hairs, & the other the devil by his side. This scaffold with the images was brought up within 8 or 10 feet of the gate with the grossest ribaldry from the mob. As they went from the gate they broke open my coach house, took my chariot out of it & carried it round the town with the images, & returned to the Fort Gate, from whence they carried them to an open place, where they had erected a gibbet, within 100 yards of the Fort Gate & there hung up the images. After hanging some time they were burnt in a fire prepared for the purpose, together with my chariot, a single horse chair and two sledges, our usual carriages when snow is on the ground, which they took out of my coach house. While this was doing a great number of gentlemen of the town if they can be called so, stood around to observe the outrage on their King's governor. The garrison was at the same time on the ramparts with preparation sufficient to destroy them, but not a single return in words or otherwise was made from any man in the fort, while this egregious insult was performing . . . It is given out that the mob will storm the fort this night. I am not apprehensive of their carrying out their purpose; probably it might be attended with much bloodshed because a great part of the mob consists of men who had been privateers & disbanded soldiers whose view it is to plunder the town.

This goes by Major James of the Royal Artillery who with much zeal for his Majesty's service put the fort in the best posture of defence he could, for reason which the mob, the same night they insulted their governor, broke open his house, burnt all his furniture, wearing clothes and every thing in it to a great value, at the same time threatening to take away his life in the most shameful manner.

<u>DOCUMENT 6</u>

Letters from a Farmer in Pennsylvania (1767–68)

John Dickinson

John Dickinson was probably the most widely read colonial pamphleteer of the prerevolutionary era. His most important work, Letters from a Farmer in Pennsylvania, *first appeared in 1767 and 1768.[6] Dickinson encouraged his readers to oppose the Townshend Act and other imperial measures. In Letter I, he condemned the New York Restraining Act. In Letter II, he initiated an extended analysis of the constitutional and economic implications Townshend Acts.*

Questions to consider:

1. Dickinson was a Philadelphia lawyer who moved in the highest circles of colonial society. Why, then, did he pose as a farmer? Was this pose convincing? Did it matter?
2. On 29 June 1767, Parliament enacted both the New York Restraining Act and the Townshend Acts. Why did Dickinson choose to inaugurate his *Letters* with an attack on the New York law?
3. How did Dickinson distinguish the Townshend Acts from the Navigation Acts? What did he fear would happen if the colonists complied with the Townshend duties?
4. Which of Dickinson's observations in these two letters were potentially the most radical?

LETTER I

My Dear Countrymen,

I am a farmer, settled after a variety of fortunes near the banks of the river Delaware, in the province of Pennsylvania. I received a liberal education and have been engaged in the busy scenes of life, but am now convinced, that a man may be as happy without bustle as with it. My farm is small, my servants are few and good, I have a little money at interest, I wish for no more, my employment in my own affairs is easy, and with a contented, grateful mind, undisturbed by worldly hopes or fears relating to myself, I am completing the number of days allotted to me by divine goodness.

Being generally master of my time, I spend a good deal of it in a library, which I think the most valuable part of my small estate; and being acquainted with two or three gentlemen of abilities and learning who honour me with their friendship, I have acquired, I believe, a greater knowledge in history and the laws and constitution of my country, than is generally attained by men of my class, many of them not being so fortunate as I have been in the opportunities of getting information.

From my infancy I was taught to love humanity and liberty. Enquiry and experience have since confirmed my reverence for the lessons then given me, by convincing me more fully of their truth and excellence. Benevolence towards mankind excites wishes for their welfare, and such wishes endear the means of fulfilling them. These can be found in liberty only, and therefore her sacred cause ought to be espoused by every man on every occasion, to the utmost of his power. As a charitable but poor person does not withhold his mite because he cannot relieve all the distresses of the miserable, so should not any honest man suppress his sentiments concerning <u>freedom,</u> however small their influence is likely to be. Perhaps he may touch some wheel that will have an effect greater than he could reasonably expect.

These being my sentiments, I am encouraged to offer to you, my countrymen, my thoughts on some late transactions that appear to me to be of the utmost importance to you . . . With a good deal of surprise I have observed, that little notice has been taken of an act of parliament, as injurious in its principle to the liberties of these colonies, as the Stamp Act was: I mean the act for suspending the legislation of New York. ← NY suspending Act

The assembly of that government complied with a former act of parliament, requiring certain provisions to be made for the troops in America, in every particular, I think, except the articles of salt, pepper, and vinegar. In my opinion they acted imprudently, considering all cir- cumstances, in not complying so far as would have given satisfaction, as several colonies did. But my dislike of their conduct in that instance has not blinded me so much that I cannot plainly perceive that they have been punished in a manner pernicious to American freedom, and justly alarming to all the colonies.

If the British Parliament has a legal authority to issue an order that we shall furnish a single article for the troops here, and to compel obedi- ence to that order, they have the same right to issue an order for us to supply those troops with arms, clothes, and every necessary and to compel obedience to that order also; in short, to lay any burdens they please upon us. What is this but taxing us at a certain sum, and leaving to us only the manner of raising it? How is this mode more tolerable than the Stamp Act? Would that act have appeared more pleasing to Americans, if being ordered thereby to raise the sum total of the taxes, the mighty privilege had been left to them, of saying how much should be paid for an instrument of writing on paper, and how much for an- other on parchment?

An act of parliament commanding us to do a certain thing, if it has any validity, is a tax upon us for the expence that accrues in complying with it, and for this reason, I believe, every colony on the continent, that chose to give a mark of their respect for Great Britain in complying with the act relating to the troops, cautiously avoided the mention of that act; lest their conduct should be attributed to its supposed obligation.

The matter being thus stated, the assembly of New York either had or had not a right to refuse submission to that act. If they had, and I imagine no American will say they had not, then the parliament had no right to compel them to execute it. If they had not that right, they had no right to punish them for not executing it; and therefore had no right to suspend their legislation, which is a punishment. In fact, if the people of New York cannot be legally taxed but by their own representatives, they cannot be legally deprived of the privileges of making laws, only for insisting on that exclusive privilege of taxation. If they may be legally deprived in such a case of the privilege of making laws, why may they not, with equal reason, be deprived of every other privilege? . . . Or what signifies the repeal of the Stamp Act, if these colonies are to lose their other privileges, by not tamely surrendering that of taxation? . . .

The cause of one is the cause of all. If the parliament may lawfully deprive New York of any of its rights, it may deprive any, or all the other colonies of their rights; and nothing can possibly so much encourage such attempts, as a mutual inattention to the interest of each other. To divide and thus to destroy, is the first political maxim in attacking those who are powerful by their union. He certainly is not a wise man who folds his arms and reposes himself at home, viewing with unconcern the flames that have invaded his neighbour's house, without using any endeavours to extinguish them . . . Small things grow great by concord.

A Farmer.

LETTER II

Beloved Countrymen,

There is another late act of parliament, which seems to me to be as destructive to the liberty of these colonies, as that inserted in my last letter; that is, the act for granting the duties on paper, glass, &c. It appears to me to be unconstitutional.

The parliament unquestionably possesses a legal authority to regulate the trade of Great Britain, and all its colonies. Such an authority is essential to the relation between a mother country and its colonies; and necessary for the common good of all. He, who considers these provinces as states distinct from the British empire, has very slender notions of justice, or of their interests. We are but parts of a whole; and therefore there must exist a power somewhere, to preside, and preserve the connection in due order. This power is lodged in the parliament; and we are as much dependent on Great Britain, as a perfectly free people can be on another.

I have looked over every statute relating to these colonies, from their first settlement to this time and find every one of them founded on this principle, till the Stamp Act administration. All before, are calculated to preserve or promote a mutually beneficial intercourse between the several constituent parts of the empire; and though many of them

imposed duties on trade, yet those duties were always imposed with design to restrain the commerce of one part, that was injurious to another,
and thus to promote the general welfare. The raising a revenue thereby
was never intended . . . Never did the British parliament, till the period above mentioned, think of imposing duties in America, FOR THE
PURPOSE OF RAISING A REVENUE. . . .

This I call an innovation; and a most dangerous innovation. It may
perhaps be objected, that Great Britain has a right to lay what duties she
pleases upon her exports, and it makes no difference to us, whether they
are paid here or there.

To this I answer. These colonies require many things for their use,
which the laws of Great Britain prohibit them from getting any where
but from her. Such are paper and glass.

That we may be legally bound to pay any general duties on these
commodities, relative to the regulation of trade, is granted; but we being
obliged by her laws to take from Great Britain, any special duties imposed on their exportation to us only, with intention to raise a revenue
from us only, are as much taxes, upon us, as those imposed by the Stamp
Act. . . .

Some persons perhaps may say, that this act lays us under no necessity to pay the duties imposed, because we may ourselves manufacture
the articles on which they are laid; whereas by the Stamp Act no instrument of writing could be good, unless made on British paper, and that
too stamped.

Such an objection amounts to no more than this, that the total disuse of British paper and glass will not be so afflicting as that which
would have resulted from the total disuse of writing among them; for by
that means even the Stamp Act might have been eluded. Why then was
it universally detested by them as slavery itself? Because it presented to
these devoted provinces nothing but a choice of calamities, embittered
by indignities, each of which was unworthy of freemen to bear. But is no
injury a violation of right but the greatest injury? If eluding the payment
of the duties imposed by the Stamp Act would have subjected us to a
more dreadful inconvenience, than the eluding the payment of those imposed by the late act, does it therefore follow that the last is no violation
of our rights, though it is calculated for the same purpose that the other
was, that is, to raise money upon us, without our consent? . . .

But the objectors may further say, that we shall sustain no injury at
all by the disuse of British paper and glass. We might not, if we could
make as much as we want. But can any man, acquainted with America,
believe this possible? I am told there are but two or three glass-houses on
this continent, and but very few paper-mills; and suppose more should be
erected, a long course of years must elapse, before they can be brought to
perfection. This continent is a country of planters, farmers, and fishermen;

not of manufacturers. The difficulty of establishing particular manufactures in such a country is almost insuperable, for one manufacture is connected with others in such a manner, that it may be said to be impossible to establish one or two, without establishing several others. The experience of many nations may convince us of this truth. . . .

Great Britain has prohibited the manufacturing of iron and steel in these colonies, without any objection being made to her right of doing it. The like right she must have to prohibit any other manufacture among us. Thus she is possessed of an undisputed precedent on that point. This authority, she will say, is founded on the original intention of settling these colonies; that is, that she should manufacture for them, and that they should supply her with materials. The equity of this policy, she will also say, has been universally acknowledged by the colonies, who never have made the least objection to statutes for that purpose; and will further appear by the mutual benefits flowing from this usage, ever since the settlement of these colonies. . . .

Here then, my dear countrymen rouse yourselves, and behold the ruin hanging over your heads . . . The single question is, whether the parliament can legally impose duties to be paid by the people of these colonies only for the sole purpose of raising a revenue, on commodities which she obliges us to take from her alone; or, in other words, whether the parliament can legally take money out of our pockets, without our consent. If they can, our boasted liberty is but . . . a sound, and nothing else.

A Farmer.

DOCUMENT 7

"Address to the Ladies" (1767)

Colonial boycotts presented women with an unusual opportunity to act politically. Although men and women alike were enthusiastic consumers of British imports, popular culture regarded fashion, ornaments, and tea-drinking as particularly feminine concerns. Accordingly, colonial leaders appealed to women to forgo such luxuries for the good of their country, and many later made women the scapegoats for the eventual disintegration of the nonimportation effort. This early version of a poem that appeared in many colonial newspapers was published in the Virginia Gazette.[7]

Questions to consider:

1. To what extent was the poet's message potentially empowering to its female readers? To what extent was it debilitating or dismissive of women's abilities or interests?
2. How did the poet define "fashion" and its purpose?

Young ladies in town, and those that live round,
Let a friend at this season advise you;
Since money's so scarce, and times growing worse,
Strange things may soon hap and surprise you.
First, then, throw aside your high topknots of pride;
Wear none but your own country linen;
Of economy boast, let your pride be your most
To show clothes of your own make and spinning.
What if homespun they say is not quite so gay
As brocades, yet be not in a passion,
For when once it is known this is much wore in town,
One and all will cry out, 'tis the fashion!
And as one all agree that you'll not married be
To such as will wear London factory,
But at first sight refuse, tell them such you do choose
As encourage our own manufactory.
No more ribands wear, nor in rich dress appear,
Love your country much better than fine things,
Begin without passion, 'twill soon be the fashion
To grace your smooth locks with a twine string.
Throw aside your Bohea, and your Green Hyson tea,
And all things with a new fashion duty;
Procure a good store of the choice Labrador,
For there'll soon be enough here to suit you.
These do without fear, and to all you'll appear,
Fair, charming, true, lovely and clever;
Though the times remain darkish, young men may be sparkish,
And love you much stronger than ever.

DOCUMENT 8

The "Liberty Song" and the Parody (1768)

Popular culture, like learned discourse, addressed the ongoing imperial controversy and promoted opinions on both sides. In 1768, the "Liberty Song," which features lyrics by John Dickinson set to a popular English tune, appeared in the Boston

Gazette, *a leading radical newspaper. The* Gazette *published an anonymous parody of the "Liberty Song" soon thereafter.*[8]

Questions to consider:

1. What did the author of *Letters from a Farmer in Pennsylvania* expect to accomplish by penning these verses?
2. What was the main message of Dickinson's lyrics?
3. What was the main message of the parody of the "Liberty Song"? How did its author portray those colonists who opposed recent imperial policies?
4. Why would a radical newspaper, such as the *Boston Gazette*, choose to publish the parody?

Come join hand in hand brave Americans all,
And rouse your bold hearts at fair Liberty's call;
No tyrannous acts shall suppress your just claim,
Or stain with dishonour America's name.

CHORUS:
In Freedom we're born and in Freedom we'll live,
Our purses are ready,
Steady, Friends, Steady,
Not as slaves, but as Freemen our money we'll give.

Our worthy forefathers, let's give them a cheer
To climates unknown did courageously steer;
Thro' oceans, to deserts, for freedom they came,
And dying bequeathed us their freedom and fame. . . .

The tree their own hands had to Liberty reared;
They lived to behold growing strong and revered;
With transport they cried, "Now our wishes we gain,
For our children shall gather the fruits of our pain. . . ."

Then join hand in hand brave Americans all,
By uniting we stand, by dividing we fall;
In so righteous a cause let us hope to succeed,
For Heaven approves of each generous deed.

All ages shall speak with amaze and applause,
Of the courage we'll show in support of our laws;
To die we can bear—but to serve we disdain,
For shame is to freedmen more dreadful than pain.

———

Come shake your dull noodles, ye pumpkins, and bawl,
And own that you're mad at fair Liberty's call;
No scandalous conduct can add to your shame,
Condemned to dishonor, inherit the same. . . .

CHORUS:
In folly you're born, and in folly you'll live,
To madness still ready,
And stupidly steady,
Not as men, but as monkeys, the tokens you give.

All ages shall speak with contempt and amaze,
Of the vilest banditti that swarmed in those days;
In defiance of halters, of whips, and of chains,
The rogues would run riot, damned fools for their pains.

Gulp down your last dram, for the gallows now groans,
And, order depressed, her lost empire bemoans;
While we quite transported and happy shall be,
From mobs, knaves and villains, protected and free.

DOCUMENT 9

An Exemplary Funeral (1769)

Funerals, like clothing and tea parties, became politicized as a result of the colonists' adoption of nonimportation. When Mary Hasell Gadsden of Charleston died in 1769, the South Carolina Gazette *praised her funeral as evidence of the patriotism of her husband, a leading advocate of uncompromising resistance to British imperial policies.[9]*

Questions to consider:

1. Why did the editors of the *South Carolina Gazette* deem the funeral of an unnamed woman potentially big news for their readers?
2. Why did cloth top the list of desirable American manufactures?

Many of the inhabitants of the north and eastern parts of [South Carolina] have this winter clothed themselves in their own manufactures; many more would purchase them, if they could be got; and a great reform is intended in the enormous expence attending funerals, [and] for mourning . . . from the patriotic example lately set by Christopher Gadsden, Esq.; when he buried one of the best of wives and most excellent of women. In short, the generality of people now seem deeply impressed with an idea of the necessity, and most heartily disposed, to use every means, to promote INDUSTRY,

ECONOMY, and AMERICAN MANUFACTURES, and to keep so much money amongst us as possible.

SUGGESTED READING FOR CHAPTER 3

BAILYN, BERNARD. *The Ordeal of Thomas Hutchinson* (1974).
COUNTRYMAN, EDWARD. *A People in Revolution: The American Revolution and Political Society in New York, 1760–1790* (1981).
EGNAL, MARC. *A Mighty Empire: The Origins of the American Revolution* (1988).
MAIER, PAULINE. *From Resistance to Revolution: Colonial Radicals and the Development of American Opposition to Britain, 1765–1776* (1972).
———. *The Old Revolutionaries: Political Lives in the Age of Samuel Adams* (1980).
MORGAN, EDMUND S. *Prologue to Revolution: Sources and Documents on the Stamp Act Crisis, 1764–1766* (1959).
———, and MORGAN, HELEN M. *The Stamp Act Crisis: Prologue to Revolution*, rev. ed. (1995).
REID, JOHN PHILLIP. *The Constitutional History of the American Revolution: The Power to Tax* (1987).
SHAW, PETER. *American Revolutionaries and the Rituals of Revolution* (1981).
THOMAS, P. D. G. *British Politics and the Stamp Act Crisis: The First Phase of the American Revolution, 1763–1767* (1975).
———. *The Townshend Duties Crisis: The Second Phase of the American Revolution, 1767–1773* (1987).
WALSH, RICHARD. *Charleston's Sons of Liberty: A Study of the Artisans, 1763–1789* (1959).

NOTES

[1]"Journal of a French Traveller in the Colonies, 1765," *American Historical Review, 26* (1920–22): 745–46.

[2]Daniel Dulany, *Considerations on the Propriety of Imposing Taxes in the British Colonies* (Annapolis, 1765), 5–8, 15.

[3]Thomas Hutchinson to Richard Jackson, 30 Aug. 1765, *Massachusetts Archives, 26:* 146–47.

[4]*Proceedings of the Congress at New York* (Annapolis, 1766), 15–16.

[5]Cadwallader Colden to Secretary Conway, 5 Nov. 1765, in E. B. O'Callaghan and Berthold Fernow, eds., *Documents Relative to the Colonial History of the State of New York*, 15 vols. (Albany, 1853–87), 7: 771.

[6]John Dickinson, *Letters from a Farmer in Pennsylvania* (Boston, 1768), 3–26.

[7]*Virginia Gazette* (Purdie and Dixon), 24 Dec. 1767.

[8]*Boston Gazette, and Country Journal*, 18 July 1768, 26 Sept. 1768.

[9]*South Carolina Gazette*, 2 Mar. 1769.

CHAPTER FOUR

THE ROAD TO REBELLION

By 1770, colonists had spent five years denouncing the real or potential oppressiveness of British policies, while imperial authorities in London and their supporters in America rued the rising lawlessness in the colonies. Depending on one's perspective, Boston was either the center of liberty-loving patriotism or a hotbed of disorder and rebellion. Imperial authorities sent troops there in 1768 to restore order, but many Bostonians saw the soldiers' presence as a prelude to the imposition of tyranny in Massachusetts and beyond. On 5 March 1770, troops and townspeople engaged in a violent confrontation. Known variously as the "King Street Riot" or the "Boston Massacre," the incident marked the beginning of a new and far more serious phase of the imperial crisis.

Although it would be more than three years before another major controversy ignited the contending parties, mutual suspicion and a series of local controversies kept tensions high in the intervening years. Then, in 1773, Parliament's passage of the Tea Act resulted in colonial attacks on British tea ships and, most famously, the dumping of 342 chests of tea into Boston harbor. The tea-dumping episode elicited the fear and outrage of more conservative colonial leaders, who regarded property rights as inviolable and resented the increasing prominence of common folk in resisting imperial policies. Destruction of the tea also resulted in swift disciplinary action from London. In May 1774, Parliament enacted a series of laws known collectively as the Coercive Acts. A major turning point in the imperial crisis, the passage of the Coercive Acts galvanized the colonists to unite to defend what they believed to be their rights.

After 1774, the troops remained in Boston, but there and elsewhere colonists organized networks of extralegal committees and congresses to mount a coordinated opposition to the Coercive Acts and other imperial policies. Extralegal bodies, which by definition lacked legal or constitutional standing, gradually assumed the functions of government. The most tangible fruit of intercolonial cooperation was the convening of the Continental Congress in Philadelphia in September 1774. From then on, de facto political authority shifted gradually from the imperial regime to extralegal bodies at the local, provincial, and continental levels. These committees and congresses articulated colonial grievances, enforced a new commercial boycott, planned military defense, and harassed those who refused to accept the emerging revolutionary order.

In colonial America, the militia was the traditional defense against both foreign and domestic threats. Because it was made up local men, the militia presumably could not become a tool of oppression—unlike a professional army, which a king or governor might deploy against his people. Historically, the English, too, had relied on a militia of citizen-soldiers to defend their island nation, raising fulltime professional forces only to fight abroad from time to time. By 1689, however, two major changes made them more willing to maintain a professional army: Parliament's attainment of constitutional supremacy as a result of the Glorious Revolution, and the need to defend an expanding empire and its commerce. In 1689, Parliament passed the Mutiny Act, which gave the Crown resources to maintain an army for one year. Parliament renewed the law each year thereafter but could refuse to do so if the king abused his power. The colonists, by comparison, had no such control over the British troops who arrived in Boston in October 1768.

Boston radicals warned that the arrival of the troops would lead to tyranny, and they encouraged their neighbors to intimidate or ridicule the soldiers and others who upheld British imperial authority. The first violence between townspeople and the troops occurred in February 1770, when an angry crowd stormed the premises of a known customs informer, who panicked and fired on the group, killing an eleven-year-old named Christopher Sneider. Samuel Adams and the Sons of Liberty made the youth's funeral a major public event, at which the soldiers were demonized as predatory minions of tyranny. The bad feeling between the troops and the townspeople became as much personal as political in the coming months, as soldiers competed with men for part-time work in a depressed economy.

Tensions finally came to a head on the evening of 5 March 1770, when a crowd began pelting a sentry from the same regiment with snowballs as he guarded the customs house on King Street. The sentry called for help, and Captain Robert Preston arrived with a small contingent of soldiers. Someone sounded the fire bell, which brought many more townspeople to the scene. For about fifteen minutes, the crowd taunted the soldiers, waving sticks and swords. Preston managed to keep his men in line until a stick or a snowball hit Private Hugh Montgomery, who fell, regained his footing, and then fired his gun. His comrades followed suit. When the smoke cleared, the soldiers had shot eleven men, of whom five would die. The first to fall was Crispus Attucks, a mulatto runaway slave.

Soldiers and townspeople gave significantly different accounts of what happened that night. While Captain Preston stressed the antipathy of the crowd and the confusion of his troops, Boston radicals portrayed the soldiers as intent on overpowering innocent, unarmed men they saw as their inferiors. Imperial authorities referred to the incident as the King Street "riot." The propaganda efforts of Samuel Adams and his associates, however, ensured that it would become widely known in America as the Boston "massacre"—a term that contemporaries used chiefly to describe Indian raids on white towns and one that denoted brutal and purposeful acts of barbarity against innocent and virtuous people. Paul Revere, a Boston silversmith and prominent radical, produced an engraving that portrayed the troops purposefully assaulting the townspeople. His image, along with the words of Adams and others, spread news of the affair and shaped the popular response to it.

The Boston Massacre evoked general fear and outrage, despite the efforts of Thomas Hutchinson—who was now governor of Massachusetts—to defuse the situation by ensuring that the soldiers who were implicated in the affair were indicted and tried for murder. The fact that a Massachusetts jury acquitted Preston and six of his men, and convicted two others of the lesser crime of manslaughter, attested to the ambiguity of events and tenacity of the soldiers' lawyers and in no way signified forgiveness on the part of Bostonians.

The Boston Massacre had three short-term consequences. First, the violent confrontation resulted in the prudent removal of the troops from Boston to an island in Boston harbor. Second, it created five martyrs to the cause of colonial liberty. Third, the episode resulted in the amendment of New England's civic calendar. Particularly in Boston, the anniversary of the massacre was observed with sober patriotism. Although Bostonians still claimed to be loyal subjects of the king, by embracing new heroes and new civic festivals that commemorated resistance to British rule, they were taking important steps in the formation of a new political identity.

The Boston Massacre, unlike the colonial response to either the Stamp Act or the Townshend Acts, had no discernible impact on British imperial policy. Lord North, who had become prime minister in early 1770, hoped to restore order in the colonies. He chose to do so, first, by repealing the Townshend Duties—except the tax on tea—and, second, by adopting no new policies that might rekindle colonial protests. At the same time, however, North in no way compromised the constitutional principle behind the Declaratory Act of 1766, which had asserted the authority of Parliament to legislate for the colonies "in all cases whatsoever." Restoration of peace and order was for North, as for the colonists, a matter of convenience.

The fact that reconciliation between Britain and the colonies was at best superficial was revealed in a series of altercations over local issues during this period. In North Carolina, South Carolina, and Georgia, royal governors engaged in unusually bitter conflicts with the colonial assemblies, which were more than ever sensitive to encroachments on what they believed to be their constitutionally sanctioned powers. In New Jersey, Pennsylvania, and Rhode Island, merchants—many of whom engaged in smuggling—attacked the collectors of the customs, and in 1772 some Rhode Islanders captured and burned the *Gaspee,* a British naval ship charged with seizing smugglers in Narragansett Bay. The special commission that investigated the *Gaspee* incident could identity none of the parties involved in it. Nevertheless, by empowering the commission to transport all suspects to England for trial, the imperial government again evoked the wrath of colonists, who regarded this tactic as a violation of the common law right to a trial by a jury of one's peers.

In response to the *Gaspee* affair, Virginia's House of Burgesses appointed a Committee of Correspondence to consult with legislators in other colonies about their growing list of grievances and urged the establishment of similar committees in the other colonies. Within a year, twelve of thirteen colonies had responded to the Virginians' initiative, thereby taking an important step in organizing subsequent resistance to imperial authority. The Committees of Correspondence became an essential intercolonial network for sharing intelligence and coordinating responses to Britain's evolving imperial policies.

Meanwhile, in Massachusetts, a series of new imperial regulations spread resistance to British rule beyond Boston and into the countryside. Although many country towns had protested the Stamp Act and Townshend Acts, they had done so on a limited basis and primarily in response to directions from Boston's radical leaders. In 1772, however, imperial authorities decided that all Massachusetts superior court judges should receive their salaries directly from London, rather than from the colonial assembly. On hearing this news, Boston radicals asked Governor Hutchinson to convene the legislature. When he refused to do so, they formed a Committee of Correspondence to prepare a manifesto of rights and grievances to be circulated among the towns of the colony. The committee printed some 600 copies of this document, and by April 1773 almost half of the towns and districts in Massachusetts were forming their own committees, passing resolutions, and urging their representatives to protest the change in the payment of judges, which undermined both their own interests and the independence of the judiciary.

During the three years following the Boston Massacre, then, mutual suspicions between colonial dissidents and their imperial governors festered and perhaps deepened, but no single episode or issue precipitated a crisis of continental proportions until May 1773, when Parliament passed the Tea Act. Primarily intended to help the financially troubled British East India Tea Company, the law's provisions nonetheless had potentially grave implications for the American colonists. Besides giving the company assorted tax breaks, the Tea Act allowed it to sell tea directly to American consumers, cutting out the middleman and enhancing the company's profits. These changes, in effect, gave this British corporation— which would now designate its own agents in the colonies—a monopoly over the tea trade, shutting most local merchants out of the business entirely. At the same time, since the 1768 tea duty remained in force, suspicious colonists regarded Parliament's purposeful reduction of the price of tea as a trick to get them to pay the tax, thereby setting a precedent for colonial acceptance of Parliamentary taxes.

Colonial radicals vigorously opposed the implementation of the Tea Act. In Philadelphia and New York, the Sons of Liberty prevented the landing of the tea and prevailed upon the local East India Company agents to resign their commissions. Residents of smaller ports along the Atlantic seaboard reenacted similar dramas. In Annapolis, outraged townspeople burned the ship *Peggy Stewart*, when they learned that its owner, a Maryland merchant, intended to pay the tax and land his cargo. The only port in which the tea cargo came ashore was Charleston, South Carolina, but even there the consignees agreed to give up their commissions and the tea was never sold.

In Boston, merchants and officials utterly rejected popular demands to refuse the hateful tea. Not only was Governor Hutchinson determined to uphold the authority of Parliament, but because the East India Company had chosen his mercantile house as its Boston agent, he and his family had a vested interest in the successful enforcement of the Tea Act. The Sons of Liberty in Boston, as elsewhere, vigorously opposed that law and were determined to do anything it took to prevent the landing of the tea that arrived aboard the *Dartmouth* on 28 November 1773. By mid-December, it was evident that Hutchinson would not compromise and that he intended to land the tea imminently. On the night of 16 December, a band of men disguised themselves as Indians, boarded the tea ships—by then there were three—and dumped 342 chests of tea into Boston harbor.

This incident, which later became known as the Boston Tea Party, angered many colonial elites, who opposed the radicals' strident lawlessness and resented the growing initiative of artisans, mechanics, and other middling folk in political life. Others correctly surmised that the destruction of the tea would bring strong reprisals from London and provoke another major crisis in imperial relations.

The response from London was swift and decisive. News of the incident, which reached England by mid-January 1774, was met with outrage, even by those in Britain who had supported the colonists since the days of the Stamp Act crisis. The wanton destruction of property belonging to the East India Company, they believed, was unjustifiable. For their parts, both the king and Lord North concluded that the conflict with the colonies had moved to a new and more perilous stage. What had been differences over specific constitutional issues—like taxation and the nature of Parliamentary representation—had become instead a question of whether the authority of the home government was still viable in Massachusetts—and, by extension, in the other colonies. To assert that authority, the king sent General Thomas Gage to Massachusetts to take command of the troops and assume the position of military governor. In addition, in the spring of 1774, on North's recommendation, Parliament enacted a series of four statutes pertaining to Massachusetts. Known collectively as the Coercive or "Intolerable" Acts, these laws imposed economic penalties on the people of Massachusetts and—more ominous still—fundamentally altered the province's frame of government.

The Coercive Acts sought to punish the people of Massachusetts and to take steps to prevent the further erosion of the authority of imperial officials in the colony. First, the Boston Port Act closed the province's chief seaport, delivering a mortal blow to an already depressed economy. Second, the Massachusetts Government Act gave the king the power to appoint the members of the governor's council—the upper house of the colonial legislature—which previously had been elected by the lower house; this law also limited town meetings to one per year and confined their discussions to local matters in order to prevent them from being used to encourage resistance to imperial policies. Third, the Administration of Justice Act provided that any royal official—including soldiers and tax collectors—accused of a capital crime be sent to England or another colony for trial, thereby escaping the vengeance of local juries. Fourth, a new Quartering Act retained the requirement that the colonists pay for housing and provisioning troops, while adding an equally offensive provision permitting the lodging of troops in private households.

In June 1774, Parliament also passed the Quebec Act, which established fundamental guidelines for the administration of much of the territory Britain had gained as a result of its great victory in the French and Indian War. From the perspective of the conquered people of what used to be French Canada, this law was liberal and enlightened. Parliament permitted these newest subjects of King George III to retain their familiar French system of civil law and offered religious toleration to the overwhelmingly Roman Catholic population. In the original thirteen colonies, however, many interpreted the Quebec Act in the context of their growing conflict with the home government. New England clergy, in particular, concluded that the passage of this statute was, in fact, a prelude to the general imposition throughout the empire of Catholicism and French law—which lacked jury trials and other common law rights—and that the absence of representative government in Quebec boded ill for the survival of their own elected assemblies.

Although they applied specifically to Massachusetts, the severity of these laws galvanized resistance throughout the colonies. As a result of the Coercive Acts, for the first time, the cause of Massachusetts became the cause of America. Patriots in other colonies expressed sympathy and support for the people of Boston, organized independent militia to defend their own liberties, and in various other ways showed their willingness to repudiate British imperial authority.

By 1774, colonists increasingly were divided into three political camps. Radicals pressed for an uncompromising defense of colonial rights and liberties. Conservatives accepted the supremacy of Parliament, but hoped to persuade imperial authorities to adopt reforms to redress the colonists' chief grievances. Finally, moderates sought to preserve both liberty and peace, though they sometimes disagreed about how they could best achieve those ends. Colonial political leaders discussed the Coercive Acts in their separate provincial legislatures and—in colonies where the assembly was not in session or the governor had dissolved it to avert protest—in special extralegal conventions or committees. Often led by political conservatives who feared the growing assertiveness of radical leaders and their largely plebeian following, these bodies nonetheless recognized the need to devise a unified response to the Coercive Acts.

The Coercive Acts led directly and swiftly to the convening of a Continental Congress. When Congress met in Philadelphia on 5 September 1774, its fifty-five delegates were mainly politically experienced men of high social status. Most were either moderate or conservative in their approach to imperial politics. Although radical leader Samuel Adams was a member of the Massachusetts delegation, neither the New York nor Pennsylvania delegation included a prominent member of the Sons of Liberty. Although Virginia sent Richard Henry Lee and Patrick Henry—both outspoken critics of British imperial policies—the Old Dominion's other spokesmen were more conservative members of the planter elite.

The First Continental Congress did not formally consider separation from Great Britain, but rather sought to defend American rights within the British Empire. Joseph Galloway of Pennsylvania introduced a plan of union that would have created an American Congress to share power with Parliament, under the general oversight of the king and a council to be appointed by the provincial assemblies. After serious consideration, the Congress rejected Galloway's proposal. A Declaration of Rights and Grievances, which carefully compromised the delegates' disagreements on several key points, sufficed to articulate the colonists' understanding of their place within the imperial constitution. Because conservatives derived colonial rights from legal and constitutional sources, while radicals asserted a theory of natural rights, Congress incorporated both views in its Declaration of Rights and Grievances, citing natural law, common law, the British constitution, and colonial charters as the bases of colonial rights. Congress rejected outright taxation without representation and Parliament's interference with jury trials and other common law rights, but—reflecting divisions among the delegates—dealt ambiguously with the Navigation Acts and Parliament's right to regulate trade.

Congress's most significant accomplishment was the adoption of the Continental Association in October 1774. Most delegates came to Philadelphia committed to some sort of commercial boycott as an orderly and seemingly effective strategy for bringing about changes in imperial policy. After much negotiation to accommodate the economic needs and interests of particular colonies, Congress adopted the Continental Association, which provided for a general stoppage of trade with Britain—in other words, nonimportation and eventually nonexportation, too—until Parliament repealed its objectionable laws. The Association also called for the establishment of local Committees of Inspection to enforce the trade boycott. In the coming months, as imperial institutions became increasingly irrelevant, such committees would gradually evolve into Committees of Safety, which assumed the authority and functions of local government, appealing to patriotism and community spirit but resorting to force and intimidation to enforce the Association.

The Committees of Safety, like the Continental Congress, were extralegal bodies that lacked legal or constitutional authority. In the eyes of imperial officials, the pretensions of these bodies were compelling evidence of mounting lawlessness. Under such circumstances, they surmised, compromise would mean the end of British authority in America. Acting on reports from General Thomas Gage and other colonial officials, who warned that challenges to imperial authority were both vigorous and widespread, the North ministry decided that only a show of force could restore the sovereignty of Parliament in America. The home government resolved to use troops to quell what appeared to be an ongoing rebellion in Massachusetts, where the assembly—now calling itself the Provincial Congress—met in defiance of Gage to organize special Minute Men militia units to provide for the common defense. Although

Gage warned his superiors in London that any military action would result in an all-out war, they nonetheless ordered him to suppress the Provincial Congress, capture its leaders, and seize its stores of ammunition and supplies. On 18 April 1775, Gage left Boston with 700 men. Their objective was to take or destroy the cache of military stores their spies had discovered some twenty miles away in the town of Concord.

By the next day, both British regulars and colonial militia were ready for action. Meanwhile, the Boston Committee of Safety had dispatched Paul Revere and William Dawes to the towns of Lexington and Concord to alert their inhabitants of the approaching regulars. In both towns, the militia stood prepared. At Lexington, about seventy Minute Men assembled on the village green at dawn on 19 April, silently protesting the soldiers' march through their community. When Major John Pitcairn ordered the Minute Men to disperse, they began to do so, but somebody fired a shot; the British fired in response, killing eight and wounding ten.

When the British arrived at Concord, the townspeople were ready, having removed much of their supplies and assembled militia from Concord and neighboring towns to resist the British advance. After destroying some supplies and tearing down the town liberty pole, the British retreated to Boston. Their losses were heavy in retreat: 73 dead, 174 wounded, and 26 missing—compared to 49 dead, 39 wounded, and 4 missing of the nearly 4,000 colonial militia. Unofficially, the war for America had begun.

In the decade since the Stamp Act crisis, colonists had moved from decorous and often deferential verbal protests to armed rebellion. In the process, resistance to British imperial authority had become not only more overt but also more widespread and inclusive. In 1765, lawyers had penned learned pamphlets, city merchants had foresworn British imports, and gentlemen had directed and sanctioned the actions of extralegal crowds. By 1775, resistance was more organized, thanks to a network of extralegal bodies that culminated in the Continental Congress. Committees and militia companies of ordinary people in towns and in the countryside now often were at the forefront of the struggle.

Lexington and Concord marked the beginning of the final phase of the imperial crisis, the point at which many Americans resorted to warfare to settle their differences with Britain. But what were the colonists fighting for? Did they seek reconciliation, redress of grievances, or royal and Parliamentary recognition of rights and liberties they had claimed since before 1765? Or did they now want something more? Beginning in May 1775, Americans addressed these questions—which would take more than a year to resolve—in the Second Continental Congress, in their provincial congresses and conventions, and in their local communities.

<small>DOCUMENT 1</small>

The Soldiers and the "Mob" (1770)

Captain Thomas Preston was officer of the day for the 29th Regiment on 5 March 1770, when the troops engaged in violent confrontation with townspeople on the snowy streets of Boston. Preston provided this account of the incident to his superiors in London.[1] He himself was arrested and remained in jail for seven months before being acquitted of a murder charge in October. Preston returned to England in December.

Questions to consider:

1. How did Preston describe the behavior of the soldiers before during, and after their altercation with the townspeople?
2. How did he describe the conduct of the townspeople?
3. Did Preston foresee any possibility of a peaceful coexistence for troops and townspeople in Boston?

It is [a] matter of too great notoriety to need any proofs that the arrival of his Majesty's troops in Boston was extremely obnoxious to its inhabitants. They have ever used all means in their power to weaken the regiments, and to bring them into contempt by promoting and aiding desertions, and with impunity, even where there has been the clearest evidence of the fact, and by grossly and falsely propagating untruths concerning them . . . The insolence as well as utter hatred of the inhabitants to the troops increased daily, insomuch that Monday and Tuesday, the 5th and 6th [of March], were privately agreed on for a general engagement, in consequence of which several of the militia came from the country armed to join their friends, menacing to destroy any who should oppose them. This plan has since been discovered.

On Monday night about 8 o'clock two soldiers were attacked and beat. But the party of the townspeople in order to carry matters to the utmost length, broke into two meeting houses and rang the alarm bells, which I supposed was for fire as usual, but was soon undeceived. About 9 some of the guard came to and informed me the town inhabitants were assembling to attack the troops, and that the bells were ringing as the signal for that purpose and not for fire, and the beacon intended to be fired to bring in the distant people of the country. This, as I was captain of the day, occasioned my repairing immediately to the main guard. In my way there I saw the people in great commotion, and heard them use the most cruel and horrid threats against the troops. In a few minutes after I reached the guard, about 100 people passed it and went towards the custom house where the king's money is lodged. They immediately surrounded the sentry posted there, and with clubs and other weapons threatened to execute their vengeance on him. I was soon informed by a townsman their intention was to carry off the soldier from his post and probably murder him. On which I desired him to return for further intelligence, and he soon came back and assured me he heard the mob declare they would murder him. This I feared might be a prelude to their plundering the king's chest.

I immediately sent a non-commissioned officer and 12 men to protect both the sentry and the king's money, and very soon followed myself to prevent, if possible, all disorder, fearing lest the officer and soldiers, by the insults and provocations of the rioters, should be thrown off their guard and commit some rash act. They soon rushed through the people, and by charging their bayonets in half-circles, kept them at a little distance. Nay, so far was I from intending the death of any person that I suffered the troops to go to the spot where the unhappy affair took place without any loading in their pieces; nor did I ever give orders for loading them. This remiss conduct in me perhaps merits censure; yet it is evidence, resulting from the nature of things, which is the best and surest that can be offered, that my intention was not to act offensively, but the contrary part, and that not without compulsion.

The mob still increased and were more outrageous, striking their clubs or bludgeons one against another, and calling out, come on you rascals, you bloody backs, you lobster scoundrels, fire if you dare, G-d damn you, fire and be damned, we know you dare not, and much more such language was used. At this time I was between the soldiers and the mob, parleying with, and endeavouring all in my power to persuade them to retire peaceably, but to no purpose. They advanced to the points of the bayonets, struck some of them and even the muzzles of the pieces, and seemed to be endeavouring to close with the soldiers. On which some well behaved persons asked me if the guns were charged. I replied yes. They then asked me if I intended to order the men to fire. I answered no, by no means, observing to them that I was advanced before the muzzles of the men's pieces, and must fall a sacrifice if they fired; that the soldiers were upon the half cock and charged bayonets, and my giving the word fire under those circumstances would prove me to be no officer. While I was thus speaking, one of the soldiers having received a severe blow with a stick, stepped a little on one side and instantly fired, on which turning to and asking him why he fired without orders, I was struck with a club on my arm, which for some time deprived me of the use of it, which blow had it been placed on my head, most probably would have destroyed me.

On this a general attack was made on the men by a great number of heavy clubs and snowballs being thrown at them, by which all our lives were in imminent danger, some persons at the same time from behind calling out, damn your bloods—why don't you fire. Instantly three or four of the soldiers fired, one after another, and directly after three more in the same confusion and hurry. The mob then ran away, except three unhappy men who instantly expired . . . one more is since dead, three others are dangerously, and four slightly wounded. The whole of this melancholy affair was transacted in almost 20 minutes. On my asking the soldiers why they fired without orders, they said they heard the word fire and supposed it came from me. This might be the case as many of the mob called out fire, fire, but I assured the men that I gave no such order; that my words were, don't fire, stop your firing.

DOCUMENT 2

The Boston Massacre (1770)

This account of the altercation between soldiers and Bostonians appeared one week later in the Boston Gazette, *a leading radical newspaper. Radical spokesmen spread the news of the incident and shaped the public's understanding of it. Among other things, radical propagandists invented the name by which the episode would be widely known: the Boston "massacre."*[2]

Questions to consider:

1. How did this account of the events of 5 March differ from that of Captain Preston? According to this account, how did the violence begin and what caused it to escalate?
2. How did this author's portrayals of the soldiers and townspeople contrast with those of Preston?
3. Why did the author believe it important to note that the soldiers "showed a degree of cruelty unknown to British troops, at least since the house of Hanover had directed their operations?"
4. Why did the *Boston Gazette* publish this account? Who was its intended audience?

On the evening of Monday . . . the fifth . . . several soldiers of the 29th Regiment were seen parading the streets with their drawn cutlasses and bayonets, abusing and wounding numbers of the inhabitants. A few minutes after nine o'clock four youths, named Edward Archbald, William Merchant, Francis Archbald, and John Leech, jun., came down Cornhill together, and separating at Doctor Loring's corner, the two former were passing the narrow alley leading to Murray's barrack in which was a soldier brandishing a broad sword of an uncommon size against the walls, out of which he struck fire plentifully. A person of mean countenance armed with a large cudgel bore him company. Edward Archbald admonished Mr. Merchant to take care of the sword, on which the soldier turned round and struck Archbald on the arm, then pushed at Merchant and pierced through his clothes inside the arm close to the armpit and grazed the skin. Merchant then struck the soldier with a short stick he had; and the other person ran to the barrack and brought with him two soldiers, one armed with a pair of tongs, the other with a shovel. He with the tongs pursued Archbald back through the alley, collared and laid him over the head with the tongs. The noise brought people together; and John Hicks, a young lad, coming up, knocked the soldier down but let him get up again; and more lads gathering, drove them back to the barrack where the boys stood some time as it were to keep them in. In less than a minute ten or twelve of them came out with drawn cutlasses, clubs, and bayonets and set upon the unarmed boys and young folk who stood them a little while but, finding the inequality of their equipment, dispersed.

On hearing the noise, one Samuel Atwood came up to see what was the matter; and entering the alley from dock square, heard the latter part of the combat; and when the boys had dispersed he met the ten or twelve soldiers aforesaid rushing down the alley towards the square and asked them if they intended to murder people? They answered Yes, by God, root and branch! With that one of them struck Mr. Atwood with a club which was repeated by another; and being unarmed, he turned to go off and received a wound on the left shoulder which reached the bone and gave him much pain. Retreating a few steps, Mr. Atwood met two officers and said, gentlemen, what is the matter? They answered, you'll see by and by. Immediately after, those heroes appeared in the square, asking where were the boogers? Where were the cowards? But notwithstanding their fierceness to naked men, one of them advanced towards a youth who had a split of a raw stave in his hand and said, damn them, here is one of them. But the young man seeing a person near him with a drawn sword and good cane ready to support him, held up his stave in defiance; and they quietly passed by him up the little alley by Mr. Silsby's to King Street where they attacked single and unarmed persons till they raised much clamour, and then turned down Cornhill Street, insulting all they met in like manner and pursuing some to their very doors.

Thirty or forty persons, mostly lads, being by this means gathered in King Street, Capt. Preston with a party of men with charged bayonets, came from the main guard to the commissioner's house, the soldiers pushing their bayonets, crying, make way! They took place by the custom house and, continuing to push to drive the people off, pricked some in several places, on which they were clamorous and, it is said, threw snow balls. On this, the Captain commanded them to fire; and more snow balls coming, he again said, damn you, fire, be the consequence what it will! One soldier then fired, and a townsman with a cudgel struck him over the hands with such force that he dropped his firelock; and, rushing forward, aimed a blow at the Captain's head which grazed his hat and fell pretty heavy upon his arm. However, the soldiers continued the fire successively till seven or eight or, as some say, eleven guns were discharged.

By this fatal maneuver three men were laid dead on the spot and two more struggling for life; but what showed a degree of cruelty unknown to British troops, at least since the house of Hanover has directed their operations, was an attempt to fire upon or push with their bayonets the persons who undertook to remove the slain and wounded! . . .

The people were immediately alarmed with the report of this horrid massacre, the bells were set a-ringing, and great numbers soon assembled at the place where this tragical scene had been acted. Their feelings may be better conceived than expressed; and while some were taking care of the dead and wounded, the rest were in consultation what to do in those dreadful circumstances. But so little intimidated were they, notwithstanding their being within a few yards of the main guard and seeing the 29th Regiment under arms and drawn up in King Street, that they kept their station and appeared, as an officer of rank expressed it, ready to run upon the very muzzles of their muskets.

The lieutenant-governor soon came into the town house and there met some of his Majesty's Council and a number of civil magistrates. A considerable body of the people immediately entered the council chamber and expressed themselves to his honour with a freedom and warmth becoming the occasion. He used his utmost endeavours to pacify them, requesting that they would let the matter subside for the night and promising to do all in his power that justice should be done and the law have its course. Men of influence and weight with the people were not wanting on their part to procure their compliance with his Honour's request by representing the horrible consequences of a promiscuous and rash engagement in the night, and assuring them that such measures should be entered upon in the morning as would be agreeable to their dignity and a more likely way of obtaining the best satisfaction for the blood of their fellow townsmen. The inhabitants attended to these suggestions; and the regiment under arms being ordered to their barracks, which was insisted upon by the people, they then separated and returned to their dwellings by one o'clock. At three o'clock

Capt. Preston was committed, as were the soldiers who fired, a few hours after him.

Tuesday morning presented a most shocking scene, the blood of our fellow citizens running like water through King Street and the Merchants' Exchange, the principal spot of the military parade for about eighteen months past. Our blood might also be tracked up to the head of Long Lane, and through divers other streets and passages.

At eleven o'clock the inhabitants met at Faneuil Hall; and after some animated speeches becoming the occasion, they chose a committee of fifteen respectable gentlemen to wait upon the lieutenant-governor in Council to request of him to issue his orders for the immediate removal of the troops.

The Bloody Massacre perpetrated in King Street Boston on March 5th 1770 by a party of the 29th Regiment. The work of radical leader Paul Revere, this engraving presented a partisan view of the event that became known as the "Boston Massacre." How did Revere portray the encounter between soldiers and townspeople? How did this image compare to Captain Preston's account of the incident? How did it compare to the written description of it in the radical *Boston Gazette*? Source: The Library of Congress, Washington, D.C.

Bostonians Oppose the Tea Act (1773)

In March 1770, Parliament repealed all the Townshend Duties except the tea tax, prompting the colonists to shelve nonimportation while continuing to boycott tea. Three years later, however, Parliament passed the Tea Act, which gave the British East India Company a monopoly on colonial tea sales and tax concessions so it could sell its tea at lower prices. Colonists resented the monopoly provision and regarded the tax cuts as a ploy to trick them into buying dutied tea. Patriots in some colonial seaports prevented the tea ships from landing their cargo; in Boston, the failure to do so led to another dramatic rejection of Parliamentary authority. In this letter, John Andrews of Boston described the tea-dumping incident to his merchant brother-in-law, William Barrell of Philadelphia.[3]

Questions to consider:

1. Was John Andrews, the author of this narrative, a supporter or a critic of those who destroyed the tea?
2. Why did the participants in the tea-dumping incident dress as Indians?
3. How did the methods and objectives of these "actors" compare to those of the Stamp Act rioters?

However precarious our situation may be, yet such is the present calm composure of the people that a stranger would hardly think that ten thousand pounds sterling of the East India Company's tea was destroyed the night, or rather evening before last, yet it's a serious truth . . . A general muster was assembled, from this and all the neighbouring towns, to the number of five or six thousand, at 10 o'clock Thursday morning in the Old South Meeting house, where they passed a unanimous vote that the tea should go out of the harbour that afternoon, and sent a committee with Mr. Rotch [the owner of the tea and its ship] to the Custom house to demand a clearance, which the collector told 'em was not in his power to give, without the duties being first paid. They then sent Mr. Rotch . . . to ask a pass from the Governor, who sent for answer, that "consistent with the rules of government and his duty to the King he could not grant one without they produced a previous clearance from the office."

By the time he returned with this message the candles were light in the [meeting] house, and upon reading it, such prodigious shouts were made, that induced me, while drinking tea at home, to go out and know the cause of it. The house was so crowded I could get no farther than the porch, when I found the moderator was just declaring the meeting to be dissolved, which caused another general shout, out doors and in, and three cheers. What with that, and the consequent noise of breaking up the meeting, you'd thought that the inhabitants of the infernal regions had broke loose. For my part, I went contentedly home and finished my tea, but was soon informed what was going forward: but still not crediting it without ocular demonstration, I went and was satisfied. They mustered, I'm told, upon Fort Hill, to the number of about two hundred, and proceeded, two by two, to Griffin's wharf, where [ships commanded by] Hall, Bruce, and Coffin lay, each with 114 chests of the ill fated article on board; the two former with only that article, but the latter . . . was freighted with a large quantity of other goods, which they took the greatest care not to injure in the least, and before nine o'clock in the evening, every chest from on board the three vessels was knocked to pieces and flung over the sides. They say the actors were Indians from Narragansett. Whether they were or not, to a transient observer they appeared as such, being clothe in blankets with the heads muffled, and copper colored countenances, being each armed with a hatchet or axe, and pair pistols, nor was their dialect different from what I conceive these geniuses to speak, as their jargon was unintelligible to all but themselves. Not the least insult was offered to any person, save one Captain Conner, a letter of horses in this place, not many years since removed from dear Ireland, who had ripped up the lining of his coat and waistcoat under the arms, and watching his opportunity had nearly filled 'em with tea, but being detected, was handled pretty roughly. They not only stripped him of his clothes, but gave him a coat of mud, with a severe bruising into the bargain; and nothing but their utter aversion to make any disturbance prevented his being tarred and feathered.

DOCUMENT 4

A Gentleman Fears the Power of the People (1774)

Like many members of the colonial ruling class, Gouverneur Morris of New York saw the necessity of resisting British violations of American rights and liberties but worried about the consequences of the growing involvement of ordinary people in the patriot movement. In this letter, written as New Yorkers pondered their response to the Coercive Acts, Morris described how the gentlemen of the province's rival political factions vied for the support of the "mobility."[4] Although he remained distrustful of popular politics, in 1776 Morris reluctantly supported American independence.

Questions to consider:

1. According to Morris, how had the imperial crisis changed New York's political culture? What sorts of changes did he expect the future would bring? Was he optimistic or pessimistic about the future of America?
2. Who did Morris blame for the transformation of New York politics?
3. How did he describe the common people of New York? What metaphors did he use to describe "the mob"?

Dear Sir:

You have heard, and you will hear a great deal about politics, and in the heap of chaff you may find some grains of good sense. Believe me, sir, freedom and religion are the only watchwords. We have appointed a committee, or rather we have nominated one. Let me give you a history of it. . . .

The troubles in America during Grenville's administration . . . stimulated some daring coxcombs to rouse the mob into an attack upon the bounds of order and decency. These fellows became . . . the leaders in all the riots, the bell-weathers of the flock . . . That we have been in hot water with the British Parliament ever since everybody knows . . . The port of Boston has been shut up. These [mobs], simple as they are, cannot be gulled as heretofore. In short, there is no ruling them, and now . . . the heads of the mobility grow dangerous to the gentry, and how to keep them down is the question. While they correspond with the other colonies, call and dismiss popular assemblies, make resolves to bind the consciences of the rest of mankind, bully poor printers, and exert with full force all their other tribunitial powers, it is impossible to curb them.

But art sometimes goes farther than force, and therefore, to trick them handsomely a committee of patricians was to be nominated, and into their hands was to be committed the majesty of the people . . . The tribunes, through the want of good legerdemain in the senatorial order, perceived the finesse; and yesterday I was present at a grand division of the city, and there I beheld my fellow-citizens very accurately counting all their chickens, not only before any of them were hatched, but before above one half of the eggs were laid. In short, they fairly contended about the future forms of our government, whether it should be founded upon aristocratic or democratic principles.

I stood in the balcony, and on my right hand were ranged all the people of property, with some few poor dependents, and on the other all the tradesmen, etc., who thought it worth their while to leave daily labour for the good of the country. The spirit of the English constitution has yet a little influence left, and but a little. The remains of it, however, will give the wealthy people a superiority this time, but would they secure it they must banish all school-masters and confine all knowledge to themselves. This cannot be. The mob begin to think and to reason. Poor reptiles! It is with them a vernal morning; they are struggling to cast off their winter's slough, they bask in the sunshine, and ere noon they will bite, depend upon it. The gentry begin to fear this. Their committee will be appointed, they will deceive the people and again forfeit a share of their confidence. And if these instances of what with one side is policy, with the other perfidy, shall continue to increase and become more frequent, farewell aristocracy. I see, and I see it with fear and trembling, that if the disputes with Great Britain continue, we shall be under the worst of all possible dominions; we shall be under the domination of a riotous mob.

DOCUMENT 5

The Continental Association (1774)

On 5 September 1774, the First Continental Congress convened in Philadelphia to respond to the Coercive Acts and other offensive imperial measures. The Continental Association, which called for an end to trade with Britain until colonial grievances were redressed, was the Congress's greatest achievement.[5] The Association called for the establishment of local committees to enforce the Association and punish violators. Although compliance was far from complete, by the spring of 1775, all thirteen colonies had these extralegal committees, whose membership totaled roughly 7,000. The creation of the committees and the enlistment of popular support for the Association were important steps in organizing resistance and mobilizing many outside the traditional governing elite.

Questions to consider:

1. Why did the Association begin with a declaration of loyalty to the king?
2. From the Congress's perspective, what were the respective benefits of nonimportation, nonexportation, and nonconsumption?
3. Why did nonimportation go into effect nine months earlier than nonexportation?

4. Why did the Association "discountenance and discourage" horse-racing, gambling, theatrical performances, and extravagant funerals? Why did it encourage sheep raising? Why did it call for an end to the Atlantic slave trade?

We, his Majesty's most loyal subjects . . . affected with the deepest anxiety, and most alarming apprehensions, at those grievances and distresses, with which his Majesty's American subjects are oppressed; and having taken under our most serious deliberation, the state of the whole continent, find, that the present unhappy situation of our affairs is occasioned by a ruinous system of colony administration, adopted by the British ministry about the year 1763, evidently calculated for enslaving these colonies, and, with them, the British empire. In prosecution of which system, various acts of parliament have been passed, for raising a revenue in America, for depriving the American subjects, in many instances, of the constitutional trial by jury, exposing their lives to danger, by directing a new and illegal trial beyond the seas, for crimes alleged to have been committed in America: and in prosecution of the same system, several late, cruel, and oppressive acts have been passed, respecting the town of Boston and the Massachusetts Bay, and also an act for extending the province of Quebec, so as to border on the western frontiers of these colonies, establishing an arbitrary government therein, and discouraging the settlement of British subjects in that wide extended country; thus, by the influence of civil principles and ancient prejudices, to dispose the inhabitants to act with hostility against the free Protestant colonies, whenever a wicked ministry shall choose so to direct them.

To obtain redress of these grievances, which threaten destruction to the lives, liberty, and property of his majesty's subjects, in North America, we are of opinion, that a non-importation, non-consumption, and non-exportation agreement, faithfully adhered to, will prove the most speedy, effectual, and peaceable measure: and, therefore, we do, for ourselves, and the inhabitants of the several colonies, whom we represent, firmly agree and associate, under the sacred ties of virtue, honour and love of our country, as follows:

1. That from and after the first day of December next, we will not import, into British America, from Great Britain or Ireland, any goods, wares, or merchandise whatsoever, or from any other place, any such goods, wares, or merchandise, as shall have been exported from Great Britain or Ireland; nor will we, after that day, import any East-India tea from any part of the world; nor any molasses, syrups, paneles, coffee, or pimento, from the British plantations or from Dominica; nor wines from Madeira, or the Western Islands; nor foreign indigo.

2. We will neither import nor purchase, any slave imported after the first day of December next; after which time, we will wholly discontinue the slave trade, and will neither be concerned in it ourselves, nor will we hire our vessels, nor sell our commodities or manufactures to those who are concerned in it.

3.   As a non-consumption agreement, strictly adhered to, will be an effectual security for the observation of the non-importation, we, as above, solemnly agree and associate, that, from this day, we will not purchase or use any tea, imported on account of the East India company, or any on which a duty hath been or shall be paid; and from and after the first day of March next, we will not purchase or use any East India tea whatever; nor will we, nor shall any person for or under us, purchase or use any of those goods, wares, or merchandise, we have agreed not to import, which we shall know, or have cause to suspect, were imported after the first day of December, except such as come under the rules and directions of the tenth article hereafter mentioned.

4.   The earnest desire we have, not to injure our fellow-subjects in Great Britain, Ireland, or the West-Indies, induces us to suspend a non-exportation, until the tenth day of September, 1775; at which time, if the said acts and parts of acts of the British parliament herein after mentioned are not repealed, we will not, directly or in-directly, export any merchandise or commodity whatsoever to Great Britain, Ireland, or the West Indies, except rice to Europe.

5.   Such as are merchants, and use the British and Irish trade, will give orders, as soon as possible, to their factors, agents and correspondents, in Great Britain and Ireland, not to ship any goods to them, on any pretence whatsoever, as they cannot be received in America; and if any merchant, residing in Great Britain or Ireland, shall directly or indirectly ship any goods, wares or merchandise, for America, in order to break the said non-importation agreement, or in any manner contravene the same, on such unworthy conduct being well attested, it ought to be made public; and, on the same being so done, we will not, from thenceforth, have any commercial connexion with such merchant.

6.   That such as are owners of vessels will give positive orders to their captains, or masters, not to receive on board their vessels any goods prohibited by the said non-importation agreement, on pain of immediate dismission from their service.

7.   We will use our utmost endeavours to improve the breed of sheep, and in-crease their number to the greatest extent; and to that end, we will kill them as seldom as may be, especially those of the most profitable kind; nor will we export any to the West Indies or elsewhere; and those of us, who are or may become over-stocked with, or can conveniently spare any sheep, will dispose of them to our neigh-bours, especially to the poorer sort, on moderate terms.

8.   We will, in our several stations, encourage frugality, economy, and indus-try, and promote agriculture, arts and the manufactures of this country, especially that of wool; and will discountenance and discourage every species of extravagance and dissipation, especially all horse-racing, and all kinds of gaming, cock-fighting, exhibitions of shows, plays, and other expensive diversions and entertainments; and on the death of any relation or friend, none of us, or any of our families, will go into any further mourning-dress, than a black crape or ribbon on the arm or hat, for gentlemen, and a black ribbon and necklace for ladies, and we will discontinue the giving of gloves and scarves at funerals.

9.   Such as are venders of goods or merchandise will not take advantage of the scarcity of goods, that may be occasioned by this association, but will sell the same at the rates we have been respectively accustomed to do, for twelve months last past. And if any vender of goods or merchandise shall sell any such goods on higher terms, or shall, in any manner, or by any device whatsoever violate or depart from this agreement, no person ought, nor will any of us deal with any such person, or his or her factor or agent, at any time thereafter, for any commodity whatever.

10.   In case any merchant, trader, or other person, shall import any goods or merchandise, after the first day of December, and before the first day of February

next, the same ought forthwith, at the election of the owner, to be either re-shipped or delivered up to the committee of the county or town, wherein they shall be imported, to be stored at the risk of the importer, until the non-importation agreement shall cease, or be sold under the direction of the committee . . . the profit, if any, to be applied towards relieving and employing such poor inhabitants of the town of Boston, as are immediate sufferers by the Boston port-bill. . . .

11.   That a committee be chosen in every county, city, and town, by those who are qualified to vote for representatives in the legislature, whose business it shall be attentively to observe the conduct of all persons touching this association; and when it shall be made to appear, to the satisfaction of a majority of any such committee, that any person within the limits of their appointment has violated this association, that such majority do forthwith cause the truth of the case to be published in the gazette; to the end, that all such foes to the rights of British-America may be publicly known, and universally contemned as the enemies of American liberty; and thenceforth we respectively will break off all dealings with him or her.

12.   That the committee of correspondence, in the respective colonies, do frequently inspect the entries of their custom-houses, and inform each other, from time to time, of the true state thereof, and of every other material circumstance that may occur relative to this association.

13.   That all manufactures of this country be sold at reasonable prices, so that no undue advantage be taken of a future scarcity of goods.

14.   And we do further agree and resolve, that we will have no trade, commerce, dealings or intercourse whatsoever, with any colony or province, in North America, which shall not accede to, or which shall hereafter violate this association, but will hold them as unworthy of the rights of freemen, and as inimical to the liberties of their country.

And we do solemnly bind ourselves and our constituents, under the ties aforesaid, to adhere to this association, until such parts of the several acts of parliament passed since the close of the last war . . . are repealed . . . And we recommend it to the provincial conventions, and to the committees in the respective colonies, to establish such farther regulations as they may think proper, for carrying into execution this association.

DOCUMENT 6

A Virginia County Committee Punishes an "Enemy to America" (1775)

On 8 November 1775, the gentlemen of the Westmoreland County Committee questioned David Wardrobe, a local tutor, about a letter he had written to a friend in Scotland in which he disparaged the colonists' ability to abide by the Continental Association.

Although Wardrobe did not return three weeks later, as ordered, to recant his offensive statements, he eventually reappeared before the committee to "implore the forgiveness" of his neighbors in the hope that he "shall be at least admitted to subsist amongst the people I greatly esteem."[6]

Questions to consider:

1. On what grounds did the committee justify its prosecution of David Wardrobe?
2. Why did the committee choose public recantation—both in person and in a published newspaper statement—as the most appropriate form of punishment?

At a meeting of the committee for the county of Westmoreland for seeing the association duly executed, November 8, 1774. Before them a certain David Wardrobe came, and being examined concerning a letter, false, scandalous, and inimical to America, published in the *Glasgow Journal* August 18, 1774, said to be written by a gentleman from Westmoreland county, in Virginia, June 30, 1774, and charged to be written by the said Wardrobe; the committee, on hearing the said Wardrobe acknowledge to have written the greatest part of said letter, and equivocating extremely concerning the rest of it, and seriously considering the fatal consequences that will infallibly be derived to the dearest rights and just liberties of America, if such enemies are suffered to proceed in this manner, of giving false and mischievous accounts to Great Britain, tending to misrepresent this country, and to deceive Great Britain, have come to the following resolutions, which they do most earnestly recommend to all those who regard the peace, the liberty, and the rights of their country:

   I.   Resolved, that the vestry of Cople parish be desired no longer to furnish the said Wardrobe with the use of the vestryhouse for his keeping school therein.

   II.   That all persons who have sent their children to school to the said Wardrobe do immediately take them away, and that he be regarded as a wicked enemy to America, and be treated as such.

   III.   That the said Wardrobe do forthwith write and publish a letter in the gazette, expressing to the world his remorse for having traduced the people here, and misrepresented their proceedings in manner as in the said letter is done.

   IV.   That the said Wardrobe be charged to appear at Westmoreland courthouse on the 29th day of this instant, to be dealt with further as the committee shall direct, to which time and place they do adjourn themselves.

The Alternative of Williams-burg, 1775. This English political cartoon showed Virginia patriots forcing merchants to choose between accepting the Continental Association or being tarred and feathered. What message did the artist, Philip Dawes, seek to convey to his audience? What was the significance of the presence of white women and African Americans among the crowd of onlookers? Source: Plate IV, Courtesy of The Library of Congress, Washington, D.C.

DOCUMENT 7

"The Testimony of the People Called Quakers" (1775)

Quakers were officially pacifists who opposed the escalation of hostilities with Britain on religious grounds, though a few wealthy merchants also did so to protect their trade. In Pennsylvania and western New Jersey, where Quakers were both numerous and influential, they found themselves under growing pressure to support increasingly militant resistance to British imperial authority. In early 1775, therefore, the Philadelphia Yearly Meeting issued this statement to explain and justify their position to their non-Quaker neighbors.[7]

Questions to consider:

1. Why did the Quakers claim to oppose resistance to British imperial authority? What did they mean by "illegal authority" and "illegal assemblies"?
2. What did they propose to do if the king continued to reject or ignore colonial petitions?
3. In 1775, how would radical readers of the *Pennsylvania Gazette* have responded to the Quakers' "Testimony"? How might they have responded ten years earlier?

Given forth by a Meeting of the Representatives of said People [called Quakers], in Pennsylvania and New Jersey, held at Philadelphia, the twenty-fourth Day of the first Month, 1775.

Having considered with real sorrow, the unhappy contest between the legislature of Great Britain and the people of these colonies, and the animosities consequent thereon, we have by repeated public advices and private admonitions, used our endeavours to dissuade the members of our religious society from joining with the public resolutions promoted and entered into by some of the people, which as we apprehended, so we now find have increased contention, and produced great discord and confusion.

The Divine Principle of grace and truth which we profess leads all who attend to its dictates to demean themselves as peaceable subjects, and to discountenance and avoid every measure tending to excite disaffection to the king, as supreme magistrate, or to the legal authority of his government;

to which purpose many of the late political writings and addresses to the people appearing to be calculated, we are led by a sense of duty to declare our entire disapprobation of them—their spirit and temper being not only contrary to the nature and precepts of the gospel, but destructive of the peace and harmony of civil society. . . .

From our past experience of the clemency of the king and his royal ancestors, we have grounds to hope and believe, that decent and respectful addresses from those who are vested with legal authority, representing the prevailing dissatisfactions, and the cause of them, would avail towards obtaining relief, ascertaining and establishing the just rights of the people and restoring the public tranquility; and we deeply lament that contrary modes of proceeding have been pursued, which have involved the colonies in confusion, appear likely to produce violence and bloodshed, and threaten the subversion of the constitutional government, and of that liberty of conscience, for the enjoyment of which our ancestors were induced to encounter the manifold dangers and difficulties of crossing the seas, and of settling in the wilderness.

We are, therefore, incited by a sincere concern for the peace and welfare of our country, publicly to declare against every usurpation of power and authority, in opposition to the laws and government, and against all combinations, insurrections, conspiracies, and illegal assemblies: and as we are restrained from them by the conscientious discharge of our duty to Almighty God, "by whom Kings reign, and princes decree justice," we hope through his assistance and favour to be enabled to maintain our testimony against any requisitions which may be made of us, inconsistent with our religious principles, and the fidelity we owe to the king and his government, as by law established; earnestly desiring the restoration of that harmony and concord which have hitherto united the people of these provinces, and been attended by the divine blessing on their labours.

DOCUMENT 8

Janet Schaw on the Mistreatment of North Carolina Loyalists (1775)

Janet Schaw, the sister of a Scottish tobacco merchant living in North Carolina, visited Wilmington in the summer of 1775. She found the town's inhabitants divided between Whigs, who were determined to resist the imperial regime, and Tories, or loyalists, who continued to uphold it. Whig leaders drilled the militia, enforced the Association, and harassed the predominantly Scottish loyalist inhabitants of eastern North Carolina.[8] The presence of a large enslaved population complicated divisions between Whigs and Tories in North Carolina, as in the other southern colonies, as Schaw perceptively noted.

Questions to consider:

1. According to Janet Schaw, what sorts of people remained loyal to the king and the empire in Wilmington and its environs?
2. How did Schaw describe the colonial soldiers? To what did she attribute popular support for the Whig movement in eastern North Carolina?
3. How did Schaw's sex affect the sort of treatment she received in Wilmington? Did gender influence her account of the town and its inhabitants?

We came down in the morning for the review [of militia] which the heat made as terrible to the spectators as to the soldiers, or what you please to call them. They had certainly fainted under it, had not the constant draughts of grog supported them. Their exercise was that of bush-fighting, but it appeared so confused and so perfectly different from any thing I ever saw, I cannot say whether they performed it well or not; but this I know that they were heated with rum till capable of committing the most shocking outrages. We stood in the balcony of Dr. Cobham's house and they were reviewed on a field mostly covered with what are called here scrubby oaks, which are only a little better than brushwood. They at last however assembled on the plain field, and I must really laugh while I recollect their figures: 2,000 men in their shirts and trousers, preceded by a very ill beat-drum and a fiddler, who was also in a shirt with a long sword and a cue at his hair, who played with all his might. They made indeed a most unmartial appearance. But the worst figure there can shoot from behind a bush and kill even a General Wolfe.

Before the review was over, I heard a cry of tar and feather. I was ready to faint at the idea of this dreadful operation. I would have gladly quitted the balcony, but was so much afraid the victim was one of my friends, that I was not able to move; and he indeed proved to be one, though in a humble station. For it was Mr Neilson's poor English groom. You can hardly conceive what I felt when I saw him dragged forward, poor devil, frighted out of his wits. However at the request of some of the officers, who had been Neilson's friends, his punishment was changed into that of mounting on a table and begging pardon for having smiled at the regiment. He was then drummed and fiddled out of the town, with a strict prohibition of ever being seen in it again. . . .

After the review . . . I went into the town, the entry of which I found closed up by a detachment of the soldiers; but as the officer immediately made way for me, I . . . advanced to the middle of the street, where I found a number of the first people of the town standing together . . . As most of them were my acquaintances, I stopped to speak to them, but they with one voice begged me for heaven's sake to get off the street, making me observe they were prisoners, adding that every avenue of the town was shut up, and that in all human probability some scene would be acted very unfit for me to witness. I could not take the friendly advice, for I became unable to move and absolutely petrified with horror.

Observing however an officer with whom I had just dined, I beckoned him to me. He came, but with no very agreeable look, and on my asking him what was the matter, he presented a paper he had folded in his hand. If you will persuade them to sign this they are at liberty, said he, but till then must remain under this guard, as they must suffer the penalties that have justly incurred. "And we will suffer every thing," replied one of them, "before we abjure our king, our country and our principles." . . . Oh Britannia, what are you doing, while your true obedient sons are thus insulted by their unlawful brethren; are they also forgotten by their natural parents? . . .

At present the martial law stands thus: An officer or committeeman enters a plantation with his posse. The alternative is proposed. Agree to join us and your persons and properties are safe; you have a shilling sterling a day; your duty is no more than once a month appearing under arms at Wilmington, which will prove only merry-making, where you will have as much grog as you can drink. But if you refuse, we are directly to cut up your corn, shoot your pigs, burn your houses, seize your Negroes and perhaps tar and feather yourself. Not to choose the first requires more courage than they are possessed of, and I believe this method has seldom failed with the lower sort. No sooner do they appear under arms on the stated day, than they are harangued by their officers with the implacable cruelty of the king of Great Britain, who has resolved to murder and destroy man, wife and child, and that he has sworn before God and his parliament that he will not spare one of them; and this those deluded people believe more firmly than their creed, and who is it that is bold enough to venture to undeceive them. The King's [proclamation that the colonies were in a state of rebellion] they never saw; but are told it was ordering the tories to murder the whigs, and promising every Negro that would murder his Master and family that he should have his Master's plantation. This last artifice they may pay for, as the Negroes have got it amongst them and believe it to be true. Tis ten to one they may try the experiment, and in that case friends and foes will all be one.

SUGGESTED READING FOR CHAPTER 4

AMMERMAN, DAVID. *In Common Cause: American Response to the Coercive Acts of 1774* (1974).

BROWN, RICHARD D. *Revolutionary Politics in Massachusetts: The Boston Committee of Correspondence and the Towns, 1772–1774* (1970).

FISCHER, DAVID H. *Paul Revere's Ride* (1994).

GROSS, ROBERT A. *The Minutemen and Their World* (1976).

HOERDER, DIRK. *Crowd Action in Revolutionary Massachusetts, 1765–1780* (1977).

HOLTON, WOODY. *Forced Founders: Indians, Debtors, Slaves, and the Making of the American Revolution in Virginia* (1999).

LABAREE, BENJAMIN W. *The Boston Tea Party* (1964).

NASH, GARY B. *The Urban Crucible: Social Change, Political Consciousness, and the Origins of the American Revolution* (1979).

RAGSDALE, BRUCE A. *A Planters' Republic: The Search for Economic Independence in Revolutionary Virginia* (1996).

RYERSON, RICHARD ALAN. *The Revolution Is Now Begun: The Radical Committees of Philadelphia, 1765–1776* (1978).

SHY, JOHN. *Toward Lexington: The Role of the British Army in the Coming of the American Revolution* (1965).

WITHINGTON, ANN FAIRFAX. *Toward a More Perfect Union: Virtue and the Formation of American Republics* (1991).

ZOBEL, HILLER B. *The Boston Massacre* (1970).

NOTES

[1]British Public Records Office, C. O. 5/759.

[2]*Boston Gazette and Country Journal,* 12 Mar. 1770.

[3]John Andrews to William Barrell, 18 Dec. 1773, in *Proceedings of the Massachusetts Historical Society,* 8 (1862–65): 325–27.

[4]Gouverneur Morris to Thomas Penn, 20 May 1774, in Peter Force, ed., *American Archives,* 4th ser., 6 vols. (Washington, 1837–53), 1: 342–43.

[5]*Journals of the Continental Congress, 1774–1789,* ed. Worthington C. Ford et al. (Washington, D.C., 1904–37), 1:75–80.

[6]*Virginia Gazette* (Pinkney), 9 Feb. 1775.

[7]*Pennsylvania Gazette,* 22 Feb. 1775.

[8]Evangeline Walker Andrews and Charles McLean Andrews, eds., *Journal of a Lady of Quality; Being the Narrative of a Journal from Scotland to the West Indies, North Carolina, and Portugal, in the years 1774 to 1776* (New Haven, 1927), 189–92, 198–99.

CHAPTER FIVE

ASSERTING
INDEPENDENCE

News of the fighting at Lexington and Concord spread first through New England and then southward, impelling Americans to action. Militia drilled and prepared to fight. Provincial congresses and other extralegal bodies gradually assumed the powers and responsibilities of government. And on 10 May 1775, just three weeks after the fateful battles, the Second Continental Congress convened in Philadelphia. For the next fourteen months, Congress acted cautiously but decisively, ultimately claiming the right of self-determination on behalf of its thirteen constituent members.

The movement toward independence involved both words and action as the continuing drama unfolded in London, Philadelphia, the colonial capitals, and many local communities. Congress restated colonial grievances to an uncompromising king who, in turn, reiterated British legal and constitutional positions to skeptical provincials. County committees formulated declarations and resolutions for their constituents and wider audiences. Colonial military activities likewise emanated from both local and continental authorities during the months following Lexington and Concord, though in June Congress took an important step toward centralization by establishing the Continental Army. Radicals and conservatives debated in Congress, in the press, and in informal face-to-face encounters. Purposeful radical leadership in all of these venues set the stage for a formal declaration of independence by mid-1776.

Local and provincial authorities provided the initial response to the military engagements at Lexington and Concord, which many Americans regarded as turning points in their relations with Great Britain and its government. The Continental Congress was not in session in April 1775, but as news of the battles spread throughout the colonies, local committees that had been established to enforce the Association stepped up recruitment and training of militia to provide for the common defense. Thousands of militia from all over New England flocked to Boston, where the British military presence was greatest. Local militia units in other colonies trained and gathered arms and ammunition, anticipating battle.

Military action initially proceeded without central coordination from the Continental Congress. On 10 May 1775, colonial militia led by Ethan Allen and Benedict Arnold seized the poorly defended British fort at Ticonderoga in New York's upper Hudson River Valley. Two days later, Allen's troops took nearby Crown Point, also located in New York, north of Ticonderoga. Meanwhile, New England militia who had gathered in the Boston area moved to fortify the hills overlooking the city in nearby Charlestown. British troops engaged colonial forces at Breed's Hill on 17 June 1775. After three frontal assaults, a force of 2,000 British regulars dislodged the colonial militia, but at a great cost: 226 dead and 828 wounded, compared to 140 dead and 271 wounded for the Americans. Although they captured both Breed's Hill and neighboring Bunker Hill—from which the engagement would take its name—the British were demoralized, while colonial militia were buoyed by the outcome of the battle.

News from Bunker Hill made its way to Philadelphia, where the Second Continental Congress had convened a month earlier. Congress responded cautiously to military and political developments as they unfolded in Massachusetts and elsewhere. Drawn overwhelmingly from the ranks of the colonial elite, most delegates did not see themselves as revolutionaries. Even the more radical delegates, who by now wanted and expected independence, did not openly pursue it in 1775. Caution was the most effective strategy in a Congress that included a significant minority of conservatives, who sought reconciliation by peaceful means, and many more moderates, who also wanted reconciliation but supported armed resistance to extract concessions from British authorities. In 1775, Congress therefore pursued a two-pronged strategy of military action and continued dialog with London, using both physical force and conciliatory rhetoric to reiterate colonial grievances and defend what they believed to be traditional liberties and rights.

The engagements at Lexington and Concord, which many colonists regarded as brutal and unjustified attacks, made military organization Congress's top priority. In May 1775, the delegates resolved to put the colonies in a state of defense; in June, they created the Continental Army. As fighting raged at Bunker Hill, Congress appointed George Washington of Virginia as the army's commander-in-chief. Washington's service in the British army during the French and Indian War gave him strong military credentials, and many delegates believed that selecting a Virginian as commander-in-chief would strengthen support for war in the southern colonies. To pay for the army and its operations, Congress issued $2 million in paper currency. This emission was the first of many, as Americans would finance much of the war by issuing paper money.

By July 1775, Congress also had adopted a short-term military strategy. Congress dispatched General Washington to command a detachment of troops in the Boston area. At Washington's urging, however, the delegates also authorized a major offensive against Canada. American leaders erroneously expected the overwhelmingly French population of Quebec to turn against their new British governors. Beginning in September 1775, American forces commanded by Richard Montgomery and Benedict Arnold held Quebec under siege for several months, only to be rebuffed.

Even as they undertook a major military offensive against the imperial regime, colonial leaders in Congress continued their dialog with British authorities. On 6 July 1775, Congress issued two documents to delineate its current position in the evolving crisis. The first explained the delegates' decision to take up arms officially in the wake of Lexington and Concord. The second reasserted the colonists' loyalty to the king, while asking him to intervene on their behalf to resolve their grievances against his government. Somewhat contradictory in tone and purpose, these documents reflected the considerable differences of opinions among members of the Continental Congress.

The Declaration of the Causes and Necessity of Taking Up Arms best represented the position of radicals in Congress, along with that of moderates who believed that imperial authorities would never concede anything to the colonists voluntarily. The authors of this document, radical Thomas Jefferson and moderate John Dickinson, characterized the actions of the British soldiers at Lexington and Concord as the most brutal of many Parliamentary abuses suffered by the king's American subjects. Accordingly, they characterized Congress's decision to take up arms as wholly defensive and therefore both legally and morally justified.

The so-called Olive Branch Petition, by contrast, appeased moderates and conservatives in Congress who still valued the imperial tie and sought reconciliation with the king's government. The Olive Branch Petition marked the last instance in which colonial leaders formally embraced the image of the king as a benevolent father who might redress their grievances and protect them from malevolent forces in the

British government. Few in Congress expected George III to grant the petitioners' requests—and thereby repudiate both Parliament and his ministers—but many believed that the failure of this last-ditch appeal to the king would persuade moderates and even conservatives of the impossibility of compromise.

Indeed, the response from London showed unequivocally that compromise was untenable. British authorities, including the king, regarded the colonists as traitors and outlaws who should be suppressed by force of arms. In August 1775, George III issued a proclamation condemning colonial leaders, and he refused to receive the Olive Branch Petition from the Continental Congress, which he regarded as both illegal and unconstitutional. In the coming months, Lord North's ministry took steps to suppress the colonial rebellion. In December, Parliament passed the Prohibitory Act, which ended all trade with the colonies and empowered the Royal Navy to seize any American ships and cargoes it encountered. In January 1776, the British government concluded treaties with several German states, which agreed to provide mercenary soldiers to fight the American war.

The home government also pressed colonial governors to act aggressively to shore up their rapidly eroding power, only to find that a show of force often accelerated the disintegration of imperial authority. Most spectacular was the blunder of John Murray, Earl of Dunmore, the governor of Virginia, who on 7 November 1775 issued a proclamation offering freedom to any able-bodied slaves who fled their masters to serve in the British army. About a thousand enslaved people seeking liberty responded to the governor's call, but in December Virginia militia defeated a combined force of British regulars, escaped slaves, and white loyalists at the Battle of Great Bridge. When the victorious militia occupied the town of Norfolk, the governor ordered a naval bombardment and burning of the town in retaliation. Dunmore's proclamation and its consequences aroused outrage and fears of slave insurrection, making even the most conservative gentry more receptive to the idea of independence.

By January 1776, then, relations between Britain and the colonies were deteriorating rapidly. George III had rebuffed Congress's conciliatory petition, while the decision to enlist both slaves and foreign mercenaries in the America war elicited new outrage among the colonists. Recent events were forcing many in America to conclude that they had only two choices: to accept the principle of Parliament sovereignty with all its implications or to withdraw their allegiance from the king and from the British Empire. In Congress and among the people at large, the latter proved to be the preferable option, though it would be another six months before American leaders took that position officially.

The formal declaration of independence in July 1776 was in some respects the logical culmination of more than a year of political pronouncements and maneuvering at the local, provincial, and continental levels. As early as May 1775, the Provincial Congress of Massachusetts had proposed the adoption of a new written constitution. Around the same time, one North Carolina county declared all royal commissions null and void and adopted a series of resolutions that established new local institutions to be controlled directly by the voting population. Clearly, there were scattered expressions—even quasi-official pronouncements—in favor of independence before July 1776.

Independence found one of its most forceful and charismatic advocates in Thomas Paine, editor of the *Pennsylvania Magazine* and a recent emigrant from England. By mid-1775, Paine was impatient with Congress's apparent moderation. In January 1776, his anonymous pamphlet, *Common Sense*, radicalized many Americans. Paine's style was plain and direct; his thesis was elegantly simple: the colonies must be independent and they must be so immediately. Had Paine taken such a radical stance just a year earlier, most colonists probably would have dismissed him as a dangerous iconoclast. But by 1776, many readers found his message not only plausible but appealing, too. *Common Sense* was an instant success, selling at least 150,000 copies and going through an unprecedented twenty-five editions in its first year of publication.

Paine's influential pamphlet transformed the terms of the ongoing political debate, both in Congress and among the general population. After January 1776, instead of pondering the best means by which to extract concessions from Britain, colonial leaders increasingly debated the timing, means, and justification for asserting the autonomy of the thirteen colonies. Military developments informed these debates, as the war continued and colonial leaders recognized that only an independent America could openly seek military support from foreign powers. In early 1776, the colonists' military prospects were promising. In late February, North Carolina militia routed a force of loyalists at Moore's Creek Bridge near Wilmington. In March, the royal governor of Georgia failed to reclaim Savannah, the colony's capital. In June, South Carolina's patriots withstood eleven hours of shelling to defend Charleston, the largest city and busiest port in the southern colonies. Meanwhile, farther north, Washington's forces besieged Boston, forcing the British to evacuate the town, which resulted in their withdrawal from New England.

Radicals in Congress were determined to pursue independence, and they saw the creation of new governments at the provincial level as the essential first step in separating the colonies from the British empire. Although Congress enjoined individual colonies to take steps to create workable and appropriate governments in May 1776, moderate and conservative delegates interpreted this resolution as an attempt to preserve order as imperial authority eroded. But John Adams proposed a

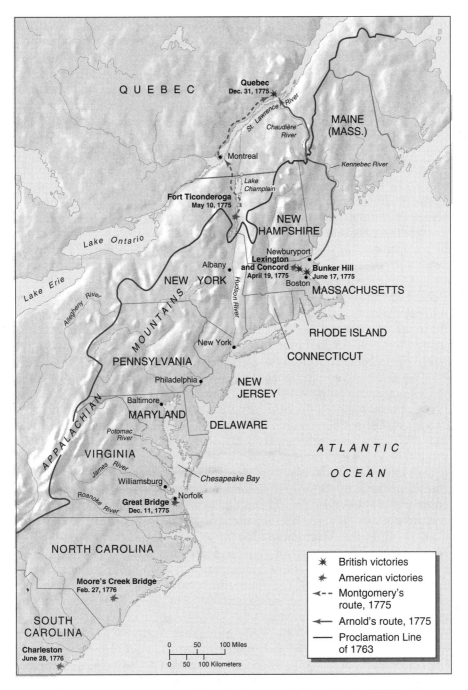

Early Military Encounters, 1775–1776. From Lexington and Concord in April 1775 to the successful defense of Charleston in June 1776, Americans engaged the British in a series of scattered confrontations.

controversial preamble to this resolution which angered many of his less radical colleagues. Adams's preamble cited the abuses of the king and Parliament as grounds for suppressing the imperial regime, thereby transforming the rationale behind the creation of new governments. Radicals in Congress capitalized on the rising popular mood in favor of independence and on the absence of many more moderate delegates to adopt Adams's preamble, which was tantamount to a declaration of independence in its author's estimation.

Three weeks later, on 7 June 1776, Richard Henry Lee, a radical leader from Virginia, proposed in Congress "that these United Colonies are, and of right ought to be, free and independent states." Although Congress postponed the vote on Lee's resolution until 2 July, in the next few days the delegates appointed two committees: one to draft a formal declaration of independence and another to draw up a collective frame of government for the thirteen states. The committee charged with writing the declaration of independence included three radicals—Thomas Jefferson, John Adams, and Benjamin Franklin—and the moderates Robert R. Livingston of New York and Roger Sherman of Connecticut. Jefferson wrote a draft of the entire document, to which Adams and Franklin contributed the most significant revisions. On 2 July 1776, Congress voted in favor of Lee's independence resolution. Two days later, the delegates adopted the Declaration of Independence.

Scholars have long debated the sources of the ideas and rhetoric of the Declaration of Independence. Some stress the influence of John Locke, the seventeenth-century English philosopher who described the origins and functions of civil government in terms strikingly similar to those Jefferson used in the preamble of the Declaration. Others, noting the influence of Scottish educators in eighteenth-century American colleges, claim that the ideals of the Scottish Enlightenment shaped the Declaration. Other historians emphasize the impact of current events on the content of the Declaration. A recent biographer of Jefferson notes his absorption in the efforts of his own state, Virginia, to draft its first constitution. In June, the Virginians adopted a preamble—written by George Mason—whose content strongly resembled that of the Declaration. Another scholar, who has studied the many resolutions, instructions, and constitutions adopted at the state and local levels, concludes that the Declaration drew on a range of conventional ideas widely shared by eighteenth-century Americans.

Scholars agree that the Declaration was designed to persuade its audience of the justice of the American cause. This first of America's founding documents announced and explained Congress's renunciation of the authority of George III as a consequence of his habitual violation of his subjects' inalienable rights. The Declaration attacked the king specifically because, by 1776, Congress regarded him as the sole remaining constitutional link between themselves and Great Britain. But to whom did Congress address its case for the overthrow of the king's government? In the text of the Declaration, Congress claimed to address "a candid world"—meaning presumably potential European allies, who needed reassurance that American leaders cautiously and responsibly chose independence as a last resort to defend their traditional rights. Of at least of equal importance, however, was informing Americans of Congress's decision to assert independence and convincing them that that decision was both wise and just.

The eloquent phrases of the Declaration of Independence probably had little effect in the courts of Europe, but they boosted American morale significantly. For many Americans, the Declaration made the ongoing disruption of trade and economic life and the continuing war with Britain more understandable and worthwhile, transforming

Pulling Down the Statue of King George III, 1848, by Johannes Adam Oertel. In 1770, an elegant equestrian statue of George III was erected in Bowling Green at the southwestern tip of Manhattan Island. During the imperial crisis, radicals often vandalized the statue. On 9 July 1776, after the first public reading of the Declaration of Independence in New York, a crowd of New Yorkers pulled it down completely. This nineteenth-century painting depicts that event. What elements of the painter's interpretation of the incident seem plausible? Which seem less so? Source: Oil on canvas, 32¾ × 42⅛ inches. Accession number 1925.6, negative number 6278, Collection of The New-York Historical Society.

tragedies and tribulations into avenues for the pursuit of substantial and specific goals. Now, American patriots sought not merely liberty and security within the British Empire—a limited objective whose attainment many considered temporary at best. Now, they instead fought for self-determination and for their inalienable rights.

In the months between the battles at Lexington and Concord and the Declaration of Independence, the Continental Congress had inched toward an unprecedented—and therefore revolutionary—assertion of colonial independence. Congress created an army and promoted the establishment of new governments. Then, finally, the delegates renounced, completely and irrevocably, America's venerable ties to the king and to the British Empire. But asserting independence, both by words and by actions, did not automatically make it reality. For more than five years, Americans would persevere—militarily, politically, and in their own lives—to attain that goal.

DOCUMENT 1

The Mecklenburg Resolves (1775)

On 31 May 1775, just three weeks after the Second Continental Congress convened in Philadelphia, leading citizens of Mecklenburg County in western North Carolina adopted a series of twenty resolutions that in their view suspended royal and imperial rule in their community.[1] In so doing, they made explicit the process that was occurring gradually and on an ad hoc basis throughout the colonies: the establishment of new political and administrative entities to supplant an increasingly intractable and untenable imperial regime.

Questions to consider:

1. What was the historical context in which the Mecklenburg County committee composed and adopted its Resolves? What recent developments impelled the committeemen to take such decisive action?
2. What did the committee members expect to be the consequences of their publication of the Resolves, both locally and in the *South Carolina Gazette*, the chief newspaper in the Carolinas?

3. What did committee members mean when they said that all officers would "hold their commissions during the pleasure of their several constituents"? To what extent did that statement suggest a dramatic break with past practice?

This day the Committee of this county met and passed the following resolves:

Whereas by an address presented to his majesty by both Houses of Parliament in February last, the American colonies are declared to be in a state of actual rebellion, we conceive that all laws and commissions confirmed by or derived from the authority of the King and Parliament are annulled and vacated and the former civil constitution of these colonies for the present wholly suspended. To provide in some degree for the exigencies of this county, in the present alarming period, we deem it proper and necessary to pass the following resolves:

1. That all commissions civil and military heretofore granted by the Crown to be exercised in these colonies are null and void and the constitution of each particular colony wholly suspended.

2. That the Provincial Congress of each Province under the direction of the great Continental Congress is invested with all legislative and executive powers within their respective Provinces and that no other legislative or executive power does or can exist at this time in any of these colonies.

3. As all former laws are now suspended in this Province and the Congress have not yet provided others we judge it necessary for the better preservation of good order, to form certain rules and regulations for the internal government of this county until laws shall be provided for us by the Congress.

4. That the inhabitants of this county do meet on a certain day appointed by the committee and having formed themselves into nine companies . . . eight in the county and one in the town of Charlotte do choose a Colonel and other military officers who shall hold and exercise their several powers by virtue of this choice and independent of the Crown of Great Britain and former constitution of this Province.

5. That for the better preservation of the peace and administration of justice each of those companies do choose from their own body two discreet freeholders who shall be empowered each by himself and singly to decide and determine all matters of controversy arising within said company under the sum of twenty shillings and jointly and together all controversies under the sum of forty shillings, that so as their decisions may admit of appeal to the convention of the selectmen of the county and also that anyone of these men shall have power to examine and commit to confinement persons accused of petit larceny.

6. That those two selectmen thus chosen do jointly and together choose from the body of their particular body two persons properly qualified to act as constables who may assist them in the execution of their office.

7. That upon the complaint of any persons to either of these selectmen he do issue his warrant directed to the constable commanding him to bring the aggressor before him or them to answer said complaint.

8. That these eighteen selectmen thus appointed do meet every third Thursday in January, April, July and October, at the Court House in Charlotte, to hear and determine all matters of controversy for sums exceeding forty shillings, also appeals, and in cases of felony to commit the person or persons convicted thereof to close confinement until the Provincial Congress shall provide and establish laws and modes of proceedings in all such cases.

9. That these eighteen selectmen thus convened do choose a clerk to record the transactions of said convention and that said clerk upon the application of any person or persons aggrieved do issue his warrant to one of the constables of the company to which the offender belongs, directing said constable to summon and warn said offender to appear before the convention at their next sitting to answer the aforesaid complaint. . . .

10. That whatever person hereafter shall receive a commission from the Crown or attempt to exercise any such commission heretofore received shall be deemed an enemy to his country and upon information being made to the captain of the company in which he resides, the said company shall cause him to be apprehended and conveyed before the two selectmen of the said company, who upon proof of the fact, shall commit him the said offender to safe custody until the next sitting of the committee, who shall deal with him as prudence may direct.

11. That any person refusing to yield obedience to the above resolves shall be considered equally criminal and liable to the same punishment as the offenders above last mentioned.

12. That these resolves be in full force and virtue until instructions from the Provincial Congress regulating the jurisprudence of the Province shall provide otherwise or the legislative body of Great Britain resign its unjust and arbitrary pretensions with respect to America.

13. That the eight Militia companies in this county provide themselves with proper arms and accoutrements and hold themselves in readiness to execute the commands and directions of the General Congress of this Province and of this Committee.

14. That the committee appoint Colonel Thomas Polk and Dr. Joseph Kennedy to purchase three hundred pounds of powder, six hundred pounds of lead and one thousand flints for the use of the militia of this county and deposit the same in such place as the committee may hereafter direct.

DOCUMENT 2

Proclamation of George III (1775)

On 23 August 1775, George III issued a royal proclamation in which he responded to the latest developments in the colonies, including Congress's recent Olive Branch Petition and Declaration of the Causes and Necessity of Taking up Arms.[2] Although this message came directly from the king, it also reflected the opinions of Lord North, most members of Parliament, and most ordinary Britons.

Questions to consider:

1. Why did George III issue this proclamation?
2. On whom did he blame the "rebellion" in America? Who did he see as its chief victims?
3. How did the king's interpretation of the events of the past decade differ from that of the Continental Congress?

Whereas many of our subjects in divers parts of our Colonies and Plantations in North America, misled by dangerous and ill designing men, and forgetting the allegiance which they owe to the power that has protected and supported them; after various disorderly acts committed in disturbance of the publick peace, to the obstruction of lawful commerce, and to the oppression of our loyal subjects carrying on the same; have at length proceeded to open and avowed rebellion, by arraying themselves in a hostile manner, to withstand the execution of the law, and traitorously preparing, ordering and levying war against us: And whereas, there is reason to apprehend that such rebellion hath been much promoted and encouraged by the traitorous correspondence, counsels and comfort of divers wicked and desperate persons within this realm: To the end therefore, that none of our subjects may neglect or violate their duty through ignorance thereof, or through any doubt of the protection which the law will afford to their loyalty and zeal, we have thought fit, by and with the advice of our Privy Council, to issue our Royal Proclamation, hereby declaring, that not only all our Officers, civil and military, are obliged to exert their utmost endeavours to suppress such rebellion, and to bring the traitors to justice, but that all our subjects of this Realm, and the dominions thereunto belonging, are bound by law to be aiding and assisting in the suppression of such rebellion, and to disclose and make known all traitorous conspiracies and attempts against us, our crown and dignity; and we do accordingly strictly charge and command all our Officers, as well civil as military, and all others our obedient and loyal subjects, to use their utmost endeavours to withstand and suppress such rebellion, and to disclose and make known all treasons and traitorous conspiracies which they shall know to be against us, our crown and dignity; and for that purpose, that they transmit to one of our principal Secretaries of State, or other proper officer, due and full information of all persons who shall be found carrying on correspondence with, or in any manner or degree aiding or abetting the persons now in open arms and rebellion against our Government, within any of our Colonies and Plantations in North America, in order to bring to condign punishment the authors, perpetrators, and abettors of such traitorous designs.

DOCUMENT 3

Lord Dunmore's Appeal to the Slaves of Virginia (1775)

In November 1775, John Murray, Earl of Dunmore, the royal governor of Virginia, issued a proclamation offering freedom to enslaved people who deserted "Rebel" plantations to serve in the king's forces.[3] Dunmore's proclamation raised the specter of race war in the minds of white Virginians and, in so doing, probably convinced many to support the Whig cause. For enslaved people, however, Dunmore's proclamation offered the prospect of freedom. About a thousand Virginia slaves escaped their masters to answer the governor's call to arms.

Questions to consider:

1. What prompted Dunmore to take such a drastic step? Why did he deem declaring martial law insufficient to restore order in Virginia?
2. Why did Dunmore offer freedom only to the slaves of "Rebels"?
3. How did he expect white Virginians to respond to his proclamation?

As I have ever entertained hopes that an accommodation might have taken place between Great Britain and this colony, without being compelled by my duty to this most disagreeable but now absolutely necessary step, rendered so by a body of armed men unlawfully assembled . . . and the formation of an army . . . now on their march to attack His Majesty's troops and destroy the well disposed subjects of this colony. To defeat such unreasonable purposes, and that all such traitors, and their abettors, may be brought to justice, and that the peace, and good order of this colony may be again restored, which the ordinary course of the civil law is unable to effect; I have thought fit to issue this my proclamation, hereby declaring, that until the aforesaid good purposes can be obtained, I do in virtue of the power and authority to me given, by His Majesty, determine to execute martial law, and cause the same to be executed throughout this colony. And to the end that peace and good order may the sooner be restored, I do require every person capable of bearing arms, to resort to His Majesty's standard, or be looked upon as traitors to His Majesty's crown and government, and thereby become liable to the penalty the law inflicts upon such offences; such as forfeiture of life, [and] confiscation of lands . . . And I do hereby further declare all indentured servants, negroes, or others, (appertaining to Rebels,) free that are able and willing to bear arms, they joining His Majesty's troops as soon as may be, for the more speedily reducing this colony to a proper sense of their duty, to His Majesty's liege subjects . . . till such time as peace may be again restored to this at present most unhappy country, or demanded of them for their former salutary purposes, by officers properly authorised to receive the same.

DOCUMENT 4

A White Virginian's Response to Dunmore's Proclamation (1775)

As this essay from the Virginia Gazette *indicates, the response of Virginia slaveowners to Dunmore's proclamation was both angry and self-serving.*[4] *Outraged by the governor's apparent willingness to incite a slave insurrection, planters united to oppose him and to defend white supremacy in Virginia. At the same time, they told themselves—and presumably their slaves, too—that only weak and foolish "negroes" would cast their lot with such brutes, despite the prospect of freedom. In fact, Dunmore had no moral objection to the institution of slavery. He used enslaved people to suit his purposes, and so did white Virginians.*

Questions to consider:

1. Who was the intended audience for this essay?
2. Why did the author find it necessary to exaggerate the supposed opposition of white Virginians to slavery and their concern for the welfare of their slaves?
3. What was the author's implicit message to his white readers?

Lord Dunmore's declaration . . . is a cruel declaration to the negroes. He does not pretend to make it out of any tenderness to them, but solely upon his own account; and should it be met with success, it leaves by far the greater number at the mercy of an enraged and injured people. But should there be any amongst the negroes weak enough to believe that lord Dunmore intends to do them a kindness, and wicked enough to provoke the fury of the Americans against their defenceless fathers and mothers, their wives, their women, and children, let them only consider the difficulty of effecting their escape, and what they must expect to suffer if they fall into the hands of the Americans. Let them farther consider what must be their fate should the English prove conquerors. If we can judge of the future from the past, it will not be much mended. Long have the Americans, moved by compassion, and actuated by sound policy, endeavoured to stop the progress of slavery. Our assemblies have repeatedly passed acts, laying heavy duties upon imported negroes, by which they meant altogether to prevent the horrid traffic; but their humane intentions have been as often frustrated by the cruelty and covetousness of a set of English merchants, who prevailed upon the king to repeal our kind and merciful acts, little, indeed, to the credit of his humanity.

Can it then be supposed that the negroes will be better used by the English, who have always encouraged and upheld this slavery, than by their present masters, who pity their condition, who wish, in general, to make it as easy and comfortable as possible, and who would, were it in their power, or were they permitted, not only prevent any more negroes from losing their freedom, but restore it to such as have already unhappily lost it? No. The ends of lord Dunmore and his party, being answered, they will either give up the offending negroes to the rigour of the laws they have broken, or sell them in the West Indies, where every year they sell many thousands of their miserable brethren, to perish, either by the inclemency of the weather, or the cruelty of barbarous masters.

Be not then, ye negroes, tempted by this proclamation to ruin yourselves. I have given you a faithful view of what you are to expect and declare, before God, in doing it I have considered your welfare, as well as that of the country. Whether you will profit by my advice I cannot tell, but this I know, that whether we suffer or not, if you desert us you most certainly will.

DOCUMENT 5

A Call to Revolution: Thomas Paine, Common Sense (1776)

Thomas Paine's early publications in America included essays attacking slavery and promoting women's rights. His greatest achievement, however, came in January 1776 with the publication of Common Sense, *the most influential and arguably the most radical pamphlet of the prerevolutionary era. Paine condemned monarchy, ridiculed the British constitution, and rejected every conceivable rationale for preserving America's ties to Britain. He drew on the Bible, English history, and Lockean natural rights theory to build what many deemed a compelling case for American independence.[5]*

Questions to consider:

1. How did Paine think his readers would respond to his pamphlet? What did he mean when he wrote, "Time makes more converts than reason?"
2. How did the language of *Common Sense* compare to that of other contemporary pamphlets on political topics? Why did Paine adopt this style of writing?
3. What did Paine mean when he asserted that "the cause of America is . . . the cause of all mankind"?
4. Did Paine really offer his readers "nothing more than simple facts"? Which of his incredibly optimistic predictions seem most far-fetched? Was *Common Sense* propaganda?

Perhaps the sentiments contained in the following pages, are not yet sufficiently fashionable to procure them general favor; a long habit of not thinking a thing wrong, gives it a superficial appearance of being right, and raises at first a formidable outcry in defence of custom. But the tumult soon subsides. Time makes more converts than reason.

As a long and violent abuse of power, is generally the means of calling the right of it in question (and in matters too which might never have been thought of, had not the sufferers been aggravated into the inquiry) and as the King of England hath undertaken in his own right, to support the Parliament in what he calls theirs, and as the good people of this country are grievously oppressed by the combination, they have an undoubted privilege to inquire into the pretensions of both, and equally to reject the usurpations of either. . . .

The cause of America is in a great measure the cause of all mankind. Many circumstances hath, and will arise, which are not local, but universal, and through which the principles of all lovers of mankind are affected, and in the event of which, their affections are interested. The laying a country desolate with fire and sword, declaring war against the natural rights of all mankind, and extirpating the defenders thereof from the face of the earth, is the concern of every man to whom nature hath given the power of feeling; of which class, regardless of party censure, is the author. . . .

In the following pages I offer nothing more than simple facts, plain arguments, and common sense; and have no other preliminaries to settle with the reader, than that he will divest himself of prejudice and prepossession, and suffer his reason and his feelings to determine for themselves; that he will put on, or rather that he will not put off, the true character of a man, and generously enlarge his views beyond the present day.

Volumes have been written on the subject of the struggle between England and America. Men of all ranks have embarked in the controversy, from different motives, and with various designs; but all have been ineffectual, and the period of debate is closed. Arms, as the last resource, decide the contest; the appeal was the choice of the king, and the continent hath accepted the challenge. . . .

By referring the matter from argument to arms, a new era for politics is struck; a new method of thinking hath arisen. All plans, proposals, &c. prior to . . . the commencement of hostilities, are like the almanacs of the last year; which, though proper then, are superceded and useless now. Whatever was advanced by the advocates on either side of the question then, terminated in one and the same point, a union with Great Britain. The only difference between the parties was the method of effecting it, the one proposing force, the other friendship; but it hath so far happened that the first hath failed, and the second hath withdrawn her influence.

As much hath been said of the advantages of reconciliation, which, like an agreeable dream, hath passed away and left us as we were, it is but right, that we should examine the contrary side of the argument, and inquire into some of the many material injuries which these colonies sustain, and always will sustain, by being connected with, and dependent on Great Britain. To examine that connexion and dependence, on the principles of nature and common sense, to see what we have to trust to, if separated, and what we are to expect, if dependent.

I have heard it asserted by some, that as America hath flourished under her former connexion with Great Britain, that the same connexion is necessary towards her future happiness, and will always have the same effect. Nothing can be more fallacious than this kind of argument. We may as well assert that because a child has thrived upon milk, that it is never to have meat, or that the first twenty years of our lives is to become a precedent for the next twenty. But even this is admitting more than is true, for I answer roundly, that America would have flourished as much, and probably much more, had no European power had any thing to do with her. The commerce, by which she hath enriched herself are the necessaries of life, and will always have a market while eating is the custom of Europe.

But she has protected us, say some. That she hath engrossed us is true, and defended the continent at our expence as well as her own is admitted, and she would have defended Turkey from the same motive . . . [for] the sake of trade and dominion.

Alas, we have been long led away by ancient prejudices, and made large sacrifices to superstition. We have boasted the protection of Great Britain, without considering, that her motive was interest not attachment; that she did not protect us from our enemies on our account, but from her enemies on her own account, from those who had no quarrel with us on any other account, and who will always be our enemies on the same account. Let Britain waive her pretensions to the continent . . . and we should be at peace with France and Spain were they at war with Britain. . . .

Much hath been said of the united strength of Britain and the colonies, that in conjunction they might bid defiance to the world. But this is mere presumption; the fate of war is uncertain, neither do the expressions mean any thing; for this continent would never suffer itself to be drained of inhabitants to support the British arms in either Asia, Africa, or Europe.

Besides, what have we to do with setting the world at defiance? Our plan is commerce, and that, well attended to, will secure us the peace and friendship of all Europe; because it is the interest of all Europe to have America a free port. Her trade will always be a protection, and her barrenness of gold and silver secure her from invaders. . . .

The authority of Great Britain over this continent, is a form of government, which sooner or later must have an end. And a serious mind can draw no true pleasure by looking forward, under the painful and positive conviction, that what he calls "the present constitution" is merely temporary. As parents, we can have no joy, knowing that this government is not sufficiently lasting to ensure any thing which we may bequeath to posterity. And by a plain method of argument, as we are running the next generation into debt, we ought to do the work of it, otherwise we use them meanly and pitifully. In order to discover the line of our duty rightly, we should take our children in our hand, and fix our station a few years farther into life; that eminence will present a prospect, which a few present fears and prejudices conceal from our sight.

Though I would carefully avoid giving unnecessary offence, yet I am inclined to believe, that all those who espouse the doctrine of reconciliation, may be included within the following descriptions. Interested men, who are not to be trusted; weak men, who cannot see; prejudiced men, who will not see; and a certain set of moderate men, who think better of the European world than it deserves; and this last class, by an ill-judged deliberation, will be the cause of more calamities to this continent, than all the other three. . . .

I have never met with a man, either in England or America, who hath not confessed his opinion, that a separation between the countries, would take place one time or other: And there is no instance, in which we have shewn less judgment, than in endeavouring to describe, what we call, the ripeness or fitness of the Continent for independence.

As all men allow the measure, and vary only in their opinion of the time, let us, in order to remove mistakes, take a general survey of things, and endeavour, if possible, to find out the very time. But we need not go far, the inquiry ceases at once, for, the time hath found us. The general concurrence, the glorious union of all things prove the fact.

'Tis is not in numbers, but in unity that our great strength lies; yet our present numbers are sufficient to repel the force of all the world. The continent hath, at this time, the largest body of armed and disciplined men of any power under Heaven; and is just arrived at that pitch of strength, in which, no single colony is able to support itself, and the whole, when united, can accomplish the matter, and either more, or, less than this, might be fatal in its effects. . . .

Debts we have none; and whatever we may contract on this account will serve as a glorious memento of our virtue. Can we but leave posterity with a settled form of government, an independent constitution of its own, the purchase at any price will be cheap. But to expend millions for the sake of getting a few vile acts repealed, and routing the present ministry only, is unworthy the charge, and is using posterity with the utmost cruelty; because it is leaving them the great work to do, and a debt upon their backs, from which, they derive no advantage. Such a thought is unworthy a man of honor, and is the true characteristic of a narrow heart and a peddling politician.

The debt we may contract doth not deserve our regard if the work be but accomplished. No nation ought to be without a debt. A national debt is a national bond; and when it bears no interest, is in no case a grievance. Britain is oppressed with a debt of upwards of one hundred and forty millions sterling, for which she pays upwards of four millions interest. And as a compensation for her debt, she has a large navy; America is without a debt, and without a navy; yet for the twentieth part of the English national debt, could have a navy as large again. . . .

To conclude, however strange it may appear to some, or however unwilling they may be to think so, matters not, but many strong and striking reasons may be given, to shew, that nothing can settle our affairs so expeditiously as an open and determined declaration for independence. Some of which are:

First—It is the custom of nations, when any two are at war, for some other powers, not engaged in the quarrel, to step in as mediators, and bring about the preliminaries of a peace: but while America calls herself the subject of Great Britain, no power, however well disposed she may be, can offer her mediation. Wherefore, in our present state we may quarrel on forever.

Secondly—It is unreasonable to suppose, that France or Spain will give us any kind of assistance, if we mean only, to make use of that assistance for the purpose of repairing the breach, and strengthening the connection between Britain and America; because, those powers would be sufferers by the consequences.

Thirdly—While we profess ourselves the subjects of Britain, we must, in the eye of foreign nations, be considered as rebels. The precedent is somewhat dangerous to their peace, for men to be in arms under the name of subjects; we, on the spot, can solve the paradox: but to unite resistance and subjection, requires an idea much too refined for the common understanding.

Fourthly—Were a manifesto to be published, and dispatched to foreign courts, setting forth the miseries we have endured, and the peaceable methods we have ineffectually used for redress; declaring, at the same time, that not being able, any longer, to live happily or safely under the cruel disposition of the British court, we had been driven to the necessity of breaking off all connections with her; at the same time, assuring all such courts of our peaceable disposition towards them, and of our desire of entering into trade with them. Such a memorial would produce more good effects to this continent, than if a ship were freighted with petitions to Britain.

<u>DOCUMENT 6</u>

An Appeal to Caution: James Chalmers, Plain Truth (1776)

Critics of Common Sense *ranged from conservative Whigs, who reluctantly accepted American independence but worried about its consequences, to Tories, who for various reasons refused to sever their ties to king and empire. Among the latter, James Chalmers of Maryland penned the most pointed reply to Paine's arguments in favor of American independence. Published in March 1776 under the pseudonym "Candidus," Chalmers's pamphlet reiterated most of the conventional economic and political rationales for reconciliation with Britain and quoted leading political theorists, such as Montesquieu and Hume, to support his claims.[6] Chalmers remained loyal to the Crown in 1776 and moved to London after the war was over.*

Questions to consider:

1. Who was Chalmers's intended audience?
2. Which of Paine's arguments did he criticize most effectively? Which did he merely ridicule? Which did he ignore?

3. What was the main argument that Chalmers advanced in *Plain Truth*?
4. Why did he see reconciliation with Britain as the best means to preserve American liberty?

I have now before me the pamphlet, entitled COMMON SENSE; on which I shall remark with freedom and candour . . . The judicious reader will . . . perceive, that malevolence only, is requisite to declaim against and arraign the most perfect governments. Our political quack [Paine] avails himself of this trite expedient, to cajole the people into the most abject slavery, under the delusive name of independence. His first indecent attack is against the English constitution, which with all its imperfections, is, and ever will be the pride and envy of mankind . . . This beautiful system (according to Montesquieu) . . . is a compound of monarchy, aristocracy, and democracy. But it is often said that the sovereign, by honours and appointments, influences the Commons. The profound and elegant Hume agitating this question, thinks, to this circumstance, we are in part indebted for our supreme felicity; since without such control in the Crown, our constitution would immediately degenerate into democracy, a government, which . . . I hope to prove ineligible. Were I asked marks of the best government and the purpose of political society, I would reply the increase, preservation, and prosperity of its members, [and] in no quarter of the globe, are those marks so certainly to be found, as in Great Britain, and her dependencies. . . .

[Paine] shamefully misrepresents facts, is ignorant of the true state of Great Britain and her colonies, utterly unqualified for the arduous task he has presumptuously assumed, and ardently intent on seducing us to that precipice on which himself stands trembling . . . In the English provinces, exclusive of negroes and other slaves, we have one hundred and sixty thousand or one hundred and seventy thousand men capable of bearing arms. If we deduct the people called Quakers, Anabaptists, and other religionists averse to arms; a considerable part of the emigrants, and those having a grateful predilection for the ancient constitution and parent state, we shall certainly reduce the first number to sixty or seventy thousand men. Now admitting those equal to the Roman legions, can we suppose them capable of defending against the power of Britain a country nearly twelve hundred miles extending on the ocean? Suppose our troops assembled in New England, if the Britons see not fit to assail them, they hasten to and desolate our other provinces, which eventually would reduce New England. If by dividing our forces, we pretend to defend our provinces, we also are infallibly undone. Our most fertile provinces, filled with unnumbered domestic enemies, slaves, intersected by navigable rivers, everywhere accessible to the fleets and armies of Britain, can make no defence. If without the medium of passion and prejudice, we view our other provinces, half armed, destitute of money and a navy, we must confess that no power ever engaged such potent antagonists under such peculiar circumstances of infelicity. . . .

With the utmost deference to the honorable Congress, I do not view the most distant gleam of aid from foreign powers. The princes alone capable of succouring us are the sovereigns of France and Spain. If according to our author, we possess an eighth part of the habitable globe, and actually have a check on the West India commerce of England, the French indigo and other valuable West India commodities, and the Spanish galleons, are in great jeopardy from our power. The French and Spaniards are therefore wretched politicians, if they do not assist England, in reducing her colonies to obedience. Pleasantry apart! Can we be so deluded, to expect aid from those princes, which inspiring their subjects with a relish for liberty, might eventually shake their arbitrary thrones. Natural avowed enemies to our sacred cause? Will they cherish, will they support the flame of liberty in America? . . .

I would blush for human nature, did I imagine that any man other than a bigot could believe [Paine's] ridiculous stories . . . respecting our numerous and best disciplined army under Heaven, about our navy, and . . . that France and Spain will not assist us . . . until . . . we declare ourselves independent. Can a reasonable being for a moment believe that Great Britain, whose political existence depends on our constitutional obedience, who but yesterday made such prodigious efforts to save us from France, will not exert herself to preserve us from our frantic schemes of independency. Can we a moment doubt that the Sovereign of Great Britain and his ministers, whose glory as well as personal safety depends on our obedience, will not exert every nerve of the British power to save themselves and us from ruin? . . .

Innumerable are the advantages of our connection with Britain; and a just dependence on her, is a sure way to avoid the horrors and calamities of war. Wars in Europe will probably than heretofore become less frequent; religious rancour, which formerly animated princes to arms, is succeeded by a spirit of philosophy extremely friendly to peace. The princes of Europe are or ought to be convinced by sad experience, that the objects of conquest, are vastly inadequate to the immense charge of their armaments. Prudential motives, therefore, in future, will often dictate negotiation, instead of war. Be it however admitted, that our speculations are nugatory, and that as usual, we are involved in war. In this case we really do not participate in a twentieth part of the misery and hardships of war, experienced by the other subjects of the empire. As future wars will probably be carried on by Britain in her proper element, her success will hardly be doubtful, nor can this be thought audacity, if we remember the great things effected by Britain in her naval wars . . . Our sailors navigating our vessels to the West Indies during war, are exempted from impressment, and if our trade to any part of Europe is then stagnated, it flows with uncommon rapidity in the West Indies, nor is the object of captures inconsiderable.

Our author surely forgets, that when independent, we cannot trade with Europe, without political connections, and that all treaties made by England or other commercial states are, or ought to be, ultimately subservient to their commerce . . . Reconciliation would conduct us to our former happy state. The happiness of the governed is without doubt the true interest of the governors, and if we aim not at independence, there cannot be a doubt, of receiving every advantage relative to laws and commerce that we can desire. . . .

Volumes were insufficient to describe the horror, misery and desolation, awaiting the people at large in the siren form of American independence. In short, I affirm that it would be most excellent policy in those who wish for true liberty to submit by an advantageous reconciliation to the authority of Great Britain. . . .

DOCUMENT 7

The Declaration of Independence (1776)

The Declaration of Independence is both a timeless statement of general principles and a historical response to specific political circumstances.[7] It begins with the assertion that government exists only to preserve the natural rights of men and ends by rhetorically dissolving a particular government that allegedly violated American rights. The Declaration of Independence was the means by which the Congress announced and explained its action both to the American people and to a "candid world."

Questions to consider:

1. What did Jefferson mean when he declared that "all men are created equal"?
2. What, according to the Declaration of Independence, are the "unalienable" rights of men? How might an American in 1776 have understood the practical meaning of those rights? Would we today share their views?
3. How did the style, tone, and content of the Declaration of Independence compare to those of *Common Sense*?
4. In *Common Sense*, Paine had ridiculed monarchy in general. Why did Jefferson attack only one king, George III of Great Britain? Why did

the Declaration say relatively little about the conduct of the British Parliament?

When in the course of human events, it becomes necessary for one people to dissolve the political bands which have connected them with another, and to assume among the powers of the earth, the separate and equal station to which the Laws of Nature and of Nature's God entitle them, a decent respect to the opinions of mankind requires that they should declare the causes which impel them to the separation.

We hold these truths to be self-evident, that all men are created equal, that they are endowed by their Creator with certain unalienable Rights, that among these are Life, Liberty and the pursuit of Happiness. That to secure these rights, Governments are instituted among Men, deriving their just powers from the consent of the governed. That whenever any Form of Government becomes destructive of these ends, it is the Right of the People to alter or to abolish it, and to institute new Government, laying its foundation on such principles and organizing its powers in such form, as to them shall seem most likely to effect their Safety and Happiness. Prudence, indeed, will dictate that governments long established should not be changed for light and transient causes; and accordingly all experience hath shewn, that mankind are more disposed to suffer, while evils are sufferable, than to right themselves by abolishing the forms to which they are accustomed. But when a long train of abuses and usurpations, pursuing invariably the same Object evinces a design to reduce them under absolute Despotism, it is their right, it is their duty, to throw off such Government, and to provide new Guards for their future security.—Such has been the patient sufferance of these Colonies; and such is now the necessity which constrains them to alter their former Systems of Government. The history of the present King of Great Britain is a history of repeated injuries and usurpations, all having in direct object the establishment of an absolute Tyranny over these States. To prove this, let Facts be submitted to a candid world.

He has refused his Assent to Laws, the most wholesome and necessary for the public good.

He has forbidden his Governors to pass Laws of immediate and pressing importance, unless suspended in their operation till his Assent should be obtained; and when so suspended, he has utterly neglected to attend to them.

He has refused to pass other Laws for the accommodation of large districts of people, unless those people would relinquish the right of Representation in the Legislature, a right inestimable to them and formidable to tyrants only.

[handwritten margin note: controversial—there was slavery. Americans = to the British]

He has called together legislative bodies at places unusual, uncomfortable, and distant from the depository of their public Records, for the sole purpose of fatiguing them into compliance with his measures.

He has dissolved Representative Houses repeatedly, for opposing with manly firmness his invasions on the rights of the people.

He has refused for a long time, after such dissolutions, to cause others to be elected; whereby the Legislative powers, incapable of Annihilation, have returned to the People at large for their exercise; the State remaining in the mean time exposed to all the dangers of invasion from without, and convulsions within.

He has endeavoured to prevent the population of these States; for that purpose obstructing the Laws for Naturalization of Foreigners; refusing to pass others to encourage their migrations hither, and raising the conditions of new Appropriations of Lands.

He has obstructed the Administration of Justice, by refusing his Assent to Laws for establishing Judiciary powers.

He has made Judges dependent on his Will alone, for the tenure of their offices, and the amount and payment of their salaries.

He has erected a multitude of New Offices, and sent hither swarms of Officers to harass our people, and eat out their substance.

He has kept among us, in times of peace, Standing Armies without the Consent of our legislatures.

He has affected to render the Military independent of and superior to the Civil power.

He has combined with others to subject us to a jurisdiction foreign to our constitution, and unacknowledged by our laws; giving his Assent to their Acts of pretended Legislation:

For Quartering large bodies of armed troops among us:

For protecting them, by a mock Trial, from punishment for any Murders which they should commit on the Inhabitants of these States:

For cutting off our Trade with all parts of the world:

For imposing Taxes on us without our Consent:

For depriving us in many cases, of the benefits of Trial by Jury:

For transporting us beyond Seas to be tried for pretended offences

For abolishing the free System of English Laws in a neighbouring Province, establishing therein an Arbitrary government, and enlarging its Boundaries so as to render it at once an example and fit instrument for introducing the same absolute rule into these Colonies:

For taking away our Charters, abolishing our most valuable Laws, and altering fundamentally the Forms of our Governments:

For suspending our own Legislatures, and declaring themselves invested with power to legislate for us in all cases whatsoever.

He has abdicated Government here, by declaring us out of his Protection and waging War against us.

He has plundered our seas, ravaged our Coasts, burnt our towns, and destroyed the lives of our people.

He is at this time transporting large Armies of foreign Mercenaries to complete the works of death, desolation and tyranny, already begun with circumstances of Cruelty & perfidy scarcely paralleled in the most barbarous ages, and totally unworthy the Head of a civilized nation.

He has constrained our fellow Citizens taken Captive on the high Seas to bear Arms against their Country, to become the executioners of their friends and Brethren, or to fall themselves by their Hands.

He has excited domestic insurrections amongst us, and has endeavoured to bring on the inhabitants of our frontiers, the merciless Indian Savages, whose known rule of warfare, is an undistinguished destruction of all ages, sexes and conditions.

In every stage of these Oppressions we have petitioned for Redress in the most humble terms: Our repeated Petitions have been answered only by repeated injury. A Prince whose character is thus marked by every act which may define a Tyrant, is unfit to be the ruler of a free people.

Nor have we been wanting in attentions to our British brethren. We have warned them from time to time of attempts by their legislature to extend an unwarrantable jurisdiction over us. We have reminded them of the circumstances of our emigration and settlement here. We have appealed to their native justice and magnanimity, and we have conjured them by the ties of our common kindred to disavow these usurpations, which, would inevitably interrupt our connections and correspondence. They too have been deaf to the voice of justice and of consanguinity. We must, therefore, acquiesce in the necessity, which denounces our Separation, and hold them, as we hold the rest of mankind, Enemies in War, in Peace Friends.

We, therefore, the Representatives of the united States of America, in General Congress, assembled, appealing to the Supreme Judge of the world for the rectitude of our intentions, do, in the Name, and by Authority of the good People of these Colonies, solemnly publish and declare, that these United Colonies are, and of Right ought to be Free and Independent States; that they are absolved from all Allegiance to the British Crown, and that all political connection between them and the State of Great Britain, is and ought to be totally dissolved; and that as Free and Independent States, they have full Power to levy War, conclude Peace, contract Alliances, establish Commerce, and to do all other Acts and Things which Independent States may of right do. And for the support of this Declaration, with a firm reliance on the protection of divine Providence, we mutually pledge to each other our Lives, our Fortunes and our sacred Honor.

SUGGESTED READING FOR CHAPTER 5

BECKER, CARL. *The Declaration of Independence* (1922).
BONWICK, COLIN. *English Radicals and the American Revolution* (1977).
ELLIS, JOSEPH J. *American Sphinx: The Character of Thomas Jefferson* (1997).
FONER, ERIC. *Tom Paine and Revolutionary America* (1976).
GREENE, JACK P.; BUSHMAN, RICHARD L.; and KAMMEN, MICHAEL. *Society, Freedom, and Conscience: The Coming of the Revolution in Virginia, Massachusetts, and New York* (1976).
MAIER, PAULINE. *American Scripture: Making the Declaration of Independence* (1997).
MARSTON, JERRILYN GREENE. *King and Congress: The Transfer of Political Legitimacy, 1774–1776* (1987).
MORGAN, EDMUND S. *The Meaning of Independence: John Adams, George Washington, and Thomas Jefferson* (1976).
WILLS, GARRY. *Inventing America: Jefferson's Declaration of Independence* (1978).

NOTES

[1]W. L. Saunders, et al., eds., *The Colonial and State Records of North Carolina*, 30 vols. (Raleigh, Winston, Goldsboro, and Charlotte, 1886–1914), 9: 1282–84.

[2]Clarence S. Brigham, ed., *British Royal Proclamations Relating to America, 1603–1783* (New York, 1911), 224–29.

[3]Broadside, Library of Virginia.

[4]*Virginia Gazette* (Pinkney), 23 Nov. 1775.

[5]Thomas Paine, *Common Sense*, in Moncure Daniel Conway, ed., *The Writings of Thomas Paine*, 4 vols. (New York, 1894–96), 1: 67–68, 84–86, 88–90, 101–2, 110–11.

[6]James Chalmers, *Plain Truth* (Philadelphia, 1776), 9–12, 16–18, 25–26, 29, 35–36, 50–52, 57–58, 74.

[7]For the Declaration of Independence see the following Website: http://www.nara.gov/ exhall/charters/declaration/declaration.html.

CHAPTER SIX

TIMES THAT TRIED MEN'S SOULS

After the commencement of hostilities at Lexington and Concord, men in every colony enthusiastically donned uniforms, took up arms, and drilled with their local militia. Some 16,000 men enlisted in the Continental Army in the first months of its existence. American patriots believed they had the innate courage, public spirit, and unity of purpose to vanquish the king's forces, whose motives they believed were largely mercenary. Such confidence and such passion for all things military, however, waned in the difficult months following the Declaration of Independence.

From mid-1776 through 1778, military engagements occurred primarily in the middle states of New York, New Jersey, and Pennsylvania. What in New England had been a series of occasional engagements in a strongly pro-American environment became in the middle states a series of sustained military campaigns fought in the midst of a deeply divided population. The revolutionaries—who were known variously as Whigs or patriots—took steps to punish those who refused to support the war and swear allegiance to their new state governments. Nevertheless, many patriots themselves became disillusioned as battlefield reverses, money and supply problems, and difficulties raising troops and taxes undermined the American war effort and took a major toll on the living conditions of soldiers and civilians alike. In various ways, the war profoundly affected the lives of men and women of all social ranks.

During this phase of the War of Independence, American forces suffered many more defeats than victories, but they held their own over-all against the British in the middle states. In 1776 and 1777, the United States won only two important battles, at Trenton and Saratoga. The British, for their part, took the major port of New York in 1776 and occupied Philadelphia, the American capital, the following year. During this phase of the war, American soldiers suffered horrific winters, most famously at Valley Forge, Pennsylvania, in 1777–78. By then, British authorities, perceiving that the war was at a stalemate, resolved to seek a decisive victory in the southern states.

Although in declaring independence Congress claimed to speak for a united people, Americans were divided on the issues of independence and the continuing war with Britain. A substantial minority of the white inhabitants of the thirteen states professed loyalty to the king, while at least as many again were apathetic or neutral. Supporters of king and empire, who were known either as Tories or loyalists, came from all social ranks. Royal officials, merchants who traded extensively with Britain, and Anglican clergymen were often loyalists, but so were many members of ethnic and religious minorities who found refuge in the British Empire and feared the majoritarian implications of revolutionary republicanism. Scots in eastern North Carolina and many Dutch New Yorkers, for example, were loyal to the king. Others sided with the British because their local political enemies were leaders or supporters of the revolutionary movement. In New York's Hudson River Valley, many tenant farmers were Tories because their landlords—against whom they had rioted as recently as 1766—were prominent Whigs. North Carolina's Regulators remained aloof from the Revolution, which was led by east-ern gentry who had supported the use of military force to suppress these western dissidents in 1771.

Although most loyalists simply refused to support the American cause and tried in various ways to assist the British when they arrived in their locales, some engaged in more concerted opposition to the Revolu-tion. At least 19,000 men served in loyalist regiments of the British army, and others fought in regular units. During and after the war, between 60,000 and 100,000 Tories left the United States rather than make their peace with the new revolutionary governments.

All forms of loyalism became criminal offenses after independence. As part of the process of creating independent republican governments, each state enacted laws requiring men to take oaths of allegiance to the new revolutionary order. Failure to do so could result in fines, imprison-ment, and eventually banishment and loss of property. During the Revo-lution, state governments confiscated significant amounts of land and other loyalist property, much of which they sold to help finance the war.

In some loyalist families, women saved property from confiscation by state authorities. Assuming that women were either apolitical or bound by their husband's political choices, state officials exempted them from taking oaths of allegiance. Many wives of Tories, who remained at home while their husbands were in the army or in exile, claimed that the war had rendered them, in effect, widows. Using this logic, some successfully petitioned the courts and state legislatures to retain the portion of their husbands' property—typically one-third—that they would have received as widows under the common law.

Despite the states' best efforts to suppress loyalism, Tory soldiers and civilians contributed significantly to British military successes after the war moved out of New England and into the middle states. After British forces evacuated Boston in March 1776, Washington moved his base of operations to New York in anticipation of an enemy assault. When the British arrived in New York in July, they encountered relatively little civilian resistance and much support in Manhattan and the surrounding region.

The campaign of 1776, which began with the battle for New York, pitted an inexperienced and outnumbered American force against the most massive military expedition in British history before the twentieth century. Washington divided his troops between Manhattan and Long Island, hoping to retain control of the economically and strategically important port of New York. By July, however, a force of some 32,000 men under General William Howe and his brother, Admiral Lord Richard Howe, had descended upon the area. In late August, the British engaged Washington's troops in battle on Long Island, forcing them to retreat across the East River to Manhattan. In September, Howe would follow up this major victory by pursuing Washington to Manhattan, nearly capturing the entire American army in the process. The Continentals managed to escape across the Hudson River to northern New Jersey, but the British occupied the city of New York, which they retained for the rest of the war. They also established outposts in the surrounding counties and throughout New Jersey, where British military presence emboldened local Tories, who periodically terrorized Whig inhabitants of the region. The Whigs returned the favor, making this area the site of partisan violence throughout the war.

In September 1776, the Howe brothers followed up their victory in New York by convening a peace conference at nearby Staten Island. There, they met with three commissioners—Benjamin Franklin, John Adams, and John Rutledge of South Carolina—representing the Continental Congress. When it became clear that British authorities would accept peace only if Congress rescinded the Declaration of Independence, the Americans rejected the Howes' overtures and resolved to continue fighting. Congress immediately dispatched Franklin and Silas Deane of

Connecticut to France to seek military assistance from Britain's long-standing nemesis.

By December 1776, Washington's defeated and downtrodden troops were encamped in eastern Pennsylvania, while Howe's victorious forces had settled into the comparatively luxurious social whirl of Tory-dominated New York. According to the conventional European rules of eighteenth-century warfare, armies retired during the winter months when conditions for formal military engagements—in which each side advanced toward the other in line formation—were not optimal. Washington, however, knew that his troops needed a victory before settling down for the winter. With short-term enlistments due to expire, he concluded that only a significant boost in the Continentals' morale could sustain an army whose membership already had dwindled to some 3,000.

Believing that the outcome of the whole war was at stake, Washington decided to use unorthodox methods to win the victory he needed. On Christmas night, he and his troops crossed the Delaware River to Trenton, New Jersey, where they surprised a garrison of roughly 1,500 Hessians in the midst of their holiday celebrations. By attacking under a cover of darkness and in winter, Washington doubly flouted the military conventions of the time. Doing so enabled him to lead his troops to a resounding victory in which two-thirds of the enemy were either killed or captured. On 3 January, the Continentals, reinforced by militia, defeated a British garrison at nearby Princeton. Washington and his troops then retired, spending the remainder of the winter in Morristown in central New Jersey. Although disease and desertion ravaged the Continentals, aggressive recruitment efforts replenished the ranks by spring, when the armies began their new campaigns.

In 1777, the war took place in two major theaters: the Philadelphia area and northern New York. In September, the Howe brothers captured Philadelphia, the American capital, forcing the Continental Congress to flee for safety. Around the same time, however, British and American forces fought a major battle at Saratoga, New York, where the latter won a decisive victory with far-reaching consequences.

In June 1777, General John Burgoyne led a combined force of British regulars, Germans, Tories, and Indian scouts southward from Canada. His objective was to march southward along the Hudson River to Albany and thereby complete New England's isolation from the rest of the United States, a process already begun by the British occupation of the ports of New York and Philadelphia. By August, however, Burgoyne had run into trouble. His supply lines were cut. A force of Tories and Indians, scheduled to meet Burgoyne's army, had been delayed to the west, and the general's foraging party sustained heavy losses in an encounter with patriot militia at Bennington, Vermont. Encumbered by supplies and by civilian personnel—including the families of many

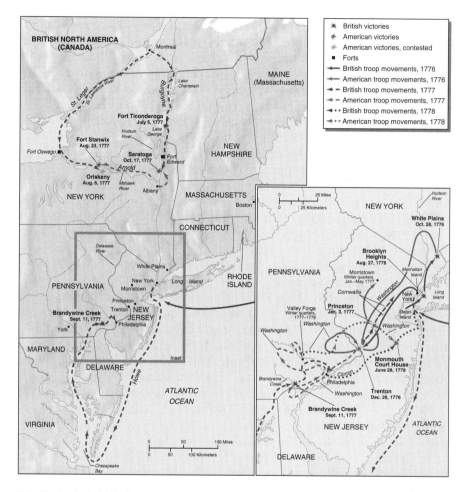

The War in the Middle States, 1776–1777.   Most of the fighting in the years immediately following the Declaration of Independence occurred in New York, New Jersey, and Pennsylvania.

officers—Burgoyne's army moved slowly through the mountainous wilderness of northern New York. The Americans, expecting his advance, felled trees and created other obstacles to impede the enemy's progress. General Horatio Gates, who, assisted by Benedict Arnold and Daniel Morgan, commanded a combined force of Continental troops and New England militia, waited for Burgoyne and surrounded him about thirty miles north of Albany. After two successful engagements, the Americans forced Burgoyne to capitulate. The British commander surrendered his entire army of some 7,000 men on 17 October 1777.

Historians regard the Battle of Saratoga as a major turning point in the War of Independence. The defeat of Burgoyne prevented British forces both from isolating New England and from attaining near-complete control over the middle states. This setback, in turn, led authorities in London to reassess their war aims and conclude that they should redirect their efforts toward regaining the southern states. For the Americans, Gates's victory provided a much-needed morale boost following the loss of Philadelphia. More important still, the Americans' impressive and utter defeat of Burgoyne at Saratoga was crucial in persuading the French government to enter the war as an ally of the United States. Although France had supplied the United States with covert assistance in the form of money, munitions, and other supplies since 1775, the French government understandably avoided a formal alliance until the Americans showed that they had reasonable chance of winning the war with Britain. Saratoga suggested that an American victory was possible, and in February 1778 the French government signed a treaty of alliance with the United States.

French entry into the war brought Americans at least two major benefits, besides the significant amounts of men, money, and materiel they could now receive openly from their new ally. First, France's entry into the war forced the British to divide their resources to engage multiple enemies in different military theaters, complicating Britain's military objectives. While the United States continued to fight the British on the North American mainland, the French forced the British to undertake additional campaigns in the Caribbean and elsewhere. In 1779, Spain entered the war as an ally of France, hoping to drive the British from Florida and Gibraltar on the southern tip of the Iberian peninsula. The Netherlands joined the war against Britain in 1780. Second, the French alliance gave Americans access to much-needed naval power. The war at sea had gone badly for the United States in the face of Britain's vastly superior fleet. The arrival of a French fleet helped address that deficiency and proved essential in achieving final victory at Yorktown in 1781.

Paradoxically, the months immediately following the Battle of Saratoga were among the most difficult of the war for the victorious Americans. Getting supplies for the army and maintaining cordial relations between soldiers and civilians were recurring problems for the American war effort, and they became particularly acute in the winter of 1777–78. Continental soldiers endured hunger, cold, and disease in their winter encampments, most famously at Valley Forge in eastern Pennsylvania. With some justification, soldiers attributed their suffering to the selfishness and callousness of the civilian population.

Accustomed to abundance, revolutionary Americans experienced scarcity and deprivation as a result of the disruption of most aspects of economic life. When men left home for military service and when armies trampled crops in the fields, agricultural productivity declined, even as the war generated increased demand for provisions. The war also resulted in the curtailment of overseas trade, causing shortages of all sorts of imported goods, including cloth and other necessities. The scarcity of both agricultural and manufactured products predictably drove prices up, despite the states' imposition of price controls to inhibit wartime profiteering.

The inflationary effects of wartime shortages were compounded by the absence of a stable currency. Because Americans had no specie reserves or commodities that could readily provide a financial basis for their new governments, Congress and the states had no choice but to finance the war on credit. To do so, they secured loans both locally and in Europe; they also printed large quantities of paper currency, which, without the backing of gold or silver, had no intrinsic value. Such currency was, in effect, a promissory note whereby the issuing government agreed to pay the holder its face value at some future date. As the war dragged on and as revolutionary governments emitted more and more paper money, however, many Americans came to doubt the ability of the issuers to make good on that promise, and the value of state and Continental currencies fell accordingly. In Massachusetts, for example, 105 dollars in paper currency were worth 100 dollars in gold and silver in January 1777; it took 742 dollars in state currency to equal 100 dollars in specie in 1779, and 2,934 dollars in 1780. Similarly, in 1777, 3 dollars in Continental currency was equivalent to 1 dollar in gold or silver. The ratio between Continentals and specie increased steadily thereafter: 7 to 1 in 1778; 42 to 1 in 1779; 100 to 1 in 1780; 146 to 1 in 1781.

Although many civilians suffered as a result of wartime shortages and inflation, soldiers felt the consequences of these conditions more than most. Soldiers' wages and enlistment bounties were fixed at the time of their enlistment. By the time they received their pay—if they ever did—its real value was significantly diminished. The army's decision to shelve one-year enlistments in favor of stints lasting for three years or for the duration of the war aggravated this problem, while inflation and wartime shortages also increasingly undermined the government's ability to procure supplies. The winter of 1777–78 was the first in which the army suffered severe deprivation as a result of currency depreciation and related economic problems. By then, many civilian farmers were hiding or hoarding their produce to negotiate higher prices or to avoid having to accept payment in depreciated paper currency. Continental troops often went hungry, in large part because local farmers preferred to deal with the British, who paid in gold and silver, rather than take the Americans' paper money.

The difficult winter after Saratoga was a formative experience for the Continental Army. The soldiers' suffering was intense. Of some

11,000 troops who began the winter at Valley Forge, for instance, more than 2,500 were dead by spring as a result of disease, starvation, and malnutrition. Each day, about ten soldiers deserted, while those soldiers and civilian camp followers who remained were forced to huddle in poorly constructed huts and forage for fuel and food in order to survive. The soldiers' suffering became the basis of their growing sense of identity as a community of patriots who believed themselves to be uniquely willing to sacrifice their own interests for the cause of American liberty. At Valley Forge, in particular, Friedrich Wilhelm August Heinrich Ferdinand, Baron von Steuben, a former Prussian army officer, worked to instill in the troops a self-conscious sense of professionalism and competence by emphasizing military discipline and pride and by teaching them the manual of arms.

As winter waned in early 1778, American and British authorities prepared for the new campaign. The American victory at Saratoga and the resulting French alliance had convinced Lord North that Britain could not win the war, but George III stubbornly refused to recognize American independence. In March 1778, the British government offered to redress American grievances prior to July 1776 in exchange for peace, but Congress rejected that proposal. As spring approached, the impact of Steuben's drills, along with Congress's promises of increased pay and bonuses and news of the French alliance, raised the Continentals' spirits as they prepared to take the field. In 1778, most of the fighting occurred in the west, where Americans inflicted heavy losses on the British and their Indian allies, and in New Jersey, as the new British commander, Sir Henry Clinton, withdrew from Philadelphia and moved his troops northeastward to New York.

By mid-1778, British leaders had reassessed their war aims and dramatically altered their military strategy. Having fought the Americans to a stalemate in the middle states, they resolved to withdraw a significant portion of their forces from that region and focus their efforts further south. British authorities believed the southern states were full of Tories who would flock to the king's standard. They were also determined to regain these valuable tobacco- and rice-producing territories.

Although the British invaded Georgia by year's end, the fighting was not over in the northern states. Large bodies of troops from both sides remained in New York and New Jersey, where they engaged in occasional inconclusive battles, and partisan violence between Whigs and Tories continued to plague the region. In 1779 and again in 1780, for instance, the British and their Tory allies burned towns along the Connecticut coast. When soldiers attacked towns—instead of engaging another army on the battlefield—civilians were often casualties. Meanwhile, Washington's troops had their worst winter ever at Morristown, New Jersey, in 1779–80. Mutinies occurred among the northern troops in 1780 and again in 1781, largely due to lack of supplies and wages and deteriorating relations with the civilian population. By then, however, the main military action was unfolding farther south.

The early phases of the War of Independence exposed both the strengths and weaknesses of the American war effort. Financing the war, supplying the army, and maintaining good relations with civilians were persistent challenges for American political and military leaders. The Continental Army sustained heavy losses and was unable to defend either New York or Philadelphia. Each winter death, desertion, and expiring enlistments thinned the army's ranks. Nevertheless, Americans persevered militarily against the British. They weathered the losses of the major northern ports, achieved a major victory at Saratoga, and finalized a military alliance with a major European power. As the final phase of the War of Independence began, each side sought a decisive victory in the southern states.

DOCUMENT 1

"The Crisis #1" (1776)

Thomas Paine

In July 1776, Thomas Paine joined the Continental Army. In the coming months, he witnessed the stalled American war effort, as General William Howe defeated Washington's forces, occupied New York, and forced the Americans to retreat across New Jersey and on to Pennsylvania. On 23 December, Paine published the first of a series of essays that aimed to boost the morale of soldiers and foster civilian support for the revolutionary cause.[1] Washington ordered Paine's essay, "The American Crisis," to be read in army camps. Perhaps not coincidentally, American forces triumphed at the Battle of Trenton, New Jersey, just three days after its publication.

Questions to consider:

1. Why did Paine believe that the center of the war had moved southward, from New England to the middle states?
2. Was he being fair to the Tories? What did he expect to gain by his vicious denunciation of those who were loyal to the king?

3. How did Paine seek to build the confidence of his comrades in arms?
4. What were his most effective arguments against civilian apathy?

dear = expensive

These are the times that try men's souls. The summer soldier and the sunshine patriot will, in this crisis, shrink from the service of their country; but he that stands it now, deserves the love and thanks of man and woman. Tyranny, like hell, is not easily conquered; yet we have this consolation with us, that the harder the conflict, the more glorious the triumph. What we obtain too cheap, we esteem too lightly: it is dearness only that gives every thing its value. Heaven knows how to put a proper price upon its goods; and it would be strange indeed if so celestial an article as freedom should not be highly rated. . . .

Why is it that the enemy have left the New England provinces, and made these middle ones the seat of war? The answer is easy: New England is not infested with Tories, and we are. I have been tender in raising the cry against these men, and used numberless arguments to show them their danger, but it will not do to sacrifice a world either to their folly or their baseness. The period is now arrived, in which either they or we must change our sentiments, or one or both must fall. And what is a Tory? Good God! what is he? I should not be afraid to go with a hundred Whigs against a thousand Tories, were they to attempt to get into arms. Every Tory is a coward; for servile, slavish, self-interested fear is the foundation of Toryism; and a man under such influence, though he may be cruel, never can be brave.

But, before the line of irrecoverable separation be drawn between us, let us reason the matter together: Your conduct is an invitation to the enemy, yet not one in a thousand of you has heart enough to join him. Howe is as much deceived by you as the American cause is injured by you. He expects you will all take up arms, and flock to his standard, with muskets on your shoulders. Your opinions are of no use to him, unless you support him personally, for 'tis soldiers, and not Tories, that he wants . . . I consider Howe as the greatest enemy the Tories have; he is bringing a war into their country, which, had it not been for him and partly for themselves, they had been clear of. Should he now be expelled, I wish with all the devotion of a Christian, that the names of Whig and Tory may never more be mentioned; but should the Tories give him encouragement to come, or assistance if he come, I as sincerely wish that our next year's arms may expel them from the continent, and the Congress appropriate their possessions to the relief of those who have suffered in well-doing. A single successful battle next year will settle the whole. America could carry on a two years' war by the confiscation of the property of disaffected persons, and be made happy by their expulsion. Say not that this is revenge, call it rather the soft resentment of a suffering people, who, having no object in view but the good of all, have staked their own all upon a seemingly doubtful event. Yet it is folly to argue against determined hardness; eloquence may strike the ear, and the language of sorrow draw forth the tear of compassion, but nothing can reach the heart that is steeled with prejudice.

Quitting this class of men, I turn with the warm ardor of a friend to those who have nobly stood, and are yet determined to stand the matter out: I call not upon a few, but upon all: not on this state or that state, but on every state: up and help us; lay your shoulders to the wheel; better have too much force than too little, when so great an object is at stake. Let it be told to the future world, that in the depth of winter, when nothing but hope and virtue could survive, that the city and the country, alarmed at one common danger, came forth to meet and to repulse it. Say not that thousands are gone, turn out your tens of thousands; throw not the burden of the day upon Providence, but "show your faith by your works," that God may bless you. It matters not where you live, or what rank of life you hold, the evil or the blessing will reach you all. The far and the near, the home counties and the back, the rich and the poor, will suffer or rejoice alike. The heart that feels not now is dead; the blood of his children will curse his cowardice, who shrinks back at a time when a little might have saved the whole, and made them happy. I love the man that can smile in trouble, that can gather strength from distress, and grow brave by reflection. 'Tis the business of little minds to shrink; but he whose heart is firm, and whose conscience approves his conduct, will pursue his principles unto death. My own line of reasoning is to myself as straight and clear as a ray of light. Not all the treasures of the world, so far as I believe, could have induced me to support an offensive war, for I think it murder; but if a thief breaks into my house, burns and destroys my property, and kills or threatens to kill me, or those that are in it, and to "bind me in all cases whatsoever" to his absolute will, am I to suffer it? What signifies it to me, whether he who does it is a king or a common man; my countryman or not my countryman; whether it be done by an individual villain, or an army of them? If we reason to the root of things we shall find no difference; neither can any just cause be assigned why we should punish in the one case and pardon in the other. Let them call me rebel and welcome, I feel no concern from it; but I should suffer the misery of devils, were I to make a whore of my soul by swearing allegiance to one whose character is that of a sottish, stupid, stubborn, worthless, brutish man. I conceive likewise a horrid idea in receiving mercy from a being, who at the last day shall be shrieking to the rocks and mountains to cover him, and fleeing with terror from the orphan, the widow, and the slain of America.

There are cases which cannot be overdone by language, and this is one. There are persons, too, who see not the full extent of the evil which threatens them; they solace themselves with hopes that the enemy, if he succeed, will be merciful. It is the madness of folly, to expect mercy from those who have refused to do justice; and even mercy, where conquest is the object, is only a trick of war; the cunning of the fox is as murderous as the violence of the wolf, and we ought to guard equally against both. Howe's first object is, partly by threats and partly by promises, to terrify or seduce the people to deliver up their arms and receive mercy. The ministry recommended the same plan to Gage, and this is what the Tories call making their peace, "a peace which passeth all understanding" indeed! A peace which would be the immediate forerunner of a worse ruin than any we have yet thought of. Ye men of Pennsylvania, do reason upon these things! Were the back counties to give up their arms, they would fall an easy prey to the Indians, who are all armed: this perhaps is what some Tories would not be sorry for. Were the home counties to deliver up their arms, they would be exposed to the resentment of the back counties who would then have it in their power to chastise their defection at pleasure. And were any one state to give up its arms, that state must be garrisoned by all Howe's army of Britons and Hessians to preserve it from the anger of the rest. Mutual fear is the principal link in the chain of mutual love, and woe be to that state that breaks the compact. Howe is mercifully inviting you to barbarous destruction, and men must be either rogues or fools that will not see it. I dwell not upon the vapors of imagination; I bring reason to your ears, and, in language as plain as A, B, C, hold up truth to your eyes. . . .

By perseverance and fortitude we have the prospect of a glorious issue; by cowardice and submission, the sad choice of a variety of evils—a ravaged country—a depopulated city—habitations without safety, and slavery without hope—our homes turned into barracks and bawdy-houses for Hessians, and a future race to provide for, whose fathers we shall doubt of. Look on this picture and weep over it! and if there yet remains one thoughtless wretch who believes it not, let him suffer it unlamented.

illegitimate children

DOCUMENT 2

Anne Terrel Addresses the Wives of Continental Soldiers (1776)

Like Tom Paine, Anne Terrel sought to awaken the patriotism of her readers. But while Paine addressed the "men of Pennsylvania," Terrel specifically wrote for "the Ladies whose husbands are now in the continental Army." She identified herself as a resident of Bedford County in western Virginia. Her letter, which asserted a female patriotism that was no less genuine than its male counterpart, appeared in the Virginia Gazette.[2]

Questions to consider:

1. To whom did Anne Terrel address her letter? Was she appealing to all American women?
2. What sorts of rhetoric and reasoning did Terrel use to persuade her readers? Did her sex—and the presumed sex of her readers—influence the tone or content of her writing?
3. What did Terrel see as women's role in the revolutionary crisis? What did she mean by claiming "another branch of American politics" as the province of women?

Ladies,

I now address myself to you who are under the same trouble of mind that I myself am. I am now absent from the tenderest husbands; but why is he absent from me? Because he is a soldier in the continental army, nobly supporting the glorious cause of liberty. I must confess, that when I hear of the dreadful wars and bloodshed, it makes me shudder. Yet, when I reflect on the wickedness of a cruel and abandoned ministry, who are forging chains, to bind not only us in the present age, but to bring our posterity into a lasting state of slavery; conspiring with our slaves to cut our throats, instigating the savage Indians to fall on our frontiers; . . . when I reflect on whole families inhumanly butchered by those savages, without regard to age or sex; the infant torn from its mother's arms; the milk in its innocent mouth; its brains dashed out against the next post; and when I consider all these cruel scenes, owing to the contrivance of a cruel and abandoned tyrant and his agents (acts too shocking in the heathen nations, but more so when perpetuated by those who profess christianity) I am not only willing to bear the absence of my dear husband for a short time, but am almost ready to start up with sword in hand to fight by his side in so glorious a cause.

But let us support ourselves under the absence of our husbands as well as we can, and as we are not well able to help them to fight, let us pay our attention to another branch of American politics, which comes more immediately under our province, namely, in frugality and industry, at home particularly in manufacturing our own wearing; and let the tyrants of Great Britain see that the American Ladies have both ingenuity and industry, and that we can dress with gentility without any of the British manufactories. Let us, in some measure, lay aside our visiting and fashions, and earnestly attend to carding, spinning, weaving, and brown our fair arms in our bleach-yards; and instead of the fine gew-gaws of Great Britain wear linen of our own manufacturing; and although it may not be so very fine, yet we may say we paid nothing for it to Great Britain, and that we are free women, and while our dear husbands are nobly struggling in the army for their freedom, let us be fervent in prayer to Almighty God for their protection and safe return, and that it may please him to support us under our present troubles, and our dear husbands under their present trials, for Christ's sake, I hope Ladies you will excuse the liberty I have taken in this short hint, as we are all greatly interested in this important affair.

DOCUMENT 3

Baroness Riedesel at Saratoga (1777)

When Baron von Riedesel, a German general in the British army, went to America to fight in 1776, he took his wife, Frederika, and their children with him. Eighteenth-century armies typically were accompanied by corps of civilians, many of whom were soldiers' relatives. The Baroness von Riedesel kept a journal describing her life among the British forces commanded by General John Burgoyne in the days leading up to their defeat by General Horatio Gates's army at Saratoga.[3] After the war, the Riedesels returned to Germany. In 1808, the baroness died in Berlin at the age of sixty-two.

Questions to consider:

1. How did the baroness assess the relative advantages of the Americans and their opponents?
2. What sorts of people were fighting for the king—or assisting those who did—in the Saratoga area?
3. What were the chief problems Burgoyne's forces and their civilian companions faced in October 1777?
4. Did the presence of so many civilians help or hinder the army's success?

When the army again moved, on the 11th of September, 1777, it was at first intended to leave me behind; but upon my urgent entreaties, and as other ladies were to follow the army, I received, finally, the same permission. We made only small day's marches, and were very often sick; yet always contented at being allowed to follow. I had still the satisfaction of daily seeing my husband. A great part of my baggage I had sent back, and had kept only a small summer wardrobe. . . .

As we were to march farther, I had a large calash made for me, in which I, my children, and both my women servants had seats; and in this manner I followed the army, in the midst of the soldiers, who were merry, singing songs, and burning with a desire for victory. We passed through boundless forests and magnificent tracts of country, which, however, were abandoned by all the inhabitants, who fled before us, and reinforced the army of the American general, Gates. In the sequel this cost us dearly, for every one of them was a soldier by nature, and could shoot very well; besides, the thought of fighting for their fatherland and their freedom, inspired them with still greater courage. . . .

Suddenly, however, on the 7th of October, my husband, with the whole general staff, decamped. Our misfortunes may be said to date from this moment. I had just sat down with my husband at his quarters to breakfast. General Frazer and, I believe, Generals Burgoyne and Phillips, also, were to have dined with me on that same day. I observed considerable movement among the troops. My husband thereupon informed me that there was to be a reconnaissance, which, however, did not surprise me, as this often happened. On my way homeward, I met many savages in their war-dress, armed with guns. To my question where they were going, they cried out to me, "War, war!," which meant that they were going to fight. This completely overwhelmed me, and I had scarcely got back to my quarters, when I heard skirmishing, and firing, which by degrees, became constantly heavier, until, finally, the noises became frightful. It was a terrible cannonade, and I was more dead than alive. About three o'clock in the afternoon, in place of the guests who were to have dined with me, they brought in to me, upon a litter, poor General Frazer (one of my expected guests), mortally wounded. Our dining table, which was already spread, was taken away, and in its place they fixed up a bed for the general. I sat in a corner of the room trembling and quaking. The noises grew continually louder. The thought that they might bring in my husband in the same manner was to me dreadful, and tormented me incessantly . . . Finally, toward evening, I saw my husband coming, upon which I forgot all my sufferings, and thanked God that he had spared him to me. He ate in great haste with me and his adjutant, behind the house. We had been told that we had gained an advantage over the enemy, but the sorrowful and down-cast faces which I beheld, bore witness to the contrary, and before my husband again went away, he drew me one side and told me that every thing might go very badly, and that I must keep myself in constant readiness for departure, but by no means to give anyone the least inkling of what I was doing. I therefore pretended that I wished to move into my new house the next morning, and had every thing packed up. My lady Ackland occupied a tent not far from our house. In this she slept, but during the day was in the camp. Suddenly one came to tell her that her husband was mortally wounded, and had been taken prisoner. At this she became very wretched. We comforted her by saying that it was only a slight wound, but as no one could nurse him as well as herself, we counseled her to go at once to him, to do which she could certainly obtain permission. She loved him very much, although he was a plain, rough man, and was almost daily intoxicated; with this exception, however, he was an excellent officer. She was the loveliest of women. I spent the night in this manner—at one time comforting her, and at another looking after my children, whom I had put to bed. . . .

The order had gone forth that the army should break up . . . and the horses were already harnessed to our calashes . . . The greatest silence had been enjoined; fires had been kindled in every direction; and many tents left standing, to make the enemy believe the camp was still there. We traveled continually the whole night. Little Frederica was afraid, and would often begin to cry. I was, therefore, obliged to hold a pocket handkerchief over her mouth, lest our whereabouts should be discovered.

At six o'clock in the morning a halt was made, at which every one wondered. General Burgoyne had all the cannon ranged and counted, which worried all of us, as a few more good marches would have placed us in security. My husband was completely exhausted, and seated himself during this delay, in my calash, where my maid servants were obliged to make room for him; and where he slept nearly three hours with his head upon my shoulder. In the mean time, Captain Willoe brought me his pocket-book containing bank bills, and Captain Geismar, his beautiful watch, a ring, and a well filled purse, and begged me to keep all these for them. I promised them to do my utmost. At last, the army again began its march, but scarcely had we proceeded an hour on the way, when a fresh halt was made, in consequence of the enemy being in sight. They were about two hundred men who came to reconnoitre, and who might easily have been taken prisoners by our troops, had not General Burgoyne lost his head. It rained ill torrents. . . .

Toward evening, we at last came to Saratoga, which was only half an hour's march from the place where we had spent the whole day. . . .

On the 10th, at seven o'clock in the morning, I drank some tea by way of refreshment; and we now hoped from one moment to another, that at last we would again get under way. General Burgoyne, in order to cover our retreat, caused the beautiful houses and mills at Saratoga, belonging to General Schuyler, to be burned. An English officer brought some excellent broth, which he shared with me, as I was not able to refuse his urgent entreaties. Thereupon we set out upon our march, but only as far as another place not far from where we had started.

The greatest misery and the utmost disorder prevailed in the army. The commissaries had forgotten to distribute provisions among the troops. There were cattle enough, but not one had been killed. More than thirty officers came to me, who could endure hunger no longer. I had coffee and tea made for them, and divided among them all the provisions with which my carriage was constantly filled; for we had a cook who, although an arrant knave, was fruitful in all expedients, and often in the night crossed small rivers, in order to steal from the country people, sheep, poultry and pigs. . . .

About two o'clock in the afternoon, the firing of cannon and small arms was again heard, and all was alarm and confusion. My husband sent me a message telling me to betake myself forthwith into a house which was not far from there. I seated myself in the calash with my children, and had scarcely driven up to the house, when I saw on the opposite side of the Hudson river, five or six men with guns, which were aimed at us. Almost involuntarily I threw the children on the bottom of the calash and myself over them. At the same instant the churls fired, and shattered the arm of a poor English soldier behind us, who was already wounded, and was also on the point of retreating into the house. Immediately after our arrival a frightful cannonade began, principally directed against the house in which we had sought shelter, probably because the enemy believed, from seeing so many people flocking around it, that all the generals made it their headquarters. Alas! it harbored none but wounded soldiers, or women! We were finally obliged to take refuge in a cellar, in which I laid myself down in a corner not far from the door. My children laid down on the earth with their heads upon my lap, and in this manner we passed the entire night. A horrible stench, the cries of the children, and yet more than all this, my own anguish, prevented me from closing my eyes.

On the following morning the cannonade again began, but from a different side. I advised all to go out of the cellar for a little while, during which time I would have it cleaned, as otherwise we would all be sick. They followed my suggestion, and I at once set many hands to work, which was in the highest degree necessary; for the women and children being afraid to venture forth, had soiled the whole cellar. After they had all gone out and left me alone, I for the first time surveyed our place of refuge. It consisted of three beautiful cellars, splendidly arched. I proposed that the most dangerously wounded of the officers should be brought into one of them; that the women should remain in another; and that all the rest should stay in the third, which was nearest the entrance. I had just given the cellars a good sweeping, and had fumigated them by sprinkling vinegar on burning coals, and each one had found his place prepared for him—when a fresh and terrible cannonade threw us all once more into alarm. Many persons, who had no right to come in, threw themselves against the door. My children were already under the cellar steps, and we would all have been crushed, if God had not given me strength to place myself before the door, and with extended arms prevent all from coming in; otherwise everyone of us would have been severely injured. Eleven cannon balls went through the house, and we could plainly hear them rolling over our heads. One poor soldier, whose leg they were about to amputate, having been laid upon a table for this purpose, had the other leg taken off by another cannon ball, in the very middle of the operation. His comrades all ran off, and when they again came back they found him in one corner of the room, where he had rolled in his anguish, scarcely breathing. I was more dead than alive, though not so much on account of our own danger, as for that which enveloped my husband, who, however, frequently sent to see how I was getting along, and to tell me that he was still safe. . . .

Our cook saw to our meals, but we were in want of water; and in order to quench thirst, I was often obliged to drink wine, and give it, also, to the children . . . As the great scarcity of water continued, we at last found a soldier's wife who had the courage to bring water from the river, for no one else would undertake it, as the enemy shot at the head of every man who approached the river. This woman, however, they never molested; and they told us afterward, that they spared her on account of her sex.

I endeavored to divert my mind from my troubles, by constantly busying myself with the wounded. I made them tea and coffee, and received in return a thousand benedictions. Often, also, I shared my noonday meal with them. One day a Canadian officer came into our cellar, who could scarcely stand up. We at last got it out of him, that he was almost dead with hunger. I considered myself very fortunate to have it in my power to offer him my mess. This gave him renewed strength, and gained for me his friendship. Afterward, upon our return to Canada, I learned to know his family. One of our greatest annoyances was the stench of the wounds when they began to suppurate. . . .

On the morning of the 16th of October, my husband was again obliged to go to his post, and I once more into my cellar.

On this day, a large amount of fresh meat was distributed among the officers, who, up to this time, had received only salted provisions, which had exceedingly aggravated the wounds of the men. The good woman who constantly supplied us with water, made us capital soup from the fresh meat. I had lost all appetite, and had the whole time taken nothing but crusts of bread dipped in wine. The wounded officers, my companions in misfortune, cut off the best piece of the beef and presented it to me, with a plate of soup. I said to them that I was not able to eat any thing, but as they saw that it was absolutely necessary I should take some nourishment, they declared that they themselves would not touch a morsel until I had given them the satisfaction of taking some. I could not longer withstand their friendly entreaties, upon which they assured me that it made them very happy to be able to offer me the first good thing which they themselves enjoyed.

On the 17th of October the capitulation was consummated. The generals waited upon the American general-in-chief, Gates, and the troops laid down their arms, and surrendered themselves prisoners of war. Now the good woman, who had brought us water at the risk of her life, received the reward of her services. Everyone threw a whole handful of money into her apron, and she received altogether over twenty guineas. At such a moment, the heart seems to be specially susceptible to feelings of gratitude. At last, my husband sent to me a groom with a message that I should come to him with our children. I, therefore, again seated myself in my dear calash; and, in the passage through the American camp, I observed, with great satisfaction, that no one cast at us scornful glances. On the contrary, they all greeted me, even showing compassion on their countenances at seeing a mother with her little children in such a situation.

DOCUMENT 4

The Burning of Fairfield, Connecticut (1779)

The boundaries between war and homefront, soldiers and civilians, often were poorly defined, especially in areas whose inhabitants included substantial numbers of both Whigs and Tories. Fairfield, Connecticut, was one such area. Although the British had withdrawn their main forces from New England in 1776, the Royal Navy occasionally raided coastal towns with the support of local Tories. The Reverend Andrew Eliot, a Congregational minister, penned this account of the British attack on Fairfield in July 1779.[4]

Questions to consider:

1. What did the British hope to achieve by burning the town of Fairfield?
2. Who were the various groups who participated in the raid and how, according to Eliot, did their conduct differ toward the town's inhabitants?
3. Why did Eliot devote so much of his narrative to describing the circumstances of the women of Fairfield?

Dear Brother,

I sit down to write you some account of the sad and awful scenes which have been exhibited in this once pleasant and delightful town, now, alas! a heap of ruins, a sad spectacle of desolation and woe.

It was in the beginning of wheat harvest, a season of extraordinary labour and festivity; a season which promised the greatest plenty that has been known for many years, if within the memory of man. Never did our fields bear so ponderous a load, never were our prospects, with regard to sustenance, so bright.

The British fleet and army, with the American refugees that had possessed and plundered New Haven, set sail from that distressed place on the 6th instant . . . Their commanding officers were Sir George Collier by sea, Generals Tryon and Garth by land. The approach of the fleet was so sudden, that but few men could be collected, though the alarm guns were fired immediately on the dissipation of the fog. There was no thought of opposing their landing, as our force was nothing to theirs.

Our little party, however, posted themselves so as to annoy them to the best advantage, expecting they would land at the Point. When our people found them landing on the left and marching in their rear to take possession of the town, they immediately retreated to the court house; and as the enemy advanced from the Beach lane, they gave them such a warm reception with a field piece; which threw both round and grape shot, and with their musketry, as quite disconcerted them for some time. The column, however, quickly recovered its solidity, and advancing rapidly, forced our small body to retreat to the heights, back of the town, where they were joined by numbers coming in from the country. The enemy were likewise galled very much, as they turned from the beach to the lane, by the cannon which played from Grover's hill.

The town was almost cleared of inhabitants. A few women, some of whom were of the most respectable families and characters, tarried, with a view of saving their property. They imagined their sex and character would avail to such a purpose. They put some confidence in the generosity of an enemy, who were once famed for generosity and politeness; and thought that kind treatment and submissive behaviour would secure them against harsh treatment and rough usage. Alas! They were miserably mistaken, and bitterly repented their confidence and presumption.

The Hessians were first let loose for rapine and plunder. They entered houses, attacked the persons of Whig and Tory indiscriminately; breaking open desks, trunks, closets, and taking away every thing of value. They robbed women of their buckles, rings, bonnets, aprons, and handkerchiefs. They abused them with the foulest and most profane language, threatened their lives without the least regard to the most earnest cries and entreaties. Looking glasses, china, and all kinds of furniture were soon dashed to pieces.

Another party that came on were the American refugees, who in revenge for their confiscated estates, carried on the same direful business. They were not, however, so abusive to the women as the former, but appeared very furious against the town and country. The Britons, by what I could learn, were the least inveterate: some of the officers seemed to pity the misfortunes of the country, but in excuse said, that they had no other way to regain their authority over us. Individuals among the British troops were, however, exceedingly abusive, especially to women. Some were forced to submit to the most indelicate and rough treatment, in defence of their virtue, and now bear the bruises of the horrid conflict.

About an hour before sunset, the conflagration began at the house of Mr. Isaac Jennings, which was consumed with the neighbouring buildings. In the evening, the house of Elijah Abel, Esq., sheriff of the county, was consumed, with a few others. In the night, several buildings in the main street. General Tryon was in various parts of the town plot, with the good women begging and entreating him to spare their houses. Mr. Sayre, the Church of England missionary, a gentleman firmly and zealously engaged in the British interest, and who has suffered considerably in their cause, joined with them in these entreaties; he begged the general to spare the town, but was denied. He then begged that some few houses might be spared as a shelter for those who could provide habitations nowhere else; this was denied also. At length Mr. Tryon consented to save the buildings of Mr. Burr and the writer of this epistle. Both had been plundered ere this. He said, likewise, that the houses for publick worship should be spared. He was far from being in good temper, during the whole affair. General Garth, at the other end of the town, treated the inhabitants with as much humanity, as his errand would admit.

At sunrise, some considerable part of the town was standing; but in about two hours the flames became general. The burning parties carried on their business with horrible alacrity, headed by one or two persons who were born and bred in the neighbouring towns. All the town from the bridge by Colonel Gold's to the Mill river, a few houses excepted, was a heap of ruin.

About eight o'clock, the enemy sounded a retreat. We had some satisfaction, amidst our sorrow and distress, to see that the meeting house and a few other buildings remained. But the rear guard, consisting of a banditti, the vilest that was ever loose among men, set fire, to every thing which General Tryon had left, the large and elegant meeting house, the ministers' houses, Mr. Burr's, and several other houses which had received protection. They tore the protection to pieces, damned Tryon, abused the women most shamefully, and then ran off in a most disgraceful manner. Happily our people came in and extinguished the flames in several houses, so that we are not entirely destitute.

The rear guard, which behaved in so scandalous a manner, were chiefly German troops, called Yaugers. They carry a small rifle gun, and fight in a skulking manner like our Indians. They may be properly called sons of plunder and devastation.

Our people on the heights, back of the town, were joined by numbers, but not equal to the numbers of the enemy. They were skirmishing all the evening, part of the night, and the next morning. The enemy were several times disconcerted and driven from their outposts. Had they continued longer in town, it must have been fatal to them; for the militia were collecting from all parts.

Our fort yet stands . . . Many were killed on both sides. The number cannot be ascertained. They carried off some prisoners, but no person of distinction.

DOCUMENT 5

A Winter Encampment (1779–80)

When the war's main theater was in the northern states, the armies retired for the winter and waited until spring to resume fighting. Although American historical memory later celebrated Valley Forge as the utmost example of soldiers' supposedly unique willingness to sacrifice and suffer for the revolutionary cause, the army's worst winter, in fact, came two years later. In the winter of 1779–80, in the aftermath of significant British victories in the southern states, Washington's forces endured an especially cold and hungry winter in Morristown, New Jersey. The author of this firsthand account of their ordeal was James Thacher, a surgeon in the Continental Army.[5]

Questions to consider:

1. What were the most pressing problems the soldiers faced? Did their morale and their conduct change over the course of this long and difficult winter?

2. What were the chief problems that Washington faced as the army's commander? To what extent were his interests and objectives different from those of the soldiers?

3. What sorts of "serious consequences" did Thacher fear would result from the soldiers' continual suffering? Who did he blame for the army's predicament?

⚬

[December 1779] General Washington has taken his headquarters at Morristown, and the whole army in this department are to be employed in building log huts for winter-quarters. The ground is marked out, and the soldiers have commenced cutting down the timber of oak and walnut, of which we have a great abundance. Our baggage has at length arrived, the men find it very difficult to pitch their tents on the frozen ground, and notwithstanding large fires, we can scarcely keep from freezing. In addition to other sufferings, the whole army has been for seven or eight days entirely destitute of the staff of life; our only food is miserable fresh beef, without bread, salt, or vegetables. . . .

Besides the evils above mentioned, we experience another, in the rapid depreciation of the continental money, which we receive for our pay; it is now estimated at about thirty for one. It is from this cause, according to report, that our commissary-general is unable to furnish the army with a proper supply of provisions. The people in the country are unwilling to sell the produce of their farms for this depreciated currency, and both the resources and the credit of our Congress appear to be almost exhausted. The year is now closed, and with it expires the term of enlistment of a considerable number of our soldiers; new conditions are offered them to encourage their reenlistment during the war, but such are the numerous evils which they have hitherto experienced, that it is feared but a small proportion of them will re-enlist. Should these apprehensions be realized, the fate of our country, and the destiny of its present rulers and friends, will soon be decided. . . . *land grants & pensions promised to soldiers*

January 1st, 1780. A new year commences, but brings no relief to the sufferings and privations of our army. Our canvas covering affords but a miserable security from storms of rain and snow, and a great scarcity of provisions still prevails, and its effects are felt even at headquarters . . . The weather for several days has been remarkably cold and stormy . . . But the sufferings of the poor soldiers can scarcely be described, while on duty they are unavoidably exposed to all the inclemency of storms and severe cold; at night they now have a bed of straw on the ground, and a single blanket to each man; they are badly clad, and some are destitute of shoes. We have contrived a kind of stone chimney outside, and an opening at one end of our tents gives us the benefit of the fire within. The snow is now from four to six feet deep, which so obstructs the roads as to prevent our receiving a supply of provisions. For the last ten days we have received but two pounds of meat a man, and we are frequently for six or eight days entirely destitute of meat, and then as long without bread. The consequence is, the soldiers are so enfeebled from hunger and cold, as to be almost unable to perform their military duty, or labor in constructing their huts. It is well known that General Washington experiences the greatest solicitude for the sufferings of his army, and is sensible that they in general conduct with heroic patience and fortitude. His excellency, it is understood, despairing of supplies from the commissary-general, has made application to the magistrates of the state of New Jersey for assistance in procuring provisions. This expedient has been attended with the happiest success. It is honorable to the magistrates and people of Jersey, that they have cheerfully complied with the requisition, and furnished for the present an ample supply, and have thus probably saved the army from destruction.

As if to make up the full measure of grief and embarrassment to the commander-in-chief, repeated complaints have been made to him that some of the soldiers are in the practice of pilfering and plundering the inhabitants of their poultry, sheep, pigs, and even their cattle, from their farms. This marauding practice has often been prohibited in general orders, under the severest penalties, and some exemplary punishments have been inflicted. General Washington possesses an inflexible firmness of purpose, and is determined that discipline and subordination in camp shall be rigidly enforced and maintained. The whole army has been sufficiently warned, and cautioned against robbing the inhabitants on any pretence whatever, and no soldier is subjected to punishment without a fair trial, and conviction by a court-martial. Death has been inflicted in a few instances of an atrocious nature; but in general, the punishment consists in a public whipping, and the number of stripes is proportioned to the degree of offence. . . .

[February] 14th. Having continued to this late season in our tents, experiencing the greatest inconvenience, we have now the satisfaction of taking possession of the log huts, just completed by our soldiers, where we shall have more comfortable accommodations.

March. The present winter is the most severe and distressing which we have ever experienced. An immense body of snow remains on the ground. Our soldiers are in a wretched condition for the want of clothes, blankets and shoes; and these calamitous circumstances are accompanied by a want of provisions. It has several times happened that the troops were reduced to one-half, or to one-quarter, allowance, and some days have passed without any meat or bread being delivered out. The causes assigned for these extraordinary deficiencies, are the very low state of public finances, in consequence of the rapid depreciation of the continental currency, and some irregularity in the commissary's department. Our soldiers, in general, support their sufferings with commendable firmness, but it is feared that their patience will be exhausted, and very serious consequences ensue.

DOCUMENT 6

The Murder of Hannah Caldwell (1780)

In the War of Independence, as in many wars, both sides committed atrocities. One of the most notorious episodes of the war in the northern states was the murder of Hannah Ogden Caldwell, wife of an outspoken Whig Presbyterian minister. Residents of Elizabethtown, New Jersey, the Caldwells sought refuge in the rural community of Connecticut Farms, near Springfield, where a battle took place on 7 June 1780. Despite her best efforts to shield herself and her children, Hannah Caldwell became a casualty of that battle. Although her death may have been unintended, her story was widely reported—and exploited—by the Whig press. This account appeared in the New Jersey Journal.[6]

Questions to consider:

1. What lesson did the author of this article seek to convey to his readers?
2. Why did Hannah Caldwell—at least as this author portrayed her—make such a sympathetic heroine?
3. In describing the Caldwell family, what did the author imply were the ideal roles of women and men in revolutionary times? Did those ideals reflect reality?

As soon as [the British, Hessian, and Tory troops] came to Connecticut Farms, seven miles from the place of their landing, they began the exercise of their awful cruelty. They first set fire to the house of Deacon Wade, and then to the Presbyterian church; but soon advancing to the house of the Rev. Mr. Caldwell, they had an opportunity of reaching the summit of that cruelty after which they have been climbing for so many years. Mr. Caldwell could not remove his property, nor all his family. His amiable wife, with a babe of eight months, and one of three years old, with the house-keeper and a little maid, were left. Mrs. Caldwell having dressed herself, and put her house in order, retired with those into a back room, which was so situated that she was entirely secured against transient shot from either party, should they dispute the ground near the house, which happened not to be the case. The babe was in the arms of the housekeeper, the other child the mother held by the hand, all sitting upon the side of the bed, when one of the barbarians advancing round the house, took the advantage of a small space, through which the room was accessible, and fired two balls into that amiable lady, so well directed that they ended her life in a moment.

This horrid deed appears the more cruel in the eyes of all who knew the lovely person, the sweet temper, and the not only inoffensive but benevolent life of that dear mother of nine children now living, the eldest of which is but just turned sixteen. From some circumstances this appears not to have been the act of one rash inconsiderate villain, but the effect of deliberate orders given previous to their coming to the place, that she should be murdered. She was stripped of part of her clothes, but her corpse was preserved from the flames by two or three of the enemy whose humanity was not yet extinct. This was a murder without provocation, and the most opposite to humanity; for although her husband has uniformly defended the American cause, yet he has not only avoided cruelty himself, but used his utmost endeavours to prevent it being done by others; and as to herself, one would have thought her sweet appearance, and amiable life, would have protected her from even British or Tory cruelty. Not satiated by this horrid deed, after stripping the house they set fire to it and eleven more dwelling-houses in the neighbourhood. . . .

Thus has British cruelty been led to perfection . . . Six widows are burnt out; some very aged, and others with small families; and almost all the houses in the neighbourhood which were not burnt were torn to pieces, and entirely plundered.

Consider Americans! what you have to expect from such enemies, and what you have to do! If the tribes of Israel rose as one man to revenge the cruelty offered an individual of no good character (Judges xix), what ought to be our conduct when the fairest innocence is no protection; when the condition of widowhood, attended with age, or a large offspring, is no defence?

DOCUMENT 7

The Sentiments of an American Woman (1780)

In 1779, some patriotic women in Philadelphia organized a funding-raising campaign to benefit the poorly supplied troops of the Continental Army. After unsuccessfully insisting that the money they raised go directly to the troops rather than to a general army account, the women decided to use their funds to make shirts for some 2,200 soldiers. This manifesto aimed to generate women's involvement in the Pennsylvania fund-raising movement, which inspired similar undertakings in New Jersey and Maryland. Its author justified women's involvement in political life and clearly articulated an ideal of female patriotism.[7]

Questions to consider:

1. What sort of woman wrote this manifesto? Whom did she envision as her prospective readers?
2. Why did the author include the stories of Biblical and European women in her brief appeal?
3. On what grounds did she declare American women "born for liberty"? What were the attributes of female patriotism and how did it differ from its masculine counterpart?

On the commencement of actual war, the Women of America manifested a firm resolution to contribute as much as could depend on them, to the deliverance of their country. Animated by the purest patriotism, they are sensible of sorrow at this day, in not offering more than barren wishes for the success of so glorious a Revolution. They aspire to render themselves more really useful; and this sentiment is universal from the north to the south of the Thirteen United States. Our ambition is kindled by the same of those heroines of antiquity, who have rendered their sex illustrious, and have proved to the universe, that, if the weakness of our constitution, if opinion and manners did not forbid us to march to glory by the same paths as the Men, we should at least equal, and sometimes surpass them in our love for the public good. I glory in all that which my sex has done great and commendable. I call to mind with enthusiasm and with admiration, all those acts of courage, of constancy and patriotism, which history has transmitted to us: The people favoured by Heaven, preserved from destruction by the virtues, the zeal and the resolution of Deborah, of Judith, of Esther! The fortitude of the mother of the Massachabees, in giving up her sons to die before her eyes: Rome saved from the fury of a victorious enemy by the efforts of Volumnia, and other Roman Ladies: So many famous sieges where the Women have been seen forgetting the weakness of their sex, building new walls, digging trenches with their feeble hands, furnishing arms to their defenders, they themselves darting the missile weapons of the enemy, resigning the ornaments of their apparel, and their fortune, to fill the public treasury, and to hasten the deliverance of their country; burying themselves under its ruins, throwing themselves into the flames rather than submit to the disgrace of humiliation before a proud enemy.

Born for liberty, disdaining to bear the irons of a tyrannic government, we associate ourselves to the grandeur of those sovereigns, cherished and revered, who have held with so much splendour the scepter of the greatest states, the Batildas, the Elizabeths, the Maries, the Catharines, who have extended the empire of liberty, and contented to reign by sweetness and justice, have broken the chains of slavery, forged by tyrants in the times of ignorance and barbarity . . . We call to mind, doubly interested, that it was a French Maid who kindled up amongst her fellow-citizens, the flame of patriotism buried under long misfortunes: It was the Maid of Orleans who drove from the kingdom of France the ancestors of those same British, whose odious yoke we have just shaken off; and whom it is necessary that we drive from this Continent. . . .

But I must limit myself to the recollection of this small number of achievements. Who knows if persons disposed to censure, and sometimes too severely with regard to us, may not disapprove our appearing acquainted even with the actions of which our sex boasts? We are at least certain, that he cannot be a good citizen who will not applaud our efforts for the relief of the armies which defend our lives, our possessions, our liberty? The situation of our soldiery has been represented to me; the evils inseparable from war, and the firm and generous spirit which has enabled them to support these. But it has been said, that they may apprehend, that, in the course of a long war, the view of their distresses may be lost, and their services be forgotten. Forgotten! Never; I can answer in the name of all my sex. Brave Americans, your disinterestedness, your courage, and your constancy will always be dear to America, as long as she shall preserve her virtue. . . .

The time is arrived to display the same sentiments which animated us at the beginning of the Revolution, when we renounced the use of teas, however agreeable to our taste, rather than receive them from our persecutors; when we made it appear to them that we placed former necessaries in the rank of superfluities, when our liberty was interested; when our republican and laborious hands spun the flax, prepared the linen intended for the use of our soldiers; when exiles and fugitives we supported with courage all the evils which are the concomitants of war. Let us not lose a moment; let us be engaged to offer the homage of our gratitude at the altar of military valour, and you, our brave deliverers, while mercenary slaves combat to cause you to share with them, the irons with which they are loaded, receive with a free hand our offering, the purest which can be presented to your virtue, by an American Woman.

SUGGESTED READING FOR CHAPTER 6

BUEL, RICHARD, JR. *Dear Liberty: Connecticut's Mobilization for War* (1980).
———, and JOY DAY BUEL. *The Way of Duty: A Woman and Her Family in Revolutionary America* (1984).
CARP, E. WAYNE. *To Starve the Army at Pleasure: Continental Army Administration and American Political Culture, 1775–1783* (1984).
CALHOON, ROBERT M. *The Loyalists in Revolutionary America, 1760–1781* (1973).
DULL, JONATHAN R. *A Diplomatic History of the American Revolution* (1985).
GRUBER, IRA D. *The Howe Brothers and the American Revolution* (1972).

HIGGINBOTHAM, DON. *War and Society in Revolutionary America: The Wider Dimensions of the Conflict* (1988).

———. *The War of American Independence: Military Attitudes, Policies, and Practice, 1763–1789* (1971).

MARTIN, JAMES KIRBY, and LENDER, MARK E. *A Respectable Army: The Military Origins of the Republic* (1982).

MAYER, HOLLY A. *Belonging to the Army: Camp Followers and Community during the American Revolution* (1996).

NELSON, WILLIAM H. *The American Tory* (1961).

NORTON, MARY BETH. *Liberty's Daughters: The Revolutionary Experience of American Women, 1750–1800.*

ROSSWURM, STEVEN. *Arms, Country, and Class: The Philadelphia Militia and the "Lower Sort" during the American Revolution* (1987).

ROYSTER, CHARLES. *A Revolutionary People at War: The Continental Army and American Character, 1775–1783* (1979).

SHY, JOHN. *A People Numerous and Armed: Reflections on the Military Struggle for American Independence* (1976).

SKEMP, SHEILA L. *William Franklin: Son of a Patriot, Servant of a King* (1990).

STINCHCOMBE, WILLIAM C. *The American Revolution and the French Alliance* (1969).

NOTES

[1]Thomas Paine, "The Crisis #1," in Moncure Daniel Conway, ed., *The Writings of Thomas Paine*, 4 vols. (New York, 1894–96) 1: 170–79.

[2]*Virginia Gazette* (Purdie and Hunter), 21 Sept. 1776.

[3]William L. Stone, trans., *Letters and Journals relating to the War of the American Revolution and the Capture of the German Troops at Saratoga, by Mrs. General Riedesel* (Albany, 1867), 113, 115–20, 122–23, 125–32, 134.

[4]Andrew Eliot to John Eliot, 15 July 1779, in *Collections of the Massachusetts Historical Society, For the Year 1794*, vol. 3 (Boston, 1810), 103–5.

[5]James Thacher, *Military Journal of the American Revolution* (Hartford, Conn., 1862), 181–86, 190–91.

[6][Chatham] *New Jersey Journal*, 14 June 1780.

[7]*The Sentiments of an American Woman* (Philadelphia, 1780).

CHAPTER SEVEN

A WORLD TURNED UPSIDE DOWN

In the southern states, the War of Independence had three distinct phases. In the first, which lasted from late 1775 through 1776, the British mustered support among slaves, native Americans, and white loyalists, but nonetheless suffered a series of military defeats that resulted in their withdrawal from the region. The war's second phase, which lasted approximately two years, was a period of relative peace, when most of the region's inhabitants felt the effects of the war primarily in the form of inflation, high taxes, and scarcities of goods and labor. In the third phase, however, the southern states became the main military theater. From the British capture of Savannah in December 1778 until their surrender at Yorktown, Virginia, nearly three years later, southerners would witness or participate in some of the Revolution's bloodiest and most consequential battles.

The southern campaign was by all accounts the nastiest and most brutal of the War of Independence. Inhabitants of the southern states were divided in their political allegiance, in part due to differences among them in ethnicity, race, and social rank. British officials correctly expected both native Americans, who felt threatened by the westward migration of white settlers, and enslaved African Americans, who sought freedom, to gravitate to the king's standard, but they badly overestimated the extent and depth of loyalist sentiment among the region's white population. Some white southerners were committed Tories, but many others were either apathetic or only mildly sympathetic to the British as a result of their antipathy toward local Whigs. In the southern backcountry especially, the brutality of the British and their Tory allies ultimately alienated these waverers and helped turn what began as an auspicious campaign for the British into a decisive victory for the United States.

In the war's first year, British authorities had anticipated widespread support among the inhabitants of the southern colonies. They expected a substantial portion of the region's white inhabitants to remain loyal to the king, and they believed that both slaves and native Americans would support them militarily. In fact, the British received support from all three of these sources in 1775–76. Scottish loyalists fought unsuccessfully for the king at Moore's Creek Bridge in eastern North Carolina in early 1776. African Americans supported Lord Dunmore's failed attempt to defeat Virginia's Whigs. The Cherokees waged an all-out war against white settlers in the Carolina backcountry, acting on their own initiative though often with the help of local Tories. But by December 1776, the Cherokees were utterly defeated. By then, too, all four southern colonial governors had fled, having suffered defeat at the hands of the revolutionaries.

Despite such abysmal precedents, British officials remained convinced that Georgia and the Carolinas, in particular, were full of active and latent opponents of the Revolution. Displaced royal officials and Tory exiles who poured into London after 1776 promoted the appealing notion that planters and lesser folk longed for a return to royal government. Refugees cherished the prospect of a full-scale invasion of the southern states as their only chance of regaining lost property and prestige, as well as a welcome opportunity to enact vengeance upon the hated Whigs. The prospect of a decisive victory, accomplished in part by mobilizing local people and resources, was increasingly tantalizing to British officials as the war dragged on indecisively in the northern states. After Saratoga, Lord George Germain, who was charged with directing the British war effort, succumbed to that vision, adopting a dramatic change in strategy. Germain decided to invade the southern states, where he expected the king's forces to capitalize on local support to defeat the Whigs and reinstate the old colonial governments.

The southern campaign began auspiciously for the British with the fall of Savannah in December 1778. In November, General Henry Clinton had sent Lieutenant Colonel Archibald Campbell and 3,500 men from New York and New Jersey to join Florida-based American loyalists under the command of General Augustin Prevost in attacking the Georgia capital. The poorly defended town fell quickly, and the victorious British, supported by some Indians and thousands of runaway slaves, subdued opposition in the countryside and restored the colonial regime. British authorities forced Georgia Whigs to choose between banishment and loss of their property or swearing allegiance to the king and the reconstituted imperial government. Some 1,400 Georgians chose the latter option, and loyalists organized twenty new militia units.

Hoping to replicate their success in neighboring South Carolina, in early 1780 British detachments from Georgia, Virginia, and New York converged outside Charleston, where General Benjamin Lincoln commanded a combined force of some 6,000 Continentals and militia. Generals Clinton and Cornwallis sailed southward to Charleston from New York, trapping Lincoln's army in the South Carolina capital and bringing the total number of British troops there to about 8,000. Bowing to pressure from Charleston's civilian leaders to resist the invaders, Lincoln fought for six weeks before surrendering the city and his entire army on 12 May 1780. Charleston was the biggest single American loss of the War of Independence. With Lincoln's surrender, every adult white man in the city became a British prisoner. Although many South Carolinians regained their freedom by swearing allegiance to the king, others were imprisoned in rank jails or on putrid prison ships in Charleston harbor. General Sir Henry Clinton, the British commander, installed a military government in Charleston. He then dispatched troops under Lord Charles Cornwallis to reestablish British control in the interior of South Carolina.

In response to these major military reverses, Congress chose General Horatio Gates, the hero of Saratoga, to command the American forces in the southern states. In early August, Gates arrived in South Carolina with his army, only to be routed in battle at Camden by Cornwallis, who forced the Americans to retreat some 160 miles to Hillsborough, North Carolina. After this disaster, Congress replaced Gates with General Nathanael Greene, a skillful strategist who, since March 1778, also had served as the army's quartermaster general. In December 1780, Greene arrived in Charlotte to assume his command. The general found his army demoralized, starving, and in utter disarray.

For nearly two years, the British enjoyed remarkable success in their southern campaign. They captured both Savannah and Charleston, the largest American cities south of Virginia. They reestablished their political control over Georgia and much of South Carolina. Moreover, as their advisors had predicted, they found significant support among the inhabitants of the region. Tories awaited the arrival of the British in the coastal towns, where other residents acquiesced in the reimposition of royal government once the king's forces and their local allies had triumphed militarily. Thousands of enslaved people in Georgia and South Carolina also fled their masters to support the British in hopes of attaining their freedom. Only the anticipated Indian support failed to materialize. Whig militia suppressed the Cherokees in 1776 and again in 1780. When Georgia Tories sought help from the Creeks in 1780–81, they demurred, fearing a similar fate.

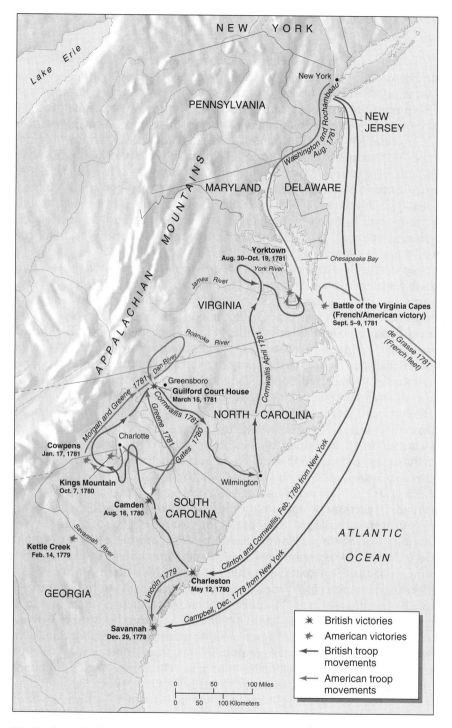

The Southern Campaign, 1778–1781. By late 1778, the British focused their military efforts in the southern states, where they expected significant support from white loyalists, slaves, and nearby native Americans. The British won the first major engagements of the campaign, which nonetheless ended with their surrender at Yorktown in October 1781.

By late 1780, however, the tide began to turn in favor of the Americans, in part as a result of the brutality of the British and their Tory allies, especially in the backcountry. When the war began, the Carolina backcountry was unstable, contentious, and for the most part beyond the control of the newly established state governments. Local grievances and animosities often influenced political allegiance in this region, whose inhabitants included Tories, Whigs, and many others who were apathetic or neutral. When the British withdrew from the area in 1776, backcountry Whigs harassed their Tory neighbors. When the British returned in 1779–80, local Tories retaliated with a vengeance. Their brutality, along with British efforts to enlist the support of Indians and slaves, converted many white backcountry people into active supporters of the revolutionary cause.

After the British victories at Savannah and Charleston, Tories and British regulars moved into the interior, where they terrorized civilians, murdering, plundering, taking prisoners, and causing chaos in many communities. Tory marauders destroyed farms and houses, leaving their dispossessed inhabitants without food and shelter. Loyalist militia tortured the families of known Whigs to obtain information and forced local patriots to witness summary executions of their relatives and neighbors. On the battlefield, the British and their Tory allies also showed unusual cruelty toward their adversaries. In May 1780, when Lieutenant Colonel Banastre Tarleton defeated a force of Continentals at the Waxhaws, he allowed his men to slaughter American soldiers after they surrendered. Appalled by the ruthlessness of the invaders and fearing that they would be compelled to serve in the British army, many previously quiescent Carolinians decided to fight back.

In 1780, Whig militia scored several important victories in the Carolina backcountry, the first defeats suffered by British forces in the southern campaign. The most important of these occurred on 7 October 1780 at Kings Mountain, where Whig militia soundly defeated a force made up largely of local Tories. Recalling Tarleton's abuse of the Continentals at the Waxhaws, Whigs at Kings Mountain continued firing on the surrendering Tories and killed most of those they captured once the battle was over. Many historians consider the Battle of Kings Mountain the turning point of the southern campaign because it showed that the British and their allies were not invincible, despite their early impressive successes in the region. More than most battles, Kings Mountain also demonstrated the extent to which the War of Independence, in some localities, assumed the guise of a civil war.

In 1781, American military fortunes continued to improve under the leadership of General Nathanael Greene. The new commander of the southern army divided his forces into four units, which he dispersed throughout the Carolinas. Recognizing that his troops lacked both the numbers and discipline to defeat Cornwallis in a conventional battle, Greene used guerrilla tactics to harass the British and engage them in a series of more limited engagements. In January 1781, Greene's subordinate, General Daniel Morgan, led a combined force of Continentals and militia to victory at Cowpens, South Carolina. Morgan then retreated into North Carolina, where he reunited with Greene; after retiring briefly to Virginia, the pair returned to North Carolina and engaged Cornwallis at Guilford Courthouse in March. While the British held the field and therefore technically won this battle, their losses were much heavier than those of the Americans. After Guilford Courthouse, Cornwallis retreated to the coastal town of Wilmington, while Greene directed his subordinates to attack British garrisons that were dispersed throughout South Carolina.

In order to prevent Greene from obtaining reinforcements from Virginia, Cornwallis decided to march his army northward to the Old Dominion, where they would join a force under the command of General Benedict Arnold. A hero of the American victories at Ticonderoga and Saratoga, Arnold turned traitor in September 1780 and had been leading a British force in Virginia since December. Together, Cornwallis and Arnold commanded some 7,200 men, significantly more than the nearby American force commanded by the Marquis de Lafayette, a French nobleman who had joined the Continental Army in 1777. Although they were outnumbered, Lafayette's troops weathered two months of indecisive fighting, after which Cornwallis moved his army to the coast.

The British commander settled his troops in Yorktown, which was situated on a peninsula. Then, in what proved to be a fatal error, he began to fortify the peninsula to protect his army. Because the American navy was small and the French fleet had not been a significant presence on the American coast, Cornwallis assumed that the British navy would retain control of the waters off Virginia. In the summer of 1781, however, Washington learned that Cornwallis had gone to Yorktown and that the French had sent a fleet of twenty ships and 3,000 men to America. Admiral de Grasse, the French naval commander, sailed to the Chesapeake, while Lafayette assembled his troops to block Cornwallis's escape. Washington and the French army commander, the Comte de Rochambeau, raced southward with the bulk of their troops, joining Lafayette in Virginia. The combined American and French force of more than 16,000 men was now vastly superior to Cornwallis's army. On 10 September, the French navy secured the coast, driving the British fleet back to New York for repairs. Cornwallis was surrounded, trapped on the peninsula.

On 9 October 1781, the allies began their assault, which continued until the British commander surrendered his army eight days later on the fourth anniversary of the American victory at Saratoga. Two days later, the defeated troops marched out to turn in their weapons and surrender formally to the victorious Americans. Cornwallis, who claimed to be indisposed, sent his second-in-command to present his sword to General Washington. The American commander responded in kind, directing Cornwallis's subordinate to give the sword to his own second-in-command, General Benjamin Lincoln, who had been forced to surrender his own army the preceding year at Charleston.

Cornwallis's surrender did not end the war, but after Yorktown many people sensed that its outcome was now certain. As Lincoln accepted the sword of surrender, the army's band played an old English song that pondered a world without logic or predictability: "The World Turned Upside Down." When British officials learned of Cornwallis's surrender, the House of Commons voted to cease offensive operations against the United States and passed a bill authorizing the Crown to seek a formal peace. While George III doggedly resisted making peace with his erstwhile subjects, in the end he had no choice. On 20 March 1782, Lord North resigned. In April, a new ministry initiated informal peace negotiations in Paris.

Diplomacy would formally establish the United States as a sovereign nation and bring about the demilitarization of the thirteen states. In part because of the continuing hostilities between Britain and its European enemies, the demilitarization of the American mainland proceeded quickly once Britain and the United States commenced their negotiations. By early December 1782, the British army had evacuated New York City, Staten Island, and Long Island—all of which they had occupied since 1776. In the coming weeks, the British likewise left the southern states. By late December, General Washington was in Annapolis, Maryland, where he resigned his commission to the Continental Congress. A month later, Washington was instrumental in ending the Newburgh Conspiracy, an attempt by Continental officers to force Congress to pay the army's wages, which were seriously in arrears. In an unequivocal assertion of the supremacy of civilian authority, Congress disbanded the Continental Army.

The departure of the British and the demobilization of the American forces unleashed a wave of migration that ultimately touched many parts of the Atlantic world. Some American soldiers returned home to their families, but others—especially those who received pay in the form of western land warrants—moved elsewhere, often settling in new frontier communities. Whig residents of New York City, Charleston, and other cities or towns that the British had occupied returned to their homes, which they often found despoiled by years of rough usage. Tories, who had taken protection from the British, now found themselves forced to leave the United States. Some white loyalists successfully petitioned the legislatures for permission to return to their respective states, while others came back quietly, eluding the attention of local authorities. Thousands of others, however, resettled in Great Britain, Canada, or the British island colonies. Nova Scotia was the main destination of the several thousand African Americans who escaped slavery by supporting the Crown during the War of Independence, though a substantial minority later moved on to establish the colony of Sierra Leone in West Africa.

On 3 September 1783, the United States and its allies signed separate treaties that ended their wars with Britain. As a result of these treaties, Spain received Florida and the Mediterranean island of Minorca, and France regained Senegal in western Africa and the Caribbean island of Tobago, both of which it had lost in 1763. American negotiators— chiefly Benjamin Franklin, John Jay, and John Adams—concluded a highly favorable peace. First and foremost, the Treaty of Paris that ended the war with Britain recognized the United States as a sovereign and independent nation. Second, it established the Mississippi River as the western boundary of the United States. In addition, the British granted Americans fishing rights off the coast of Newfoundland, which were of vital interest to New Englanders. The Americans, in return, promised only that Congress would recommend that the states return confiscated loyalist property and impose no legal obstacles to the collection of debts transacted with British merchants prior to independence. In sum, the American negotiators had given Britain only two carefully worded and possibly unenforceable concessions, while attaining all of their own most pressing objectives.

In 1776, no one would have predicted precisely the course of America's War of Independence. The British and most Tories, of course, wholly doubted the rebels' ability to defeat the world's leading military, naval, and economic power. American patriots, who were more confident of their own success, nonetheless overestimated their supposed military, economic, and moral advantages at the outset. Those on both sides expected that, one way or the other, the whole affair would be settled relatively quickly; no one expected that it would take more than six years of difficult and exhausting war.

In the end, the United States triumphed by persevering, by continuing to fight until they got the two decisive victories they needed to make peace on their terms. The first, at Saratoga, resulted in the French alliance. The second, at Yorktown, led to Cornwallis's surrender, which caused the British government to withdraw its support from the American war. The revolutionaries were motivated variously by love of liberty, hatred for their enemies, and a desire to defend themselves and their communities. These mixed motives informed their conduct toward the British, as well as their relations with each other.

DOCUMENT 1

The British Capture Savannah (1778)

In December 1778, the southern campaign began auspiciously for the British with the capture of Savannah, Georgia's capital. In the process, they captured 186 men, including Mordecai Sheftall, the author of this narrative, and his teenaged son.[1] Sheftall was a leader of the revolutionary movement in Savannah and a prominent member of its Jewish community. He remained a prisoner until he was freed by exchange, whereupon he went to Philadelphia, where he was involved in privateering ventures against the British until the war was over.

Questions to consider:

1. What sorts of men made up the force that attacked and captured the town of Savannah?
2. How did the victors treat their prisoners? What were some of the variables that may have influenced the treatment received by any individual?
3. How did civilians experience the occupation of Savannah? In what ways did they interact with the British soldiers and their prisoners?

❧ ☙

This day the British troops, consisting of about three thousand five hundred men, including two battalions of Hessians, under the command of Lieutenant-Colonel Archibald Campbell, of the 71st Regiment of Highlanders, landed early in the morning at Brewton Hill, two miles below the town of Savannah, where they met with very little opposition before they gained the height. At about three o'clock, P. M., they entered, and took possession of the town of Savannah, when I endeavoured, with my son Sheftall, to make our escape across Musgrove Creek . . . but on our arrival at the creek, after having sustained a very heavy fire of musketry from the light infantry under the command of Sir James Baird, during the time we were crossing the Common, without any injury to either of us, we found it high water; and my son, not knowing how to swim, and we, with about one hundred and eighty-six officers and privates, being caught, as it were, in a pen, and the Highlanders keeping up a constant fire on us, it was thought advisable to surrender ourselves prisoners, which we accordingly did, and which was no sooner done than the Highlanders plundered everyone amongst us, except Major Low, myself and son, who, being foremost, had an opportunity to surrender ourselves to the British officer . . . who disarmed us as we came into the yard formerly occupied by Mr. Moses Nunes . . . This over, we were marched in files, guarded by the Highlanders and [New] York Volunteers, who had come up before we were marched, when we were paraded before Mrs. Goffe's door, on the bay, where we saw the greatest part of the army drawn up. From there, after some time, we were all marched through the town to the courthouse, which was very much crowded, the greatest part of the officers they had taken being here collected, and indiscriminately put together. I had been here about two hours, when an officer, who I afterwards learned to be Major Crystie, called for me by name, and ordered me to follow him, which I did, with my blanket and shirt under my arm, my clothing and my son's, which were in my saddle-bags, having been taken from my horse, so that my wardrobe consisted of what I had on my back.

On our way to the white guard-house we met with Colonel Campbell, who inquired of the Major who he had got there. On his naming me to him, he desired that I might be well guarded, as I was a very great rebel. The Major obeyed his orders, for, on lodging me in the guard-house, he ordered the sentry to guard me with a drawn bayonet, and not to suffer me to go without the reach of it . . . He asked me if I knew that Charlestown was taken, I told him no. He then called us poor, deluded wretches, and said, "Good God! how are you deluded by your leaders!" When I inquired of him who had taken it, and when he said General Grant, with ten thousand men, and that it had been taken eight or ten days ago, I smiled, and told him it was not so, as I had a letter in my pocket that was wrote in Charlestown but three days ago by my brother. He replied, we had been misinformed. I then retorted that I found they could be misinformed by their leaders as well as we could be deluded by ours. This made him so angry, that . . . he ordered me to be confined amongst the drunken soldiers and negroes, where I suffered a great deal of abuse, and was threatened to be run through the body, or, as they termed it, skivered by one of the York Volunteers; which threat he attempted to put into execution three times during the night, but was prevented by one Sergeant Campbell.

In this situation I remained two days without a morsel to eat, when a Hessian officer named Zaltman, finding I could talk his language, removed me to his room, and sympathized with me on my situation. He permitted me to send to Mrs. Minis, who sent me some victuals. He also permitted me to go and see my son, and to let him come and stay with me. He introduced me to Captain Kappel, also a Hessian, who treated me very politely. In this situation I remained until Saturday morning, the 2d of January 1779, when . . . I met with Captain Stanhope, of the *Raven* sloop of war, who treated me with the most illiberal abuse; and . . . ordered me on board the prison-ship, together with my son. I made a point of giving Mr. Stanhope suitable answers to his impertinent treatment, and then turned from him, and inquired for Colonel Innis. I got his leave to go to Mrs. Minis for a shirt she had taken to wash for me, as it was the only one I had left, except the one on my back, and that was given me by Captain Kappel, as the British soldiers had plundered both mine and my son's clothes. This favour he granted me under guard; after which I was conducted on board one of the flat-boats, and put on board the prison-ship *Nancy*, commanded by Captain Samuel Tait, when the first thing that presented itself to my view was one of our poor Continental soldiers laying on the ship's main deck in the agonies of death, and who expired in a few hours after. After being presented to the Captain with mine and the rest of the prisoners' names, I gave him in charge what paper money I had, and my watch. My son also gave him his money to take care of. He appeared to be a little civiller after this confidence placed in him, and permitted us to sleep in a state-room—that is, the Rev. Moses Allen, myself and son. In the evening we were served with what was called our allowance, which consisted of two pints and a half and a half-gill of rice, and about seven ounces of boiled beef per man.

<u>Document 2</u>

Eliza Wilkinson's Wartime Experience (1779)

> *In June 1779, when the British invasion of Charleston seemed imminent, Eliza Wilkinson and her sisters-in-law sought refuge at a family plantation outside the city, only to be harassed by British troops who traversed the area. Indignation pervades Wilkinson's account of her ordeal, suggesting that she expected her sex to shield her and her companions from the soldiers' worst abuse. Yet Wilkinson clearly did not regard women as passive or apolitical. "I won't have it thought," she wrote elsewhere, "that because we are the weaker sex as to* bodily *strength . . . we are capable of nothing more than minding the dairy, visiting the poultry-house, and all such domestic concerns."[2]*

Questions to consider:

1. What was Wilkinson's attitude toward the several slaves or "negroes" who appear in her narrative? What roles did African Americans play in the conflict between the British and white Americans in this plantation region?
2. How could civilians distinguish friendly from enemy troops? What were their options when dealing with the latter?

3. Why did Wilkinson repeatedly characterize the British soldiers as "inhuman"?

All this time we had not seen the face of an enemy, not an open one—for I believe private ones were daily about. One night, however, upwards of sixty dreaded red-coats, commanded by Major Graham, passed our gate, in order to surprise Lieut. Morton Wilkinson at his own house, where they understood he had a party of men. A negro wench was their informer, and also their conductor; but (thank heaven) some how or other they failed in their attempt, and repassed our avenue early in the morning, but made a halt at the head of it, and wanted to come up; but a negro fellow, whom they had got at a neighbor's not far from us to go as far as the ferry with them, dissuaded them from it, by saying it was not worth while, for it was only a plantation belonging to an old decrepit gentleman, who did not live there; so they took his word for it, and proceeded on. You may think how much we were alarmed when we heard this, which we did the next morning; and how many blessings the negro had from us for his consideration and pity. . . .

Well, now comes the day of terror—the 3d of June . . . In the morning, fifteen or sixteen horsemen rode up to the house; we were greatly terrified, thinking them the enemy, but from their behavior, were agreeably deceived, and found them friends. They sat a while on their horses, talking to us; and then rode off, except two, who tarried a minute or two longer, and then followed the rest, who had nearly reached the gate. One of the said two must needs jump a ditch—to show his activity I suppose; for he might as well, and better, have gone in the road. However, he got a sad fall; we saw him, and sent a boy to tell him, if he was hurt, to come up to the house, and we would endeavor to do something for him. He and his companion accordingly came up; he looked very pale, and bled much; his gun somehow in the fall, had given him a bad wound behind the ear, from whence the blood flowed down his neck and bosom plentifully. We were greatly alarmed on seeing him in this situation, and had gathered around him, some with one thing, some with another, in order to give him assistance. We were very busy examining the wound, when a negro girl ran in, exclaiming "O! The king's people are coming, it must be them, for they are all in red." Upon this cry, the two men that were with us snatched up their guns, mounted their horses, and made off; but had not got many yards from the house, before the enemy discharged a pistol at them. Terrified almost to death as I was, I was still anxious for my friends' safety. I tremblingly flew to the window, to see if the shot had proved fatal. When, seeing them both safe, "Thank heaven;" said I, "they've got off without hurt!" I'd hardly uttered this, when I heard the horses of the inhuman Britons coming in such a furious manner, that they seemed to tear up the earth, and the riders at the same time bellowing out the most horrid curses imaginable; oaths and imprecations, which chilled my whole frame. Surely, thought I, such horrid language denotes nothing less than death; but I'd no time for thought—they were up to the house—entered with drawn swords and pistols in their hands; indeed, they rushed in, in the most furious manner, crying out, "Where're these women rebels?" (Pretty language to ladies from the once famed Britons!) That was the first salutation! The moment they espied us, off went our caps . . . And for what, think you? Why, only to get a paltry stone and wax pin, which kept them on our heads; at the same time uttering the most abusive language imaginable, and making as if they'd hew us to pieces with their swords. But it's not in my power to describe the scene. It was terrible to the last degree; and, what augmented it, they had several armed negroes with them, who threatened and abused us greatly. They then began to plunder the house of every thing they thought valuable or worth taking; our trunks were split to pieces, and each mean, pitiful wretch crammed his bosom with the contents, which were our apparel, &c.

I ventured to speak to the inhuman monster who had my clothes. I represented to him the times were such we could not replace what they'd taken from us, and begged him to spare me only a suit or two; but I got nothing but a hearty curse for my pains; nay, so far was his callous heart from relenting, that, casting his eyes towards my shoes, "I want them buckles," said he, and immediately knelt at my feet to take them out, which, while he was busy about, a brother villain, whose enormous mouth extended from ear to ear, bawled out "Shares there, I say; shares." So they divided my buckles between them. The other wretches were employed in the same manner; they took my sister's earrings from her ears; hers, and Miss Samuells's buckles. They demanded her ring from her finger; she pleaded for it, told them it was her wedding ring, and begged they'd let her keep it; but they still demanded it, and, presenting a pistol at her, swore if she did not deliver it immediately, they'd fire. She gave it to them, and, after bundling up all their booty, they mounted their horses. But such despicable figures! Each wretch's bosom stuffed so full, they appeared to be all afflicted with some dropsical disorder; had a party of rebels (as they called us) appeared, we should soon have seen their circumference lessen.

They took care to tell us, when they were going away, that they had favored us a great deal—that we might thank our stars it was no worse. But I had forgot to tell you, that, upon their first entering the house, one of them gave my arm such a violent grasp, that he left the print of his thumb and three fingers, in black and blue, which was to be seen, very plainly, for several days after. I showed it to one of our officers, who dined with us, as a specimen of British cruelty. If they call this favor, what must their cruelties be? . . .

After a few words more, they rode off, and glad was I . . . After they were gone, I began to be sensible of the danger I'd been in, and the thoughts of the vile men seemed worse (if possible) than their presence; for they came so suddenly up to the house, that I'd no time for thought; and while they staid, I seemed in amaze! Quite stupid! I cannot describe it. But when they were gone, and I had time to consider, I trembled so with terror, that I could not support myself. I went into the room, threw myself on the bed, and gave way to a violent burst of grief, which seemed to be some relief to my full-swollen heart.

For an hour or two I indulged the most melancholy reflections. The whole world appeared to me as a theatre, where nothing was acted but cruelty, bloodshed, and oppression; where neither age nor sex escaped the horrors of injustice and violence; where the lives and property of the innocent and inoffensive were in continual danger, and lawless power ranged at large.

Document 3

Partisan War in the Carolina Backcountry (1779–81)

Many inhabitants of the Carolina backcountry were either hostile or indifferent to the revolutionary cause. Although some backcountry people became Whigs or Tories as a result of principled commitment, other chose sides on the basis of local rivalries and animosities. David Ramsay, a prominent South Carolina Whig, wrote the first history of the Revolution in his home state. Published in 1785, Ramsay's account of the war was based both on documentary research and the reminiscences of eyewitnesses. This passage describes in gory detail the bitter "civil war" between Whig and Tory partisans in western South Carolina.[3]

Questions to consider:

1. Was Ramsay's pro-Whig bias evident in his work? What was the main point he sought to convey to readers about the war in the backcountry?
2. To what factors did he attribute the unusual brutality of the war in western Carolina?
3. In Ramsay's opinion, to what extent was the local war between Whigs and Tories connected to and shaped by the larger struggle between Britain and its former colonies?

The distinction of Whig and Tory took its rise in the year 1775 . . . In the interval between . . . 1775, and the year 1780, the Whigs were occasionally plundered by parties who attempted insurrections in favour of the royal government. But all that was done prior to the surrender of Charleston was trifling when compared to what followed. After that event political hatred raged with uncommon fury, and the calamities of civil war desolated the state. The ties of nature were in several instances dissolved, and that reciprocal good-will and confidence, which hold mankind together in society, was in a great degree extinguished. Countrymen, neighbours, friends and brothers, took different sides, and ranged themselves under the opposing standards of the contending factions. In every little precinct, more especially in the interior parts of the state, King's-men and Congress-men were names of distinction. The passions on both sides were kept in perpetual agitation, and wrought up to a degree of fury which rendered individuals regardless, not only of the laws of war but of the principles of humanity. While the British had the ascendancy, their partizans gave full scope to their interested and malicious passions. People of the worst characters emerged from their hiding-places in the swamps—called themselves King's-men—and began to appropriate to their own use whatsoever came in their way. Every act of cruelty and injustice was sanctified, provided the actor called himself a friend to the King, and the sufferer was denominated a rebel. Of those who were well-disposed to the claims of America, there were few to be found who had not their houses and plantations repeatedly rifled. Under the sanction of subduing rebellion, private revenge was gratified. Many houses were burned, and many people inhumanly murdered. Numbers for a long time were obliged, either entirely to abandon their homes, or to sleep in the woods and swamps. Rapine, outrage and murder became so common, as to interrupt the free intercourse between one place and another. That security and protection, which individuals expect by entering into civil society, ceased almost totally. Matters remained in this situation for the greatest part of a year after the surrender of Charleston.

When General Greene returned to South Carolina, in the spring of 1781, every thing was reversed. In a few weeks he dispossessed the British of all their polls in the upper country, and the exasperated Whigs once more had the superiority. On their return to their homes, they generally found starving families and desolate plantations. To reimburse their losses and to gratify revenge, they, in their turn, begin to plunder and to murder. The country was laid waste, and private dwellings frequently stained with the blood of husbands and fathers inhumanly shed in the presence of their wives and children. . . .

In the close of the year 1781, when the successes of the American army had confined the [British] to the vicinity of Charleston, a desperate band of Tories adopted the infernal scheme of taking their last revenge, by carrying fire and sword into the settlements of the Whig militia. To this end Major William Cunningham, of the British militia, collected a party, and having furnished them with every thing necessary for laying waste the country, sallied from Charleston. He and his associates concealed themselves till they arrived in the back settlements, far in the rear of the American army, and there began to plunder, burn and murder. In the unsuspecting hour of sleep and domestic security, they entered the houses of the solitary farmers, and sacrificed to their revenge the obnoxious head of the family. Their cruelties induced some small parties to associate and arm in self-defence. Captain Turner and twenty men had, on these principles, taken post in a house, and defended themselves till their ammunition was nearly expended. After which they surrendered on receiving assurances that they would be treated as prisoners of war. Notwithstanding this solemn agreement, Captain Turner and his party were put to instant death by Cunningham and the men under his command.

Soon after this massacre the same party of Tories attacked a number of the American militia, in the district of Ninety-Six, commanded by Colonel Hayes, and set fire to the house in which they had taken shelter. The only alternative left was either to be burned, or to surrender themselves as prisoners. The last being preferred, Colonel Hayes and Captain Daniel Williams were hung at once on the pole of a fodder-stack. This breaking, both fell, on which Major William Cunningham cut them into pieces with his own sword, when, turning upon the others, he continued on them the operations of his savage barbarity, till the powers of nature being exhausted, and his enfeebled limbs refusing to administer any longer to his insatiate fury, he called upon his comrades to complete the dreadful work by killing whichsoever of the prisoners they pleased. They instantly put to death such of them as they personally disliked. Only two fell in action, but fourteen were deliberately cut to pieces after their surrender. . . .

About the same time, and under the same influence, emissaries from the British induced the Cherokee Indians to commence hostilities . . . When the co-operation of the Indians could be of the least service to the British forces, they were induced to break through their agreement of neutrality. They, with a number of disguised white men, who called themselves the King's friends, made an incursion into the district of Ninety-Six, massacred some families, and burned several houses. . . .

In consequence of these civil wars between the Whigs and the Tories— the incursions of the savages—and the other calamities resulting from the operations of the British and American armies, South Carolina exhibited scenes of distress which were shocking to humanity. The single district of Ninety-Six, which is only one of six districts into which the state of South-Carolina is divided, has been computed, by well-informed persons residing therein, to contain within its limits fourteen hundred widows and orphans, made so by the war.

DOCUMENT 4

Life and Death on the British Prison Ships (1780–81)

During the war, thousands of prisoners were housed in squalid prison ships docked in major ports. Although the Americans kept some prisoners-of-war on ships off the New England coast, this practice was more common among the British, who had sixteen prison ships in and around New York City. Some 11,000 men perished aboard the Jersey, the most notorious. The British also employed prison ships during the southern campaign. In Charleston, more than three-quarters of the ships' inmates died during their incarceration. Peter Fayssoux, a patriot physician who had visited the prison ships, described the conditions there to historian David Ramsay, who was also a medical doctor.[4]

Questions to consider:

1. Why were the British more likely than the Americans to house their prisoners aboard ships?
2. What were the chief hardships the prisoners encountered? How might their conditions have been improved? In Fayssoux's view, what circumstances hindered the improvement of conditions on the prison ships?

After the defeat of General Gates [at Camden in August 1780] our sufferings commenced. The British appeared to have adopted a different mode of conduct toward their prisoners, and proceeded from one step to another until they fully displayed themselves, void of faith, honor or humanity, and capable of the most savage acts of barbarity.

The unhappy men who belonged to the militia, were taken prisoners on Gates' defeat, experienced the first effects of the cruelty of their new system.

These men were confined on board of prison-ships, in numbers by no means proportioned to the size of the vessels, immediately after a march of one hundred and twenty miles, in the most sickly season of this unhealthy climate.

These vessels were in general infected with the small-pox; very few of the prisoners had gone through that disorder. A representation was made to the British commandant of their situation, and permission was obtained for one of our surgeons to inoculate them—this was the utmost extent of their humanity—the wretched objects were still confined on board of the prison-ships, and fed on salt provisions, without the least medical aid, or any proper kind of nourishment. The effect that naturally followed was a small-pox with a fever of the putrid type; and to such as survived the small-pox, a putrid dysentery—and, from these causes, the deaths of at least one hundred and fifty of the unhappy victims. Such were the appearances, and such was the termination of the generality of the cases brought to the general hospital after the eruption of the small-pox. Before the eruption, not a single individual was suffered to be brought on shore. If any thing can surpass the above relation in barbarity, it is the following account.

The Continental troops, by the articles of capitulation, were to be detained prisoners in some place contiguous to Charleston. The barracks were pitched on as the proper place; this was agreed to by both parties. The British, in violation of their solemn compact, put these people on board of prison-ships. Confined in large numbers on board of these vessels, and fed on salt provisions in this climate in the months of October and November, they naturally generated a putrid fever from the human miasma. This soon became highly contagious. The sick brought into the general hospital from the prison-ships generally died in the course of two or three days, with all the marks of a highly septic* state. Application was made to Mr. De Rosette, the British commissary of prisoners; the vast increase of the numbers of deaths was pointed out, and he was requested to have proper steps taken to check the progress of a disorder that threatened to destroy the whole of the prisoners.

In consequence of this application Mr. Fisher, our commissary of prisoners, and Mr. Fraser, who formerly practised physic in this country but then acted as a British deputy commissary, were ordered to inspect the state of the prisoners in the vessels. This report confirmed the truth of what had been advanced—this can be proved by a very particular circumstance. My hopes were very sanguine that something would be done for the relief of those unhappy persons, but they were entirely frustrated by a person from whom I did not and ought not to have expected it. Dr. John M'Namara Hays, physician to the British army, a person who had been taken by the Americans on the capture of Burgoyne, who had received the politest treatment from the Americans when a prisoner, and who had the generosity to acknowledge the usage he had met with—this person was ordered to report on the state of the prisoners. To my astonishment, I was informed his report was, that the prison-ships were not crowded, perfectly wholesome, and no appearance of infectious disorders amongst the prisoners. . . .

It was scarcely possible for men to support such an accumulated misery; but when least expected, a relief was administered to us. A subscription for the support of the sick was filled by people of every denomination with amazing rapidity. Several of the ladies of Charleston, laying aside the distinction of Whig and Tory, were instrumental and assiduous in procuring and preparing every necessary article of clothing and proper nourishment for our poor, worn-out and desponding soldiers.

A Common Soldier's Account of the Battle of Yorktown (1781)

In late September 1781, a combined French and American force converged on the Virginia community of Yorktown. By mid-October, the allies had trapped the army of Lord Charles Cornwallis on Yorktown's peninsula, forcing him to surrender in what would be the war's last major offensive. Ebenezer Denny of Pennsylvania was one of many troops who marched to coastal Virginia to prepare for this decisive battle. Denny had a keen eye for people and places. His diary includes a good description of Virginia's decayed colonial capital of Williamsburg, as well as his impressions of Washington, Steuben, and other army luminaries.[5]

Questions to consider:

1. How did Washington interact with his troops? How did the soldiers feel about him and other leading military men they encountered?
2. What sorts of jobs did soldiers do in order to prepare for a major engagement?
3. What was the soldiers' mood before and after the battle? Did Denny and his comrades realize that after Cornwallis surrendered, the war was effectively over?

Sept. 1st. Army encamped on the bank of the James river—part of French fleet, with troops on board, in view. Recrossed James river and encamped at Williamsburg. Army in high spirits—reinforcements coming on.

14th. General Washington arrived; our brigade was paraded to receive him; he rode along the line-quarters in Williamsburg.

15th. Officers all pay their respects to the Commander-in-chief; go in a body; those who are not personally known, their names given by General Hand and General Wayne. He stands in the door, takes every man by the hand—the officers all pass in, receiving his salute and shake. This the first time I had seen the General. We have an elegant encampment close to town, behind William and Mary College. This building occupied as an hospital. Williamsburg a very handsome place, not so populous as Richmond, but situate on evenly, pretty ground; streets and lots spacious—does not appear to be a place of much business, rather the residence of gentlemen of fortune; formerly it was the seat of government and Dunmore's late residence. A neat public building, called the capitol, fronts the principal street; upon the first floor is a handsome marble statue of William Pitt.

The presence of so many general officers, and the arrival of new corps, seem to give additional life to everything; discipline the order of the day. In all directions troops seen exercising and maneuvering. Baron Steuben, our great military oracle. The guards attend the grand parade at an early hour, where the Baron is always found waiting with one or two aids on horseback. These men are exercised and put through various evolutions and military experiments for two hours—many officers and spectators present; excellent school, this. At length the duty of the parade comes on. The guards are told off; officers take their posts, wheel by platoons to the right; fine corps of music detailed for this duty, which strikes up; the whole march off, saluting the Baron and field officer of the day, as they pass. Pennsylvania brigade almost all old soldiers, and well disciplined when compared with those of Maryland and Virginia. But the troops from the eastward far superior to either. . . .

28th. The whole army moved in three divisions toward the enemy, who were strongly posted at York [town], about twelve miles distant. Their pickets and light troops retire. We encamped about three miles off—change ground and take a position within one mile of York. . . .

At length, everything in readiness, a division of the army broke ground on the night of the 6th of October, and opened the first parallel about six hundred yards from the works of the enemy. Every exertion to annoy our men, who were necessarily obliged to be exposed about the works; however, the business went on, and on the 9th our cannon and mortars began to play. The scene viewed from the camp now was grand, particularly after dark—a number of shells from the works of both parties passing high in the air, and descending in a curve, each with a long train of fire, exhibited a brilliant spectacle. Troops in three divisions manned the lines alternately. We were two nights in camp and one in the lines; relieved about ten o'clock. Passed and repassed by a covert way leading to the parallel.

Oct. 11th. Second parallel thrown up within three hundred yards of the main works of the enemy; new batteries erected, and additional number of cannon brought forward some twenty-four pounders and heavy mortars and howitzers. A tremendous fire now opened from all the new works,

French and American. The heavy cannon directed against the embrasures and guns of the enemy. Their pieces were soon silenced, broke and dismantled. Shells from behind their works still kept up. Two redoubts advanced of their lines, and within rifle shot of our second parallel, much in the way. These forts or redoubts were well secured by a ditch and picket, sufficiently high parapet, and within were divisions made by rows of casks ranged upon end and filled with earth and sand. On tops of parapet were ranged bags filled with sand—a deep narrow ditch communicating with their main lines. On the night of the 14th, shortly after dark, these redoubts were taken by storm; the one on our right, by the Marquis [de Lafayette], with part of his light infantry—the other, more to our left, but partly opposite the centre of the British lines, by the French. Our batteries had kept a constant fire upon the redoubts through the day. Belonged this evening to a command detailed for the purpose of supporting the Marquis. The night was dark and favorable. Our batteries had ceased—there appeared to be a dead calm; we followed the infantry and halted about half way—kept a few minutes in suspense, when we were ordered to advance. The business was over, not a gun was fired by the assailants; the bayonet only was used; ten or twelve of the infantry were killed. French had to contend with a post of more force—their loss was considerable. Colonel Hamilton led the Marquis' advance; the British sentries hailed them—no answer made. They also hailed the French, "Who comes there?" were answered, "French grenadiers." Colonel Walter Stewart commanded the regiment of reserve which accompanied the Marquis; they were immediately employed in connecting, by a ditch and parapet, the two redoubts, and completing and connecting the same with our second parallel. The British were soon alarmed; some from each of the redoubts made their escape. The whole enemy were under arms—much firing round all their lines, but particularly toward our regiment, where the men were at work; the shot passed over. In about three quarters of an hour we were under cover. Easy digging; light sandy ground.

15th. Heavy fire from our batteries all day. A shell from one of the French mortars set fire to a British frigate; she burnt to the water's edge, and blew up—made the earth shake. Shot and shell raked the town in every direction. Bomb-proofs the only place of safety.

16th. Just before day the enemy made a sortie, spiked the guns in two batteries and retired. Our troops in the parallel scarcely knew of their approach until they were off; the thing was done silently and in an instant. The batteries stood in advance of the lines, and none within but artillery. This day, the 16th, our division manned the lines—firing continued without intermission. Pretty strong detachments posted in each battery over night.

17th. In the morning, before relief came, had the pleasure of seeing a drummer mount the enemy's parapet, and beat a parley, and immediately an officer, holding up a white handkerchief, made his appearance outside their works; the drummer accompanied him, beating. Our batteries ceased. An officer from our lines ran and met the other, and tied the handkerchief over his eyes. The drummer sent back, and the British officer conducted to a house in rear of our lines. Firing ceased totally.

18th. Several flags pass and repass now even without the drum. Had we not seen the drummer in his red coat when he first mounted, he might have beat away till doomsday. The constant firing was too much for the sound of a single drum; but when the firing ceased, I thought I never heard a drum equal to it—the most delightful music to us all.

19th. Our division man the lines again. All is quiet. Articles of capitulation signed; detachments of French and Americans take possession of British forts. Major Hamilton commanded a battalion which took possession of a fort immediately opposite our right and on the bank of York river. I carried the standard of our regiment on this occasion. On entering the fort, Baron Steuben, who accompanied us, took the standard from me and planted it himself. The British army parade and march out with their colors furled; drums beat as if they did not care how. Grounded their arms and returned to town. Much confusion and riot among the British through the day; many of the soldiers were intoxicated; several attempts in course of the night to break open stores; an American sentinel killed by a British soldier with a bayonet; our patrols kept busy. Glad to be relieved from this disagreeable station. Negroes lie about, sick and dying, in every stage of the small pox. Never was in so filthy a place—some handsome houses, but prodigiously shattered. Vast heaps of shot and shells lying about in every quarter, which came from our works. The shells did not burst, as was expected. Returns of British soldiers, prisoners six thousand, and seamen about one thousand. Lord Cornwallis excused himself from marching out with the troops; they were conducted by General O'Hara. Our loss said to be about three hundred; that of the enemy said not more than five hundred and fifty. Fine supply of stores and merchandise had; articles suitable for clothing were taken for the use of the army. A portion furnished each officer to the amount of sixty dollars.

DOCUMENT 6

Petition of the Whig Women of Wilmington, North Carolina (1782)

As British forces planned to depart in the wake of Cornwallis's surrender, American loyalists were forced to choose between perpetual exile and prosecution at the hands of the victorious Whigs. The Whig women of Wilmington had to leave their homes when the British occupied their town in February 1781. A year later, twenty-one women from the town's leading Whig families sought to spare their Tory counterparts a similar fate, petitioning the governor of North Carolina on their behalf.[6] Neither the governor nor the assembly acted on the women's petition.

Questions to consider:

1. What did the petitioners believe should become of the Tories after the war was over?
2. Did the fact that the petitioners were women strengthen or undermine the legitimacy of their petition?

We, the subscribers, inhabitants of the town of Wilmington, warmly attached to the state of North Carolina, and strenuously devoted to our best wishes and endeavours to the achievement of its independence, feeling for the honor of, and desirous that our enemies should not have the smallest pretext to brand them as cruel or precipitate, that the dignity of our public characters may not be degraded to the imitation of examples of inhumanity exhibited by our enemies.

Humbly shew to His Excellency, the Governor, and the Honorable the Council, that we have been informed that orders have issued from your honorable board that the wives and children of [Tory] absentees should depart the state with a small part of their property in forty eight hours after notice given them.

It is not the province of our sex to reason deeply upon the policy of the order, but as it must affect the helpless and innocent, it wounds us with the most sincere distress and prompts our earnest supplication that the order may be arrested, and the officers forbid to carry it into execution. If it is intended as retaliation for the expulsion of some of us, the subscribers, by the British from the town of Wilmington, and to gratify a resentment which such inhumanity to us may be supposed to have excited, its object is greatly mistaken.

Those whom your proclamation holds forth as marks of public vengeance neither prompted the British order nor aided the execution of it. On the contrary, they expressed the greatest indignation at it, and with all their power strove to mitigate our sufferings. Still some instances attended which made the execution of it less distressing to us than yours must be to those upon whom it is intended to operate. We were ordered without the British lines and then our friends were ready to receive us. They received us with a cordial welcome, and ministered to our wants with generosity and politeness. With pleasure we bear this public testimony. But our town women now ordered out must be exposed to the extreme of human wretchedness. Their friends are in [Charleston]; they have neither carriages nor horses to remove them by land, nor vessels to transport them by water, and the small pittance allotted them of their property, could they be procured, would be scarce equal to the purchase of them. It is beneath the character of the independent state of North Carolina to war with women and children. The authors of our ill treatment are the proper subjects of our own and the resentment of the public. Does their barbarity strike us with abhorrence? Let us blush to imitate it; not justify by our own practice what we so justly condemn in others. . . .

If we may be allowed to claim any merit with the public for our steady adherence to the Whig principles of America; if our sufferings induced by that attachment have given us favor and esteem with your honorable body, we beg leave to assure you that we shall hold it as a very signal mark of your respect for us if you will condescend to suffer to remain amongst us our old friends and acquaintances whose husbands, though estranged from us in political opinions, have left wives and children much endeared to us, and who may live to be an honor to the state and to society if permitted to continue here. The safety of this state, we trust in God, is now secured beyond the most powerful exertions of our enemies, and it would be a system of abject weakness to fear the feeble efforts of women and children.

Document 7

The British Evacuate Charleston (1782)

In 1776, General William Moultrie led the successful defense of the fort guarding Charleston harbor. Four years later, when the British captured Charleston, he was taken prisoner, along with its other defenders. Like most officers, Moultrie was spared the horrors of the prison ships, but he remained a prison of war until 1782, when he witnessed the British evacuation of Charleston, which he recounted in his memoirs.[7]

Questions to consider:

1. What was the purpose of the carefully orchestrated maneuvers of General Leslie's British forces and their American counterparts, which were under the command of Generals Wayne and Lee?

2. Who participated in the celebratory procession? Who watched the procession? What message did it seek to convey?
3. To whom was Moultrie referring when he wrote of "citizens" and "soldiers?"

On Saturday, the fourteenth day of December, 1782, the British troops evacuated Charlestown, after having possession two years, seven months, and two days.

The evacuation took place in the following manner: Brigadier General Wayne was ordered to cross Ashley-river, with three hundred light-infantry, eighty of Lee's cavalry, and twenty artillery, with two six-pounders, to move down towards the British lines . . . General Leslie, who commanded in town, sent a message to General Wayne, informing him, that he would next day leave the town, and for the peace and security of the inhabitants, and of the town, would propose to leave their advanced works next day at the firing of the morning gun; at which time, General Wayne should move on slowly, and take possession; and from thence to follow the British troops into town, keeping at a respectful distance (say about two hundred yards;) and when the British troops after passing through the town gates, should file off to Gadsden's wharf, General Wayne was to proceed into town, which was done with great order and regularity, except now and then the British called to General Wayne that he was too fast upon them, which occasioned him to halt a little. About 11 o'clock, a.m. the American troops marched into town and took post at the state house.

At 3 o'clock, p.m. General Greene conducted Governor Mathews, and the council, with some other of the citizens into town. We marched in, in the following order: an advance of an officer and thirty of Lee's dragoons; then followed the governor and General Greene; the next two were General Gist and myself; after us followed the council, citizens and officers, making altogether about fifty. One hundred and eighty cavalry brought up the rear. We halted in Broad-street . . . there we alighted, and the cavalry discharged to quarters. Afterwards, everyone went where they pleased; some in viewing the town, others in visiting their friends. It was a grand and pleasing sight, to see the enemy's fleet (upwards of three hundred sail) . . . ready to depart from the port. The great joy that was felt on this day, by the citizens and soldiers, was inexpressible: the widows, the orphans, the aged men and others, who, from their particular situations, were obliged to remain in Charlestown, many of whom had been cooped up in one room of their own elegant houses for upwards of two years, whilst the other parts were occupied by the British officers, many of whom where a rude uncivil set of gentlemen; their situations, and the many mortifying circumstances occurred to them in that time, must have been truly distressing. I cannot forget that happy day when we marched into Charlestown with the American troops; it was a proud day to me, and I felt myself much elated, at seeing the balconies, the doors, and windows crowded with the patriotic fair, the aged citizens and others, congratulating us on our return home, saying, 'God bless you, gentlemen! You are welcome home, gentlemen!' Both citizens and soldiers shed mutual tears of joy.

It was an ample reward for the triumphant soldier, after all the hazards and fatigues of war, which he had gone through, to be the instrument of releasing his friends and fellow citizens from captivity, and restoring to them their liberties and possession of their city and country again.

America Triumphant and Britannia in Distress, 1782.   Published in Boston, this print celebrated America's triumph over Great Britain. The image featured "America . . . holding in one hand the olive branch, inviting the ships of all nations to partake in her commerce, and in the other hand supporting the Cap of Liberty" and Britannia "weeping at the loss of the trade of America, attended with an evil genius." Directly below the American flag, Benedict Arnold is shown hanging himself in remorse for betraying his country. Why do you think the artist used female figures to represent both America and Britain? Why was America personified by Minerva, the Roman goddess of handicrafts and the arts? Source: Etching on laid paper; 18 × 20.5 cm (sheet, trimmed irregularly). The Library of Congress, Washington, D.C.

SUGGESTED READING FOR CHAPTER 7

CALLOWAY, COLIN G. *The American Revolution in Indian Country: Crisis and Diversity in Native American Communities* (1995).

DANN, JOHN C., ed. *The Revolution Remembered: Eyewitness Accounts of the War for Independence* (1980).

DULL, JONATHAN R. *The French Navy and American Independence: A Study of Arms and Diplomacy, 1774–1787* (1975).

FREY, SYLVIA R. *Water From the Rock: Black Resistance in a Revolutionary Age* (1991).

HIGGINBOTHAM, DON. *Daniel Morgan, Revolutionary Rifleman* (1961).

HOFFMAN, RONALD; TATE, THAD W.; and ALBERT, PETER J., eds., *An Uncivil War: The Southern Backcountry during the American Revolution* (1985).

KIERNER, CYNTHIA A. *Southern Women in Revolution, 1776–1800: Personal and Political Narratives* (1998).

LEE, JEAN B. *The Price of Nationhood: The American Revolution in Charles County* (1994).

NADELHAFT, JEROME J. *The Disorders of War: The Revolution in South Carolina* (1981).

O'DONNELL, JAMES H. *Southern Indians and the American Revolution* (1973).

RANKIN, HUGH F. *The North Carolina Continentals* (1971).

SELBY, JOHN E. *The Revolution in Virginia, 1763–1783* (1988).

SMITH, PAUL H. *Loyalists and Redcoats: A Study in British Revolutionary Policy* (1964).

SOSIN, JACK M. *The Revolutionary Frontier, 1763–1783* (1967).

STOURZH, GERALD. *Benjamin Franklin and American Foreign Policy* (1954).

NOTES

[1]"Capture of Mordecai Sheftall," in George White, ed., *Historical Collection of Georgia* (New York, 1854), 340–42.

[2]Caroline Gilman, ed., *Letters of Eliza Wilkinson* (New York, 1839), 24, 27–31, 60–61.

[3]David Ramsay, *The History of the Revolution of South Carolina*, 2 vols. (Trenton, N.J., 1785), 2: 269–75.

[4]Peter Fayssoux to David Ramsay, 26 Mar. 1785, in R. W. Gibbes, ed., *Documentary History of the American Revolution*, 3 vols. (New York and Columbia, S.C., 1853–57), 3: 117–21.

[5]Ebenezer Denny, *Military Journal of Major Ebenezer Denny* (Philadelphia, 1859), 38–45.

[6]Petition of Anne Hooper, et al., 1782, in W. L. Saunders, et al., eds., *The Colonial and State Records of North Carolina*, 30 vols. (Raleigh, Winston, Goldsboro, and Charlotte, 1886–1914), 16: 467–49.

[7]William Moultrie, *Memoirs of the American Revolution*, 2 vols. (New York, 1802), 2: 358–60.

CHAPTER EIGHT

WHO SHOULD RULE
AT HOME

From the imperial crisis through the 1790s, Americans debated two great and transcendent questions. The first, the question of independence, was resolved by military victory over Britain. The second question was more difficult to answer: what was the meaning of independence? How would it affect American politics and society? Were all men, indeed, created equal? American patriots debated these issues initially at the state level after 1776, particularly as they drafted their first constitutions. If conflict on the battlefield decided the question of home rule, battles in state politics, in the famous words of one historian, addressed the question of "who should rule at home."[*]

In the decades following 1776, Americans redefined political society. They created republican governments in which citizens, through their representatives, were sovereign. They made political life more inclusive by easing the economic, religious, and geographical impediments to political participation that had applied during the colonial era. Some reconsidered the status of women, while others questioned the propriety of slavery in a republic purportedly based on liberty and natural rights. Revolutionary ideals and rhetoric, which impelled the colonists ultimately to reject the customary authority of king and empire, led some Americans to question other inherited traditions. Like the struggle for home rule, the reallocation of authority "at home" was contested at

197

every turn. And while the War of Independence ended in triumph, the outcome of America's internal revolution was less decisive.

As Americans inched toward independence in 1776, they began to construct political institutions to supplant the disintegrating imperial regime. Throughout the colonies, Whigs established extralegal conventions and committees, which functioned increasingly as de facto governments. Political leaders in Massachusetts, New Hampshire, South Carolina, and Rhode Island began writing constitutions that formally defined a new political order. Constitution-making became pervasive after May 1776, when the Continental Congress instructed the colonies to establish governments to supplant crumbling imperial institutions. Virginia, New Jersey, Delaware, Pennsylvania, Connecticut, Maryland, and North Carolina had drafted new constitutions by the end of 1776. Georgia and New York did so in 1777.

The Declaration of Independence destroyed the imperial regime without establishing—or even suggesting—alternative political arrangements for the independent states. In 1776, the Continental Congress began drafting articles of confederation to create a loose union of states to wage war and conduct diplomacy, but the pressures of war and disagreement among the states delayed their ratification until 1781. As a result, the most important political and constitutional work of the revolutionary years occurred at the state level.

The constitutional crisis that led to the break-up of Britain's American empire profoundly influenced the political choices that American leaders made immediately after independence. Colonists had trusted the British constitution to safeguard their rights and liberties only to have imperial authorities claim that they misunderstood their constitutional status within the empire. Once they declared their independence, Americans therefore insisted on writing constitutions to delineate the powers of government and the rights of citizens. Having recently suffered tyranny at the hands of a distant central government, they overwhelmingly favored a more decentralized political system in which their states were sovereign. Having ultimately identified the king himself as the source of their worst problems, Americans also universally agreed that they would have no monarch. Their new governments would be wholly republican, meaning that the representatives of the people in each state would be sovereign.

But who were "the people" and how could political institutions best express their sovereignty? When Americans went beyond the fundamentals of republicanism and state sovereignty, they disagreed on many issues, most of which revolved around the central question of how much citizens should control government and its policies. Simply put, Americans disagreed about just how democratic their republics ought to be. Some Whigs believed that the Revolution should achieve American independence, or home rule, but change little else. The hierarchical, deferential politics and society of the colonial period, these conservatives maintained, were perfectly acceptable once divorced from their oppressive imperial context. Other supporters of the American Revolution, however, believed that independence and republicanism should bring wide-ranging changes to American politics and society. In particular, these radicals Whigs wanted more people—or at least more white men— from different social backgrounds to participate in the decision-making aspects of political life.

Although the specific agenda of conservative Whigs varied from state to state, conservatives everywhere attempted to limit popular participation in government. Above all, they wished to retain the property qualifications for voting and officeholding that had been in force during the colonial period. While most conceded that economic self-sufficiency qualified a man to vote, conservatives—most of whom had belonged to the colonial elite—insisted that the wealthy and well-born were best equipped to exercise real political power. Accordingly, they tried to limit the number of elective offices, hoping that having fewer offices would increase likelihood that they would be filled disproportionately by members of the gentry elite. In most states, conservatives also supported the continued overrepresentation of gentry-dominated eastern counties at the expense of newer western settlements. Finally, conservative Whigs believed that giving the governor, judiciary, and upper legislative house substantial powers might effectively dilute the more popular or democratic influence of the lower house. The conservatives' greatest fear was anarchy, which they regarded as the inevitable consequence of excessive democracy.

Radical Whigs, by contrast, wanted to make political institutions representative of a broader cross section of the white male population. To that end, they pushed to decrease or even eliminate property qualifications for voting and officeholding. They also supported the reapportionment of legislative seats to give adequate representation to newer settlements, which were typically in the west. Radicals sought to increase the number of elective offices to bring more men into the decision-making process. For example, they promoted the enlargement of the assemblies to lower the ratio between the legislators and their constituents. Because they wanted government to be more democratic, radicals also advocated expanding the powers of the assembly relative to those of the governor, the judiciary, and the upper house.

Radical Whigs scored their biggest victory in Pennsylvania, where the elite was divided in 1776, affording radicals from Philadelphia and the western counties a unique opportunity to draft their ideal constitution. Pennsylvania's constitution-makers adopted unusually liberal criteria for political participation: all taxpaying freemen over the age of twenty-one could vote and hold any political office in the Commonwealth. They also reallocated political representation to reflect the growing population of the state's western settlements. Finally, and most strikingly, Pennsylvania's radicals prevented the dilution of the democratic power of the assembly by eliminating both the governor and the upper house. The state's unicameral legislature, moreover, was accountable to the voters in annual elections, and every seven years a Council of Censors reevaluated—and, if necessary, revised—the entire constitution.

By contrast, Maryland's first constitution was the work of wealthy planter elites who sought to preserve many aristocratic features of the old colonial government. Under its 1776 constitution, Maryland's governor, upper house, and judiciary retained substantial powers to counterbalance those of the state assembly, which was the only directly elected portion of the government. Maryland's constitution-makers did not reapportion legislative seats to equalize representation between the eastern plantation districts and the newer western counties. Although they eased the property requirements for voting, they adopted highly restrictive qualifications for holding political office. A man had to own £5,000 worth of property—at least £1,000 of which had to be in land—in order to be governor; an estate worth £1,000 was required for election to the senate or upper house. Only 7 percent of Maryland's white males could meet the property qualifications to serve as senators; only 11 percent had enough property to be eligible to sit in the lower house.

Most states adopted constitutions that were neither as inclusive as Pennsylvania's nor as restrictive as Maryland's, in part because political leaders recognized the need for compromise to generate wide support for the revolutionary governments. As a result, most decreased but did not eliminate property qualifications for voting and officeholding. State legislatures were typically larger than their colonial predecessors and included some seats—though usually not enough—for areas that previously lacked political representation. Most states increased the powers of the assembly, while diminishing but not eliminating those of the governor, judiciary, and upper house. Although they retained some significant checks on popular involvement, these state constitutions created political institutions that were more democratic than their colonial counterparts.

In most states, revolutionary leaders also reassessed the relationship between Church and State, either as part of the constitution-making process or in separate legislation. Religious establishments survived the Revolution only in Massachusetts and Connecticut, where the overwhelming majority of inhabitants belonged to the tax-supported Congregational Church. In states where the Church of England enjoyed a privileged status during the colonial period, Whig leaders dismantled the religious establishment. All of the states protected liberty of conscience—meaning that political authorities would not persecute citizens for their religious beliefs—though most retained some religious qualification for holding political office. Almost every state required officeholders to be Christians, and many further stipulated that they must be Protestants. Only Virginia explicitly separated Church and State. Adopted in 1786, the Virginia Statute for Religious Freedom guaranteed liberty of conscience, prohibited all religious tests, and made religion a private matter in which government had no role or influence.

The cumulative effect of all these changes in political rules and rhetoric was to democratize political life. More men were voting, and voters were playing a more active role in politics after the elections were over. Revolutionary Americans embraced the notion of actual representation, the idea that an individual legislator spoke for the particular interests of those who elected him and not those of the larger polity. In keeping with that view, they routinely issued detailed instructions to their representatives, whom they held accountable for what they did or did not accomplish in their respective state assemblies. The expansion of the assemblies and of state governments generally also enabled more men to hold political office at the state level. New York's moderately democratic state constitution, for example, increased the membership of the assembly from thirty-one to sixty-five and created a new popularly elected twenty-four–seat upper house. Voters in New York often chose men like themselves to fill these new political offices. The result was that of the 290 men who sat in the state assembly between 1777 and 1789, only six had served in the colonial legislature; only six of fifty-five state senators had been legislators during the colonial era.

Those who believed they lacked representation in their state government could nonetheless exercise their right to petition, as they had done during the colonial era. Petitioning presupposed an unequal relationship between those who sought favor and the officials who determined the fate of their requests—an inequality that was evident, for instance, in petitions colonists addressed to the king and his governors before 1776. The ancient practice of petitioning survived the profound changes of the revolutionary era, though petitioners' rhetoric adapted to changing political values. When disenfranchised religious minorities petitioned for political rights or westerners sought legislative representation, they were polite but assertive, reflecting revolutionary changes in the way Americans conceived the relationship between citizens and political authority.

But who counted as citizens in revolutionary America? The republican ideal of citizenship was based on a duality of rights and obligations: voting, serving on juries, and bearing arms in the militia were both prerogatives of citizens and obligations they fulfilled for the good of the polity. Most Americans considered personal independence, typically derived from property ownership, a prerequisite for exercising the rights and obligations of republican citizenship. That rationale, which was rooted in centuries of English and colonial constitutional thought and custom, justified the retention of property qualifications for political participation in revolutionary America.

Coupled with longstanding Anglo-American assumptions about race and gender, that rationale also prevented African Americans and white women from attaining full membership in political society during and after the Revolution. Although slaves, free blacks, and white women were active participants in the revolutionary movement and the War of Independence, most Americans regarded their involvement in public life as a temporary aberration. White women and African Americans could petition their governors—as, indeed, they could during the colonial period—and the fact that they increasingly did so was indicative of enhanced political consciousness. Nevertheless, both remained on the margins of political society and, with the significant exception of the abolition of slavery in the northern states, the Revolution brought them no new civil or political rights.

White women had been prominent participants in the prerevolutionary boycotts and home manufacturing efforts, and they had contributed heroically to the war effort, both with the army and at home. Hundreds of women traveled with the army as nurses, cooks, and laundresses. Others served as spies or couriers, and a few dressed as men and enlisted in the army. On the home front, women ran their families' farms and businesses while their husbands served in the army or in government. Women in Philadelphia raised money to aid the Continental troops. Others, like playwright and historian Mercy Otis Warren and poet Phillis Wheatley, used their pens to promote the cause of American liberty.

Some educated and articulate women called for a degree of political inclusion or empowerment for their sex during and after the Revolution. The political changes that resulted from independence had not lessened the legal disabilities of married women under the common law of coverture. Wives still could not control property, sign contracts, file suits in court, or control their own earnings. Abigail Adams privately admonished her congressman husband to reconsider married women's legal status. Judith Sargent Murray made the case against coverture in a series of published essays. Such appeals for general reform were unsuccessful, however, until the middle of the nineteenth century.

Although there is no evidence that American women of the revolutionary generation demanded the right to vote, events in New Jersey suggest that many would have exercised that right, given the opportunity. In 1776, New Jersey's constitution-makers defined the state's electorate as "all free inhabitants" who met the property and residence qualifications for voting. Married women were not free persons under the terms of coverture, but widows and single women who possessed property worth £50 or more could and did vote in local elections from 1776 until 1807, when their votes appeared to decide a particularly close contest. That year, the state legislature disenfranchised all women on the grounds that they supposedly lacked the knowledge and independence to vote responsibility. In reality, women's disenfranchisement was the result of men's partisan vengeance and their fears of women's real and potential political power.

White women's gains as a result of the Revolution were informal and limited. Americans' belief that the survival of republican government depended on the virtue of its citizens led to an increased emphasis on education and a new appreciation for the potential influence of mothers on future generations. Moralists and social critics called on women to promote virtue and public spirit within their families, and they urged improvements in women's education to that end. Although other factors, such as the rise of gentility, had resulted in better education for elite females by the end of the colonial period, revolutionary republicanism accelerated this trend and spread educational improvements to the middling strata of society. Republican ideals of womanhood endowed the roles of mother and wife with new political or public significance, even as they sought to circumscribe women's influence and activities within the household.

While the status of women elicited only limited public debate and few significant changes in law or public policy, revolutionary Americans paid considerable attention to the legal status of slavery and African Americans. Even before 1776, African Americans had begun pressing Whig leaders to extend the natural rights of liberty and equality to enslaved people and free blacks, and they continued to assert their claims to freedom in the coming years. While some white patriots conceded the incompatibility of liberty and chattel slavery, others tried their best to ignore the contradiction. For his part, Thomas Jefferson contended that the British Crown had imposed slavery on the colonists—a wishful fantasy that the Congress wisely deleted from his original draft of the Declaration of Independence.

African Americans participated militarily in the War of Independence on both sides. A few blacks served in the Massachusetts militia at Concord and Bunker Hill. In November 1775, however, under pressure from southern delegates, Congress voted to bar all African Americans, whether slave or free, from serving in the Continental Army. That policy changed in the wake of Lord Dunmore's successful recruitment of Virginia slaves to serve with the king's forces. By 1778, all the states except South Carolina and Georgia—whose black populations were proportionately largest—allowed at least some African Americans to serve in the military. In the end, some 5,000 of the soldiers and sailors who fought for the patriots were African Americans, free and slave, drawn disproportionately from the northern states. Thousands of southern blacks also participated in the war, though most of those who did were escaped slaves who fought for the British, who were more likely to offer them freedom.

During and after the war, Africans Americans and antislavery whites pressured state governments to abolish the institution of slavery. As a result of their efforts, all of the northern states had addressed the issue by 1804, but the ambivalence with which they did so spoke volumes about the racial attitudes and priorities of white Americans. In 1777, Vermont claimed its independence from New York and adopted a state constitution that explicitly banned slavery. In 1783, the Supreme Court of Massachusetts declared slavery unconstitutional, thereby effectively ending it throughout the state. The other northern states preferred the option of gradual emancipation by statute, which enabled them to delay what many regarded as a controversial violation of the property rights of white citizens. In 1780, Pennsylvania passed the first statute that provided for the gradual abolition of slavery. Rhode Island, Connecticut, New York, and New Jersey adopted versions of gradual emancipation in the coming decades. None of these laws required the emancipation of those currently held in bondage, providing only for the manumission of future generations.

Not surprisingly, opposition to slavery was less successful farther south, where the black population was larger and where whites benefited more substantially from the employment of bonded labor. In Delaware, Maryland, Virginia, and North Carolina, state legislatures passed laws that made it easier for individual masters to free their slaves. Hundreds did so, especially in areas where wheat was supplanting the more labor intensive tobacco as the staple crop. The free black population of the Chesapeake states grew significantly during this period as a result of these manumissions, increasing sixfold in Virginia alone between 1782 and 1790. The growing numbers and increased visibility of free blacks, in turn, resulted in a white backlash against manumissions in Virginia and elsewhere. South Carolina and Georgia planters, by contrast, consistently and firmly opposed manumission. When the war ended, these two states imported more than 250,000 slaves from Africa, both to replace those who had escaped during the war and to exploit the profitability of a new cash crop following the invention of the cotton gin in 1793. The cotton boom perpetuated slavery and expanded it ever further westward in the coming decades.

North and south, moreover, free blacks did not possess rights and opportunities comparable to those enjoyed by whites. Some southern states forced free blacks to leave, others required that they pay extra taxes, and free blacks in the slave states risked the possibility of being forced back into slavery. In the northern states, free blacks typically were barred from public schools and relegated to the lowest-paying jobs. Most states eventually prohibited or discouraged them from voting. In New Jersey, for instance, the same law that disenfranchised widows and single women in 1807 also took the vote away from free African Americans, even if they met the property and residency qualifications. Excluded from white celebrations of America's Independence Day, free blacks would instead commemorate the Haitian Revolution of 1793, which resulted in the creation of a black republic by former slaves.

American revolutionaries invoked the heady but imprecise concepts of liberty and equality when they declared their independence from Great Britain. They were then forced to define their terms more carefully as they constructed their new political order. In revolutionary America, the initial debates on the nature and limits of political society occurred in the states. Revolutionaries created new institutions that sought to express the will of the people through their representatives. In the process, they empowered many Americans, rendered some marginal, and excluded others entirely.

DOCUMENT 1

"A Dialogue between Orator Puff and Peter Easy" (1776)

One of the most hotly debated issues among those who drafted the first state constitutions was whether to lessen or even abolish property requirements for voting and office-holding. Pennsylvania's first constitution stipulated that a man could vote if he was twenty-one, had lived in his locality for one year, and had paid taxes. As this fictional dialog from a Philadelphia newspaper shows, some Pennsylvanians feared the prospect of such an extremely liberal suffrage.[1]

Questions to consider:

1. What was the significance of the names of these fictional characters?
2. Which character—Orator Puff or Peter Easy—advocated the more inclusive suffrage? What did each character consider the essential prerequisites for voting?

3. Why did these characters see voting as "a grand right" and reform of the suffrage as "a great step?"

Orator: Now all men will be put on a level with respect to this grand right of voting at elections, and that may in time bring them to a level in every other respect, as has happened in other countries.

Peter: This is a great step, neighbour Puff, and may have very extraordinary consequences. Thou must be convinced, I believe, that a large majority of Pennsylvania, at present, consists of free-holders, and honest, industrious, frugal people, who are worth at least fifty pounds each.

Orator: I am convinced of that truth; but what would you argue from that?

Peter: Why, I cannot perceive the propriety or prudence of putting these inhabitants upon a level with the indolent or prodigal, who have not acquired such a small sum as fifty pounds, in a country where the acquiring of such a sum is not difficult, especially for a single man. If the privilege [of voting] extended only to those who had families, here there would not be so much in it; or if there was any other "sufficient evidence" of their attachment to the state required. Besides, it appears clearly to be an injury to all the inhabitants of the state, who are worth fifty pounds in real or personal estate. For the right of electing is vested in them, by the laws of Pennsylvania, and in them alone, and therefore the extending the same right to all men without distinction . . . takes away so much of their right, from those who are worth fifty pounds, and proportionately lessens their influence in elections, and therefore in the state. What necessity is there for this general alteration? Can't the liberties and happiness of Pennsylvania be trusted to those men in it, who are worth fifty pounds each? And should we go to wreck and ruin, unless we are saved by those who are not worth that sum? . . . Such people, having nothing to lose, and a prospect of gaining by public convulsions, are always the most ready to engage in seditions, tumultuous and factious proceedings. They are the people to whom artful, delighting, selfish, ambitious, daring, wicked men apply themselves, and make use of to promote their pernicious projects. They are generally the most illiterate and ignorant of the whole of society, and therefore, the most easily imposed on by such men as I have described. . . On the other hand, while the rights of election, that is of sovereignty, as I said, are lodged in those who possess the general property, landed and personal within this state, it will ever be in their interest to keep things quiet, and to have officers go on with regularity; and if the other class grows turbulent, the whole force and dignity of the government can be exerted to keep them in order.

DOCUMENT 2

A Vindication of the . . . Inhabitants of Vermont (1779)

Ethan Allen

Beginning in 1747, the governor of New Hampshire issued titles for land in what he believed was the western part of his colony. In 1763, however, the government of New York, supported by the imperial administration in London, established that the land in fact fell within the boundaries of New York and thus belonged to the absentee landlords who had received their titles from its governor. Led by Ethan Allen, the Green Mountain Boys defended their claims militarily against the New Yorkers. In 1777, after fighting at Ticonderoga and Saratoga, they declared the land in question the separate state of Vermont and adopted a constitution modeled on that of Pennsylvania.[2]

Questions to consider:

1. Why did Ethan Allen write his *Vindication*? To whom did he address it?
2. On what grounds did Allen justify the creation of Vermont as a separate state? How did he use the rhetoric and the ideology of the Revolution to enhance the legitimacy of his claims? What did he consider attributes of good government? Why, in his view, was the New York government even worse than the government of Great Britain?
3. What sorts of readers in Vermont, and elsewhere, would find Allen's views most appealing? Who would find his ideas horrifying?

Usurpation and injustice was the primary cause of the separation and revolt of the English American colonies from Great Britain; and this was also their grand reason and justification for so doing, and consequently the ground of their right to independency. These reasons are abundantly conclusive and satisfactory . . . and there appears to be a great degree of similarity in the controversy with the British government with that of Vermont against the government of New York, except in this respect, that the territory of Vermont was never under the jurisdiction of New York . . . The British government claimed an exclusive right of taxing the colonies in all cases whatsoever; such a prerogative would unavoidably have terminated finally in abject slavery, as has been fully illustrated by many ingenious writers, and verified by the universal experience of mankind; but the government of New York took a more direct and immediate method, for at one blow they struck at the landed property of every of the inhabitants of Vermont, by stretching their subsequent interfering patents over them. This was more like a combination of land thieves, than a government who coveting the lands and labors of the inhabitants, which, but a little before by iniquitous concerted measures at the British court (instead of slaves) they proved to be denominated their subjects.

The local distance of Vermont from the seat of government in the state of New York, is near four hundred and fifty miles from its extreme parts, which would make government chargeable and inconvenient; and abstracted from all other considerations, would constitute a sufficient reason for the independence of Vermont; nevertheless, provided those inhabitants were obliged to submit to the government of New York, they would wish to have the distance ten times greater.

The people of Vermont consider themselves as being virtually in union with the united states, from the time that they took possession of Lake Champlain, and the garrisons [at Ticonderoga and Crown Point] depending thereon, in behalf of the united states, in May 1775; from which early period of the revolution, they have taken an active part with them, and have pursued invariable, the same object, . . . liberty; have participated in all their troubles; and with them have hazarded all that is worth living or dying for; such a combination of interests, and mutual cooperation, in securing and defending the same, constitutes the very nature and essence of union and confederation, nor can there be more than a mere formal declaration requisite to fully establish a confederation between them.

And lastly, a confederation of the state of Vermont with the other free and independent states, cannot fail of being attended with salutary consequences to the confederacy at large, for ages yet to come. What a nursery of hardy soldiers may in future be nourished and supported in this fertile country, (which is one hundred and fifty miles in length, and near sixty in breadth,) stimulated with the spirit of liberty, having a perfect detestation and abhorrence of arbitrary power, from the exertions whereof they have suffered so much evil; will instill the principles of liberty and social virtue in their children, which will be perpetuated to future generations. Their climate and interior remove from the sea coast, will naturally be productive of a laborious life, by which means they will be in great measure exempted from luxury and effeminacy, and be a valuable support to the rising empire of the new world.

DOCUMENT 3

Petition of the Inhabitants of the Western Country (1785)

Residents of newer settlements in many states pressed for the reallocation of legislative seats to reflect their region's growing population. Some dissatisfied westerners went farther, attempting to form their separate own government. In 1784, after North Carolina ceded its western lands to the United States, the inhabitants of that western territory asked the state legislature to support their bid for admission to the Union as a separate state.[3] Although the legislators withheld their support, the westerners founded the self-styled state of Franklin. In 1788, North Carolina resumed jurisdiction in the area, which eventually became part of Tennessee.

Questions to consider:

1. On what basis did the petitioners believe they deserved to have their own state? To what extent did they invoke the ideals of the Revolution to support their objectives?
2. Why did the North Carolina legislature not support this petition? Did the North Carolinians break with the ideals of the Revolution when they refused to accede to the petitioners' requests?
3. Were the grievances of the petitioners similar to those of Ethan Allen and the Vermonters? Which group made the more compelling case for the creation of a new state government?

The Inhabitants of the Western Country humbly sheweth:

That it is with sincere concern we lament the unhappy disputes that have long subsisted between us and our brethren on the eastern side of the mountains, respecting the erecting of a new government . . . Being influenced by your acts and constitution and at the same time considering that it is our undeniable right to obtain for ourselves and posterity a proportionable and adequate share of the blessings, rights, privileges, and immunities allotted with the rest of mankind, we have thought that the erecting of a new government would greatly contribute to our welfare and convenience and that the same could not militate against your interest and future welfare as a government. Hoping that mutual and reciprocal advantages would attend each party, and that cordiality and unanimity would permanently subsist between us ever after, we earnestly request that an impartial view of our remoteness be taken into consideration; that the great inconveniency attending your seat of government, and also the great difficulty in ruling well and giving protection to so remote a people, to say nothing of the almost impassable mountains Nature has placed between, which renders it impracticable for us to furnish ourselves with a bare load of the necessaries of life, except we in the first instance travel from one to two hundred and more miles through another state ere we can reach your government.

Every tax paid you from this country would render us that sum the poorer, as it is impossible from the nature of our situation, that any part could return into circulation, having nothing that could bear the carriage, or encourage purchasers to come so great a distance; for which reasons were we to continue under your government a few years, the people here must pay a greater sum than the whole of the medium now in circulation for the exigencies and support of your government which would be a sum impossible for us to secure, would we be willing to give you our all; and of course we must be beholden to other states for any part we could raise; and by these means our property would gradually diminish, and we at last be reduced to mere poverty and want by not being able equally to participate with the benefits and advantages of your government.

We hope that having settled west of the Appalachian mountains ought not to deprive us of the natural advantages designed by the bountiful Providence for the convenience and comfort of all those who have spirit and sagacity enough to seek after them. When we reflect on our past and indefatigable struggles, both with savages and our other enemies during our late war, and the great difficulty we had to obtain and withhold this country from those enemies at the expense of the lives and fortunes of many of our dearest friends and relations; and the happy conclusion of peace having arrived, North Carolina has derived great advantages from our alertness in taking and securing a country, from which she has been able to draw into her treasury, immense sums of money, and thereby become enabled to pay off, if not wholly, yet a great part, and sink her national debt. We therefore humbly conceive you will liberally think that it will be nothing more than paying a debt in full to us for only to grant what God, Nature, and our locality entitles us to receive. Trusting that your magnanimity will not consider it a crime in any people to pray their rights and privileges, we call the world to testify our conduct and exertion in behalf of American independency; and the same to judge whether we ask more than free people ought to claim, agreeable to republican principles, the great foundation whereon our American fabric now stands. . . .

We hope to be enabled by the concurrence of your state to participate in the fruits of the Revolution; and to enjoy the essential benefits of civil society under a form of government which ourselves alone can only calculate for such a purpose. It will be a subject of regret that so much blood and treasure have been lavished away for no purpose to us; that so many sufferings have been encountered without compensation, we hope what hath been mentioned will be sufficient for our purpose, adding only that Congress hath, from time to time, explained their ideas so fully and with so much dignity and energy that if their arguments and requisitions will not produce conviction, we know of nothing that will have a greater influence, especially when we recollect that the system referred to is the result of the collected wisdom of the United States, and, should it not be considered as perfect, must be esteemed as the least objectionable.

DOCUMENT 4

Virginia Baptists Oppose Religious Privilege (1776)

In the decades preceding independence, first Presbyterians and then Baptists began attracting converts in Virginia. The Baptists became especially vocal opponents of the established Church of England and its gentry patrons in the colony. In June 1776, forty-nine Baptists from Prince William County sent this petition to Virginia's revolutionary convention. It was the first of many petitions the state's legislators received from religious dissenters during the revolutionary years.[4]

Questions to consider:

1. What penalties and disabilities did the Virginia Baptists suffer as a result of their refusal to conform to the Church of England?
2. Why, in June 1776, did they believe that the time was right to ask that their grievances be redressed?
3. Why did the legislators reject this petition, as well as the many similar ones they received in the ensuing decade?

To the honourable Speaker, and other Members of the honourable Convention of Virginia, the petition of a Baptist Church at Occaquon Prince William County hereby sheweth.

That whereas this colony with others, is now contending for the civil rights & liberties of mankind against the enslaving scheme of a powerful enemy, we being convinced, that the strictest unanimity among ourselves is very necessary in this most critical juncture of public affairs, and that every remaining cause of animosity and division may if possible be removed, have thought it our duty as peaceable Christians, to petition for several religious privileges which assets we have not been indulged in this part of the world: 1. That we be allowed to worship God in our own way, without interruption. 2. That we be permitted to maintain our own ministers . . . and no other. 3. That we and our friends who desire it, may be married, buried, and the like, without paying the parsons of any other denomination. These things granted, we will gladly unite with our brethren of other denominations, and to the utmost of our ability, promote the cause of freedom, always praying for your welfare & success.

DOCUMENT 5

Philadelphia Jews Seek
Civil Rights (1784)

Although most states disbanded their religious establishments, some limited voting or officeholding to Protestants and others made belief in the Scriptures a condition for participation in political life. The latter rule excluded Jews, who accepted only the Old

Petition of the Members of the Baptist Church at Occaquan, 20 June 1776. In the revolutionary era, religious dissenters were among those who petitioned their legislatures to express their grievances and claim what they believed to be their rights. In this early petition, a Virginia Baptist congregation promised to "unite with our Brethren of other denominations . . . to . . . promote the common cause of Freedom," if the legislature permitted them to maintain their own ministers and "worship God in our own way without interruption." The Virginia legislature either ignored or rejected this petition and many others like it. How could its members do so, while maintaining that they were fighting for America's liberties and rights? Source: Revolutionary Government 1774–1795 (RG2) Revolutionary Conventions Box 174, May 1776, Petition of the Members of the Baptist Church at Occaquan, June 20 1776. The Library of Virginia.

> Testament. *In 1784, leaders of Philadelphia's Jewish community petitioned for the removal of this religious requirement from Pennsylvania's otherwise liberal constitution. The authorities did not respond to their petition, but in 1790 a new state constitution provided that "no person, who acknowledges the being of a God and a future state of rewards and punishments, shall, on account of his religious sentiments, be disqualified to hold any office or place of trust or profit under this commonwealth."*[5]

Questions to consider:

1. On what basis did the Jews of Philadelphia make their case for political inclusion?
2. Did the petitioners emphasize how they differed from other Pennsylvanians or how they were similar to the other inhabitants of the state? Why?

To the honourable, the Council of Censors, assembled agreeable to the constitution of the State of Pennsylvania. The memorial of Rabbi Ger. Seixas of the synagogue of the Jews at Philadelphia, Simon Nathan, their . . . president, Asher Myers, Bernard Gratz, and Haym Salomon, the . . . associates of their council, in behalf of themselves and their bretheren Jews, residing in Pennsylvania, most respectfully sheweth:

That by the tenth section of the frame of government of this commonwealth, it is ordered that each member of the general assembly of representatives of the freemen of Pennsylvania, before he takes his seat, shall make and subscribe a declaration which ends in these words, "I do acknowledge the Scriptures of the Old and New Testament to be given by divine inspiration," to which is added an assurance that "no further or other religious test shall ever hereafter be required of any civil officer or magistrate in this state."

Your memorialists beg leave to observe that this clause seems to limit the civil rights of your citizens to one very special article of the creed, whereas, by the second paragraph of the declaration of the rights of the inhabitants, it is asserted without any other limitation than the professing the existence of God, in plain words, "that no man who acknowledges the being of a God can be justly deprived or abridged of any civil rights as a citizen on account of his religious sentiments." But certainly this religious test deprives the Jews of the most eminent rights of freemen, solemnly ascertained to all men who are not professed atheists.

May it please your Honors: Although the Jews in Pennsylvania are but few in number, yet liberty of the people in one country, and the declaration of the government thereof, that these liberties are the rights of the people, may prove a powerful attractive to men who live under restraints in another country. Holland and England have made valuable acquisitions of men, who, for their religious sentiments, were distressed in their own countries.

And if Jews in Europe or elsewhere should incline to transport themselves to America, and would, for reason of some certain advantage of the soil, climate, or the trade of Pennsylvania, rather become inhabitants thereof, than of any other state, yet the disability of Jews to take seat among the representatives of the people, as worded by the said religious test, might determine their free choice to go to New York, or to any other of the United States of America, where there is no such like restraint laid upon the nation and religion of the Jews, as in Pennsylvania.

Your memorialists cannot say that the Jews are particularly fond of being representatives of the people in assembly or civil officers and magistrates in the state, but with great submission they apprehend that a clause in the constitution, which disables them to be elected by their fellow citizens to represent them in assembly, as a stigma upon their nation and their religion, and it is inconsonant with the second paragraph of the said bill of rights. Otherwise, Jews are as fond of liberty as other religious societies can be, and it must create in them a displeasure when they perceive that for their professed dissent to a doctrine, which is inconsistent with their religious sentiments, they should be excluded from the most important and honourable part of the rights of a free citizen.

Your memorialists beg farther leave to represent that in the religious books of the Jews, which are or may be in every man's hands, there are no such doctrines or principles established as are inconsistent with the safety and happiness of the people of Pennsylvania, and that the conduct and behaviour of the Jews in this and the neighbouring states, has always tallied with the great design of the Revolution; that the Jews of Charlestown, New York, Newport, and other posts occupied by the British troops, have distinguishedly suffered for their attachment to the Revolution principles. . . .

The Jews of Pennsylvania, in proportion to the number of their members, can count with any religious society whatsoever the Whigs among either of them. They have served some of them in the Continental army; some went out in the militia to fight the common enemy; all of them have chearfully contributed to the support of the militia and of the government of this state.

They have no inconsiderable property in lands and tenements, but particularly in the way of trade, some more, some less, for which they pay taxes. They have, upon every plan formed for public utility, been forward to contribute as much as their circumstances would admit of, and as a nation or a religious society, they stand unimpeached of any matter whatsoever against the safety and happiness of the people.

And your memorialists humbly pray that if your honours, from any other consideration than the subject of this address, should think proper to call a convention for revising the constitution, you would be pleased to recommend this to the notice of that convention.

The Virginia Statute for Religious Freedom (1786)

Virginia's postrevolutionary religious settlement ultimately went far beyond merely dismantling the state's established church. Although some Virginians supported the preservation of the Anglican establishment and others wanted citizens to pay taxes to support the church of their choice, secular-minded liberals and religious dissenters joined together to enact the Statute for Religious Freedom. In the words of its author, Thomas Jefferson, this famous law erected a "wall of separation" between Church and State.[6] The Virginia Statute for Religious Freedom became the model for the First Amendment to the United States Constitution, which established the formal neutrality of the national government in all matters pertaining to religion.

Questions to consider:

1. How does the Statute define "religious liberty?"
2. What does the Statute imply was the purpose of religion? Would all Americans—then or now—accept that view?
3. The preamble of the Statute gives many reasons why Church and State should be separate. Which were probably the most compelling reasons for Jefferson and those who shared his deist views? For the Baptists and other Protestant evangelicals?

Whereas Almighty God hath created the mind free; that all attempts to influence it by temporal punishments or burthens, or by civil incapacitations, tend only to beget habits of hypocrisy and meanness, and are a departure from the plan of the Holy author of our religion, who being Lord both of body and mind, yet chose not to propagate it by coercions on either, as it was in his Almighty power to do; that the impious presumption of legislators and rulers, civil as well as ecclesiastical, who being themselves but fallible and uninspired men, have assumed dominion over the faith of others, setting up their own opinions and modes of thinking as the only true and infallible, and as such endeavouring to impose them on others, hath established and maintained false religions over the greatest part of the world, and through all time; that to compel a man to furnish contributions of money for the propagation of opinions which he disbelieves, is sinful and tyrannical; that even the forcing him to support this or that teacher of his own religious persuasion, is depriving him of the comfortable liberty of giving his contributions to the particular pastor, whose morals he would make his pattern, and whose powers he feels most persuasive to righteousness, and is withdrawing from the ministry those temporary rewards, which proceeding from an approbation of their personal conduct, are an additional incitement to earnest and unremitting labours for the instruction of mankind; that our civil rights have no dependence on our religious opinions, any more than our opinions in physics or geometry; that therefore the proscribing any citizen as unworthy the public confidence by laying upon him an incapacity of being called to offices of trust and emolument, unless he profess or renounce this or that religious opinion, is depriving him injuriously of those privileges and advantages to which in common with his fellow-citizens he has a natural right; that it tends only to corrupt the principles of that religion it is meant to encourage, by bribing with a monopoly of worldly honours and emoluments, those who will externally profess and conform to it; that though indeed these are criminal who do not withstand such temptation, yet neither are those innocent who lay the bait in their way; that to suffer the civil magistrate to intrude his powers into the field of opinion, and to restrain the profession or propagation of principles on supposition of their ill tendency, is a dangerous fallacy, which at once destroys all religious liberty, because he being of course judge of that tendency will make his opinions the rule of judgment, and approve or condemn the sentiments of others only as they shall square with or differ from his own; that it is time enough for the rightful purposes of civil government, for its officers to interfere when principles break out into overt acts against peace and good order; and finally, that truth is great and will prevail if left to herself, that she is the proper and sufficient antagonist to error, and has nothing to fear from the conflict, unless by human interposition disarmed of her natural weapons, free argument and debate, errors ceasing to be dangerous when it is permitted freely to contradict them:

Be it enacted by the General Assembly, That no man shall be compelled to frequent or support any religious worship, place, or ministry whatsoever, nor shall be enforced, restrained, molested, or burthened in his body or goods, nor shall otherwise suffer on account of his religious opinions or belief; but that all men shall be free to profess, and by argument to maintain, their opinion in matters of religion, and that the same shall in no wise diminish, enlarge, or affect their civil capacities.

And though we well know that this assembly elected by the people for the ordinary purposes of legislation only, have no power to restrain the acts of succeeding assemblies, constituted with powers equal to our own, and that therefore to declare this act to be irrevocable would be of no effect in law; yet we are free to declare, and do declare, that the rights hereby asserted are of the natural rights of mankind, and that if any act shall be hereafter passed to repeal the present, or to narrow its operation, such act shall be an infringement of natural right.

DOCUMENT 7

"Remember the Ladies" (1776)

Abigail Adams spent the war years running her family's farm and household in Braintree, Massachusetts, while her husband, John, represented their state in the Continental Congress and then served Congress abroad as a diplomat. During their separation, the Adamses exchanged frequent letters full of political, military, and family news. In this famous letter, Abigail Adams pondered both the evils of slavery and the debased legal status of women.[7]

Questions to consider:

1. Whom did Abigail Adams characterize as "vassals"? What was the significance of that characterization?
2. Was Adams exaggerating when she decried the "unlimited power" of husbands?
3. Abigail Adams did not believe women should have the right to vote. What, then, did she want when she warned that women would be bound only by laws in which they had a "voice or representation?"

I wish you would ever write me a letter half as long as I write you, and tell me, if you may, where your fleet are gone; what sort of defense Virginia can make against our common enemy; whether it is so situated as to make an able defense. Are not the gentry lords, and the common people vassals? Are they not like the uncivilized vassals Britain represents us to be? . . . I have sometimes been ready to think that the passion for liberty cannot be equally strong in the breasts of those who have been accustomed to deprive their fellow-creatures of theirs. Of this I am certain, that it is not founded upon that generous and Christian principle of doing to others as we would that others should do unto us. . . .

I long to hear that you have declared an independency. And, by the way, in the new code of laws which I suppose it will be necessary for you to make, I desire you would remember the ladies and be more generous and favorable to them than your ancestors. Do not put such unlimited power into the hands of the husbands. Remember, all men would be tyrants if they could. If particular care and attention is not paid to the ladies, we are determined to foment a rebellion, and will not hold ourselves bound by any laws in which we have no voice or representation.

That your sex is naturally tyrannical is a truth so thoroughly established as to admit of no dispute; but such of you as wish to be happy willingly give up the harsh title of master for the more tender and endearing one of friend. Why, then, not put it out of the power of the vicious and the lawless to use us with cruelty and indignity with impunity? Men of sense in all ages abhor those customs which treat us only as the vassals of your sex; regard us then as beings placed by Providence under your protection, and in imitation of the Supreme Being make use of that power only for our happiness.

DOCUMENT 8

"On the Equality of the Sexes" (1790)

Judith Sargent Murray

Judith Sargent Murray was an early and forceful advocate for women's education and economic independence. In the 1780s, she published occasional essays on women's issues and other topics, and she was a regular contributor to the Massachusetts Magazine *after 1790. "On the Equality of the Sexes" was the first and best-known essay Murray wrote for the* Massachusetts Magazine.[8] *Although many readers probably rejected her ideas, between 1792 and 1794 the* Magazine *also published her monthly essays—titled "The Gleaner"—on public affairs, in which she often promoted equal education and other improvements in the status of women.*

Questions to consider:

1. What, according to Murray, was the source of women's alleged inferiority?
2. What was Murray's opinion of housework? To whom might this characterization of women's domestic work be either inappropriate or irrelevant?
3. Did Murray want the rights and responsibilities of women and men to be the same? What was her definition of "equality"?

Is it upon mature consideration that we adopt the idea, that nature is . . . partial in her distributions? Is it indeed a fact, that she hath yielded to one half of the human species so unquestionable a mental superiority? I know that to both sexes elevated understandings, and the reverse, are common. But, suffer me to ask, in what the minds of females are so notoriously deficient, or unequal. . . .

Now, was [woman] permitted the same instructors as her brother, (with an eye however to their particular departments) for the employment of a rational mind an ample field would be opened. In astronomy she might catch a glimpse of the immensity of the Deity, and thence she would form amazing conceptions of the august and supreme Intelligence. In geography she would admire Jehovah in the midst of his benevolence; thus adapting this globe to the various wants and amusements of its inhabitants. In natural philosophy she would adore the infinite majesty of heaven, clothed in condescension; and as she traversed the reptile world, she would hail the goodness of a creating God. A mind, thus filled, would have little room for the trifles with which our sex are, with too much justice, accused of amusing themselves, and they would thus be rendered fit companions for those, who should one day wear them as their crown. Fashions, in their variety, would then give place to conjectures, which might perhaps conduce to the improvement of the literary world; and there would be no leisure for slander or detraction. Reputation would not then be blasted, but serious speculations would occupy the lively imaginations of the sex. Unnecessary visits would be precluded, and that custom would only be indulged by way of relaxation, or to answer the demands of consanguinity and friendship. Females would become discreet, their judgments would be invigorated, and their partners for life being circumspectly chosen, an unhappy Hymen would then be as rare, as is now the reverse.

Will it be urged that those acquirements would supersede our domestic duties? I answer that every requisite in female economy is easily attained; and, with truth I can add, that when once attained, they require no further *mental attention*. Nay, while we are pursuing the needle, or the superintendency of the family, I repeat, that our minds are at full liberty for reflection; that imagination may exert itself in full vigor; and that if a just foundation is early laid, our ideas will then be worthy of rational beings. If we were industrious we might easily find time to arrange them upon paper, or should avocations press too hard for such an indulgence, the hours allotted for conversation would at least become more refined and rational. Should it still be vociferated, "Your domestic employments are sufficient"—I would calmly ask, is it reasonable, that a candidate for immortality, for the joys of heaven, an intelligent being, who is to spend an eternity in contemplating the works of Deity, should at present be so degraded, as to be allowed no other ideas, than those which are suggested by the mechanism of a pudding, or the sewing the seams of a garment? Pity that all such censurers of female improvement do not go one step further, and deny their future existence; to be consistent they surely ought.

Yes, ye lordly, ye haughty sex, our souls are by nature *equal* to yours; the same breach of God animates, enlivens, and invigorates us; . . . I know there are who assert, that as the animal powers of the one sex are superiour, of course their mental faculties also must be stronger: thus attributing strength of mind to the transient organization of this earth born tenement. But if this reasoning is just, man must be content to yield the palm [to] many of the brute creation, since by not a few of his brethren of the field, he is far surpassed in bodily strength. Moreover, was this argument admitted, it would prove too much, for occular demonstration evinces that there are many robust masculine ladies, and effeminate gentlemen . . . Besides, were we to grant that animal strength proved any thing, taking into consideration the accustomed impartiality of nature, we should be induced to imagine, that she had invested the female mind with superiour strength as an equivalent for the bodily powers of man. But waving this however palpable advantage, for *equality only,* we wish to contend.

DOCUMENT 9

Massachusetts Antislavery Petition (1777)

In an age of libertarian rhetoric and republican reforms, slavery seemed incongruous— and increasing numbers of African Americans were willing to say so publicly. In Massachusetts, where Crispus Attucks, an escaped mulatto slave, became a martyr to liberty in the Boston Massacre, free blacks repeatedly petitioned the legislature for the outright abolition of slavery.[9] Although the legislators consistently ignored those petitions, in 1783, the Supreme Court of Massachusetts declared slavery unconstitutional.

Questions to consider:

1. How would you characterize the tone of the petitioners?
2. What arguments did they use to support their case against slavery?
3. Why did they concede that children might be held as slaves until they reached the age of twenty-one?

The petition of a great number of blacks detained in a state of slavery in the bowels of a free & Christian country humbly sheweth that your petitioners apprehend that they have in common with all other men a natural and un-alienable right to that freedom which the great parent of the universe that bestowed equally on all mankind and which they have never forfeited by any compact or agreement whatever—but that were unjustly dragged by the hand of cruel power and their dearest friends and some of them even torn from the embraces of their tender parents—from a populous pleasant and plentiful country and in violation of Laws of Nature and of Nations and in defiance of all the tender feelings of humanity brought here either to be sold like beasts of burthen & like them condemned to slavery for life—among a people professing the mild religion of Jesus, a people not insensible of the secrets of rational being nor without spirit to resent the unjust endeavors of others to reduce them to a state of bondage and subjugation. Your honour need not to be informed that a life of slavery like that of your petitioners deprived of every social privilege of every thing requisite to render life tol[er]able is far worse than nonexistance.

[In imitat]ion of the laudable example of the good people of these states your petitioners have long and patiently waited the event of petition after petition by them presented to the legislative body of this state and can-not but with grief reflect that their success hath been but too similar. They cannot but express their astonishment that it has never been considered that every principle from which America has acted in the course of their unhappy difficulties with Great Britain pleads stronger than a thousand arguments in favor of your petitioners. They therefore humbly beseech your honours to give this petition its due weight and consideration & cause an act of the legislature to be past whereby they may be restored to the enjoy-ments of that which is the natural right of all men—and their children who were born in this land of liberty may not be held as slaves after they arrive at the age of twenty one years so may the inhabitants of this state no longer chargeable with the inconstancy of acting themselves that part which they condemn and oppose in others be prospered in their present glorious struggle for liberty and have those blessings to them.

DOCUMENT 10

Virginia Proslavery Petition (1785)

In 1782, Virginia enacted a private manumission law that empowered individual slaveholders to emancipate their bondpeople. In the next few years, several religious denominations—particularly the Quakers and the Methodists—called for an end to slavery in Virginia and elsewhere. In 1784 and 1785, however, more than a thousand Virginians from eight leading tobacco-producing counties reacted to this antislavery activism by petitioning their legislature. This petition, which was signed by 161 inhabitants of Lunenburg County, includes an early invocation of white women's alleged vulnerability as a justification for the enslavement of African Americans.[10]

Questions to consider:

1. How would you characterize the tone of the petitioners? Did they appear to regard the legislators as their equals—or as their superiors or inferiors?
2. How was the issue of paper money relevant to what was essentially a petition for repeal of the private manumission law?
3. What did the petitioners expect would be the result of emancipation?
4. Given that Virginia remained a slaveholding state until the end of the Civil War, why do you think the state legislature rejected this and other proslavery petitions?

When the British Parliament usurped a right to dispose of our property, it was not the matter, but the manner adopted for that purpose, that alarmed us, as it tended to establish a principle which might one day prove fatal to our rights of property. In order therefore to fix a tenure in our property on a basis of security not to be shaken in future, we dissolved our union with our parent country, and by a self-erected power bravely and wisely established a Constitution and form of government, grounded on a full and clear declaration of such rights as naturally pertain to men born free and determined to be respectfully and absolutely so as human institutions can make them. This we effected by our representatives, to whom we delegated our power, in General Convention, whose wisdom, integrity, fortitude, and patriotic zeal will ever reflect glory on them and honor on their constituents. In support of this happy establishment, with its attendant blessings we have cheerfully sacrificed our ease, lives and fortunes, and waded through deluges of civil blood to that unequivocal liberty, which alone characterises the free independent citizen, and distinguishes him from the subjugated vassal of despotic rule.

Thus happily possessed of all the rational rights of freedom, this country might have stood the envy of admiring nations, to the end of the time, had the same wisdom, fidelity and patriotic zeal, which gave being to this glorious work, continued to guide the public councils of the state. But how far this has, or had not, been our happy lot, let past violations of our sacred rights of property, and the recent invasions of them from such examples, testify to the world. And here we could wish not to call to mind, particulars. Suffice it therefore only to mention the Act for funding our Paper Money, which not only involved thousands of our most valuable citizens in irretrievable ruin, but stabbed the very vitals of public faith. But it was said to be expedient, and we acquiesced in it. But never did, nor ever will, admit it as a ruling precedent [for] the wanton disposal of our property, of any kind, whenever the chimerical flights of a fanatic spirit, or the venal views of a corrupted heart shall prompt to the rash attempt—No! We have sealed with our blood, a title to the full, free, and absolute enjoyment of every species of our property, whensoever, or howsoever legally acquired; a purchase of too great value to be sacrificed to the caprice, or interest of any rank or description of men, however dignified, or distinguished, either by the confidential suffrages of their fellow-citizens, or otherwise.

To this free, and we trust, inoffensive, as well as necessary communication of our sentiments, on the most important subject that ever arrested the attention of a free people, we are enforced by a daring attempt now on foot in several counties in this state by petitions warmly advocated by some men of considerable weight to wrest from us, by an act of the legislature, the most valuable and indispensable article of our property, our slaves, by a general emancipation of them. An attempt that involves in it not only a flagrant contempt of the constituent powers of the Commonwealth, in which its majesty resides and which we are sorry to have occasion to observe seem to be forgotten by too many, and a daring attack on that sacred Constitution thereby established; but also, want, poverty, distress and ruin to the free citizen; the horrors of all the rapes, robberies, murders, and outrages, which an innumerable host of unprincipled, unpropertied, vindictive, and remorseless banditti are capable of perpetrating; neglect, famine and death to the abandoned black infant, and superannuated parent; inevitable bankruptcy to the revenue; desparation and revolt to the disappointed, oppressed citizen; and sure and final ruin to this once happy, free, and flourishing country. And all this . . . to answer no one civil, religious, or national purpose, whatever. . . .

No language can express our indignation . . . For though we admit it to be the indisputable right of the citizen to apply to the legislature by petition on any or otherwise subject within the cognizance of their constitutional powers, yet we positively deny a right in any man or description of men, even to move the legislature in any manner, to violate the smallest article of our Constitution, as it is not only a contempt of that, but strongly implies a want of wisdom, integrity, or spirit in our representatives, to discharge the high trust found in them, want of either of which would render them very unfit objects of the confidence of their constituents, and of course, dangerous and contemptible. It therefore cannot be admitted that any man has a right, to petition or otherwise press the legislature to divest us of our known rights of property, which are so clearly defined, so fully acknowledged, and so solemnly ratified and confirmed, by our Bill of Rights, as not to admit of an equivocal construction, nor of the smallest alteration or diminution, by any power, but that which originally authorised its establishment.

To an unequivocal construction therefore of this Bill of Rights we now appeal, and claim the utmost benefits of it; not doubting the hearty concurrence of our faithful representatives in what ever may tend to promote our mutual interests; preserve our rights inviolate; secure to us all the blessings of a free, undisturbed, independent government; and so, an indiscriminate diffusion of peace, wealth, and happiness among the free citizens of this Commonwealth. And as the lasting welfare of our country, and the happiness of its citizens depend [on the] invariable adherence to our Constitution, we most solemnly adjure, and humbly pray, that you, gentlemen, to whom we have committed the guardianship of our rights of property, will in no instance, permit them to be called in question; particularly, that you will discountenance, and utterly reject every motion and proposal for emancipating our slaves; that you will immediately, and totally repeal the act for permitting owners of slaves to emancipate them; that you will provide effectually for the good government, and due restraint of those already set free, whose disorderly conduct, and thefts and outrages, are so generally the just subject of complaint; but particularly whose insolences, and violences so frequently of late committed to and on our respectable maids and matrons, which are a disgrace to government.

SUGGESTED READING FOR CHAPTER 8

ADAMS, WILLI PAUL. *The First American Constitutions: Republican Ideology and the Making of the State Constitutions in the Revolutionary Era* (1980).

BELLESILES, MICHAEL A. *Revolutionary Outlaws: Ethan Allen and the Struggle for Independence on the Early American Frontier* (1993).

BERLIN, IRA. *Many Thousands Gone: The First Two Centuries of Slavery in North America* (1998).

BUCKLEY, THOMAS E. *Church and State in Revolutionary Virginia, 1776–1787* (1977).

CURRY, THOMAS J. *The First Freedoms: Church and State in America to the Passage of the First Amendment* (1986).

DAVIS, DAVID BRION. *The Problem of Slavery in the Age of Revolution, 1770–1823* (1983).

DOUGLASS, ELISHA P. *Rebels and Democrats: The Struggle for Equal Political Rights and Majority Rule during the American Revolution* (1955).

GUNDERSEN, JOAN R. "Independence, Citizenship, and the American Revolution." *Signs*, 13 (1987): 59–77.

KERBER, LINDA K. *Women of the Republic: Intellect and Ideology in Revolutionary America* (1980).

KRUMAN, MARC W. *Between Authority and Liberty: State Constitution Making in Revolutionary America* (1997).

McCOLLEY, ROBERT. *Slavery and Jeffersonian Virginia* (1964).

McLEOD, DUNCAN. *Slavery, Race, and the American Revolution* (1974).

NASH, GARY B.; and SODERLUND, JEAN R. *Freedom by Degrees: Emancipation in Pennsylvania and its Aftermath* (1991).
QUARLES, BENJAMIN. *The Negro in the American Revolution* (1961).
SALMON, MARYLYNN. *Women and the Law of Property in Early America* (1986).
WHITE, SHANE. "'It Was a Proud Day': African Americans, Festivals, and Parades in the North, 1741–1834." *Journal of American History*, 81 (1994): 13–50.
ZILVERSMIT, ARTHUR. *The First Emancipation: The Abolition of Slavery in the North* (1961).

NOTES

*Carl Lotus Becker, *The History of Political Parties in the Province of New York, 1760–1776* (Madison, Wisc., 1909), 22.

[1]"A Dialogue between Orator Puff and Peter Easy," *Pennsylvania Evening Post*, 24 Oct. 1776.

[2]Ethan Allen, *A Vindication of the Opposition of the Inhabitants of Vermont to the Government of New York, and of Their Right to Form an Independent State* (Dresden, Vt., i.e., Hanover, N.H., 1779), 47–51, 55–56.

[3]W. L. Saunders, et al., eds., *The Colonial and State Records of North Carolina*, 30 vols. (Raleigh, Winston, Goldsboro, and Charlotte, 1886–1914), 22: 705–7.

[4]"Virginia Legislative Petitions," *Virginia Magazine of History and Biography*, 18 (1910): 38–39.

[5]*The Freeman's Journal: or, the North-American Intelligencer*, 21 Jan. 1784; Pennsylvania constitution, 1790, in Francis Newton Thorpe, ed., *The Federal and State Constitutions, Colonial Charters, and Other Organic Laws of the States . . .* , 7 vols. (Washington, 1909), 5:3100.

[6]W. W. Hening, ed., *Statutes at Large of Virginia*, 13 vols. (Richmond, 1813–23), 12: 84–86; Jefferson to Danbury Baptist Association, 1 Jan. 1802, in Andrew A. Lipscomb, ed., *The Writings of Thomas Jefferson*, 20 vols. (Washington, 1904), 16: 281–82.

[7]Abigail Adams to John Adams, 31 Mar. 1776, in Charles Francis Adams, ed., *Familiar Letters of John Adams and his Wife Abigail Adams, During the Revolution* (New York, 1876), 149–50.

[8]Judith Sargent Murray, "On the Equality of the Sexes," *Massachusetts Magazine, or Monthly Museum*, 2 (1790): 132–34.

[9]"Negro Petitions for Freedom," in *Collections of the Massachusetts Historical Society*, 5th ser., (Boston, 1877), 3: 436–37.

[10]Petition of the inhabitants of Lunenburg County, 29 Nov. 1785, Legislative Petitions, Library of Virginia, Richmond.

CHAPTER NINE

CONFEDERATION AND CONSTITUTION

In 1776, American patriots had imagined that independence would bring them peace, prosperity, and happiness. Their removal from the British Empire, they reasoned, would enable them to avoid involvement in European wars. Withdrawal from the British navigation system would allow them to trade with whomever they chose, thereby encouraging virtually limitless agricultural and commercial development. Republican political institutions would secure their liberties and empower virtuous citizens. A decentralized federal system, in which the states were sovereign, would enhance liberty by making government less remote from its constituents and more accountable to them.

As it turned out, in the years following the stunning victory at Yorktown, the United States experienced political uncertainty and economic dislocation, leaving many Americans disillusioned and unsure of the fate of their experiment in republicanism. At the continental level, Congress could not pay its debts, negotiate credibly with foreign nations, or promote and protect American commerce. As a result, some Americans concluded that political authority was too weak and decentralized under the Articles of Confederation. At the same time, state politics grew increasingly contentious, as governments grappled with controversial economic issues, such as taxes, currency, and the confiscation of loyalist property. Many members of the gentry, now forced to share political authority with middling newcomers, decried what they deemed an excess of democracy.

In the 1780s, two important and sometimes overlapping groups believed that the republic was in crisis. A nationalist bloc centered in Congress bemoaned the weakness of the Confederation government and sought to increase its powers to advance the fiscal and foreign policy interests of the United States and encourage economic development. A second group, composed mainly of wealthy, educated, and often displaced elites, located their grievances primarily at the state level. They wanted a stronger central authority to restrain or counterbalance the democracy of the states. In 1787, fifty-five men, nearly all of whom espoused one or both of these perspectives, convened in Philadelphia, ostensibly to revise the Articles of Confederation. Instead, they drafted a whole new constitution that transformed the assumptions and practice of American republicanism.

Though not officially ratified until March 1781, the Articles of Confederation described political arrangements that were in effect since Americans asserted their independence. Under those arrangements, the collective government of the united states was extremely limited, in terms of both visibility and power. The unicameral Congress was the only continental or national political body under the Articles of Confederation; there was no executive or judiciary. The state legislatures, not the voters, chose the delegates to Congress, who represented the sovereign states. For that reason, members of Congress voted not as individuals but as unitary state delegations. In the Confederation era, Congress was less a governing body than a forum for discussion and consensus-building among a loose alliance of states.

Consensus was critical because, under the terms of the Articles, disunity paralyzed the entire Confederation. The concurrence of nine states was required for the passage of many types of acts—including fiscal and war-related measures—and unanimous approval of the states was necessary to amend the Articles. Congressional measures also needed the support of state authorities because when the Congress enacted a resolution or ordinance, it was up to the states to enforce it. For example, though the Articles of Confederation gave Congress full authority over foreign policy and Indian affairs, the states, in practice, decided whether or not to enforce the treaties it made. The Articles also left Congress dependent on the states for revenue. Lacking the power to tax, Congress sent requests, or requisitions, for funding to the states, which could comply or not as they saw fit.

At the beginning of the Revolution, the overwhelming majority of Americans, still smarting from their recent brush with British tyranny, would not have accepted a significantly stronger central government.

Most Americans still adhered to that position in 1781, when an increasingly vocal minority of nationalists began arguing that for fiscal, diplomatic, and commercial reasons, Congress needed more power. The most important members of this group were Robert Morris, Gouverneur Morris, James Duane, James Wilson, and Alexander Hamilton—all of whom were from the middle states—and James Madison of Virginia.

Fiscal reform was the first major objective of the nationalist coalition, and the Impost Plan of 1781 was their most important project. By the war's end, nationalists concluded that Congress needed the power to tax. Even in wartime, the states had filled less than half of Congress's requisitions, leaving many to wonder how Congress would be able to pay its debts after the war was over. Nationalists proposed an amendment to the Articles of Confederation that would empower Congress to levy a 5 percent impost on all imports, a proposal which, if adopted, would have yielded sufficient revenue to fund the national debt. Congress approved the proposal, but its implementation depended on the unanimous consent of the state legislatures. Robert Morris, the wealthy Philadelphia merchant who served as Congress's Superintendent of Finance from 1781, contended that the continued existence of the United States depended on the adoption of the impost. The amendment became a dead letter, however, when Rhode Island rejected it in 1782.

With the failure of the impost, nationalists sought new ways to fund and pay the debt. Morris spearheaded the chartering of the Bank of North America, which he hoped could make loans to Congress to ease its short-term financial problems. He and his nationalist allies also unsuccessfully proposed other forms of federal taxation—a land tax, a poll tax, an excise tax—to fund and pay a debt that totaled about $27 million in specie in 1782. Without a dependable source of revenue, the Confederation government sunk even further into debt, neither meeting its own operating expenses nor making payments to its domestic creditors. Congress managed to make interest payments to its foreign creditors— chiefly the French government and Dutch bankers—whose continued trust they regarded as essential if the United States hoped to turn to them for future supplies of hard money.

Nationalists insisted that Congress needed the power to tax because they believed that settling the debt was essential to the survival of the American republic. Payment of the foreign debt, they asserted, was a matter of honor for the fledgling republic, an opportunity for Americans to prove their trustworthiness on an international stage, as well as a fiscal priority. Nationalists also contended that paying the domestic debt, especially that portion of it owed to wealthy creditors, could promote both political stability and economic development. Satisfying such creditors, nationalists argued, would make them firm supporters of the republic and thereby safeguard its continued existence. Having profited by their investment in the Revolution, moreover, such men would be inclined to reinvest their profits in land, trade, and manufactures. Not surprisingly, the nationalist agenda attracted the support of many large-scale public creditors who, whatever their other motives, would profit by the implementation of more aggressive fiscal policies.

Foreign policy was the second broad area on which nationalists focused when they assailed the deficiencies of the Articles of Confederation. The central government's weakness under the Articles, they contended with justification, undermined its ability to conduct a credible foreign policy. In the 1780s, the most pressing foreign policy issues involved relations with Britain, Spain, and various native American nations, all of whom still had claims or interests in the western territory awarded to the United States by the Treaty of Paris.

Although the Confederation Congress passed a series of ordinances to organize the trans-Appalachian west and prepare for its eventual division into new states, Congress had difficulty establishing its authority in the region. After 1783, for instance, American diplomats engaged in fruitless negotiations to evacuate British troops from a string of seven forts they maintained on United States soil, stretching from central New York westward to the Mississippi River. The British wanted to retain a military presence in the region to protect their valuable trade with the Indians and to shield their native allies from westward-moving white settlers. By doing so, they clearly violated both the sovereignty of the United States and the Treaty of Paris. Nevertheless, Congress's inability to ensure that the individual American states would comply with the treaty compromised the position of its own diplomats when they sought to dislodge the British from the western territories. Congress lacked the authority to compel the states to return loyalist property or acknowledge the validity of prewar British debts, both of which were provisions of the treaty that ended the War of Independence. The states' unwillingness to abide by these terms gave the British a convenient excuse for refusing to vacate the American west. The disbanding of the Continental Army, which resulted in part from Congress's inability to pay the soldiers, meant that American diplomats could not threaten military reprisals against the British, who consequently retained the western forts for the rest of the Confederation era.

In the 1780s, the United States also sought to secure its authority over native peoples who resided within its borders, primarily in the west. The peace negotiations that ended the war established the Mississippi River as the western boundary of the United States, though the Indians did not recognize the authority of the British to give away land they regarded as their own. After 1783, Congress's commissioners prevailed on Indian nations to cede their lands to the United States, but most either refused to treat with the commissioners or repudiated the agreements once they signed them. Native Americans skirmished intermittently with the United States and its westward-moving settlers during the 1780s. Although Congress formed a 700-man regiment, drawn from state militias, specifically to fight the western Indians in 1784, this force was insufficient. United States control of the land the Indians claimed remained at best tenuous.

The well-known weakness of the United States government also undermined its attempts to negotiate with the Spanish, who controlled the territory west of the Mississippi River and, after 1783, the entire gulf coast from New Orleans to Florida. Spain also claimed exclusive navigation rights to the Mississippi River, as well as a portion of the southwestern lands ceded by Britain to the United States in the Treaty of Paris. As settlers from the United States poured into this territory, establishing American sovereignty and access to the Mississippi became a top priority. Negotiating from a position of weakness, Congress's Secretary for Foreign Affairs, John Jay of New York, made no headway in his attempts to persuade the Spanish government to accede to American demands. The Spanish had no incentive to compromise with a government whose fiscal and military debility precluded offensive or retaliatory action.

Finally, a third major source of discontent with the Articles of Confederation was Congress's inability to make commercial policy. Expecting independence to result in free trade, most Americans in 1776 neither anticipated the need for commercial regulations nor wished them to be imposed by a remote central government, as had been the case during the colonial era. In the 1780s, however, the economy suffered as state regulations impeded domestic commerce, while Americans found themselves shut out of most lucrative foreign markets. American merchants resumed their trade with Britain, but the Navigation Acts excluded their goods from the British West Indies, the most important export market for North American foodstuffs during the colonial era. Congress negotiated commercial treaties with the Netherlands, Sweden, and Prussia. Spain and especially Britain, however, rejected American overtures in part because they doubted the ability of Congress to enforce the international agreements it made. As a result, American exports plummeted, and British goods flooded the American market.

By the mid-1780s, many merchants and artisans, especially in the northern states, believed that Congress should be empowered to enact protective tariffs and, more generally, to make and enforce national commercial policies. Their concerns, though more specific, fit nicely with those of the nationalists who sought a more general expansion of the powers of the central government. In January 1786, at James Madison's suggestion, the Virginia legislature invited all thirteen states to send delegates to a meeting at Annapolis, Maryland, to discuss the commercial and economic problems the states faced, both individually and collectively. Because representatives from only five states attended this meeting, no substantive business was conducted. Nevertheless, Alexander Hamilton of New York introduced a resolution to invite delegates to convene in Philadelphia in May 1787 to consider a more wide-ranging reform agenda. This time, fifty-five men from every state except Rhode Island would heed the nationalists' call.

The men who gathered in Philadelphia in 1787 bore little resemblance to the state legislators who chose them. While roughly two-thirds of those who sat in the state assemblies in the Confederation era were farmers, artisans, or other middling men without prior legislative experience, the fifty-five delegates to the convention at Philadelphia included some of the republic's most accomplished leaders. George Washington and Benjamin Franklin were the most famous men in America. James Madison and Alexander Hamilton were rising stars, aged thirty-six and thirty-two, respectively. Of the fifty-five delegates, thirty-nine had sat in the Continental Congress, twenty-one had been officers in the army, and eight were signers of the Declaration of Independence. At a time when many Americans had no formal education at all, twenty-six of the delegates were college graduates. Most were lawyers, merchants, or planters, and nineteen of them owned slaves. About half were government creditors and, in state politics, the vast majority were aligned with the conservative Whigs. Indeed, most of these men came to Philadelphia at least in part because they resented the increasingly democratic tone of politics in their respective states. By creating a stronger central government, many hoped to reverse or at least stay the trend toward popular government that had resulted from the institutional and ideological changes of the revolutionary years.

The most divisive issues at the state level during the Confederation era were taxation, currency, and the confiscation of loyalist property. In most states, the Whig remnant of the colonial elite took unpopular positions on all three issues, which hastened the erosion of their political power. The War of Independence necessitated the levying of extraordinarily high taxes, which reformers sought to impose more equitably than had been the case during the colonial era. The wealthy, vastly undertaxed before 1776, now found themselves assuming the lion's share of the tax burden, including, in most states, an unprecedented levy on unimproved lands. Conservative gentlemen opposed the new tax laws, and they condemned inflationary currency policies, which benefited debtors by allowing them to pay off their obligations in depreciated paper money. Creditors and other conservative-minded Americans argued that paying off debts in cheap money amounted to a violation of the property rights of creditors, who had given credit in the expectation that they would be repaid in full. Substantial property owners also generally opposed the states' confiscation of loyalist estates, which seemed to set another ominous precedent for the government's abridgement of individual property rights.

In most states, however, a majority of voters supported tax reform, inflationary currency, and the seizure and redistribution of loyalist property, all of which benefited ordinary Americans during difficult economic times, either directly or indirectly. Citizens instructed their representatives to adopt such policies, and the new men in the legislatures—many of whom were themselves debtors of middling social origins—typically acted on those instructions. Proponents of tax reform, inflation, and confiscation of loyalist property believed that they were implementing the will of the people—or at least that of the majority of voters—and so they were.

Conservatives, by contrast, complained that such policies were born of self-interest and reflected a lamentable lack of public spirit—also known as civic virtue—among citizens and their elected representatives. The situation was particularly worrisome, many believed, because conventional wisdom deemed civic virtue essential to the survival of a republic, a government of the people. In the 1780s, conservative Whigs bemoaned what they called democratic despotism, or the tyranny of the majority, and looked for ways to check its power. Some made concerted efforts to reform their state constitutions to dilute the power of the legislatures. In the end, however, most decided that only a stronger central government might restrain the democratic despotism they believed to be increasingly prevalent at the state level.

In early 1787, a rebellion in western Massachusetts helped convince some wavering conservatives that reform at the national level might be the only way to restrain the excesses of an increasingly unruly people. Massachusetts had waited until 1780 to adopt its first constitution. Ratified by a slim margin, that document reflected the priorities of the state's eastern commercial and creditor interests, who subsequently succeeded in dominating the state government. After 1780, the Massachusetts legislature imposed high land and poll taxes and stipulated that all taxes be paid in specie rather than in depreciated paper currency. Statutes also required the payment of private debts in hard money on demand. Such policies caused genuine hardship for the state's western farmers, who typically used paper money or agricultural produce to pay their debts. In 1786, as many farmers lost their land and others languished in debtors' prison, westerners appealed to the legislature for relief. When the legislators did nothing, three western counties erupted in rebellion.

In the winter of 1786–87, under the leadership of Captain Daniel Shays, a veteran of the Continental Army, the insurgents closed the courts to prevent further debt litigation and stormed the jails to free their friends and neighbors. When the state had difficulty fielding militia sufficient to suppress a rebel force that swelled to as many as 2,000 men, the governor appealed to Congress for military assistance. Congress agreed, but by the time help arrived the insurrection had dissipated. In Massachusetts, Shays's Rebellion led to the election of a new governor and many new legislators, as well as some significant changes in the state's fiscal policies. Beyond the Bay State, however, news of the uprising and of the state's apparent inability to restore order heightened conservative fears of impending anarchy and led many to conclude that order could be restored only by the creation of a stronger central government.

While the turnout for the Annapolis convention had been light in 1786, twelve states sent delegates to Philadelphia in 1787. The rebellion in Massachusetts, coupled with the more general agenda of the Philadelphia meeting, caused many to believe that something decisive was bound to happen. Congress had charged the convention's delegates with the sole specific task of revising the Articles of Confederation. Perhaps because they knew that the Articles could be amended only with the states' unanimous consent, state legislators were willing to appoint many men whose political sensibilities differed significantly from their own to represent them in Philadelphia.

Within a few days of the convention's first formal session, it became clear that the delegates would far exceed their mandate. Instead of revising the Articles of Confederation, they would draft an entirely new frame of government. After four months of debate and negotiation, the delegates completed their work. They chose to submit the fruit of their labors not to the state legislatures—where rejection was all but certain—but rather to special state conventions elected for the sole purpose of considering the proposed constitution.

In Philadelphia, the delegates drafted and approved a blueprint for a government that differed profoundly from that which had existed since 1776. The constitution proposed a national government consisting of three branches: a powerful executive, a bicameral legislature, and a judiciary. Although the voters would directly elect only the lower legislative house, in theory at least, each branch of the government represented the sovereign people—and not the sovereign states. Although the states retained substantial powers under the proposed arrangements, the central government also possessed impressive powers. Above all, it had the power to tax and, more generally, to enact laws and policies and enforce them once they were made. For all these reasons, the proposed constitution was arguably the most controversial issue of the revolutionary era.

Did the proposed constitution fulfill or repudiate of the ideals of the Revolution? Most historians agree that when the convention adjourned on 17 September 1787, the majority of Americans would have regarded the proposed plan of government as unacceptable. Despite widespread recognition that the Articles of Confederation needed revision to address an array of fiscal and diplomatic problems, most Americans were reasonably content with their state governments and with the democratization of politics that had occurred as a result of the republican revolution. The main objective of the Revolution, they believed, was to preserve liberty by putting the power of government into the hands of its constituents. By contrast, those who supported the proposed constitution concluded that citizens could not be trusted to act for the public good. The Revolution, they surmised, sought to secure independence and liberty, both of which were jeopardized by the self-interest of citizens and the weakness of government. In September 1787, the onus was on such men to persuade a skeptical citizenry of the probity of their views.

DOCUMENT 1

Liberty and Peace: A Poem (1784)

Phillis [Wheatley] Peters

The woman who became known as Phillis Wheatley was born on the western coast of Africa in 1753. At the age of seven, she was kidnapped and enslaved; John Wheatley, a prominent Boston tailor, bought her as a servant for his wife in 1761. The Wheatleys taught Phillis to read and write. An apt pupil, she also studied the Bible, Greek and Latin, English literature, history, astronomy, and geography. In 1767, she published her first poem in a Rhode Island newspaper; she published a book entitled Poems on Various Subjects *in 1773, the same year she received her freedom. By 1778, when she married John Peters, Phillis Wheatley was one of the best-known poets in America, though she and her family lived in poverty in Boston until her death in 1784. This poem, one of her last, reflects the optimism many Americans felt after the war was over.*[1]

Questions to consider:

1. Many of Wheatley's poems had antislavery themes. Does this poem contain any evidence of its author's race or of her personal history in bondage?
2. What, according to Wheatley, were some of the expected "charms" of peace and freedom?

3. What were some of the metaphors she used to describe the anticipated
    course of American history in the postrevolutionary era?

O! Freedom comes. The prescient Muse foretold,
All Eyes the accomplished Prophecy behold:
Her Port described "She moves divinely fair,
"Olive and Laurel bind her golden Hair."
She, the bright Progeny of Heaven, descends,
And every Grace her sovereign Step attends;
For now kind Heaven, indulgent to our Prayer,
In smiling Peace resolves the Din of War.
Fixed in Columbia her illustrious Line,
And bids in thee her future Councils shine.
To every Realm her Portals opened wide,
Receives from each the full commercial Tide.
Each Art and Science now with rising Charms,
The expanding Heart with Emulation warms . . .
Descending Peace the Power of War Confounds;
From every Tongue celestial Peace resounds:
As from the East the illustrious King of Day,
With rising Radiance drives the Shades away,
So Freedom comes arrayed with Charms divine,
And in her Train Commerce and Plenty shine . . .
Auspicious Heaven shall fill with favoring Gales,
Where e'er Columbia spreads her swelling Sails:
To every Realm shall Peace her Charms display,
And Heavenly Freedom spread her golden Ray.

Document 2

"The Continentalist, No. VI" (1782)

Alexander Hamilton

*Even before the Articles of Confederation were ratified, nationalists wanted to revise
them to strengthen the government they established. Although nationalists championed an array of policies to promote commercial and industrial development, they*

contended that giving the central government the power to tax was particularly crucial to America's economic and political survival. A native of the West Indies who served as Washington's aide-de-camp and later represented New York in Congress, Alexander Hamilton was one of the most articulate spokesmen for the nationalist position. In 1781–82, his "Continentalist" essays appeared in the New-York Packet *and other newspapers.[2]*

Questions to consider:

1. What was Congress's current method of obtaining funding? What did Hamilton believe were its shortcomings?
2. Why, according to Hamilton, should the federal government "neither be independent nor too much dependent"? Would most Americans have agreed with that observation?

The public . . . must always have large demands upon its constituents, and the only question is whether these shall be satisfied by annual grants perpetually renewed—by a perpetual grant once for all or by a compound of permanent and occasional supplies. The last is the wisest course. The federal government should neither be independent nor too much dependent. It should neither be raised above responsibility or control, nor should it want the means of maintaining its own weight, authority, dignity and credit. To this end permanent funds are indispensable, but they ought to be of such a nature and so moderate in their amount, as never to be inconvenient. Extraordinary supplies can be the objects of extraordinary grants; and in this salutary medium will consist our true wisdom.

It would seem as if no mode of taxation could be relished but that worst of all modes which now prevails, by assessment. Every proposal for a specific tax is sure to meet with opposition. It has been objected to a poll tax, at a fixed rate, that it will be unequal, as the rich will pay no more than the poor. In the form under which it has been offered in these papers, the poor properly speaking are not comprehended, though it is true that beyond the exclusion of the indigent the tax has no reference to the proportion of property; but it should be remembered that it is impossible to devise any specific tax, that will operate equally on the whole community. It must be the province of the legislature to hold the scales with a judicious hand and balance one by another. The rich must be made to pay for their luxuries; which is the only proper way of taxing their superior wealth.

Do we imagine that our assessments operate equally? Nothing can be more contrary to the fact. Wherever a discretionary power is lodged in any set of men over the property of their neighbours, they will abuse it. Their passions, prejudices, partialities, dislikes, will have the principal lead in measuring the abilities of those over whom their power extends; and assessors will ever be a set of petty tyrants, too unskillful, if honest, to be possessed of so delicate a trust, and too seldom honest to give them the excuse of want of skill. The genius of liberty reprobates every thing arbitrary or discretionary in taxation. It exacts that every man by a definite and general rule should know what proportion of his property the state demands. Whatever liberty we may boast in theory, it cannot exist in fact, while assessments continue. The admission of them among us is a new proof, how often human conduct reconciles the most glaring opposites; in the present case the most vicious practice of despotic governments, with the freest constitutions and the greatest love of liberty.

The establishment of permanent funds would not only answer the public purposes infinitely better than temporary supplies; but it would be the most effectual way of easing the people. With this basis for procuring credit, the amount of present taxes might be greatly diminished. Large sums of money might be borrowed abroad at a low interest, and introduced into the country to defray the current expences and pay the public debts; which would not only lessen the demand for immediate supplies, but would throw more money into circulation, and furnish the people with greater means of paying the taxes. Though it be a just rule, that we ought not to run in debt to avoid present expence, so far as our faculties extend; yet the propriety of doing it cannot be disputed when it is apparent, that these are incompetent to the public necessities. Efforts beyond our abilities can only tend to individual distress and national disappointment.

DOCUMENT 3

"Primitive Whig, No. II" (1786)

William Livingston

In New Jersey, as in most other states, the emission of paper currency was a divisive issue, especially after the war was over. As states increased taxes to pay their debts, taxpayers sought relief in the form of inflationary paper currency. Creditors, by contrast, opposed the emission of legal-tender paper money, which allowed debtors to satisfy their claims with devalued currency. In a series of anonymous essays, New Jersey governor William Livingston presented the case against paper money.[3] His arguments did not persuade the majority of the state's legislators who, in 1786, authorized the printing of an additional £100,000 in currency.

Questions to consider:

1. How did Livingston portray debtors? Do you think his characterization was fair and unbiased?
2. Livingston admitted that both debtors and creditors were motivated by self-interest. On what grounds did he argue that the interests of creditors—and not those of debtors—corresponded with those of society generally? Do you agree?
3. Why, according to Livingston, did some of the state's political leaders support an inflationary prodebtor policy? In your opinion, were such legislators rejecting or reaffirming the ideals of the Revolution?

The question about the expediency of another edition of bills of credit is of such importance that it behooves every man who has a real concern for the prosperity of his country, and I may venture to say, for the very existence of the state, most seriously to resolve in his mind this momentous subject; and to oblige the public with his speculations upon it. . . .

Who are the men that are in favour of paper money? They are, generally, debtors; and debtors, by their own confession, utterly irretrievable without this iniquitous device. Iniquitous I call it, because, unless they pay their debts in money greatly depreciated at the time of payment, it can afford them no relief. How in the name of common sense should it? They are indebted. To pay their debts, they must take this money upon loan. For the repayment of this loan, they must mortgage their lands. And how is this mortgage to be discharged? In what better situation for being enabled to pay A, by running in debt to B? How is the last debt to be paid? Surely unless they annually raise out of those lands so much more than they spend, as will lessen part of the principal as well as discharge the interest, and by that means quiet the creditor, the premises mortgaged must be taken in execution at last. But that, I can tell them, they never can do, unless they will be really industrious and frugal; and oblige their wives and daughters to dress like the wives and daughters of poor distressed debtors, instead of parading in all the foppery and finery of the most opulent and independent fortunes. It is therefore their hopes of the depreciation of this money, that is the whole burden of the song.

And thus the business is eventually to terminate in the shifting the creditor instead of paying the debt, or the finally sham payment of it in depreciated currency, to their great consolation indeed as to the saving their bodies from imprisonment, but to the evident exposition of their souls to eternal perdition for such bare-faced knavery . . . For where is the man of property, the man *out* of debt, the industrious man (excepting perhaps a very few individuals, who, for the sake of popularity, or for want of better knowledge, countenances the scheme) that does not reprobate this ruinous measure?

But it will be reported, that those who are against an emission of paper money, being creditors and men of property, are also self-interested in their opposition to it. Granted. But great is the difference between the self-interest and honesty of these and that of the debtors in question. The interest of the creditor coincides with that of the community. Not so the interest of the debtor. The former desires no more than his own. The latter wants to pocket the property of another. The one, by opposing a further emission of an intended fraudulent medium, labours to restore our national credit. The other, by making it a continual resource for his own convenience, prolongs the disease and inflames the malady. Surely therefore the self-interest of the one is just and laudable: that of the other knavish and infamous. And will any legislature, so far pervert the solemn and scared trust of legislation, as to enable, under the august sanction of law, such debtors to triumph over such creditors? By what motives must such legislatures be influenced? I desire to be excused from answering the question.

DOCUMENT 4

Shays's Rebellion (1786)

In Massachusetts, state leaders used deflationary currency policies and high taxes to pare down the revolutionary debt. In 1786, the state legislature, which was dominated by eastern commercial and creditor interests, imposed still higher taxes, which many western farmers were unable to pay. That September, some 1,100 debt-ridden farmers, many of whom had fought in the Revolution, arose in Hampshire and other western counties to protest the government's fiscal policies. Led by Daniel Shays, a former captain in the Continental Army, the insurgents freed their neighbors from debtors' prison and closed the county courts to prevent the seizure of property for debt and taxes. As this manifesto shows, they also formed conventions to state their grievances and justify their conduct.[4]

Questions to consider:

1. How did the farmers' portrayal of themselves contrast with Governor Livingston's description of debtors and supporters of inflationary policies?
2. On what grounds did the insurgents argue that prosecution of debtors was counter to the public good?
3. Whom did they regard as "enemies to our liberties"?
4. Why did they feel obliged to address the people of Hampshire County?

An Address to the People of the several towns in the county of Hampshire, now at arms.

Gentlemen,

We have thought it proper to inform you of some of the principal causes of the late risings of the people, and also of their present movement:

1st. The present expensive mode of collecting debts, which by reason of the great scarcity of cash, will of necessity fill our jails with unhappy debtors, and thereby a reputable body of people rendered incapable of being serviceable either to themselves or the community.

2nd. The monies raised by impost and excise being appropriated to discharge the interest of governmental securities, and not the foreign debt, when these securities are not subject to taxation.

3rd. A suspension of the writ of Habeas Corpus, by which those persons who have stepped forth to assert and maintain the rights of the people, are liable to be taken and conveyed even to the most distant part of the Commonwealth, and thereby subjected to an unjust punishment.

4th. The unlimited power granted to Justices of the Peace and Sheriffs, Deputy Sheriffs, and Constables, by the Riot Act, indemnifying them to the prosecution thereof; when, perhaps wholly actuated from a principle of revenge, hatred, and envy. *[handwritten: ✻ protecting them from prosecution.]*

Furthermore, be assured, that this body, now at arms, despise the idea of being instigated by British emissaries, which is so strenuously propagated by the enemies of our liberties, and also wish the most proper and speedy measures may be taken, to discharge both our foreign and domestic debt.

DOCUMENT 5

"Our Affairs Are Drawing Rapidly to a Crisis" (1786)

In retirement at Mount Vernon, George Washington grew anxious over the fate of the American republic. In this letter to John Jay, the secretary of foreign affairs, Washington pondered the consequences of the states' violation of the terms of the Treaty of Paris by refusing to return confiscated property to loyalists and impeding the collection of British debts.[5] Both Washington and Jay believed that a credible foreign policy, along with the divisive and irresponsible behavior of state authorities, necessitated the creation of a stronger central government.

Questions to consider:

1.   What was Washington's mood when he wrote to John Jay in 1786?
2.   What did Washington mean when he said, "we have probably had too good an opinion of human nature in forming our confederation"?
3.   What were the most "disastrous contingencies" he envisioned as resulting from the current "crisis"?

I am sorry to be assured, of what indeed I had little doubt before, that we have been guilty of violating the treaty in some instances. What a misfortune it is the British should have so well grounded a pretext for their palpable infractions; and what a disgraceful part, out of the choice of difficulties before us, are we to act.

Your sentiments, that our affairs are drawing rapidly to a crisis, accord with my own. What the event will be, is also beyond the reach of my foresight. We have errors to correct; we have probably had too good an opinion of human nature in forming our confederation. Experience has taught us, that men will not adopt and carry into execution measures the best calculated for their own good, without the intervention of a coercive power. I do not conceive we can exist long as a nation without having lodged somewhere a power, which will pervade the whole Union in as energetic a manner, as the authority of the state governments extends over the several states.

To be fearful of investing Congress, constituted as that body is, with ample authorities for national purposes, appears to me the very climax of popular absurdity and madness. Could Congress exert them for the detriment of the public, without injuring themselves in an equal or greater proportion? Are not their interests inseparably connected with those of their constituents? By the rotation of appointment, must they not mingle frequently with the mass of citizens? Is it not rather to be apprehended, if they were possessed of the powers before described, that the individual members would be induced to use them, on many occasions, very timidly and inefficaciously for fear of losing their popularity and future election? We must take human nature as we find it: perfection falls not to the share of mortals. Many are of opinion that Congress have too frequently made use of the suppliant humble tone of requisition, in applications to the states, when they had a right to assert their imperial dignity and command obedience. Be that as it may, requisitions are a perfect nihility where thirteen sovereign independent disunited states are in the habit of discussing and refusing compliance with them at their option. Requisitions are actually little better than a jest and a bye word throughout the land. If you tell the legislatures they have violated the Treaty of Peace, and invaded the prerogatives of the confederacy, they will laugh in your face. What then is to be done? Things cannot go on in the same train forever. It is much to be feared, as you observe, that the better kind of people, being disgusted with the circumstances, will have their minds prepared for any revolution whatever. We are apt to run from one extreme into another. To anticipate and prevent disastrous contingencies, would be the part of wisdom and patriotism.

What astonishing changes a few years are capable of producing. I am told that even respectable characters speak of a monarchical form of government without horror. From thinking proceeds speaking, thence to acting is often but a single step. But how irrevocable and tremendous! What a triumph for our enemies to verify their predictions! What a triumph for the advocates of despotism to find that we are incapable of governing ourselves, and that systems founded on the basis of equal liberty are merely ideal and fallacious! Would to God that wise measures may be taken in time to avert the consequences we have but too much reason to apprehend.

Document 6

The Constitution of the United States (1787)

In May 1787, fifty-five delegates from twelve states convened in Philadelphia. After nearly four months' work, the convention, which was dominated by nationalists, did not revise the Articles of Confederation but instead produced an entirely new frame of government. Rather than submitting their work to the state legislatures for approval, they decided to have it ratified by specially elected state conventions. Popular sovereignty and separation of powers were the key ideas behind the proposed constitution. The powers of government would be divided into three branches—the legislative, executive, and judicial—each of which would represent the sovereign will of "we, the people."[6]

Questions to consider:

1. To Americans who approved of the democratizing trends of the revolutionary era, what would have been the least appealing features of the proposed constitution?
2. How did the new frame of government address the fiscal, economic, and diplomatic problems of the immediate postrevolutionary years?
3. Why is Article I, which defines the powers of the legislative branch, by far the longest of the Constitution's seven articles? What would have been the most controversial features of the proposed national legislature?
4. What sorts of constitutional restraints on executive power prevented the president from becoming a tyrant? How did the executive, conversely, limit the power of the legislature?
5. Why did the framers of the Constitution choose to submit the document to special conventions for ratification? Why did they decide that ratification by only nine states would be "sufficient for the Establishment of this Constitution between the States so ratifying the Same"?

We the People of the United States, in Order to form a more perfect Union, establish Justice, insure domestic Tranquility, provide for the common defense, promote the general Welfare, and secure the Blessings of Liberty to ourselves and our Posterity, do ordain and establish this Constitution for the United States of America.

ARTICLE I

Section. 1. All legislative Powers herein granted shall be vested in a Congress of the United States, which shall consist of a Senate and House of Representatives.

Section. 2. The House of Representatives shall be composed of Members chosen every second Year by the People of the several States, and the Electors in each State shall have the Qualifications requisite for Electors of the most numerous Branch of the State Legislature.

No Person shall be a Representative who shall not have attained to the Age of twenty five Years, and been seven Years a Citizen of the United States, and who shall not, when elected, be an Inhabitant of that State in which he shall be chosen.

Representatives and direct Taxes shall be apportioned among the several States which may be included within this Union, according to their respective Numbers, which shall be determined by adding to the whole Number of free Persons, including those bound to Service for a Term of Years, and excluding Indians not taxed, three fifths of all other Persons. The actual Enumeration shall be made within three Years after the first Meeting of the Congress of the United States, and within every subsequent Term of ten Years, in such Manner as they shall by Law direct. The Number of Representatives shall not exceed one for every thirty Thousand, but each State shall have at Least one Representative; and until such enumeration shall be made, the State of New Hampshire shall be entitled to choose three, Massachusetts eight, Rhode Island and Providence Plantations one, Connecticut five, New York six, New Jersey four, Pennsylvania eight, Delaware one, Maryland six, Virginia ten, North Carolina five, South Carolina five, and Georgia three.

When vacancies happen in the Representation from any State, the Executive Authority thereof shall issue Writs of Election to fill such Vacancies.

The House of Representatives shall chuse their Speaker and other Officers; and shall have the sole Power of Impeachment.

Section. 3. The Senate of the United States shall be composed of two Senators from each State, chosen by the Legislature thereof for six Years; and each Senator shall have one Vote.

Immediately after they shall be assembled in Consequence of the first Election, they shall be divided as equally as may be into three Classes. The Seats of the Senators of the first Class shall be vacated at the Expiration of the second Year, of the second Class at the Expiration of the fourth Year, and of the third Class at the Expiration of the sixth Year, so that one third may be chosen every second Year; and if Vacancies happen by Resignation, or otherwise, during the Recess of the Legislature of any State, the Executive thereof may make temporary Appointments until the next Meeting of the Legislature, which shall then fill such Vacancies.

No Person shall be a Senator who shall not have attained to the Age of thirty Years, and been nine Years a Citizen of the United States, and who shall not, when elected, be an Inhabitant of that State for which he shall be chosen.

The Vice President of the United States shall be President of the Senate, but shall have no Vote, unless they be equally divided.

The Senate shall choose their other Officers, and also a President pro tempore, in the Absence of the Vice President, or when he shall exercise the Office of President of the United States.

The Senate shall have the sole Power to try all Impeachments. When sitting for that Purpose, they shall be on Oath or Affirmation. When the

President of the United States is tried, the Chief Justice shall preside: And no Person shall be convicted without the Concurrence of two thirds of the Members present.

Judgment in Cases of Impeachment shall not extend further than to removal from Office, and disqualification to hold and enjoy any Office of honor, Trust or Profit under the United States: but the Party convicted shall nevertheless be liable and subject to Indictment, Trial, Judgment and Punishment, according to Law.

Section. 4. The Times, Places and Manner of holding Elections for Senators and Representatives, shall be prescribed in each State by the Legislature thereof; but the Congress may at any time by Law make or alter such Regulations, except as to the Places of choosing Senators.

The Congress shall assemble at least once in every Year, and such Meeting shall be on the first Monday in December, unless they shall by Law appoint a different Day.

Section. 5. Each House shall be the Judge of the Elections, Returns and Qualifications of its own Members, and a Majority of each shall constitute a Quorum to do Business; but a smaller Number may adjourn from day to day, and may be authorized to compel the Attendance of absent Members, in such Manner, and under such Penalties as each House may provide.

Each House may determine the Rules of its Proceedings, punish its Members for disorderly Behaviour, and, with the Concurrence of two thirds, expel a Member.

Each House shall keep a Journal of its Proceedings, and from time to time publish the same, excepting such Parts as may in their Judgment require Secrecy; and the Yeas and Nays of the Members of either House on any question shall, at the Desire of one fifth of those Present, be entered on the Journal.

Neither House, during the Session of Congress, shall, without the Consent of the other, adjourn for more than three days, nor to any other Place than that in which the two Houses shall be sitting.

Section. 6. The Senators and Representatives shall receive a Compensation for their Services, to be ascertained by Law, and paid out of the Treasury of the United States. They shall in all Cases, except Treason, Felony and Breach of the Peace, be privileged from Arrest during their Attendance at the Session of their respective Houses, and in going to and returning from the same; and for any Speech or Debate in either House, they shall not be questioned in any other Place.

No Senator or Representative shall, during the Time for which he was elected, be appointed to any civil Office under the Authority of the United States, which shall have been created, or the Emoluments whereof shall have been increased during such time; and no Person holding any Office under the United States, shall be a Member of either House during his Continuance in Office.

Section. 7. All Bills for raising Revenue shall originate in the House of Representatives; but the Senate may propose or concur with Amendments as on other Bills.

Every Bill which shall have passed the House of Representatives and the Senate, shall, before it become a Law, be presented to the President of the United States: If he approve he shall sign it, but if not he shall return it, with his Objections to that House in which it shall have originated, who shall enter the Objections at large on their Journal, and proceed to reconsider it. If after such Reconsideration two thirds of that House shall agree to pass the Bill, it shall be sent, together with the Objections, to the other House, by which it shall likewise be reconsidered, and if approved by two thirds of that House, it shall become a Law. But in all such Cases the Votes of both Houses shall be determined by yeas and Nays, and the Names of the Persons voting for and against the Bill shall be entered on the Journal of each House respectively. If any Bill shall not be returned by the President within ten Days (Sundays excepted) after it shall have been presented to him, the Same shall be a Law, in like Manner as if he had signed it, unless the Congress by their Adjournment prevent its Return, in which Case it shall not be a Law.

Every Order, Resolution, or Vote to which the Concurrence of the Senate and House of Representatives may be necessary (except on a question of Adjournment) shall be presented to the President of the United States; and before the Same shall take Effect, shall be approved by him, or being disapproved by him, shall be repassed by two thirds of the Senate and House of Representatives, according to the Rules and Limitations prescribed in the Case of a Bill.

Section. 8. The Congress shall have Power To lay and collect Taxes, Duties, Imposts and Excises, to pay the Debts and provide for the common Defence and general Welfare of the United States; but all Duties, Imposts and Excises shall be uniform throughout the United States;

To borrow Money on the credit of the United States;

To regulate Commerce with foreign Nations, and among the several States, and with the Indian Tribes;

To establish an uniform Rule of Naturalization, and uniform Laws on the subject of Bankruptcies throughout the United States;

To coin Money, regulate the Value thereof, and of foreign Coin, and fix the Standard of Weights and Measures;

To provide for the Punishment of counterfeiting the Securities and current Coin of the United States;

To establish Post Offices and post Roads;

To promote the Progress of Science and useful Arts, by securing for limited Times to Authors and Inventors the exclusive Right to their respective Writings and Discoveries;

To constitute Tribunals inferior to the supreme Court;

To define and punish Piracies and Felonies committed on the high Seas, and Offences against the Law of Nations;

To declare War, grant Letters of Marque and Reprisal, and make Rules concerning Captures on Land and Water;

To raise and support Armies, but no Appropriation of Money to that Use shall be for a longer Term than two Years;

To provide and maintain a Navy;

To make Rules for the Government and Regulation of the land and naval Forces;

To provide for calling forth the Militia to execute the Laws of the Union, suppress Insurrections and repel Invasions;

To provide for organizing, arming, and disciplining, the Militia, and for governing such Part of them as may be employed in the Service of the United States, reserving to the States respectively, the Appointment of the Officers, and the Authority of training the Militia according to the discipline prescribed by Congress;

To exercise exclusive Legislation in all Cases whatsoever, over such District (not exceeding ten Miles square) as may, by Cession of particular States, and the Acceptance of Congress, become the Seat of the Government of the United States, and to exercise like Authority over all Places purchased by the Consent of the Legislature of the State in which the Same shall be, for the Erection of Forts, Magazines, Arsenals, dock-Yards, and other needful Buildings;—And To make all Laws which shall be necessary and proper for carrying into Execution the foregoing Powers, and all other Powers vested by this Constitution in the Government of the United States, or in any Department or Officer thereof.

Section. 9. The Migration or Importation of such Persons as any of the States now existing shall think proper to admit, shall not be prohibited by the Congress prior to the Year one thousand eight hundred and eight, but a Tax or duty may be imposed on such Importation, not exceeding ten dollars for each Person.

The Privilege of the Writ of Habeas Corpus shall not be suspended, unless when in Cases of Rebellion or Invasion the public Safety may require it.

No Bill of Attainder or ex post facto Law shall be passed.

No Capitation, or other direct, Tax shall be laid, unless in Proportion to the Census or enumeration herein before directed to be taken.

No Tax or Duty shall be laid on Articles exported from any State.

No Preference shall be given by any Regulation of Commerce or Revenue to the Ports of one State over those of another; nor shall Vessels bound to, or from, one State, be obliged to enter, clear, or pay Duties in another.

No Money shall be drawn from the Treasury, but in Consequence of Appropriations made by Law; and a regular Statement and Account of the Receipts and Expenditures of all public Money shall be published from time to time.

No Title of Nobility shall be granted by the United States: And no Person holding any Office of Profit or Trust under them, shall, without the Consent of the Congress, accept of any present, Emolument, Office, or Title, of any kind whatever, from any King, Prince, or foreign State.

Section. 10. No State shall enter into any Treaty, Alliance, or Confederation; grant Letters of Marque and Reprisal; coin Money; emit Bills of Credit; make any Thing but gold and silver Coin a Tender in Payment of Debts; pass any Bill of Attainder, ex post facto Law, or Law impairing the Obligation of Contracts, or grant any Title of Nobility.

No State shall, without the Consent of the Congress, lay any Imposts or Duties on Imports or Exports, except what may be absolutely necessary for executing it's inspection Laws: and the net Produce of all Duties and Imposts, laid by any State on Imports or Exports, shall be for the Use of the Treasury of the United States; and all such Laws shall be subject to the Revision and Control of the Congress.

No State shall, without the Consent of Congress, lay any Duty of Tonnage, keep Troops, or Ships of War in time of Peace, enter into any Agreement or Compact with another State, or with a foreign Power, or engage in War, unless actually invaded, or in such imminent Danger as will not admit of delay.

ARTICLE II

Section. 1. The executive Power shall be vested in a President of the United States of America. He shall hold his Office during the Term of four Years, and, together with the Vice President, chosen for the same Term, be elected, as follows:

Each State shall appoint, in such Manner as the Legislature thereof may direct, a Number of Electors, equal to the whole Number of Senators and Representatives to which the State may be entitled in the Congress: but no Senator or Representative, or Person holding an Office of Trust or Profit under the United States, shall be appointed an Elector.

The Electors shall meet in their respective States, and vote by Ballot for two Persons, of whom one at least shall not be an Inhabitant of the same State with themselves. And they shall make a List of all the Persons voted for, and of the Number of Votes for each; which List they shall sign and certify, and transmit sealed to the Seat of the Government of the United States, directed to the President of the Senate. The President of the Senate shall, in the Presence of the Senate and House of Representatives, open all the Certificates, and the Votes shall then be counted. The Person having the greatest Number of Votes shall be the President, if such Number be a Majority of the whole Number of Electors appointed; and if there be more than one who have such Majority, and have an equal Number of Votes, then the House of

Representatives shall immediately choose by Ballot one of them for President; and if no Person have a Majority, then from the five highest on the List the said House shall in like Manner choose the President. But in choosing the President, the Votes shall be taken by States, the Representation from each State having one Vote; A quorum for this purpose shall consist of a Member or Members from two thirds of the States, and a Majority of all the States shall be necessary to a Choice. In every Case, after the Choice of the President, the Person having the greatest Number of Votes of the Electors shall be the Vice President. But if there should remain two or more who have equal Votes, the Senate shall choose from them by Ballot the Vice President.

The Congress may determine the Time of choosing the Electors, and the Day on which they shall give their Votes; which Day shall be the same throughout the United States.

No Person except a natural born Citizen, or a Citizen of the United States, at the time of the Adoption of this Constitution, shall be eligible to the Office of President; neither shall any Person be eligible to that Office who shall not have attained to the Age of thirty five Years, and been fourteen Years a Resident within the United States.

In Case of the Removal of the President from Office, or of his Death, Resignation, or Inability to discharge the Powers and Duties of the said Office, the Same shall devolve on the Vice President, and the Congress may by Law provide for the Case of Removal, Death, Resignation or Inability, both of the President and Vice President, declaring what Officer shall then act as President, and such Officer shall act accordingly, until the Disability be removed, or a President shall be elected.

The President shall, at stated Times, receive for his Services, a Compensation, which shall neither be increased nor diminished during the Period for which he shall have been elected, and he shall not receive within that Period any other Emolument from the United States, or any of them.

Before he enter on the Execution of his Office, he shall take the following Oath or Affirmation:—"I do solemnly swear (or affirm) that I will faithfully execute the Office of President of the United States, and will to the best of my Ability, preserve, protect and defend the Constitution of the United States."

Section. 2. The President shall be Commander in Chief of the Army and Navy of the United States, and of the Militia of the several States, when called into the actual Service of the United States; he may require the Opinion, in writing, of the principal Officer in each of the executive Departments, upon any Subject relating to the Duties of their respective Offices, and he shall have Power to grant Reprieves and Pardons for Offences against the United States, except in Cases of Impeachment.

He shall have Power, by and with the Advice and Consent of the Senate, to make Treaties, provided two thirds of the Senators present concur; and he shall nominate, and by and with the Advice and Consent of the

Senate, shall appoint Ambassadors, other public Ministers and Consuls, Judges of the supreme Court, and all other Officers of the United States, whose Appointments are not herein otherwise provided for, and which shall be established by Law: but the Congress may by Law vest the Appointment of such inferior Officers, as they think proper, in the President alone, in the Courts of Law, or in the Heads of Departments.

The President shall have Power to fill up all Vacancies that may happen during the Recess of the Senate, by granting Commissions which shall expire at the End of their next Session.

Section. 3. He shall from time to time give to the Congress Information of the State of the Union, and recommend to their Consideration such Measures as he shall judge necessary and expedient; he may, on extraordinary Occasions, convene both Houses, or either of them, and in Case of Disagreement between them, with Respect to the Time of Adjournment, he may adjourn them to such Time as he shall think proper; he shall receive Ambassadors and other public Ministers; he shall take Care that the Laws be faithfully executed, and shall Commission all the Officers of the United States.

Section. 4. The President, Vice President and all civil Officers of the United States, shall be removed from Office on Impeachment for, and Conviction of, Treason, Bribery, or other high Crimes and Misdemeanors.

ARTICLE III

Section. 1. The judicial Power of the United States shall be vested in one supreme Court, and in such inferior Courts as the Congress may from time to time ordain and establish. The Judges, both of the supreme and inferior Courts, shall hold their Offices during good Behaviour, and shall, at stated Times, receive for their Services a Compensation, which shall not be diminished during their Continuance in Office.

Section. 2. The judicial Power shall extend to all Cases, in Law and Equity, arising under this Constitution, the Laws of the United States, and Treaties made, or which shall be made, under their Authority;—to all Cases affecting Ambassadors, other public Ministers and Consuls;—to all Cases of admiralty and maritime Jurisdiction;—to Controversies to which the United States shall be a Party;—to Controversies between two or more States;—between a State and Citizens of another State;—between Citizens of different States;—between Citizens of the same State claiming Lands under Grants of different States, and between a State, or the Citizens thereof, and foreign States, Citizens or Subjects.

In all Cases affecting Ambassadors, other public Ministers and Consuls, and those in which a State shall be Party, the supreme Court shall have original Jurisdiction. In all the other Cases before mentioned, the supreme

Court shall have appellate Jurisdiction, both as to Law and Fact, with such Exceptions, and under such Regulations as the Congress shall make.

The Trial of all Crimes, except in Cases of Impeachment, shall be by Jury; and such Trial shall be held in the State where the said Crimes shall have been committed; but when not committed within any State, the Trial shall be at such Place or Places as the Congress may by Law have directed.

Section. 3. Treason against the United States, shall consist only in levying War against them, or in adhering to their Enemies, giving them Aid and Comfort. No Person shall be convicted of Treason unless on the Testimony of two Witnesses to the same overt Act, or on Confession in open Court.

The Congress shall have Power to declare the Punishment of Treason, but no Attainder of Treason shall work Corruption of Blood, or Forfeiture except during the Life of the Person attainted.

ARTICLE IV

Section. 1. Full Faith and Credit shall be given in each State to the public Acts, Records, and judicial Proceedings of every other State. And the Congress may by general Laws prescribe the Manner in which such Acts, Records and Proceedings shall be proved, and the Effect thereof.

Section. 2. The Citizens of each State shall be entitled to all Privileges and Immunities of Citizens in the several States.

A Person charged in any State with Treason, Felony, or other Crime, who shall flee from Justice, and be found in another State, shall on Demand of the executive Authority of the State from which he fled, be delivered up, to be removed to the State having Jurisdiction of the Crime.

No Person held to Service or Labour in one State, under the Laws thereof, escaping into another, shall, in Consequence of any Law or Regulation therein, be discharged from such Service or Labour, but shall be delivered up on Claim of the Party to whom such Service or Labour may be due.

Section. 3. New States may be admitted by the Congress into this Union; but no new State shall be formed or erected within the Jurisdiction of any other State; nor any State be formed by the Junction of two or more States, or Parts of States, without the Consent of the Legislatures of the States concerned as well as of the Congress.

The Congress shall have Power to dispose of and make all needful Rules and Regulations respecting the Territory or other Property belonging to the United States; and nothing in this Constitution shall be so construed as to Prejudice any Claims of the United States, or of any particular State.

Section. 4. The United States shall guarantee to every State in this Union a Republican Form of Government, and shall protect each of them against Invasion; and on Application of the Legislature, or of the Executive (when the Legislature cannot be convened), against domestic Violence.

ARTICLE V

The Congress, whenever two thirds of both Houses shall deem it necessary, shall propose Amendments to this Constitution, or, on the Application of the Legislatures of two thirds of the several States, shall call a Convention for proposing Amendments, which, in either Case, shall be valid to all Intents and Purposes, as Part of this Constitution, when ratified by the Legislatures of three fourths of the several States, or by Conventions in three fourths thereof, as the one or the other Mode of Ratification may be proposed by the Congress; Provided that no Amendment which may be made prior to the Year One thousand eight hundred and eight shall in any Manner affect the first and fourth Clauses in the Ninth Section of the first Article; and that no State, without its Consent, shall be deprived of its equal Suffrage in the Senate.

ARTICLE VI

All Debts contracted and Engagements entered into, before the Adoption of this Constitution, shall be as valid against the United States under this Constitution, as under the Confederation.

This Constitution, and the Laws of the United States which shall be made in Pursuance thereof; and all Treaties made, or which shall be made, under the Authority of the United States, shall be the supreme Law of the Land; and the Judges in every State shall be bound thereby, any Thing in the Constitution or Laws of any State to the contrary notwithstanding.

The Senators and Representatives before mentioned, and the Members of the several State Legislatures, and all executive and judicial Officers, both of the United States and of the several States, shall be bound by Oath or Affirmation, to support this Constitution; but no religious Test shall ever be required as a Qualification to any Office or public Trust under the United States.

ARTICLE VII

The Ratification of the Conventions of nine States, shall be sufficient for the Establishment of this Constitution between the States so ratifying the Same.

Done in Convention by the Unanimous Consent of the States present the Seventeenth Day of September in the Year of our Lord one thousand seven hundred and Eighty seven and of the Independence of the United States of America the Twelfth. In witness whereof We have hereunto subscribed our Names.

SUGGESTED READING FOR CHAPTER 9

BEEMAN, RICHARD; BOTEIN, STEPHEN; and CARTER, EDWARD C., II, eds., *Beyond Confederation: Origins of the Constitution and American National Identity* (1987).
BERNSTEIN, RICHARD B.; and RICE, KYM S. *Are We to be One Nation?: The Making of the Constitution* (1987).
BROWN, ROGER H. *Redeeming the Republic: Federalists, Taxation, and the Origins of the Constitution* (1993).
GROSS, ROBERT A., ed. *In Debt to Shays: The Legacy of an Agrarian Rebellion* (1991).
JENSEN, MERRILL. *The New Nation: A History of the United States during the Confederation, 1781–1789* (1950).
MAIN, JACKSON TURNER. "Government by the People: The American Revolution and the Democratization of the Legislatures." *William and Mary Quarterly*, 3rd ser., 23 (1966): 391–407.
MASON, JULIAN D., JR. *The Poems of Phillis Wheatley* (1966).
MCDONALD, FORREST. *E Pluribus Unum: The Formation of the American Republic* (1965).
———. *Novus Ordo Seclorum: The Intellectual Origins of the Constitution* (1985).
ONUF, PETER S. *The Origins of the Federal Republic: Jurisdictional Controversies in the United States* (1983).
RAKOVE, JACK N. *The Beginnings of National Politics: An Interpretive History of the Continental Congress* (1979).
SZATMARY, DAVID P. *Shays' Rebellion: The Making of an Agrarian Insurrection* (1980).
WOOD, GORDON S. *The Creation of the American Republic, 1776–1787* (1969).

NOTES

[1]Phillis [Wheatley] Peters, *Liberty and Peace: A Poem* (Boston, 1784), 2–4.
[2][Alexander Hamilton], "The Continentalist No. VI," *The New-York Packet*, 4 July 1782.
[3][William Livingston], "Primitive Whig, No. II," *New Jersey Gazette*, 16 Jan. 1786.
[4]George R. Minot, *The History of the Insurrection in Massachusetts in 1786 and of the Rebellion Consequent Thereon* (Worcester, Mass., 1788), 82–83.
[5]George Washington to John Jay, 1 Aug. 1786, in John C. Fitzpatrick, ed., *The Writings of George Washington*, 39 vols. (Washington, 1931–44), 28: 501–4.
[6]For the Constitution of the United States, see the following Website: www.nara.gov/exhall/charters/constitution/constitution.html

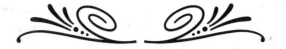

CHAPTER TEN

FEDERALISTS AND ANTIFEDERALISTS

As Americans assessed the merits and shortcomings of the proposed constitution, they divided into two camps that engaged in a bitter struggle over the issue of ratification. Those who supported the constitution became known as Federalists. Fearing anarchy above all else and deeply distrustful of popular passions, Federalists argued that a strong central government insulated from the turbulent interests of the people was essential to the survival of liberty. By contrast, critics of the proposed constitution, known as Antifederalists, viewed tyranny, or the coercive power of government, as the greatest threat to liberty. The best safeguard against tyranny, they asserted, was popular control of government.

The Federalists emerged triumphant from the struggle for ratification, but their victory was by no means inevitable. In 1787, most Americans probably espoused Antifederalist views, and, even after months of aggressive campaigning by the Federalists, the vote for ratification was excruciatingly close in many states. In the end, the superior resources, organization, and prestige of the Federalists prevailed. Although the Antifederalists could not prevent ratification, they persuaded the Federalists to amend their constitution to include a bill of rights.

The vast majority of delegates to the Philadelphia convention agreed on three key points. First, they were committed to strengthening the central government, both to make it more effective and to enable it to restrain what they believed to be the excessive democracy of the states. Second, they believed that the new government should be republican—or, in other words, a government of made up of representatives of the people. Third, drawing on their English constitutional inheritance and on their more recent experiences with institution-building at the state level, they agreed that political authority should be divided among several constituent institutions or branches to prevent any one from becoming too powerful. For although they believed that political institutions had to be insulated from the citizens' changing passions, they also remained deeply distrustful of those who wielded political power.

The delegates also disagreed on several major points, the first of which was how to allocate legislative representation among the states. Edmund Randolph of Virginia presented a comprehensive proposal, probably drafted by James Madison, who would come to play the leading role in the convention's proceedings and in the subsequent campaign for ratification. This proposal, which came to be known as the Virginia Plan, called for the establishment of a government consisting of three branches: a bicameral legislature, as well as an executive and a judiciary, both of which would be elected by the legislature. Under the Virginia Plan, the central government's authority would be extensive, including even the power to overturn state laws. But by far the most controversial part of the Virginia Plan was the proposal that representation in both legislative houses be apportioned by population, with the lower house elected directly by the voters and the upper house chosen by the members of the lower house.

This proposal alarmed delegates from small states, who understandably feared being rendered powerless under a system of proportionate representation. William Paterson of New Jersey presented an alternative proposal that became known as the New Jersey Plan. Paterson also wished to jettison the Articles of Confederation in favor of a stronger central government, but he supported the creation of a unicameral legislature in which each state would have equal representation to safeguard the interests of the smaller states. In the end, the delegates compromised after intense debate. The proposed constitution provided for a bicameral legislature. Although representation in the House of Representatives would be apportioned by population, each state, regardless of size, would have two seats in the Senate or upper house.

The second major source of division among the convention's delegates was an array of concerns related to the institution of slavery. Delegates who opposed slavery on moral grounds did not call for its abolition because they recognized that doing so would alienate southerners and make the success of the convention virtually impossible. Accordingly, the delegates never considered a constitutional provision to abolish slavery—either immediately or in the long term—and they specifically prohibited Congress from curtailing the international slave trade until at least twenty years after the constitution took effect. Northern and southern delegates compromised on the thorny issue of how enslaved people would be counted for the purposes of representation and taxation. Northern delegates agreed to count each enslaved person as equivalent to three-fifths of a free person in apportioning representation in the lower legislative house. For their part, delegates from the slaveholding states accepted the provision that slaves be considered as property for the purpose of apportioning taxes. By evading slavery's moral implications, the delegates served their larger purpose of fostering unity among nationalists across regional lines.

The constitution that emerged from months of compromise and debate had as its fundamental premise the concept of popular sovereignty. Deciding who was sovereign—or who wielded ultimate political authority—had troubled colonial Americans, who tried unsuccessfully to divide sovereignty between the Parliament of Great Britain and their own provincial legislatures. As colonial leaders soon discovered, sovereignty was by definition indivisible; only one entity could exercise ultimate or final authority. The War of Independence was fought largely over the question of whose authority—Parliament's or that of the colonial assemblies—would be paramount. In 1776, American revolutionaries made their states sovereign. In 1787, however, Federalists wanted to end state sovereignty, while nonetheless preserving the states as political entities. How could they divide political power of between the state and national governments without attempting to divide sovereignty itself? The Federalists resolved this dilemma by deciding that under their new system, neither the states nor the national government would be sovereign. Both instead would govern on behalf of—and be accountable to—the sovereign people.

The concept of popular sovereignty was instrumental in solving the problem of how best to divide and balance power within the proposed government. Many Americans still admired the concept of balance—the division of power between the three social orders of King, Lords, and Commons—that lay at the heart of the British constitution. At the same time, they had no desire to establish either a monarchy or an aristocracy, thus leaving their government bereft of two of the three constituent parts of a balanced constitution in its classical form. How could Americans achieve the benefits of balanced government in a society without legally distinct orders or ranks? Although some states tried to simulate the classical social hierarchy by making the property qualifications for prospective governors higher than those for members of the upper house—whose qualifications were higher, in turn, than those for members of the assembly—in practice, the sorts of men who held these offices were often indistinguishable. By the 1780s, efforts to reform the state governments focused on balancing the powers of the legislative, executive, and judicial branches. Typically, reformers sought to strengthen the governor and judiciary to dilute or check the power of the legislature. As they debated constitutional revisions, these reformers moved haltingly toward a redefinition of government's constituent parts. American republicans would divide or balance power among functionally specialized branches of government rather than among unequal social orders.

The Federalists made this concept of separation of powers the core of their constitution. The new government would be composed of three branches—executive, legislative, and judicial—whose functions and personnel would be separate and distinct. In keeping with the idea of popular sovereignty, they maintained, each of these branches would represent the sovereign people.

On 17 September 1787, the constitutional convention adjourned, and the thirty-nine delegates who remained in Philadelphia to approve the constitution's final draft returned to their respective states to promote its ratification. The struggle for ratification was the first nationwide political contest in the history of the United States, though the drama unfolded in the thirteen separate states over an extended period. On 7 December 1787, Delaware became the first state to ratify the constitution; Rhode Island was the last, on 29 May 1790.

What sorts of people were likely to favor ratification and what sorts were likely to oppose it? Before the twentieth century, historians of the United States, who tended to be nationalist authors of celebratory narratives, typically regarded the adoption of the constitution as the inevitable and wholly salutary achievement of godlike patriots. In 1913, however, Charles A. Beard offered a startling reassessment of the so-called Founding Fathers, declaring that they were mere mortals who, like other humans, were motivated by self-interest. For Beard, who wrote in the reform-minded Progressive Era, it was important to desacralize the constitution's origins in order to justify the sorts of legal and political changes that he and other Progressives wanted. In *An Economic Interpretation of the Constitution of the United States*, Beard argued specifically that the delegates to the constitutional convention were government creditors—especially holders of Continental securities—who expected to benefit financially by the establishment of a strong and fiscally responsible central government. Their opponents, he maintained, were mainly farmers and small planters, whose wealth was mainly in land and slaves. In Beard's view, the constitution was an economic document, designed to promote the specific interests of an economic elite.

Subsequent research has refuted many of Beard's specific arguments, but his central premise remains influential. Most of the delegates, as it turns out, were great landholders with no interest in Continental securities. Nevertheless, the constitution was bitterly contested, as Beard suggested, and social identities and economic interests helped shape voters' response to the proposed frame of government. While Progressive historians of Beard's generation downplayed the significance of ideas, which they considered mere rationalizations for the pursuit of economic interest, more recent historians posit a more complex relationship between ideas and interests, or rhetoric and reality. For example, voting data from each of the state ratifying conventions suggests that Federalists tended to be disproportionately urban, educated, and enmeshed in personal or economic networks that reached beyond their local communities. Antifederalists, conversely, were typically residents of rural areas that were isolated from outside commercial, political, and cultural influences. Varying economic and social circumstances, in turn, encouraged the development of disparate worldviews, which historian Jackson Turner Main, in his book *Political Parties Before the Constitution*, characterized as "cosmopolitan" and "localist," respectively. These worldviews, rather than narrowly construed economic interests, informed Americans' response to the proposed constitution.

Most historians believe that proponents of the cosmopolitan or nationalizing position were in the minority as the constitutional convention drew to a close in September 1787. Despite their minority status, however, supporters of the constitution had four important advantages in the campaign for ratification. First, they appropriated for themselves the name "Federalist," leading their opponents to identify themselves as "Antifederalists." These labels were misleading insofar as the word *federalism* implies decentralized authority, which was the opposite of what the self-styled Federalists truly wanted. By adopting this nomenclature, the constitution's supporters shrewdly forced its critics to be negative and defensive from the outset. Second, the Federalists could draw on interstate organizational networks that originated with the nationalist bloc in Congress and expanded and solidified at the convention in Philadelphia. Third, the constitution's champions had the support of America's best-known and widely respected leaders: that of Washington, the military hero who voluntarily resigned his commission at the war's end, was especially crucial. Finally, Federalists controlled the overwhelming majority of newspapers, which were typically based in their urban and commercial strongholds.

Exploiting all of these advantages, Federalists moved quickly to get out their message to voters in every state as they prepared to choose delegates to their special ratifying conventions. Federalists used national networks to exchange information and coordinate strategy. Their efforts included an impressive interstate newspaper campaign that featured publication in most states of many of the eighty-five *Federalist* essays, penned by Alexander Hamilton and John Jay of New York and James Madison of Virginia.

The Antifederalist effort, by contrast, was dispersed and loosely organized, reflecting the largely localist orientation and experience of its leaders. Antifederalist leaders included some prominent and influential men, most notably Samuel Adams and Elbridge Gerry of Massachusetts, George Clinton of New York, and Patrick Henry and George Mason of Virginia. But the fact that all of these men attained their prestige and influence in state and local politics—rather than at the Continental level—meant that most had few political contacts outside their own states. As a result, when Antifederalists published their often trenchant criticisms of the constitution, they typically addressed only residents of their own states.

Antifederalists interpreted the great debate over the constitution as a struggle between aristocracy and democracy. With justification, they regarded the proposed frame of government as aristocratic, by which they meant that it aimed to place political power in the hands of the few—rather than allowing the many to govern, as they did currently in the states. Antifederalists criticized the vast powers of the proposed executive and the Senate—neither of which citizens directly elected—and those of an appointive federal judiciary. They also condemned as aristocratic the nature of representation in the popularly elected House of Representatives, where each member would represent no fewer than 30,000 constituents, a significantly higher ratio between representatives and constituents than in any state legislature at that time. Antifederalists believed that such a high ratio would make it nearly impossible for ordinary men to aspire to national office and enable representatives to insulate themselves from their constituents' influence once they went to Congress.

Because they viewed the proposed national government as fundamentally aristocratic, as friends of democracy the Antifederalists necessarily opposed endowing it with varied and wide-ranging powers. While some Antifederalist authors worried about the proposed government's power to tax, others feared its potentially coercive military power. Drawing on conventional political theory, Antifederalists also asserted that the United States was too big to be a single republic. The government of so large a territory, they maintained, would degenerate into rivalries between contending interests, which would undermine the virtue of citizens and inflict tyranny on minorities. Finally, Antifederalists were nearly universal in their criticism of the constitution's lack of a bill of rights to restrain the power of the central government by protecting the rights of citizens and states. On this key issue they remained firm, utterly rejecting the Federalists' contention that the sovereignty of the people rendered superfluous additional constitutional safeguards for their rights.

The constitution's supporters responded to the Antifederalists' reservations and criticisms in pamphlets and newspaper essays. They did so most effectively and comprehensively in the series of essays that came to be known as *The Federalist Papers*. Published initially in New York, where Antifederalists were known to have an early advantage, the *Federalist* essays methodically explained the benefits of national union, the powers and responsibilities of the government's three constituent branches, and the theoretical basis of what proved to be a new and distinctively American approach to politics.

In the tenth and fifty-first essays, in particular, Madison summarized the central tenets of the Federalist perspective. Having abandoned their faith in the innate virtue of the citizens of the republic, the Federalists concluded that all human beings were motivated by self-interest. Consequently, the main task of government, Madison argued, was to preserve liberty by protecting government and society from domination by one interest or faction. Madison challenged the conventional assumption—often invoked by Antifederalists—that only small homogenous republics could protect liberty, declaring instead that a large republic with a diversity of competing interests provided the best check against the tyranny of the majority. At the same time, Federalist political institutions, with their checks and balances both among the three branches and between the state and national governments, would provide additional protection for the individual and collective liberties of the sovereign people.

Although *The Federalist Papers* have proved invaluable to future generations seeking to comprehend their authors' understanding of the constitution, in 1787–88 the Federalists' political momentum swayed more votes than the eloquence of Madison and his associates. Skillful management enabled the Federalists to secure ratification in Delaware, Pennsylvania, and New Jersey by the end of 1787, with Georgia and Connecticut following in January 1788. At this point, the Federalists had won lopsided victories in all but Pennsylvania, and delegates had proposed amendments to their constitution in none of these five states.

The Federalists encountered their first potential setback in the crucial state of Massachusetts, where their failure to orchestrate a quick convention gave Antifederalist forces sufficient time to organize an effective campaign that netted them a roughly twenty-seat advantage in a convention of more than 350 delegates. Federalist leaders in Massachusetts had to agree to support amendments—specifically the addition of a bill of rights—in order to secure ratification. They also had to woo Governor John Hancock, suggesting that he might win the presidency if Virginia's failure to ratify rendered Washington ineligible. As a result of these concessions, Massachusetts voted to ratify by a count of 187 to 168 in February 1788. Maryland and South Carolina followed, in April and May, respectively. But these and all subsequent state conventions followed the example of Massachusetts in proposing that the constitution be amended after ratification.

The proposed constitution stated that the new frame of government would go into effect when nine states ratified it. On 26 June 1788, New Hampshire became the ninth state to ratify when its delegates did so by a ten-vote margin. Nevertheless, the Federalists knew that the constitution could not be implemented without the support of the major states of Virginia and New York. In both states, however, ratification appeared doubtful. In Virginia, only Washington's vast influence and Madison's promise to support an added bill of rights got the Federalists the votes they needed: eighty-nine delegates voted for ratification, while seventy-nine opposed it. News from Virginia influenced the outcome in New York, where Antifederalists claimed forty-six of sixty-five seats when the convention gathered. Faced with the impending certainty of a Federalist victory and with the

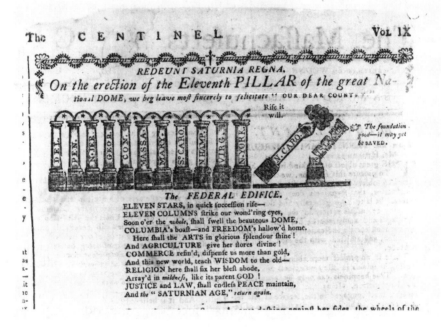

On the erection of the Eleventh Pillar of the great National dome, 1788. This cartoon, which appeared in the Federalist *Massachusetts Centinel*, celebrated New York's ratification of the U.S. Constitution, which left only North Carolina and Rhode Island outside the "Federal Edifice." Why did the author of the accompanying poem predict that New York's ratification would bring a "Saturnian Age"—or an era of peace and prosperity? Why did the author use terms like "dome" and "edifice" as metaphors for the new union of states under the Constitution? Source: "The Massachusetts Centinel." [Boston] Massachusetts: Warden & Russell, 1784–1790. Vol. 2, no. 8 (October 16, 1784)–v. 12, no. 26 (June 12, 1790). Courtesy of The Library of Congress, Washington, D.C.

additional threat of secession by New York City and its surrounding counties, some Antifederalists abstained and others switched sides. On 26 July 1788, New York voted for ratification by a three-vote margin. The reluctant acquiescence of North Carolina in November 1789 and of Rhode Island the following May completed the new federal union. In 1791, Vermont, whose inhabitants had agitated for separate statehood since 1776, was admitted to the union as its fourteenth state.

When the new government commenced operation in the spring of 1789, one of its first orders of business was to address Antifederalist demands for a bill of rights. In June, James Madison, now representing his central Virginia district in the House of Representatives, presented a total of nineteen amendments for his colleagues' consideration, based on those that the various state conventions had proposed. On 25 September, after considerable debate and revision, Congress adopted twelve of these amendments, ten of which were ratified by the requisite three-quarters of the states. Known collectively as the Bill of Rights, these first ten amendments to the Constitution went into effect on 15 December 1791.

The Federalists drafted and promoted a constitution that was antidemocratic and counterrevolutionary in intent, but one that at the same time radically broke with conventional political theory in ways that could be interpreted as decidedly democratic. On the one hand, Federalists aimed to reverse the trend toward popular government that revolutionary ideals and rhetoric had inspired in the sovereign states. To that end, they circumscribed the authority of the avowedly democratic states by creating a strong central government whose institutions would be more distant from and less directly accountable to the people. On the other hand, Federalists used the language of popular sovereignty both to justify the establishment of a powerful central government and to explain the division of labor between state and national authorities. They also embraced a conception of politics and society that accepted the pursuit of self-interest, both collectively and individually. In the process, they forged the theoretical justification for liberal interest-group politics, which, for better or worse, has become the hallmark of American democracy.

Finally, the Federalists crafted a constitution that was amendable and adaptable in ways even the most insightful could not have imagined in 1787. When the Federalists vested sovereignty in "the people," they meant simply that the representatives of a majority of white adult propertied men would wield ultimate political authority. Although the political theory of popular sovereignty could not preclude recurrent jurisdictional controversies between the state and national governments, it did offer the promise of a more inclusive polity than the Federalists ever envisioned. Americans would redefine what they meant by the sovereign "people" repeatedly in the centuries following 1787, extending political rights to propertyless white men, African-American males, and finally to women.

Most accounts of the American Revolution conclude with the adoption of the United States Constitution, which appears to have settled several fundamental questions raised by the assertion and attainment of independence. Would the United States be one nation, a loose confederation of states, or several regional confederations? Would Americans be able to preserve their independence? Would they be able to sustain their republic, a form of government that throughout history had been notoriously fragile? Yet contemporaries did not consider these issues settled in 1789, when the new government opened for business in New York, the temporary capital. Americans continued to contest these basic issues in the 1790s.

DOCUMENT 1

The Federalist, #1 (1787)

Alexander Hamilton

Led by the popular Governor George Clinton, the Antifederalists were strong in New York, and they lost no time attacking the proposed constitution in the local press. Knowing that New York's acceptance of the constitution would be crucial to its success, Alexander Hamilton solicited the help of Virginian James Madison and fellow New Yorker John Jay to write a series of essays to explain and promote the proposed constitution. Appearing under the pseudonym "Publius" and addressed to the people of the state of New York, the Federalist *papers were widely reprinted in other states. In this inaugural essay, Hamilton told his readers that the stakes were high in the struggle for ratification.[1]*

Questions to consider:

1. Describe the tone of Hamilton's essay. Which "people" of New York constituted his intended audience?
2. What did Hamilton suggest would happen if the constitution were not ratified? In what sense did he believe that the struggle for ratification

would have consequences that reached beyond New York—indeed,
beyond America?

3. How did he attempt to discredit his opponents? Among what sorts of
readers would these tactics be the most and least effective?

the Confedera-
✓ tion

After an unequivocal experience of the inefficiency of the subsisting federal
government, you are called upon to deliberate on a new Constitution for
the United States of America. The subject speaks its own importance; comprehending in its consequences nothing less than the existence of the Union,
the safety and welfare of the parts of which it is composed, the fate of an
empire in many respects the most interesting in the world. It has been frequently remarked that it seems to have been reserved to the people of this
country, by their conduct and example, to decide the important question,
whether societies of men are really capable or not of establishing good government from reflection and choice, or whether they are forever destined to
depend for their political constitutions on accident and force. If there be any
truth in the remark, the crisis at which we are arrived may with propriety be
regarded as the era in which that decision is to be made; and a wrong election of the part we shall act may, in this view, deserve to be considered as the
general misfortune of mankind.

This idea will add the inducements of philanthropy to those of patriotism, to heighten the solicitude which all considerate and good men must
feel for the event. Happy will it be if our choice should be directed by a judicious estimate of our true interests, unperplexed and unbiased by considerations not connected with the public good. But this is a thing more ardently to
be wished than seriously to be expected. The plan offered to our deliberations affects too many particular interests, innovates upon too many local
institutions, not to involve in its discussion a variety of objects foreign to its
merits, and of views, passions and prejudices little favorable to the discovery
of truth.

Among the most formidable of the obstacles which the new Constitution will have to encounter may readily be distinguished the obvious interest of a certain class of men in every state to resist all changes which may
hazard a diminution of the power, emolument, and consequence of the
offices they hold under the state establishments; and the perverted ambition
of another class of men, who will either hope to aggrandize themselves
by the confusions of their country, or will flatter themselves with fairer
prospects of elevation from the subdivision of the empire into several partial
confederacies than from its union under one government.

It is not, however, my design to dwell upon observations of this nature.
I am well aware that it would be disingenuous to resolve indiscriminately

the opposition of any set of men (merely because their situations might subject them to suspicion) into interested or ambitious views. Candor will oblige us to admit that even such men may be actuated by upright intentions. . . .

And yet, however just these sentiments will be allowed to be, we have already sufficient indications that it will happen in this as in all former cases of great national discussion. A torrent of angry and malignant passions will be let loose. To judge from the conduct of the opposite parties, we shall be led to conclude that they will mutually hope to evince the justness of their opinions, and to increase the number of their converts by the loudness of their declamations and the bitterness of their invectives. An enlightened zeal for the energy and efficiency of government will be stigmatized as the off-spring of a temper fond of despotic power and hostile to the principles of liberty. An over-scrupulous jealousy of danger to the rights of the people, which is more commonly the fault of the head than of the heart, will be represented as mere pretense and artifice, the stale bait for popularity at the expense of the public good. It will be forgotten, on the one hand, that jealousy is the usual concomitant of love, and that the noble enthusiasm of liberty is apt to be infected with a spirit of narrow and illiberal distrust. On the other hand, it will be equally forgotten that the vigor of government is essential to the security of liberty; that, in the contemplation of a sound and well-informed judgment, their interest can never be separated; and that a dangerous ambition more often lurks behind the specious mask of zeal for the rights of the people than under the forbidden appearance of zeal for the firmness and efficiency of government. History will teach us that the former has been found a much more certain road to the introduction of despotism than the latter, and that of those men who have overturned the liberties of republics, the greatest number have begun their career by paying an obsequious court to the people; commencing demagogues, and ending tyrants.

In the course of the preceding observations, I have had an eye, my fellow-citizens, to putting you upon your guard against all attempts, from whatever quarter, to influence our decision in a matter of the utmost moment to your welfare, by any impressions other than those which may result from the evidence of truth. You will, no doubt, at the same time, have collected from the general scope of them, that they proceed from a source not unfriendly to the new Constitution. Yes, my countrymen, I own to you that, after having given it an attentive consideration, I am clearly of opinion it is your interest to adopt it. I am convinced that this is the safest course for your liberty, your dignity, and your happiness. I affect not reserves which I do not feel. I will not amuse you with an appearance of deliberation when I have decided. I frankly acknowledge to you my convictions, and I will freely lay before you the reasons on which they are founded. The consciousness of good intentions disdains ambiguity. I shall not, however, multiply professions on this head. My motives must remain in the depository of my own breast. My arguments will be open to all, and may be judged of by all. They shall at least be offered in a spirit which will not disgrace the cause of truth.

I propose, in a series of papers, to discuss the following interesting particulars: *The utility of the UNION to your political prosperity—The insufficiency of the present Confederation to preserve that Union—The necessity of a government at least equally energetic with the one proposed, to the attainment of this object—The conformity of the proposed Constitution to the true principles of republican government—Its analogy to your own state constitution—and lastly, The additional security which its adoption will afford to the preservation of that species of government, to liberty, and to property.*

DOCUMENT 2

The Federalist, #10 (1787)

James Madison

Most critics of the constitution espoused the conventional view that a republic's success depended on the virtue of its citizenry. Because factions were based on self-interest, these Antifederalists contended, they signified the antithesis of public virtue. It followed, then, that republican virtue and the unanimity it presupposed could be sustained only in small, homogeneous communities. In Federalist #10, *James Madison took issue with these key points in the Antifederalist critique of the constitution.² Of the eighty-five* Federalist *essays, Madison's #10 is the most well-known, and it is generally regarded as the most original and insightful.*

Questions to consider:

1. How did Madison define "factions"? What did he mean when he wrote that the "latent causes of faction" are inherent in human nature?
2. For Madison, was diversity an advantage or a drawback? What sources of diversity or "faction" did he see as most significant in postrevolutionary America?
3. How did Madison distinguish between a democracy and a republic? Would the Antifederalists have accepted his distinction?
4. Why did Madison believe that each member of Congress should represent a larger constituency of voters than did their counterparts at the

state level? Who would have been likely to accept his preference for larger electoral districts? Who would have been likely to oppose his ideal of representation?

Among the numerous advantages promised by a well-constructed Union, none deserves to be more accurately developed than its tendency to break and control the violence of faction. The friend of popular governments never finds himself so much alarmed for their character and fate, as when he contemplates their propensity to this dangerous vice. He will not fail, therefore, to set a due value on any plan which, without violating the principles to which he is attached, provides a proper cure for it. The instability, injustice, and confusion introduced into the public councils, have, in truth, been the mortal diseases under which popular governments have everywhere perished; as they continue to be the favorite and fruitful topics from which the adversaries to liberty derive their most specious declamations. The valuable improvements made by the American constitutions on the popular models, both ancient and modern, cannot certainly be too much admired; but it would be an unwarrantable partiality, to contend that they have as effectually obviated the danger on this side, as was wished and expected . . .

By a faction, I understand a number of citizens, whether amounting to a majority or a minority of the whole, who are united and actuated by some common impulse of passion, or of interest, adverse to the rights of other citizens, or to the permanent and aggregate interests of the community.

There are two methods of curing the mischiefs of faction: the one, by removing its causes; the other, by controlling its effects.

There are again two methods of removing the causes of faction: the one, by destroying the liberty which is essential to its existence; the other, by giving to every citizen the same opinions, the same passions, and the same interests.

It could never be more truly said than of the first remedy, that it was worse than the disease. Liberty is to faction what air is to fire, an aliment without which it instantly expires. But it could not be less folly to abolish liberty, which is essential to political life, because it nourishes faction, than it would be to wish the annihilation of air, which is essential to animal life, because it imparts to fire its destructive agency.

The second expedient is as impracticable as the first would be unwise. As long as the reason of man continues fallible, and he is at liberty to exercise it, different opinions will be formed. As long as the connection subsists between his reason and his self-love, his opinions and his passions will have a reciprocal influence on each other; and the former will be objects to which the latter will attach themselves. The diversity in the faculties of men, from which the rights of property originate, is not less an insuperable obstacle to a uniformity of interests. The protection of these faculties is the first object of government. From the protection of different and unequal faculties of acquiring property, the possession of different degrees and kinds of property immediately results; and from the influence of these on the sentiments and views of the respective proprietors, ensues a division of the society into different interests and parties.

The latent causes of faction are thus sown in the nature of man; and we see them everywhere brought into different degrees of activity, according to the different circumstances of civil society. A zeal for different opinions concerning religion, concerning government, and many other points, as well of speculation as of practice; an attachment to different leaders ambitiously contending for pre-eminence and power; or to persons of other descriptions whose fortunes have been interesting to the human passions, have, in turn, divided mankind into parties, inflamed them with mutual animosity, and rendered them much more disposed to vex and oppress each other than to co-operate for their common good. So strong is this propensity of mankind to fall into mutual animosities, that where no substantial occasion presents itself, the most frivolous and fanciful distinctions have been sufficient to kindle their unfriendly passions and excite their most violent conflicts. But the most common and durable source of factions has been the various and unequal distribution of property. Those who hold and those who are without property have ever formed distinct interests in society. Those who are creditors, and those who are debtors, fall under a like discrimination. A landed interest, a manufacturing interest, a mercantile interest, a moneyed interest, with many lesser interests, grow up of necessity in civilized nations, and divide them into different classes, actuated by different sentiments and views. The regulation of these various and interfering interests forms the principal task of modern legislation, and involves the spirit of party and faction in the necessary and ordinary operations of the government. . . .

It is in vain to say that enlightened statesmen will be able to adjust these clashing interests, and render them all subservient to the public good. Enlightened statesmen will not always be at the helm. Nor, in many cases, can such an adjustment be made at all without taking into view indirect and remote considerations, which will rarely prevail over the immediate interest which one party may find in disregarding the rights of another or the good of the whole.

The inference to which we are brought is, that the causes of faction cannot be removed, and that relief is only to be sought in the means of controlling its effects.

If a faction consists of less than a majority, relief is supplied by the republican principle, which enables the majority to defeat its sinister views by regular vote. It may clog the administration, it may convulse the society; but it will be unable to execute and mask its violence under the forms of the

Constitution. When a majority is included in a faction, the form of popular government, on the other hand, enables it to sacrifice to its ruling passion or interest both the public good and the rights of other citizens. To secure the public good and private rights against the danger of such a faction, and at the same time to preserve the spirit and the form of popular government, is then the great object to which our inquiries are directed. Let me add that it is the great desideratum by which this form of government can be rescued from the opprobrium under which it has so long labored, and be recommended to the esteem and adoption of mankind.

By what means is this object attainable? Evidently by one of two only. Either the existence of the same passion or interest in a majority at the same time must be prevented, or the majority, having such coexistent passion or interest, must be rendered, by their number and local situation, unable to concert and carry into effect schemes of oppression. If the impulse and the opportunity be suffered to coincide, we well know that neither moral nor religious motives can be relied on as an adequate control. They are not found to be such on the injustice and violence of individuals, and lose their efficacy in proportion to the number combined together, that is, in proportion as their efficacy becomes needful.

From this view of the subject it may be concluded that a pure democracy, by which I mean a society consisting of a small number of citizens, who assemble and administer the government in person, can admit of no cure for the mischiefs of faction. A common passion or interest will, in almost every case, be felt by a majority of the whole; a communication and concert result from the form of government itself; and there is nothing to check the inducements to sacrifice the weaker party or an obnoxious individual. Hence it is that such democracies have ever been spectacles of turbulence and contention; have ever been found incompatible with personal security or the rights of property; and have in general been as short in their lives as they have been violent in their deaths. Theoretic politicians, who have patronized this species of government, have erroneously supposed that by reducing mankind to a perfect equality in their political rights, they would, at the same time, be perfectly equalized and assimilated in their possessions, their opinions, and their passions.

A republic, by which I mean a government in which the scheme of representation takes place, opens a different prospect, and promises the cure for which we are seeking. Let us examine the points in which it varies from pure democracy, and we shall comprehend both the nature of the cure and the efficacy which it must derive from the Union.

The two great points of difference between a democracy and a republic are: first, the delegation of the government, in the latter, to a small number of citizens elected by the rest; secondly, the greater number of citizens, and greater sphere of country, over which the latter may be extended.

The effect of the first difference is, on the one hand, to refine and enlarge the public views, by passing them through the medium of a chosen body of citizens, whose wisdom may best discern the true interest of their country, and whose patriotism and love of justice will be least likely to sacrifice it to temporary or partial considerations. Under such a regulation, it may well happen that the public voice, pronounced by the representatives of the people, will be more consonant to the public good than if pronounced by the people themselves, convened for the purpose. On the other hand, the effect may be inverted. Men of factious tempers, of local prejudices, or of sinister designs, may, by intrigue, by corruption, or by other means, first obtain the suffrages, and then betray the interests, of the people. The question resulting is, whether small or extensive republics are more favorable to the election of proper guardians of the public weal; and it is clearly decided in favor of the latter by two obvious considerations:

In the first place, it is to be remarked that, however small the republic may be, the representatives must be raised to a certain number, in order to guard against the cabals of a few; and that, however large it may be, they must be limited to a certain number, in order to guard against the confusion of a multitude. Hence, the number of representatives in the two cases not being in proportion to that of the two constituents, and being proportionally greater in the small republic, it follows that, if the proportion of fit characters be not less in the large than in the small republic, the former will present a greater option, and consequently a greater probability of a fit choice.

In the next place, as each representative will be chosen by a greater number of citizens in the large than in the small republic, it will be more difficult for unworthy candidates to practice with success the vicious arts by which elections are too often carried; and the suffrages of the people being more free, will be more likely to centre in men who possess the most attractive merit and the most diffusive and established characters.

It must be confessed that in this, as in most other cases, there is a mean, on both sides of which inconveniences will be found to lie. By enlarging too much the number of electors, you render the representatives too little acquainted with all their local circumstances and lesser interests; as by reducing it too much, you render him unduly attached to these, and too little fit to comprehend and pursue great and national objects. The federal Constitution forms a happy combination in this respect; the great and aggregate interests being referred to the national, the local and particular to the state legislatures.

The other point of difference is, the greater number of citizens and extent of territory which may be brought within the compass of republican than of democratic government; and it is this circumstance principally which renders factious combinations less to be dreaded in the former than in the latter. The smaller the society, the fewer probably will be the distinct parties and interests composing it; the fewer the distinct parties and interests, the more frequently will a majority be found of the same party; and the smaller the number of individuals composing a majority, and the smaller the compass within which they are placed, the more easily will they concert and execute their plans of oppression. Extend the sphere, and you take in a greater variety of parties and interests; you make it less probable that a majority of the whole will have a common motive to invade the rights of other citizens; or if such a common motive exists, it will be more difficult for all who feel it to discover their own strength, and to act in unison with each other. Besides other impediments, it may be remarked that, where there is a consciousness of unjust or dishonorable purposes, communication is always checked by distrust in proportion to the number whose concurrence is necessary.

Hence, it clearly appears, that the same advantage which a republic has over a democracy, in controlling the effects of faction, is enjoyed by a large over a small republic—is enjoyed by the Union over the states composing it. Does the advantage consist in the substitution of representatives whose enlightened views and virtuous sentiments render them superior to local prejudices and schemes of injustice? It will not be denied that the representation of the Union will be most likely to possess these requisite endowments. Does it consist in the greater security afforded by a greater variety of parties, against the event of any one party being able to outnumber and oppress the rest? In an equal degree does the increased variety of parties comprised within the Union, increase this security. Does it, in fine, consist in the greater obstacles opposed to the concert and accomplishment of the secret wishes of an unjust and interested majority? Here, again, the extent of the Union gives it the most palpable advantage.

The influence of factious leaders may kindle a flame within their particular states, but will be unable to spread a general conflagration through the other states . . .

In the extent and proper structure of the Union, therefore, we behold a republican remedy for the diseases most incident to republican government. And according to the degree of pleasure and pride we feel in being republicans, ought to be our zeal in cherishing the spirit and supporting the character of Federalists.

DOCUMENT 3

The Federalist, #51 (1787)

James Madison

After a series of essays delineating the respective powers of the national and state governments, Madison summarized the checks and balances between branches or "departments" within the proposed system, including the continued viability of the states as checks on centralized power. In response to Antifederalist critics who claimed that the new system amounted to a foolhardy and ultimately impracticable effort to divide sovereignty between the state and national governments, Madison asserted that an undivided sovereignty would be vested in the people.[3]

Questions to consider:

1. What, according to Madison, should be the purpose of all political institutions? What did he mean when he asked, "What is government itself, but the greatest of all reflections on human nature?"
2. Why did "the legislative authority necessarily predominate" in a republican government?
3. How, according to Madison, did the "federal system of America" further safeguard the liberties of citizens?

To what expedient, then, shall we finally resort, for maintaining in practice the necessary partition of power among the several departments, as laid down in the Constitution? The only answer that can be given is, that as all these exterior provisions are found to be inadequate, the defect must be supplied, by so contriving the interior structure of the government as that its several constituent parts may, by their mutual relations, be the means of keeping each other in their proper places. Without presuming to undertake a full development of this important idea, I will hazard a few general observations, which may perhaps place it in a clearer light, and enable us to form a more correct judgment of the principles and structure of the government planned by the convention.

In order to lay a due foundation for that separate and distinct exercise of the different powers of government, which to a certain extent is admitted on all hands to be essential to the preservation of liberty, it is evident that each department should have a will of its own; and consequently should be so constituted that the members of each should have as little agency as possible in the appointment of the members of the others. . . .

It is equally evident, that the members of each department should be as little dependent as possible on those of the others, for the emoluments annexed to their offices. Were the executive magistrate, or the judges, not independent of the legislature in this particular, their independence in every other would be merely nominal. But the great security against a gradual concentration of the several powers in the same department, consists in giving to those who administer each department the necessary constitutional means and personal motives to resist encroachments of the others. The provision for defense must in this, as in all other cases, be made commensurate to the danger of attack. Ambition must be made to counteract ambition. The interest of the man must be connected with the constitutional rights of the place. It may be a reflection on human nature, that such devices should be necessary to control the abuses of government. But what is government itself, but the greatest of all reflections on human nature? If men were angels, no government would be necessary. If angels were to govern men, neither external nor internal controls on government would be necessary. In framing a government which is to be administered by men over men, the great difficulty lies in this: you must first enable the government to control the governed; and in the next place oblige it to control itself. A dependence on the people is, no doubt, the primary control on the government; but experience has taught mankind the necessity of auxiliary precautions. . . .

But it is not possible to give to each department an equal power of self-defense. In republican government, the legislative authority necessarily predominates. The remedy for this inconveniency is to divide the legislature into different branches; and to render them, by different modes of election and different principles of action, as little connected with each other as the nature of their common functions and their common dependence on the society will admit. It may even be necessary to guard against dangerous encroachments by still further precautions. As the weight of the legislative authority requires that it should be thus divided, the weakness of the executive may require, on the other hand, that it should be fortified. An absolute negative on the legislature appears, at first view, to be the natural defense with which the executive magistrate should be armed. But perhaps it would be neither altogether safe nor alone sufficient. On ordinary occasions it might not be exerted with the requisite firmness, and on extraordinary occasions it might be perfidiously abused. May not this defect of an absolute negative be supplied by some qualified connection between this weaker department and the weaker branch of the stronger department, by which the latter may be led to support the constitutional rights of the former, without being too much detached from the rights of its own department?

If the principles on which these observations are founded be just, as I persuade myself they are, and they be applied as a criterion to the several state constitutions, and to the federal Constitution it will be found that if the latter does not perfectly correspond with them, the former are infinitely less able to bear such a test.

There are, moreover, two considerations particularly applicable to the federal system of America, which place that system in a very interesting point of view.

First. In a single republic, all the power surrendered by the people is submitted to the administration of a single government; and the usurpations are guarded against by a division of the government into distinct and separate departments. In the compound republic of America, the power

surrendered by the people is first divided between two distinct governments, and then the portion allotted to each subdivided among distinct and
separate departments. Hence a double security arises to the rights of the
people. The different governments will control each other, at the same time
that each will be controlled by itself.

Second. It is of great importance in a republic not only to guard the society against the oppression of its rulers, but to guard one part of the society
against the injustice of the other part. Different interests necessarily exist in
different classes of citizens. If a majority be united by a common interest, the
rights of the minority will be insecure. There are but two methods of providing against this evil: the one by creating a will in the community independent of the majority that is, of the society itself; the other, by comprehending
in the society so many separate descriptions of citizens as will render an unjust combination of a majority of the whole very improbable, if not impracticable. The first method prevails in all governments possessing an hereditary
or self-appointed authority. This, at best, is but a precarious security; because a power independent of the society may as well espouse the unjust
views of the major, as the rightful interests of the minor party, and may possibly be turned against both parties. The second method will be exemplified
in the federal republic of the United States. Whilst all authority in it will be
derived from and dependent on the society, the society itself will be broken
into so many parts, interests, and classes of citizens, that the rights of individuals, or of the minority, will be in little danger from interested combinations of the majority.

DOCUMENT 4

"Brutus," #3 (1787)

From October 1787 through April 1788, the New York Journal *published sixteen
essays criticizing the proposed constitution. Most historians attribute these essays,
written under the pseudonym "Brutus," to Robert Yates of Albany. A moderate Whig
of middling social origins, Yates was one of his state's delegates to the constitutional
convention. He returned home in July, when it became clear that the majority intended
to go far beyond proposing changes to the Articles of Confederation. Yates's essays,
which were widely reprinted, forcefully stated many of the chief Antifederalist criticisms of the constitution and its framers.[4]*

Questions to consider:

1. How did Yates's vision of the ideal representative differ from that of Madison?
2. What were his chief objections to the composition of the proposed House of Representatives? Did Yates oppose slavery or merely the awarding of political representation to the southern states on the basis of their combined free and enslaved population? Was he uniformly consistent in his argument that "those who are not free agents" should not be represented?
3. What sort of future did Yates foresee for Americans if they ratified the proposed constitution? How would the Federalists have responded to his predictions?

In the investigation of the constitution under your consideration, great care should be taken, that you do not form your opinions respecting it, from unimportant provisions, or fallacious appearances.

On a careful examination, you will find, that many of its parts, of little moment, are well formed; in these it has a specious resemblance of a free government—but this is not sufficient to justify the adoption of it. The gilded pill, is often found to contain the most deadly poison. . . .

The first important object that presents itself in the organization of this government, is the legislature. This is to be composed of two branches; the first to be called the general assembly, and is to be chosen by the people of the respective states, in proportion to the number of their inhabitants, and is to consist of sixty five members, with powers in the legislature to increase the number, not to exceed one for every thirty thousand inhabitants. The second branch is to be called the senate, and is to consist of twenty-six members, two of which are to be chosen by the legislatures of each of the states.

In the former of these there is an appearance of justice, in the appointment of its members—but if the clause, which provides for this branch, be stripped of its ambiguity, it will be found that there is really no equality of representation, even in this house.

The words are "representatives and direct taxes, shall be apportioned among the several states, which may be included in this union, according to their respective numbers, which shall be determined by adding to the whole number of free persons, including those bound to service for a term of years, and excluding Indians not taxed, three fifths of all other persons." What a strange and unnecessary accumulation of words are here used to conceal from the public eye what might have been expressed in the following concise manner. Representatives are to be proportioned among the states respectively, according to the number of freemen and slaves inhabiting them, counting five slaves for three free men.

"In a free state," says the celebrated Montesquieu, "every man, who is supposed to be a free agent, ought to be concerned in his own government, therefore the legislature should reside in the whole body of the people, or their representatives." But it has never been alleged that those who are not free agents, can, upon any rational principle, have any thing to do in government, either by themselves or others. If they have no share in government, why is the number of members in the assembly, to be increased on their account? Is it because in some of the states, a considerable part of the property of the inhabitants consists in a number of their fellow men, who are held in bondage, in defiance of every idea of benevolence, justice, and religion, and contrary to all the principles of liberty, which have been publicly avowed in the late glorious revolution? If this be a just ground for representation, the horses in some of the states, and the oxen in others, ought to be represented—for a great share of property in some of them, consists in these animals; and they have as much control over their own actions, as these poor unhappy creatures, who are intended to be described in the above recited clause, by the words, "all other persons." By this mode of apportionment, the representatives of the different parts of the union will be extremely unequal. In some of the southern states, the slaves are nearly equal in number to the free men; and for all these slaves, they will be entitled to a proportionate share in the legislature. This will give them an unreasonable weight in the government, which can derive no additional strength, protection, nor defence from the slaves, but the contrary. Why then should they be represented? What adds to the evil is, that these states are to be permitted to continue the inhuman traffic of importing slaves, until the year 1808—and for every cargo of these unhappy people, which unfeeling, unprincipled, barbarous, and avaricious wretches, may tear from their country, friends and tender connections, and bring into those states, they are to be rewarded by having an increase of members in the general assembly. . . .

It has been observed, that the happiness of society is the end of government—that every free government is founded in compact and that because it is impracticable for the whole community to assemble, or when assembled, to deliberate with wisdom, and decide with dispatch, the mode of legislating by representation was devised.

The very term, representative, implies, that the person or body chosen for this purpose, should resemble those who appoint them. A representation of the people of America, if it be a true one, must be like the people. It ought to be so constituted, that a person, who is a stranger to the country, might be able to form a just idea of their character, by knowing that of their representatives. They are the sign—the people are the thing signified. It is absurd to speak of one thing being the representative of another, upon any other principle. The ground and reason of representation, in a free government, implies the same thing. Society instituted government to promote the happiness of the whole, and this is the great end always in view in the delegation of powers. It must then have been intended, that those who are placed instead of the people, should possess their sentiments and feelings, and be governed by their interests, or, in other words, should bear the strongest resemblance of those in whose room they are substituted. It is obvious, that for an assembly to be a true likeness of the people of any country, they must be considerably numerous. One man, or a few men, cannot possibly represent the feelings, opinions, and characters of a great multitude. In this respect, the new constitution is radically defective. The house of assembly, which is intended as a representation of the people of America, will not, nor cannot, in the nature of things, be a proper one—sixty-five men cannot be found in the United States, who hold the sentiments, possess the feelings, or are acquainted with the wants and interests of this vast country. This extensive continent is made up of a number of different classes of people; and to have a proper representation of them, each class ought to have an opportunity of choosing their best informed men for the purpose; but this cannot possibly be the case in so small a number. . . .

According to the common course of human affairs, the natural aristocracy of the country will be elected. Wealth always creates influence, and this is generally much increased by large family connections. This class in society will for ever have a great number of dependents; besides, they will always favour each other—it is their interest to combine. They will therefore constantly unite their efforts to procure men of their own rank to be elected. They will concenter all their force in every part of the state into one point, and by acting together, will most generally carry their election. It is probable, that but few of the merchants, and those the most opulent and ambitious, will have a representation from their body—few of them are characters sufficiently conspicuous to attract the notice of the electors of the state in so limited a representation. The great body of the yeomen of the country cannot expect any of their order in this assembly—the station will be too elevated for them to aspire to—the distance between the people and their representatives, will be so very great, that there is no probability that a farmer, however respectable, will be chosen. The mechanics of every branch, must expect to be excluded from a seat in this Body. It will and must be esteemed a station too high and exalted to be filled by any but the first men in the state, in point of fortune; so that in reality there will be no part of the people represented, but the rich, even in that branch of the legislature, which is called the democratic. The well born, and highest orders in life, as they term themselves, will be ignorant of the sentiments of the middling class of citizens, strangers to their ability, wants, and difficulties, and void of sympathy, and fellow feeling . . . It will literally be a government in the hands of the few to oppress and plunder the many.

DOCUMENT 5

"Objections to the Constitution of Government Formed by the Convention" (1787)

George Mason

George Mason was one of Virginia's delegates to the constitutional convention in Philadelphia. Although he was an active participant in the convention's deliberations, Mason refused to sign the finished constitution. His grounds for disapproval were numerous, but his most weighty criticism was that it lacked a bill of rights.[5] After the convention, Mason emerged as an Antifederalist leader in Virginia. His concerns and those of other Antifederalists, some of whom ultimately voted to ratify, helped ensure that a bill of rights would be one of the first orders of business for the new federal Congress.

Questions to consider:

1. Why did Mason describe the proposed government as a "moderate aristocracy"? Why was he so pessimistic about the future of American government under this constitution?
2. Why was Mason especially suspicious of the power of the executive branch? Why did he stress the need for a "constitutional council"?
3. How did Mason describe the various regions of the United States? Did he articulate concerns that were peculiar to Virginians or to southerners?

There is no declaration of rights, and the laws of the general government being paramount to the laws and constitutions of the several states, the declarations of rights, in the separate states, are no security. Nor are the people secured even in the enjoyment of the benefit of the common law, which stands here upon no other foundation than its having been adopted by the respective acts forming the constitutions of the several states.

In the House of Representatives there is not the substance, but the shadow only of representation; which can never produce proper information in the legislature, or inspire confidence in the people. The laws will, therefore, be generally made by men little concerned in, and unacquainted with their effects and consequences.

The Senate have the power of altering all money-bills, and of originating appropriations of money, and the salaries of the officers of their appointment, in conjunction with the President of the United States—although they are not the representatives of the people, or amenable to them. These, with their other great powers, . . . their influence upon, and connection with, the supreme executive from these causes, their duration of office, and their being a constant existing body, almost continually sitting, joined with their being one complete branch of the legislature, will destroy any balance in the government, and enable them to accomplish what usurpations they please, upon the rights and liberties of the people.

The judiciary of the United States is so constructed and extended, as to absorb and destroy the judiciaries of the several states; thereby rendering laws as tedious, intricate, and expensive, and justice as unattainable by a great part of the community, as in England; and enabling the rich to oppress and ruin the poor.

The President of the United States has no constitutional council (a thing unknown in any safe and regular government). He will therefore be unsupported by proper information and advice; and will generally be directed by minions and favorites—or he will become a tool to the Senate—or a council of state will grow out of the principal officers of the great departments— the worst and most dangerous of all ingredients for such a council, in a free country; for they may be induced to join in any dangerous or oppressive measures, to shelter themselves, and prevent an inquiry into their own misconduct in office. Whereas, had a constitutional council been formed (as was proposed) of six members, . . . two from the eastern, two from the middle, and two from the southern states, to be appointed by vote of the states in the House of Representatives, with the same duration and rotation of office as the Senate, the executive would always have had safe and proper information and advice; the president of such a council might have acted as Vice-President of the United States . . . From this fatal defect of a constitutional council, has arisen the improper power of the Senate, in the appointment of the public officers, and the alarming dependence and connexion between that branch of the legislature and the supreme executive. Hence, also, sprung that unnecessary officer, the Vice-President, who, for want of other employment, is made President of the Senate; thereby dangerously blending the executive and legislative powers; besides always giving to some one of the states an unnecessary and unjust pre-eminence over the others.

The President of the United States has the unrestrained power of granting pardon for treason; which may be sometimes exercised to screen from punishment those whom he had secretly instigated to commit the crime, and thereby prevent a discovery of his own guilt. By declaring all treaties supreme laws of the land, the executive and the Senate have, in many cases, an exclusive power of legislation, which might have been avoided, by proper distinctions with respect to treaties, and requiring the assent of the House of Representatives, where it could be done with safety.

By requiring only a majority to make all commercial and navigation laws, the five southern states (whose produce and circumstances are totally different from those of the eight northern and eastern states) will be ruined. For such rigid and premature regulations may be made, as will enable the merchants of the northern and eastern states not only to demand an exorbitant freight, but to monopolize the purchase of the commodities, at their own price, for many years, to the great injury of the landed interest, and the impoverishment of the people: and the danger is the greater, as the gain on one side will be in proportion to the loss on the other. Whereas, requiring two-thirds of the members present in both houses, would have produced mutual moderation, promoted the general interest, and removed an insuperable objection to the adoption of the government.

Under their own construction of the general clause at the end of the enumerated powers, the Congress may grant monopolies in trade and commerce, constitute new crimes, inflict unusual and severe punishments, and extend their power as far as they shall think proper; so that the state legislatures have no security for the powers now presumed to remain to them; or the people for their rights. There is no declaration of any kind for preserving the liberty of the press, the trial by jury in civil cases, nor against the danger of standing armies in time of peace. . . .

This government will commence in a moderate aristocracy. It is at present impossible to foresee whether it will, in its operation, produce a monarchy, or a corrupt oppressive aristocracy. It will most probably vibrate some years between the two, and then terminate in one or the other.

DOCUMENT 6

Patrick Henry's Speech to the Virginia Ratifying Convention (1788)

Patrick Henry achieved both fame and popularity as a strident opponent of British imperial policies, and after independence he served as governor of Virginia. As an Antifederalist member of his state's ratifying convention in 1788, Henry deployed his superb oratorical skills against the Federalists and their constitution.[6] The delegates

nevertheless voted to ratify by the narrow vote of 89 to 79, some Antifederalists acqui-
escing when leading Federalists in the state promised to support the addition of a bill of
rights.

Questions to consider:

1. Why did Henry object to the secrecy of the deliberations in Philadelphia?
2. What was a "consolidated government" and how did it differ from a "confederation"? Why did Henry prefer the latter? Why did he predict that "our Republic will be lost"?
3. Henry was a famous and inspirational orator. In this speech, did he appeal to his audience's intellect or emotion—to their heads or to their hearts?

This proposal of altering our Federal Government is of a most alarming nature . . . I beg you Gentlemen to consider, that a wrong step made now will plunge us in misery, and our Republic will be lost. It will be necessary for this Convention to have a faithful historical detail of the facts that preceded the session of the Federal Convention, and the reasons that actuated members in proposing an entire alteration of Government and to demonstrate the dangers that awaited us. If they were of such awful magnitude, as to warrant a proposal so extremely perilous as this, I must assert, that this Convention has an absolute right to a thorough discovery of every circumstance relative to this great event. And here I would make this enquiry of those worthy characters who composed a part of the late Federal Convention. I am sure they were fully impressed with the necessity of forming a great consolidated Government, instead of a confederation. That this is a consolidated Government is demonstrably clear, and the danger of such a Government, is, to my mind, very striking. I have the highest veneration of those Gentlemen, but, Sir, give me leave to demand, what right had they to say, *We, the People.* My political curiosity, exclusive of my anxious solicitude for the public welfare, leads me to ask who authorised them to speak the language of, *We, the People,* instead of *We, the States?* States are the characteristics, and the soul of a confederation. If the States be not the agents of this compact, it must be one great consolidated National Government of the people of all the States . . . The people gave them no power to use their name. That they exceeded their power is perfectly clear . . . The Federal Convention ought to have amended the old system—for this purpose they were solely delegated. The object of their mission extended to no other consideration.

DOCUMENT 7

A Procession in Honor of the Constitution of the United States (1788)

In New York, as in some other American cities, a great "procession" was orchestrated to celebrate the adoption of the federal constitution.[7] Then, as now, such civic rituals reflected the ideals and aspirations of those who staged them. They also sought to differentiate members of the polity from those who were excluded and to dramatize and thereby reinforce distinctions within political society.

Questions to consider:

1. Who do you think organized New York's great "procession" and why did they do so?
2. Who were the various groups included in the procession? Who were excluded?
3. Why did so many people parade as members of occupational groups? Was there any logic behind the organization and order of the ten divisions of participants?

At 8 o'clock this morning . . . 10 guns will fire, when the Procession will parade, and proceed . . . down Broadway to Great Dock-Street, thence through Hanover-square, Queen, Chatham, Division and Arundul streets; and from thence through Bullock-street to Bayard's house.

2 Horsemen with Trumpets. 1 piece of Artillery.

First Division. Foresters in frocks, carrying axes; Columbus in his ancient dress, on horseback. 6 Foresters . . . A Plough. A Harrow. Farmers. United States' Arms, borne by Col. White. Gardners. A Band of Music. Taylors. Measurers of Grain. Millers. Inspectors of Flour. Bakers. Brewers. Distillers.

Second Division. Coopers. Butchers. Tanners and Curriers. Leather Dressers.

Third Division. Cordwainers.

Fourth Division. Carpenters. Farriers. Hatters. Peruke-makers and Hair-dressers.

Fifth Division. White Smiths. Cutlers. Stone Masons. Brick Layers. Painters and Glaziers. Cabinet Makers. Windsor Chair Makers. Upholsterers. Fringe Makers. Paper Stainers. Civil Engineers.

Sixth Division. Ship Wrights. Black Smiths. Ship Joiners. Boat Builders. Block and Pump Makers. Sail Makers. Riggers.

Seventh Division. Ship and crew. Pilot Boat and Barges. Pilots. Mariner Society. Printers, Book-binders and Stationers.

Eighth Division. Cartmen. Mathematical Instrument Makers. Carvers and Engineers. Coach Makers. Coach Painters. Copper Smiths and Brass Founders. Tin Plate Workers. Pewterers. Gold and Silver Smiths. Potters. Chocolate Makers. Tobacconists. Dyers. Brush Makers. Tallow Chandlers. Saddlers, Harness, and Whip-Makers.

Ninth Division. Gentlemen of the Bar. Philological Society. President and Students of the College. Merchants and Traders.

Tenth Division. [Former Continental Army Officers.] Physicians. Strangers. Militia Officers. 1 piece of Artillery. . . .

On the discharge of 10 guns at 8 o'clock in the morning, the various classes of citizens which are to compose the Procession, will please to repair to the Fields, under their proper officers, formed and told off in the manner they propose marching—and immediately on their arrival, an adjutant or orderly person from each, will be sent to St. Paul's Church, to receive directions from the superintendent, who will be designated by a blue coat, red sash, and white feather tipped with black, by way of distinction from the . . . gentlemen who are assistants . . . who will each be clad in a uniform white coat with blue cape and sash, wear a white feather tipped with blue, and carry a speaking trumpet.

One cannon will be posted on the right and another on the left, the first will fire on the commencement of the formation, and the second for the completion of the line—afterwards the ship will fire 13 guns as a signal for marching, when the whole procession will face the right, advance and march. . . . This being done, the committee of arrangements, followed by Congress, Ministers, Foreigners of distinction, and the gentlemen on horseback, will pass along the line of Procession, and review it, each division afterwards marching off to its table, after proper guards for their insignias . . . are posted, the artillery will close the rear, and fire two guns upon coming to their station, where the flag is displayed as a signal for dining. While at dinner 10 guns will be fired for each toast. . . .

It is sincerely to be wished, that the greatest decorum may prevail on the day of Procession. Every person who is interested in the event which is then to be celebrated, will doubtless consider, that much of the honor of the day depends upon the harmony which subsists among the different orders of citizens, who compose the Procession. Every man should esteem each other as a Brother, engaged in testifying their joy on the commencement of the "EPOCHA OF LIBERTY AND JUSTICE."

SUGGESTED READING FOR CHAPTER 10

BEARD, CHARLES. *An Economic Interpretation of the Constitution* (1913).

BOYD, STEVEN R. *The Politics of Opposition: Antifederalists and the Acceptance of the Constitution* (1979).

DEPAUW, LINDA GRANT. *The Eleventh Pillar: New York State and the Federal Constitution* (1966).

KAMMEN, MICHAEL. *A Machine That Would Go of Itself: The Constitution in American Culture* (1986).

MAIN, JACKSON TURNER. *The Antifederalists: Critics of the Constitution, 1781–1788* (1961).

———. *Political Parties before the Constitution* (1973).

MORGAN, EDMUND S. *Inventing the People: The Rise of Popular Sovereignty in England and America* (1988).

MORRIS, RICHARD B. *Witnesses at the Creation: Hamilton, Madison, Jay, and the Constitution* (1985).

POLE, J. R. *Political Representation in England and the Origins of the America Republic* (1966).

RAKOVE, JACK N. *Original Ideas: Politics and Ideas in the Making of the Constitution* (1996).

RUTLAND, ROBERT ALLEN. *The Birth of the Bill of Rights, 1776–1791* (1955).

———. *The Ordeal of the Constitution: The Antifederalists and the Ratification Struggle of 1787–1788* (1966).

STORING, HERBERT. *What the Antifederalists Were For* (1981).

NOTES

[1] Paul Leicester Ford, ed., *The Federalist: A Commentary on the Constitution of the United States*, by Alexander Hamilton, James Madison, and John Jay (New York, 1898), 1–7.

[2] Paul Leicester Ford, ed., *The Federalist: A Commentary on the Constitution of the United States*, by Alexander Hamilton, James Madison, and John Jay (New York, 1898), 54–63.

[3] Paul Leicester Ford, ed., *The Federalist: A Commentary on the Constitution of the United States*, by Alexander Hamilton, James Madison, and John Jay (New York, 1898), 342–48.

[4] *New York Journal*, 15 Nov. 1787.

[5] George Mason, "Objections to the Constitution of Government Formed by the Convention," in Paul Leicester Ford, ed., *Pamphlets of the Constitution of the United States, Published during its Discussion by the People, 1787–1788* (Brooklyn, N.Y., 1888), 329–32.

[6] Jonathan Elliot, ed., *The Debates in the Several State Conventions on the Adoption of the Federal Constitution, as recommended by the General Convention at Philadelphia in 1787*, 5 vols. (Philadelphia, 1836–59), 3: 22–23.

[7] *The New-York Journal, and Daily Patriotic Register*, 23 July 1788.

CHAPTER ELEVEN

THE FEDERALIST ERA

The Constitution established the framework for a national government. How that framework would be interpreted and implemented, however, remained an open question in April 1789, when George Washington arrived in New York to assume the presidency. American political leaders faced three major challenges in the next few years: constructing a viable government from the Constitution's blueprint; finding revenue to support the government and pay its debts; and stabilizing relations between the United States and foreign powers. As they addressed these issues, divisions emerged, first within the government and then later among citizens at-large. The 1790s became a decade of bitter conflict between two new political parties, the Federalists and Republicans.

Unlike the Federalists and Antifederalists of 1787–88, who contested a single issue and then dispersed, these parties were more broadly based and more enduring at both the state and national levels. Led by Alexander Hamilton and John Adams and generally supported by President Washington, the Federalists chose their name to identify themselves with the new Constitution—and, by extension, to cast aspersions on their opponents' commitment to the new government. The Federalists favored a strong central government, which they hoped could promote economic development and social stability. Their horrified opposition to the French Revolution reflected their distrust of democracy and disorder. After 1793, when war in Europe forced them to choose, Federalists favored Britain over France in their foreign policy. Federalist hostility toward the French republic and their fear of democracy at home and abroad led some Americans to the erroneous but perhaps understandable conclusion that they were monarchists at heart.

Although the Federalists controlled the presidency and both houses of Congress in the 1790s, they faced increasingly organized opposition to both their domestic and foreign policies. An opposition party—led by James Madison and Thomas Jefferson and known as the Republicans or Democratic-Republicans—criticized Federalist efforts to expand the government's powers and to use them inequitably. The Republicans' support for the French Revolution, as well as their willingness to mobilize ordinary citizens politically, reflected their affinity for popular liberty—at least for white men—and their fear of centralized power. Jefferson and Madison called their party "Republican" to invite comparison with their supposedly monarchical rivals. The Federalists, for their part, saw their opponents as dangerous demagogues and fomenters of disorder.

The first Congress under the Constitution, which convened in New York in 1789, had a full and varied agenda. The first order of business was to count the ballots from the Electoral College and to confirm the election of George Washington and John Adams as president and vice-president, respectively. Congress debated matters of etiquette, deciding, for instance, that the chief executive should be addressed not as "His Highness," as some preferred, but simply as "Mr. President." The legislature authorized the creation of three executive departments—Treasury, State, and War—and the post of Attorney General. The Judiciary Act of 1789 established a federal judiciary that included a Supreme Court composed of six justices. The Tariff Act gave the government a dependable source of revenue, as did the Tonnage Act, which imposed duties on ships entering American ports.

The most controversial business the First Congress undertook was to establish a sound financial footing for the new government. Alexander Hamilton, who Washington chose as his Secretary of the Treasury, was well known as champion of commercial and manufacturing interests, as well as a promoter of activist government. In October 1789, Congress asked Hamilton to prepare a report on the public credit. Three months later, he presented them with the first of four reports in which he described his vision for the future of America.

Hamilton advocated an aggressive program of fiscal reorganization and economic development. In his First Report on the Public Credit, he made two proposals to address the issue of debt, perhaps the most difficult problem facing the new government. First, Hamilton argued that the government should fund both the foreign and domestic debts at full face value by issuing new interest-bearing certificates to public creditors. Second, he contended that the national government should assume the remaining war debts of the states. In his next report, issued in December 1790, Hamilton proposed imposing a federal excise tax on whiskey, both to raise revenue for interest payments to public creditors and also to establish the government's authority to levy internal taxes. Hamilton's third report urged Congress to charter a national bank to mobilize capital for investment, aid in the development of a stable currency, and assure the government of a dependable source of money. Finally, in December 1791, Hamilton issued his Report on Manufactures, which called for high protective tariffs and other more elaborate measures for encouraging the development of American manufactures.

In preparing his prescription for the economic future of the United States, Hamilton clearly looked to Great Britain as his model. Hamilton wanted the United States to be a bigger and better version of Britain, which was at the time the world's most dynamic and prosperous economy, as well as its preeminent military power. Hamilton maintained that the United States could not be a great and fully independent power until it diversified its overwhelmingly agricultural economy, and he argued that the national government had the power to adopt the measures needed to foster such economic development. Hamilton contended that high tariffs and a central bank could spur economic growth and diversification in the United States, just as the Navigation Acts and the Bank of England had aided commerce and industry in Britain. His fiscal program unabashedly promoted the interests of the wealthy because he believed that they were most likely to invest in commercial and manufacturing ventures and because he deemed the support of the monied classes essential to the success of the new government.

Although Congress adopted all of Hamilton's proposals except the Report on Manufactures, his program generated significant opposition in Congress. Many Americans regarded Britain—with its entrenched social hierarchy, squalid industrial conditions, and decadent politics—as the antithesis of what they wanted for United States. Hamilton's proposals therefore challenged what many held to be the ideals of revolutionary republicanism. On both political and ideological grounds, three points in Hamilton's program proved to be the most controversial: the national bank, the assumption of state debts, and the plan to fund the domestic debt at full face value.

James Madison, who had collaborated with Hamilton to produce *The Federalist Papers*, led the opposition to his funding and assumption schemes in Congress. Madison and his supporters believed that Hamilton's plan to fund the domestic debt benefited wealthy speculators at the expense of ordinary citizens who had advanced goods and services to the government in wartime, only to find themselves forced to sell their certificates at hugely depreciated prices during the 1780s. Although they agreed that the domestic debt should be funded in full, they argued that the new interest-bearing government certificates should be divided among original and current holders of the public debt. Such a plan, they suggested, would be more equitable, and it would also undermine the nascent alliance between the government and the monied classes which Hamilton sought to foster. Hamilton's critics also saw his plan for the assumption of state debts as a move to strengthen the national government and to enhance the profits of speculators. Representatives from the southern states regarded the assumption plan as especially unfair because their states had already paid most of their debts. In the end, Congress adopted Hamilton's funding plan without revision. To get crucial southern votes for the assumption scheme, however, Hamilton had to promise to deliver northern votes in favor of moving the republic's permanent capital further south, to a site on the Potomac River.

Although Madison also led the opposition to the proposed national bank in Congress, the final battle over the Bank of the United States was waged in Washington's Cabinet. In unsuccessfully opposing the bill to charter the bank, Madison had argued that this measure—like all of Hamilton's policies—favored commercial and industrial interests over agricultural ones; he also maintained that the bill was unconstitutional. After Congress passed the bank bill, Washington asked his Cabinet to advise him on its constitutionality. Secretary of State Thomas Jefferson argued that the Constitution gave the national government only those powers it expressly stated, a view that became known as a "strict construction" of the Constitution. Because the Constitution did not expressly empower the government to charter corporations, Jefferson asserted, the bank bill was obviously unconstitutional. Hamilton, by contrast, espoused a "loose construction" of the Constitution, contending that the government could do most anything it did not explicitly prohibit to promote the general welfare. Since the Constitution did not prohibit Congress from chartering corporations and since, in Hamilton's view, the bank was a beneficial undertaking, the bill was constitutional. Attorney General Edmund Randolph supported Jefferson, while Secretary of War Henry Knox allied with Hamilton in this first great debate over how to interpret the United States Constitution. Washington accepted Hamilton's position, and the Bank of the United States commenced operation with a twenty-year charter in 1791.

Between 1789 and 1791, then, debates over fiscal policy had resulted in the emergence of political divisions both in Congress and in Washington's Cabinet. The president himself, however, had for the most part remained aloof from political controversy. In 1792, Washington was reelected without opposition. In his second term, party lines would begin to solidify and move beyond the government to the general population. The Whiskey Rebellion of 1794 showed the extent to which at least some citizens resented the Federalists' policies.

Because transporting grain to eastern markets was costly and inconvenient, western farmers typically converted their grain to whiskey to make their crops more profitable. Consequently, they bitterly resented the federal excise tax on whiskey, which they viewed as the work of a Congress dominated by eastern creditor interests seeking to fill their pockets at the westerners' expense. Throughout the United States, back-country people vigorously opposed the excise tax, but resistance came to a head in western Pennsylvania, where farmers who likened themselves to the Stamp Act rioters violently opposed the collection of the excise. Washington and his advisors interpreted western opposition to the excise as a challenge to the legitimacy and viability of their government. Acting decisively, the president asked governors of nearby states to call out their militias. In October 1794, a 13,000-man army—larger than any force Americans had deployed against the British–marched to western Pennsylvania to suppress the remnants of the rebellion.

The Federalists' firm response to the western uprising was important for two reasons. First, the use of troops against American citizens helped spread party divisions among the general population. After 1794, the Federalists' critics, the Republicans, won major electoral victories in western Pennsylvania and throughout the West and became an increasingly vocal minority in Congress. Second, the actions of Washington and his advisors revealed their concern about the government's perceived vulnerability to internal threats, as well as their willingness to use force to preserve its authority.

The Federalists increasingly equated dissent with disloyalty as more Americans came to criticize their conduct of foreign policy. The first aim of American foreign policy under the new Constitution was to stabilize relations with other nations, ideally on terms favorable to the United States. Washington's administration, in particular, sought to negotiate favorable relationships with Europe's leading powers and with nearby native Americans.

In the 1790s, the United States made significant progress toward securing its western territories. In 1790 and 1791, the republic suffered humiliating defeats at the hands of the Miami Confederacy of western Indians. In 1794, however, General Anthony Wayne led his army to a decisive victory over the Indians, which resulted in their withdrawal from the Ohio territory. In addition, by 1795, the United States had negotiated a treaty with Spain which fixed the northern boundary of Spanish Florida and, more important still, gave Americans access to both the Mississippi River and the port of New Orleans. Access to water transportation was essential to the westward expansion of American agriculture because farmers needed an inexpensive way to get their crops to market.

Responding to the French Revolution and the resulting war in Europe was the other foreign policy concern of the 1790s. While most Americans had praised the French Revolution when it began in 1789, conservative Federalists soon were horrified by the increasing radicalism of French republicans, who toppled the monarchy, challenged the church, and beheaded those they regarded as enemies of the Revolution. American relations with both France and Great Britain were more complicated after 1793, when Britain declared war on the French republic. The United States sought to avoid involvement, while nonetheless preserving its interests and rights. Secretary of State Thomas Jefferson urged Washington to retain the 1778 Franco-American military and commercial alliance as leverage in exacting commercial concessions from Britain. Hamilton, by contrast, wanted to invalidate the alliance and refuse diplomatic recognition of the ambassador from the French republic. Hamilton urged the president to issue a proclamation of American neutrality, but Jefferson believed that power belonged not to the executive but to Congress. Following Hamilton's advice, on 22 April 1793, Washington issued his Neutrality Proclamation, but he also recognized the French republic and formally received its ambassador, Edmond Genêt, as Jefferson recommended.

Genêt's arrival in Charleston, South Carolina, in April 1793 aroused a groundswell of popular support for the French Revolution. Enthusiastic crowds greeted the ambassador as he made his way to Philadelphia, which had replaced New York as the nation's temporary capital. In 1793 and 1794, voluntary associations known as Democratic-Republican societies were established in many communities to celebrate the French revolutionary values of democracy and equality and to ensure that the United States lived up to its own revolutionary origins. Although Jefferson and the Republicans generally welcomed Genêt and supported the Democratic-Republican societies, Federalists found both French republicanism and its American admirers doubly alarming. On the one hand, Washington feared that the French ambassador's overt attempts to rally popular support for France would lead the United States into an unwanted war. On the other hand, Federalists saw the Democratic-Republican societies, which drew much of their membership from the middling and lower social orders, as dangerous harbingers of domestic anarchy and rebellion. Indeed, Washington and other Federalists genuinely believed that the societies were in large part responsible for the Whiskey Rebellion.

After Jefferson resigned his Cabinet post in late 1793, Federalists assumed full control of American foreign policy. Above all, they sought to reach an accommodation with the British, whose military objectives in their war with France often jeopardized American interests and rights. British naval vessels blockaded France and its Caribbean colonies, seizing American ships and cargoes. British naval commanders claimed the right to board and search American ships to seize sailors they believed to be deserters, a practice known as impressment. Washington sent John Jay to London to negotiate a treaty to address these and other issues, but

British military superiority and American financial dependence on tariffs from British imports put him at a distinct disadvantage. The British refused concessions on the issues of impressment and the rights of neutral shippers, though they agreed to vacate their six western forts, pay reparations for the ships and cargoes they seized in 1794–95, and give the United States minor trading concessions in the British West Indies. In return, however, Jay had to accord Great Britain most-favored-nation

English Cotton Bedcover, ca. 1790.   Postrevolutionary Americans showed their patriotism in everyday objects. This bedcover features images of Washington and Franklin, along with inscriptions commemorating the Stamp Act and the Declaration of Independence. Why would English manufacturers produce goods that celebrated the American Revolution so soon after it was over? Why would American consumers buy such goods from English producers? Source: Collection of the Museum of Early Southern Decorative Arts. Artist Unknown, "Bedcover," 1715–1800. Cotton, 85 x 83 inches. Winston-Salem, North Carolina. Accession No.: 4179. Old Salem, Inc./MESDA. Neg. No.: S–17732. Courtesy of the Museum of Early Southern Decorative Arts.

status in American trade and guarantee the payment of prerevolutionary debts Americans owed to British creditors.

Seen by many as indefensibly pro-British, the Jay Treaty was the most controversial foreign policy issue of Washington's presidency. After its terms became widely known in March 1795, Jay and Hamilton were burnt in effigy in many American communities. Southerners, who owed huge prewar debts to British merchants and wanted reparations for slaves lost in wartime, and urban artisans, who wanted commercial concessions, were especially outraged. The Senate divided along both partisan and sectional lines to ratify the treaty, and Washington reluctantly signed it. Along with Hamilton's fiscal system and the suppression of the Whiskey Rebellion, Jay's Treaty set the stage, in 1796, for the first truly partisan election in American history.

Even James Madison, who in *Federalist* #10 asserted the inevitability of interest-based factions, did not foresee the emergence of what historians call the first party system. Federalists and Republicans were organized coalitions of class, occupational, and regional interests that were transforming American political culture by the mid-1790s. Nascent party rivalries fueled the dramatic growth of the newspaper business in the postrevolutionary era. For instance, the state of Virginia, which had just two newspapers in 1776, had fourteen by 1793, most of which were increasingly openly allied with either the Federalists or Republicans. New civic rituals also promoted partisan culture in the 1790s. Federalist leaders staged genteel balls to commemorate Washington's birthday, Republicans sponsored popular gatherings to honor the French Revolution, and both parties organized Fourth of July celebrations. By 1796, each party had a caucus in every state to nominate candidates for Congress, influence the election of senators, and give institutional support for their standard-bearers in state and national contests.

Washington's retirement from the presidency after two terms unleashed unrestrained party conflict. Although the opposition press had criticized Washington for some of the policies of his administration, both Hamilton and Jefferson agreed that his prestige was still sufficient to unite the bulk of both parties behind him. With Washington's refusal to seek a third term, however, the election of 1796 became an openly partisan contest between Federalist John Adams and Republican Thomas Jefferson. Adams won, but Jefferson received the second highest number of electoral votes. By the original terms of the Constitution, the second-place candidate became vice-president.

As president, Adams inherited the problem of the European war and increasingly widespread opposition to Federalist policies. Despite his integrity and experience, Adams lacked Washington's stature and was forced to preside over a divided administration. Not only was his vice-president, Jefferson, the leader of the opposition party, but the

Federalists were themselves divided between Adams's supporters and those who remained loyal to Hamilton. Although the latter had left the Cabinet in 1795, he wielded influence through his friends, repeatedly undermining Adams's control of the government.

Party politics intertwined with foreign policy to bring the United States to the brink of war and domestic crisis during the troubled Adams presidency. In 1796, the French government responded to the Jay Treaty by rescinding its commercial treaty with the United States and ordering the seizure of American ships carrying goods to Britain or its colonies. In 1797, after the French had captured more than three hundred American ships and cargoes, Adams broke off diplomatic relations. Despite calls for war within his own party, however, he sent three commissioners to Paris to commence negotiations, but the French refused to meet the commissioners without first receiving a $250,000 bribe and a promise of a $12 million loan from the United States government. The commissioners refused, returning home, where Federalist politicians and newspaper editors publicized the insulting treatment they had received to drum up anti-French sentiment. Federalists in Congress also used the incident to justify upgrading and expanding the navy and creating a 50,000-man provisional army, along with a regular force of 10,000 troops. Republicans vigorously opposed the establishment of such a large professional army, both because of the exorbitant taxes it necessitated and because of the threat it potentially posed to American civil liberties.

Although Adams resisted Federalist pressure to undertake an all-out war with France, he accepted the proposition that the war scare offered his administration a legitimate opportunity to curtail domestic dissent. In the summer of 1798, Congress passed four laws known collectively as the Alien and Sedition Acts. The first three pertained to immigrants, who typically supported the Republicans. These laws empowered the president to deport citizens of countries at war with the United States and to expel any alien he even suspected of subversion. They also extended the residency requirement for naturalization from five to fourteen years, thereby delaying the enfranchisement of immigrant men. The most ominous, however, was the fourth law, the Sedition Act, which criminalized both oral and written criticism of the government and its officers. Under this law, the government indicted twenty-five people, most of whom were Republican newspaper editors. Ten were convicted, including Benjamin Franklin Bache, grandson of Benjamin Franklin and editor of the Philadelphia *Aurora*, an outspoken opposition paper.

Republican leaders vigorously opposed the Alien and Sedition Acts on both ideological and constitutional grounds. They did not, however, ask the Supreme Court to assess the laws' constitutionality both because the justices were all Federalists and because the Court had not yet established its authority to review congressional legislation; that precedent was set in 1803 with the landmark ruling of *Marbury v. Madison*. In 1798–99, Jefferson and Madison took their grievance to the state legislatures of Kentucky and Virginia, both of which were overwhelmingly Republican. The two Virginians secretly drafted resolutions for the legislatures, challenging the constitutionality of the Alien and Sedition Acts and the Federalists' larger vision of an activist central government. The Kentucky and Virginia resolutions were the first important statements of the states' rights position under the new Constitution, although neither Jefferson nor Madison believed that states could nullify or invalidate federal legislation.

Republicans rode popular discontent with Federalist tyranny and taxes to a major electoral victory in 1800. With particularly strong support from southern planters, western farmers, and urban artisans, Jefferson won the presidency and his party assumed control of both houses of Congress. Although the Federalists would remain a viable opposition party at the national level and the majority party in most of New England for more than a decade, they would never again control the national government.

The politics of the Federalist era exposed serious disagreements among Americans about the meaning of their Revolution and their expectations for the future of the republic. The Federalists wanted order, expected deference, and feared anarchy as the inevitable result of the people's direct control of government. Republicans wanted liberty, trusted the citizenry, and feared tyranny as the inevitable consequence of too much government power. The Federalists put the new government on a sound financial and administrative footing, but their penchant for equating opposition to their policies with disloyalty to the nation led to their political decline and eventual defeat in 1800.

DOCUMENT 1

"First Report on the Public Credit" (1790)

Alexander Hamilton

Secretary of the Treasury Alexander Hamilton was responsible for establishing a strong fiscal foundation for the American republic. In January 1790, he presented his proposal for funding the national debt to Congress.[1] Hamilton planned to fund the domestic debt by issuing interest-bearing certificates to its current holders, instead of issuing certificates to both original and current government creditors. This plan was controversial, but Congress nonetheless adopted it, along with Hamilton's proposal for the assumption of state debts by the central government.

Questions to consider:

1. Whose respect and trust did Hamilton hope the United States would secure as a result of his proposals?
2. Why did he believe that his plan suited the particular needs of the United States in 1790?
3. Hamilton was an early adherent to the "trickle down" theory of economics. How did he believe his plan would benefit those who were not government creditors?
4. Who might have objected to Hamilton's proposals—and on what grounds?

While the observance of that good faith, which is the basis of public credit, is recommended by the strongest inducements of political expediency, it is enforced by considerations of still greater authority. There are arguments for it, which rest on the immutable principles of moral obligation. And in proportion as the mind is disposed to contemplate, in the order of Providence, as intimate connection between public virtue and public happiness, will be its repugnancy to a violation of those principles.

This reflection derives additional strength from the nature of the debt of the United States. It was the price of liberty. The faith of America has been repeatedly pledged for it, and with solemnities, that give peculiar force to the obligation. There is indeed reason to regret that it has not hitherto been kept; that the necessities of the war, conspiring with inexperience in the subjects of finance, produced direct infractions; and that the subsequent period has been a continued scene of negative violation, or non-compliance. But a diminution of this regret arises from the reflection, that the last seven years have exhibited an earnest and uniform effort, on the part of the government of the union, to retrieve the national credit, by doing justice to the creditors of the nation; and that the embarrassments of a defective constitution, which defeated this laudable effort, have ceased.

From this evidence of a favorable disposition, given by the former government, the institution of a new one, clothed with powers competent to calling forth the resources of the community, has excited correspondent expectations. A general belief, accordingly, prevails, that the credit of the

United States will quickly be established on the firm foundation of an effectual provision for the existing debt. The influence, which this has had at home, is witnessed by the rapid increase that has taken place in the market value of the public securities. From January to November, they rose thirty-three and a third per cent, and from that period to this time, they have risen fifty per cent more. And the intelligence from abroad announces effects proportionably favourable to our national credit and consequence.

It cannot but merit particular attention, that among ourselves the most enlightened friends of good government are those whose expectations are the highest.

To justify and preserve their confidence; to promote the increasing respectability of the American name; to answer the calls of justice; to restore landed property to its due value; to furnish new resources both to agriculture and commerce; to cement more closely the union of the states; to add to their security against foreign attack; to establish public order on the basis of an upright and liberal policy. These are the great and invaluable ends to be secured, by a proper and adequate provision, at the present period, for the support of public credit.

To this provision we are invited, not only by the general considerations, which have been noticed, but by others of a more particular nature. It will procure to every class of the community some important advantages, and remove some no less important disadvantages.

The advantage to the public creditors from the increased value of that part of their property which constitutes the public debt, needs no explanation.

But there is a consequence of this, less obvious, though not less true, in which every other citizen is interested. It is a well known fact, that in countries in which the national debt is properly funded, and an object of established confidence, it answers most of the purposes of money. Transfers of stock or public debt are there equivalent to payments in specie; or in other words, stock, in the principal transactions of business, passes current as specie. The same thing would, in all probability happen here, under the like circumstances.

The benefits of this are various and obvious:

First. Trade is extended by it; because there is a larger capital to carry it on, and the merchant can at the same time, afford to trade for smaller profits; as his stock, which, when unemployed, brings him in an interest from the government, serves him also as money, when he has a call for it in his commercial operations.

Secondly. Agriculture and manufactures are also promoted by it. For the like reason, that more capital can be commanded to be employed in both; and because the merchant, whose enterprize in foreign trade, gives to them activity and extension, has greater means for enterprize.

Thirdly. The interest of money will be lowered by it; for this is always in a ratio, to the quantity of money, and to the quickness of circulation. This circumstances will enable both the public and individuals to borrow on easier and cheaper terms. . . .

The effect, which the funding of the public debt, on right principles, would have upon landed property, is one of the circumstances attending to such an arrangement, which has been the least adverted to, though it deserves the most particular attention . . . The decrease, in the value of lands, ought, in a great measure, to be attributed to the scarcity of money. Consequently whatever produces an augmentation of the monied capital of the country, must have a proportional effect in raising that value. The beneficial tendency of a funded debt, in this respect, has been manifested by the most decisive experience in Great Britain.

The proprietors of lands would not only feel the benefit of this increase in the value of their property, and of a more prompt and better sale, when they had occasion to sell; but the necessity of selling would be, itself, greatly diminished. As the same cause would contribute to the facility of loans, there is reason to believe, that such of them as are indebted, would be able through that resource, to satisfy their more urgent creditors. . . .

Having now taken a concise view of the inducements to a proper provision for the public debt, the next enquiry which presents itself is, what ought to be the nature of such a provision? This requires some preliminary discussions.

It is agreed on all hands, that that part of the debt which has been contracted abroad, and is denominated the foreign debt, ought to be provided for, according to the precise terms of the contracts relating to it. The discussions, which can arise, therefore, will have reference essentially to the domestic part of it, or to that which has been contracted at home. It is to be regretted, that there is not the same unanimity of sentiment on this part, as on the other.

The Secretary [of the Treasury] has too much deference for the opinions of every part of the community not to have observed one which has, more than once, made its appearance in the public prints, and which is occasionally to be met with in conversation. It involves this question, whether a discrimination ought not be made between original holders of the public securities, and present possessors, by purchase. Those who advocate a discrimination are for making a full provision for the securities of the former, at their nominal value; but contend, that the latter ought to receive no more than the cost to them, and the interest. And the idea is sometimes suggested of making good the difference to the primitive possessor.

In favor of this scheme, it is alleged, that it would be unreasonable to pay twenty shillings in the pound, to one who had not given more for it than three or four. And it is added, that it would be hard to aggravate the misfortune of the first owner, who, probably through necessity, parted with his property at so great a loss, by obliging him to contribute to the profit of the person, who had speculated on his distresses.

The Secretary, after the most mature reflection on the force of this argument, is induced to reject the doctrine it contains, as equally unjust and impolitic, as . . . ruinous to public credit.

"Public Opinion" (1791)

By 1791, divisions had emerged in Congress over Hamilton's fiscal policies. That October, the National Gazette *was established under the editorship of Philip Freneau to express opposition viewpoints and to arouse popular outcry against the Washington administration's policies. James Madison, one of Hamilton's most articulate critics in Congress, was a frequent contributor to the* National Gazette. *In this anonymous essay, he argued forcefully for the crucial role of public opinion in a republican government.*[2]

Questions to consider:

1. What did Madison mean by "public opinion"? How did he envision the relationship between public opinion and government?
2. Was Madison's position a partisan one? Did the thesis of this essay support or contradict the position he took in his discussion of factions in *Federalist*, #10?

Public opinion sets bounds to every government, and is the real sovereign in every free one.

As there are cases where the public opinion must be obeyed by the government, so there are cases, where not being fixed, it may be influenced by the government. This distinction, if kept in view, would prevent or decide many debates on the respect due from the government to the sentiments of the people. . . .

The larger a country, the less easy for its real opinion to be ascertained, and the less difficult to be counterfeited; when ascertained or presumed, the more respectable it is in the eyes of individuals. This is favorable to the authority of government. For the same reason, the more extensive a country, the more insignificant is each individual in his own eyes. This may be unfavorable to liberty.

Whatever facilitates a general intercourse of sentiments, as good roads, domestic commerce, a free press, and particularly a circulation of newspapers through the entire body of the people, and representatives going from, and returning among, every part of them, is equivalent to a contraction of territorial limits, and is favorable to liberty, where these may be too extensive.

DOCUMENT 3

"The Union: Who Are Its Real Friends?" (1792)

In his capacity as opposition leader, Madison penned many polemical essays for Freneau's National Gazette. *In this piece, which he published anonymously in March 1792, Madison summarized the opposition's assessment of the wider significance of Hamilton's fiscal system and other Federalist policies. While Federalists deemed opposition criticism self-serving or even subversive, other citizens clearly shared Madison's views. The growing ranks of Hamilton's opponents soon became known as Republicans.[3]*

Questions to consider:

1. Who was Madison's intended audience? Who and what were the targets of his criticism? What did he believe was at stake for Americans in 1792?
2. Why did Madison believe that Hamilton's fiscal policies encouraged "corruption in government"?
3. On what grounds did Madison accuse his adversaries of promoting monarchy, aristocracy, and "a system of measures . . . accommodated to the depraved examples of those hereditary forms"?

THE UNION. WHO ARE ITS REAL FRIENDS?

Not those who charge others with not being its friends, whilst their own conduct is wantonly multiplying its enemies.

Not those who favor measures, which by pampering the spirit of speculation within and without the government, disgust the best friends of the Union.

Not those who promote unnecessary accumulations of the debt of the Union, instead of the best means of discharging it as fast as possible; thereby increasing the causes of corruption in the government, and the pretexts for new taxes under its authority, the former undermining the confidence, the latter alienating the affection of the people.

Not those who study, by arbitrary interpretations and insidious precedents, to pervert the limited government of the Union, into a government of unlimited discretion, contrary to the will and subversive of the authority of the people.

Not those who avow or betray principles of monarchy and aristocracy, in opposition to the republican principles of the Union, and the republican spirit of the people; or who espouse a system of measures more accommodated to the depraved examples of those hereditary forms, than to the true genius of our own.

Not those, in a word, who would force on the people the melancholy duty of choosing between the loss of the Union, and the loss of what the Union was meant to secure.

THE REAL FRIENDS TO THE UNION ARE THOSE,

Who are friends to the authority of the people, the sole foundation on which the Union rests.

Who are friends to liberty, the great end, for which the Union was formed.

Who are friends to the limited and republican system of government, the means provided by that authority, for the attainment of that end.

Who are enemies to every public measure that might smooth the way to hereditary government; for resisting the tyrannies of which the Union was first planned, and for more effectually excluding which, it was put into its present form.

Who considering a public debt as injurious to the interests of the people, and baneful to the virtue of the government, are enemies to every contrivance for *unnecessarily* increasing its amount, or protracting its duration, or extending its influence.

In a word, these are the real friends of the Union, who are friends to that republican policy throughout, which is the only cement for the Union of a republican people.

Washington's Indian Policy (1791)

Stabilizing relations between the United States and native American nations was a high priority for the Washington administration. Government officials wanted to secure United States authority in the West without having to go to war with the Indians. The Indian Intercourse Act of 1790 aimed to promote peaceful relations between whites and Indians by regulating trade, curtailing white land purchases in Indian territory, and mandating that whites be punished for crimes committed against native Americans. Nevertheless, as President Washington reported in his message to Congress in 1791, the law was ineffective.[4] White settlers kept moving westward, and native Americans continued to resist the settlers' encroachment on their lands.

Questions to consider:

1. What was Washington's opinion of the Indians and their culture?
2. How did he expect an "intimate intercourse" with the United States to "advance the happiness" of native Americans?
3. Who—besides the Indians themselves—would have disapproved of Washington's policies, as he described them in 1791?
4. What was the main objective of United States Indian policy in 1790–91?

In the interval of your recess due attention has been paid to the execution of the different objects which were specially provided for by the laws and resolutions of the last session.

Among the most important of these is the defense and security of the western frontiers. To accomplish it on the most humane principles was a primary wish.

Accordingly, at the same time the treaties have been provisionally concluded and other proper means used to attach the wavering and to confirm in their friendship the well-disposed tribes of Indians, effectual measures have been adopted to make those of a hostile description sensible that a pacification was desired upon terms of moderation and justice.

Those measures having proved unsuccessful, it became necessary to convince the refractory of the power of the United States to punish their depredations. Offensive operations have therefore been directed, to be conducted, however, as consistently as possible with the dictates of humanity.

Some of these have been crowned with full success and others are yet depending. The expeditions which have been completed were carried on under the authority and at the expense of the United States by the militia of Kentucky, whose enterprise, intrepidity, and good conduct are entitled of peculiar commendation.

Overtures of peace are still continued to the deluded tribes, and considerable numbers of individuals belonging to them have lately renounced all further opposition, removed from their former situations, and placed themselves under the immediate protection of the United States.

It is sincerely to be desired that all need of coercion in future may cease and that an intimate intercourse may succeed, calculated to advance the happiness of the Indians and to attach them firmly to the United States.

In order to this it seems necessary—

That they should experience the benefits of an impartial dispensation of justice.

That the mode of alienating their lands, the main source of discontent and war, should be so defined and regulated as to obviate imposition and as far as may be practicable controversy concerning the reality and extent of the alienations which are made.

That commerce with them should be promoted under regulations tending to secure an equitable deportment toward them, and that such rational experiments should be made for imparting to them the blessings of civilization as may from time to time suit their condition.

That the Executive of the United States should be enabled to employ the means to which the Indians have been long accustomed for uniting their immediate interests with the preservation of peace.

And that efficacious provision should be made for inflicting adequate penalties upon all those who, by violating [Indian] rights, shall infringe the treaties and endanger the peace of the Union.

A system corresponding with the mild principles of religion and philanthropy toward an unenlightened race of men, whose happiness materially depends on the conduct of the United States, would be as honorable to the national character as conformable to the dictates of sound policy.

DOCUMENT 5

Virginians Celebrate the French Republic (1794)

Civic rituals were an important part of the partisan culture of the Federalist era. Although militia parades, artillery salutes, and drinking toasts on the Fourth of July became the standard civic rituals of the early republic, in the 1790s Americans were still experimenting with other forms of public celebration, many of which promoted partisan political values. Federalists organized genteel balls to mark Washington's birthday, thereby demonstrating both admiration for the president and a preference for a socially exclusive polity. Republicans, by contrast, orchestrated more socially inclusive tributes to the French Revolution. In May 1794, the Virginia Herald and Fredericksburg Advertiser *published a detailed report of one such celebration.*[5]

Questions to consider:

1. Does this report contain any evidence of partisanship on the part of either the organizers of this celebration or its participants? Which toasts would have been considered controversial in 1794? Which would have been acceptable to the vast majority of Americans?
2. Who were the main participants in this celebration? Who were the spectators? What was the message and purpose of the Fredericksburg celebration?

On Saturday last, there was a numerous assemblage of the citizens of this place and neighbourhood, in order to commemorate the late glorious successes of our sister republic of France. The amusements of the day were conducted in the following manner:

At 10 o'clock the different companies of cavalry, artillery and infantry, appeared on the parade, where they were reviewed by Gen. Poley, who took command of the whole, and a number of military evolutions were performed to the great entertainment of the spectators. At 1 o'clock the several companies repaired to the spacious bower erected for the purpose, where they were met by the citizens and a large collection of the fair daughters of Columbia, and mutual congratulations took place upon the happy occasion of the meeting. The front of the bower was adorned with the national cockades, at equal distances; and the flags of the two republics, with the liberty cap between them, beautified the centre. At 3 o'clock a federal salute was fired, and the company sat down to a plentiful barbecue; after which the ladies retired to the market house, where they were entertained with dancing and music till evening, when the whole separated. We do not recollect on any occasion so numerous an assemblage, or where greater unanimity, hilarity and cheerfulness prevailed.

During the entertainment the following toasts were drank, accompanied with discharges from the artillery and infantry.

1. The People of the United States.
2. The French Republic—may the success of her armies be the means of establishing a government on the broad basis of equal liberty.
3. George Washington, our illustrious President—may he long enjoy health, and continue the guardian of liberty and of his country.
4. May the peace and happiness of a free country never be disturbed by foreign influence or domestic commotions.
5. The immortal memory of all those who have fallen in defence of liberty.
6. May the posterity of those patriots who laid the foundation of our liberty, long support the glorious fabric.
7. The agriculture, manufactures and commerce of the United States.
8. The fair daughters of Columbia.
9. May the chains of slavery be ever suspended round the neck of tyranny.
10. The state of Virginia.
11. May talents and virtue be the only road to preferment.
12. May the principles of liberty and truth prevail throughout the globe.
13. The rights of man well understood.
14. May executive influence be counteracted, judicial sophistry exposed, and legislative purity maintained, by the force of reason.
15. The great family of mankind—may all political and religious distinctions cease, and our freedom and friendship be established in their place.

DOCUMENT 6

"Thoughts on the Excise Law" (1792)

Hugh Henry Brackenridge

In 1791, Congress had enacted an excise tax on whiskey to raise the revenue needed to begin paying interest to holders of government securities. The excise tax aroused little serious opposition in Congress. In the West, however, farmers, who often converted their grain to whiskey for sale, bitterly opposed the excise. Hugh Henry Brackenridge, a Pittsburgh lawyer who had strongly supported ratification of the Constitution, explained why westerners would resist collection of the whiskey tax and argued against its enforcement in Freneau's National Gazette.[6]

Questions to consider:

1. What, besides the excise, were the westerners' chief grievances?
2. In what sense, according to Brackenridge, was the West both politically and economically crucial to the future of the United States?
3. On what grounds did Brackenridge argue for the repeal of the excise law? What did he think would happen if the westerners suffered continued mistreatment at the hands of the United States government?

I consider the Western country as the . . . third estate, of the Union and as necessary to hold the balance in the interest of the East and South parts. There is nothing in my contemplation [that] will contribute more to the duration of our empire than such a balance. It will also serve to counterbalance the weight of the monied interests and germ of aristocracy in the richer capitals by preserving a bed of simplicity and true republicanism. In this point of view every politician who wishes a long date to what we have acquired by our wars and victories will countenance these ideas.

I have been silent in the Western country, not willing to incur the suspicion of being a mover of sedition or to be so. I state my opinions here that they may come before the eyes of those who may give redress, the representatives of the United States. The ultramontane inhabitants are in fact but hewers of wood and drawers of water at this moment; so far from luxury that they are not above want. The great proportion on the frontier that, on alarms, are obliged to desert their fields and leave them uncultivated, feel the distress of this in the want of food for themselves or cattle. The more inland people are like troops called constantly from the center of the camp to protect the front line. The collecting revenue from this quarter ought not therefore to be thought of so soon. Let the tax be suspended or a sale made proportioned to these circumstances.

I profess had I it in my power and was answerable for the success of provision for the public debt, I would adopt this policy because, with respect to these people, the thing is palpably so unequal and oppressive that it cannot be borne. It amounts to a prohibition of distillation altogether; and opposition necessarily generated in one quarter may communicate to another and take flame where there are not the same strokes of the steel originally to produce it. These thoughts I submit respectfully to the Secretary of the Treasury or the representatives of the people, if an eye should be cast on this paper. I have just to add further, let peace be given to the Western country, let the use of the waters to the ocean be established, let them have a little time to breathe and recover loss and feel vigor; and if they do not submit to every demand of contribution to the revenue, I shall be the first to bear testimony against them in their country, as I have done heretofore when I thought them wrong. But I know the yeomanry are honest, though sometimes misled, and in due time that country will afford both by trade and tax a substantial revenue to these States, but oppression will make the wise mad and induce them to resist with intemperance what they ought to resist with reason. The Western country is a glorious garden to cultivate, and the fairest blossoms will bloom and richest fruit will grow there for the benefit of this government. It will enable these States to hold both Britain and Spain at bay and engage the most reasonable treaties of commerce, lest the one lost Canada or the other the Floridas and the South Mines. Your strength is here, countrymen; cast this anchor to windward, you are safe.

DOCUMENT 7

"Incendiaries of Public Peace" (1794)

Washington and his chief advisors regarded the enforcement of the excise tax of 1791 as a test of the power of the new national government. Accordingly, they were willing to use military force to suppress the western insurgents who sought to prevent the collection of the excise tax on their whiskey. In this letter to a friend, written from Philadelphia shortly after dispatching troops to western Pennsylvania, Washington reflected on what he believed was at stake for the United States in the Whiskey Rebellion.[7]

Questions to consider:

1. What did Washington envision as the proper relationship between the citizenry and their representatives in Congress?
2. Who, according to Washington, was responsible for the western uprising? What evidence did he provide to support this view?
3. The insurgents saw their activities as analogous to those of colonists who thwarted the implementation of the Stamp Act and other unconstitutional taxes under British rule. Why did Washington and many other Americans not view their actions in this light?

I hear with the greatest pleasure of the spirit which so generally pervades the militia of every state that has been called upon on the present occasion, and of the decided discountenance the incendiaries of public peace and order have met within their attempt to spread their nefarious doctrines with a view to poison and discontent the minds of the people against the government; particularly by endeavouring to have it believed that their liberties were assailed, and that all the wicked and abominable measures that co[ul]d be devised (under specious guises) are practiced to sap the Constitution, and lay the foundation of future slavery.

The Insurrection in the Western counties of this state is a striking evidence of this and may be considered as the first *ripe fruit* of the Democratic Societies. I did not, I must confess, expect their labours would come to maturity so soon; though I never had a doubt, that such conduct would produce some such issue, if it did not meet the frown of those who were well disposed to order and good government, in time. For can anything be more absurd, more arrogant, or more pernicious to the peace of society, than for a self created, *permanent* body, (for no one denies the right of the people to meet occasionally, to petition for, or to remonstrate against, any act of the legislature, &c) to declare that *this act* is unconstitutional, and *that* act is pregnant of mischief, and that all who vote contrary to their dogmas are actuated by selfish motives, or under foreign influence, nay in plain terms are traitors to their Country? [This] is such a stretch of arrogant presumption as is not to be reconciled with laudable motives, especially when we see the same set of men endeavouring to destroy all confidence in the administration by arraigning all its acts without knowing on what ground or with what information it proceeds, and this without regard to decency or truth. These things were evidently intended, and could not fail without counteraction, to disquiet the public mind; but I hope, and trust, they will work their own cure, especially when it is known, more generally than it is, that the Democratic Society of this place (from which the others have emanated) was instituted by Mr. Genet for the express purpose of dissent, and to draw a line between the people and the government, after he found the officers of the latter would not yield to the hostile measures in which he wanted to embroil this country.

DOCUMENT 8

The Sedition Act (1798)

In the midst of the war scare of 1798, the Federalists enacted four laws designed to undermine the influence of the opposition Republicans. The most notorious of these, the

Sedition Act of 1798, made it a crime to speak or publish anything critical of the federal government or its officers.[8] Twenty-five men were indicted and ten were convicted under the Sedition Act; all of those prosecuted were Republicans and most were editors of or contributors to opposition newspapers. The Republicans let the Sedition Act expire after they took control of both Congress and the presidency in 1801. Only during World War I did the United States again adopt this sort of legislation.

Questions to consider:

1. How did the authors of the Sedition Act envision their political opponents?
2. Why did they specifically seek to regulate the spoken and written word? What did they believe would happen without such regulations?
3. Why were these regulations only temporary? Why do you think the law's authors chose to have it expire in March 1801?

Congressional Pugilists, 1798. This political cartoon shows a brawl that took place between Republican Matthew Lyon of Vermont (right) and Federalist Roger Griswold of Connecticut on the floor of Congress in February 1798. What does this image convey about party politics in the 1790s? Can you deduce the political sentiments of the cartoon's unknown artist? Source: The Library of Congress, Washington, D.C.

SEC. I. Be it enacted by the Senate and House of Representatives of the United States of America, in Congress assembled, That if any persons shall unlawfully combine or conspire together, with intent to oppose any measure or measures of the government of the United States, which are or shall be directed by proper authority, or to impede the operation of any law of the United States, or to intimidate or prevent any person holding a place or office in or under the government of the United States, from undertaking, performing or executing his trust or duty; and if any person or persons, with intent as aforesaid, shall counsel, advise or attempt to procure any insurrection, riot, unlawful assembly, or combination, whether such conspiracy, threatening, counsel, advice, or attempt shall have the proposed effect or not, he or they shall be deemed guilty of a high misdemeanor, and on conviction, before any court of the United States having jurisdiction thereof, shall be punished by a fine not exceeding five thousand dollars, and by imprisonment during a term not less than six months nor exceeding five years; and further, at the discretion of the court may be holden to find sureties for his good behaviour in such sum, and for such time, as the said court may direct.

SEC. 2. And be it further enacted, That if any person shall write, print, utter or publish, or shall cause or procure to be written, printed, uttered or published, or shall knowingly and willingly assist or aid in writing, printing, uttering or publishing any false, scandalous and malicious writing or writings against the government of the United States, or either house of the Congress of the United States, or the President of the United States, with intent to defame the said government, or either house of the said Congress, or the said President, or to bring them, or either of them, into contempt or disrepute; or to excite against them, or either or any of them, the hatred of the good people of the United States, or to excite any unlawful combinations therein, for opposing or resisting any law of the United States, or any act of the President of the United States, done in pursuance of any such law, or of the powers in him vested by the constitution of the United States, or to resist, oppose, or defeat any such law or act, or to aid, encourage or abet any hostile designs of any foreign nation against the United States, their people or government, then such person, being thereof convicted before any court of the United States having jurisdiction thereof, shall be punished by a fine not exceeding two thousand dollars, and by imprisonment not exceeding two years.

SEC. 3. And be it further enacted, and declared, That if any person shall be prosecuted under this act, for the writing or publishing any libel aforesaid, it shall be lawful for the defendant, upon the trial of the cause, to give in evidence in his defence, the truth of the matter contained in the publication charged as a libel. And the jury who shall try the cause, shall have a right to determine the law and the fact, under the direction of the court, as in other cases.

SEC. 4. And be it further enacted, That this act shall continue and be in force until the third day of March, one thousand eight hundred and one, and no longer: Provided. That the expiration of the act shall not prevent or defeat a prosecution and punishment of any offence against the law, during the time it shall be in force.

SUGGESTED READING FOR CHAPTER 11

APPLEBY, JOYCE. *Capitalism and a New Social Order: The Republican Vision of the 1790s* (1984).

COOKE, JACOB E. *Alexander Hamilton* (1982).

CORNELL, SAUL. *The Other Founders: Anti-Federalism and the Dissenting Tradition in America, 1788–1828* (1999).

ELKINS, STANLEY; and MCKITRICK, ERIC. *The Age of Federalism: The Early American Republic, 1788–1800* (1993).

FLEXNER, JAMES T. *George Washington and the New Nation, 1783–1793* (1969).

———. *George Washington: Anguish and Farewell, 1793–1799* (1972).

HORSMAN, REGINALD. *The Frontier in the Formative Years, 1783–1815* (1970).

KOHN, RICHARD H. *Eagle and Sword: The Federalists and the Creation of the Military Establishment in America, 1783–1802* (1975).

MCCOY, DREW R. *The Elusive Republic: Political Economy in Jeffersonian America* (1980).

SHARP, JAMES ROGER. *American Politics in the Early Republic: The New Nation in Crisis* (1993).

SHAW, PETER. *The Character of John Adams* (1976).

SLAUGHTER, THOMAS P. *The Whiskey Rebellion: Frontier Epilogue to the American Revolution* (1986).

SMITH, JAMES MORTON. *Freedom's Fetters: The Alien and Sedition Laws and American Civil Liberties* (1966).

TAYLOR, ALAN. *William Cooper's Town: Power and Persuasion on the Frontier of the Early American Republic* (1995).

WALDSTREICHER, DAVID. *In the Midst of Perpetual Fetes: The Making of American Nationalism, 1776–1820* (1997).

NOTES

[1]"First Report on the Public Credit," 9 Jan. 1790, in Henry Cabot Lodge, ed., *The Works of Alexander Hamilton*, 12 vols. (New York, 1904), 2: 230–37.

[2][James Madison], "Public Opinion," *National Gazette*, 19 Dec. 1791.

[3][James Madison], "The Union: Who are its Real Friends?," *National Gazette*, 31 Mar. 1792.

[4]George Washington, "Third Annual Address," 25 Oct. 1791, in James D. Richardson, comp., *A Compilation of the Messages and Papers of the Presidents*, 11 vols. (New York, 1911), 1: 96–97.

[5]*Virginia Herald and Fredericksburg Advertiser*, 15 May 1794.

[6][Hugh Henry Brackenridge], "Thoughts on the Excise Law," *National Gazette*, 9 Feb. 1792.

[7]George Washington to Burges Ball, 25 Sept. 1794, in John C. Fitzpatrick, ed., *The Writings of George Washington*, 39 vols. (Washington, 1931–44), 33: 505–7.

[8]"An Act in addition to the act, entitled 'An act for the punishment of certain crimes against the United States,'" 14 July 1798, in *United States Statutes at Large*, 46 vols. (Boston and Washington, 1848–1925), 1: 596–97.

CHAPTER TWELVE

FORGING A NATIONAL CULTURE

After the Revolution, American political and intellectual leaders, aware of the historic fragility of republics, sought to construct a national culture to foster unity amid diversity and promote shared civic values. The federal Constitution and the national capital under construction on the banks of the Potomac River were significant artifacts of the American nation-state and highly visible attempts to cultivate a sense of shared national identity among its citizens. Many nationally minded leaders also emphasized the centrality of education in creating the stable and virtuous society they deemed essential to the success of Americans' experiment in republicanism. Some promoted public education, while others explored the use of literature and the arts to cultivate national consciousness. In the end, however, ordinary citizens chose selectively from elite prescriptions and for the most part rejected efforts to homogenize American culture and make it subservient to the interests of the polity.

The most basic attributes of American identity emerged from the crisis that culminated in the Declaration of Independence. While colonists typically had compared American culture unfavorably to that of Britain, the process of severing the bonds of empire encouraged them to view their deviation from European norms in a more positive light. Revolutionary Americans denounced luxury and fashion, patronage and privilege, as emblems of corruption, and they resisted the creation of what they considered artificial privileges and social distinctions. There would be no titled nobility in republican America, where even the efforts of Continental Army officers to form a hereditary fraternal organization provoked a public outcry on the grounds that it was an incipient aristocracy.

Many Americans expected a "natural aristocracy"—an elite based on talent, wisdom, and public spirit—to emerge to lead the republic. Indeed, in *The Federalist Papers*, James Madison argued that the system of representation embodied in the Constitution would encourage a "filtration of talent" that would result in the elevation of members of the natural aristocracy to leadership posts at the national level. Although Americans would disagree about the specific attributes of their ideal leaders, they agreed that merit, not heredity, would be the prerequisite for attaining prestige and power.

If attitudes about aristocracy helped Americans to distinguish themselves from Europeans, institution-building was an even more positive manifestation of their evolving sense of themselves as a cohesive political community. Most Americans identified politically with their states during the Confederation era, when a weak Congress and an unpopular army—neither of which inspired much loyalty or affection—were the only institutional embodiments of a larger continental union. The drafting and ratification of the United States Constitution was the first great victory for American nationalists. Establishing a government that at least in theory derived its power from a unitary and sovereign people, the Constitution gave the concept of American nationhood its institutional form.

Once in place, the new government enacted policies that aimed to promote a sense of shared national identity among citizens. Beginning in 1790, a constitutionally mandated decennial federal census was a compelling representation of the demographic and territorial expanse the United States. The Post Office Act of 1792, which created an expansive postal system and established special cheap postage rates for newspapers, facilitated the dissemination of information throughout the country, an achievement nationalists considered essential for promoting a shared national identity among its dispersed and growing population. Nationalists believed that a new and carefully planned seat of government would be an even more powerful representation of American nationhood for citizens and foreign visitors alike. While Thomas Jefferson and his Republican associates envisioned the seat of the republic as rustic and pristinely anticommercial, in keeping with their agrarian and antiurban ideals, Federalists preferred a more refined cultural style to reflect and reinforce both social hierarchy and the authority of the central government.

Contemporaries acknowledged that regional and ethnic affinities posed significant obstacles to the formation of a homogenized national identity among Americans. According to the First Federal Census, in 1790 the United States had nearly 4 million inhabitants dispersed among thirteen states and territories. The overall population of the area that now constituted the United States had almost doubled since 1770, mostly due to natural increase, and population was spread over a much larger area. By 1790, at least 100,000 people made their homes in the western territories. Among white Americans, ethnic diversity remained pronounced, as it had been during the colonial era. Although the roots of New Englanders were overwhelmingly English, Germans accounted for nearly 40 percent of Pennsylvania's inhabitants, 15 percent of white New Yorkers claimed Dutch ancestry, and the Scots-Irish were prominent in every area except New England.

The territorial extent and demographic diversity of the United States were formidable obstacles to the construction of a unifying national identity in the postrevolutionary era. Institution-building was one important aspect of the nation-building project. Institutional mechanisms like a strong central government, an ambitious postal system, and a federal census mitigated physical and cultural distance among scattered and diverse citizens of the republic. Nevertheless, nationalists recognized that institutions alone could not produce the results they wanted. Accordingly, they turned their attention to education and the arts, seeking to create a didactic culture to further the goals of nation-building in a republican political order.

Postrevolutionary leaders assumed a reciprocal relationship between politics and their wider cultural context. Acting on this assumption, they hoped to deploy aesthetics and education in their effort to construct and promote an American national identity. Many believed that political liberty, coupled with America's obvious prosperity and potential for growth, would give rise to a neoclassical golden age of achievement in science, the arts, and government. In encouraging this development, their objectives were threefold. First, they would educate and improve their own citizens. Second, they would show the world—by which they meant skeptical Europeans—that American artists could use themes and images from their own history and environment to create great literature and art. Third, they would use art, literature, and cultural life generally to stimulate patriotism and national consciousness.

Because most postrevolutionary artists self-consciously sought to inspire national feeling and civic virtue in their audiences, their work drew heavily on themes and incidents from American history. And because the Revolution was the defining moment in the story of American republicanism and nationhood, its events and heroes were especially appealing subjects. The best-known paintings of the revolutionary generation of American artists—most notably Charles Willson Peale, Gilbert Stuart, and John Trumbull—glorified the American nation and its leaders. For instance, in 1779, Peale portrayed Washington as the confident and victorious commander at the Battle of Trenton, while in 1797, Gilbert Stuart painted a more somber—but no less authoritative—portrait of Washington, now clothed as the civilian president of the republic. John Trumbull's *Declaration of Independence* (1787) shows a gathering of well-dressed, orderly, and like-minded gentlemen purposefully receiving Jefferson's declaration. Although declaring independence was a contested process expedited in large part by radicals outside Congress, Trumbull romanticized this founding moment of American nationhood as the result of consensus among great men.

American writers and editors, too, enlisted their talents in the nationalist project in the postrevolutionary years. By 1787, two-Philadelphia-based periodicals, the *Columbian Magazine* and the *American Museum*, sought to adapt the model of the English genteel periodical to new American circumstances, providing elite readers in every state with a combination of reprinted English pieces and original American writing. Two years later, David Ramsay, a South Carolina Federalist, published the first history of the Revolution that did not focus exclusively on a single state. In his *History of the American Revolution*, Ramsay told a story of nation-building that began with the first settlement of the colonies, recounted the struggles of the War of Independence, and ended optimistically with the adoption of the Constitution and Washington's elevation to the presidency. Around the same time, Mercy Otis Warren of Massachusetts constructed a different story of American nationhood, one more in keeping with her New England, Antifederalist, Jeffersonian perspective. Meanwhile, dramatists like William Dunlap and novelists like Charles Brockden Brown experimented with themes and topics they deemed suitable for American audiences. Brown's 1798 gothic novel, *Wieland*, for instance, was a cautionary tale about the need for family, religion, and other traditional constraints on individual freedom. Set in the seemingly idyllic Pennsylvania countryside, Brown's novel was a Federalist meditation on the political and civil unrest of the 1790s.

Most American intellectuals recognized the need to cultivate national feeling at the grassroots level, and they turned to education both as a remedy for regional and ethnic diversity and as a way to promote a universal standard for American political and social values. Influenced by the psychological theories of the Enlightenment—and especially by John Locke's *Essay on Human Understanding*—they believed that the human mind at birth was a blank slate that would be filled, over time, by information supplied by the senses. Accordingly, human reason and character were, at least to some extent, the products of environment, so it

George Washington (Lansdowne portrait), 1796 by Gilbert Stuart.
While earlier portraits showed Washington as a vigorous and
affable gentleman, typically in military dress, this image of him
became more common in decades following the Revolution.
Reproduced more than one hundred times before 1830, Stuart's
portrait hung in the White House and was the only painting saved
when British forces burned that building during the War of 1812.
Why did Stuart paint Washington in somber civilian dress—but
nonetheless with a sword at his side? What other significant
objects did he place in this portrait? Why did Stuart's image
become the standard representation of Washington in the
postrevolutionary era? Source: Gilbert Stuart (1755–1828), "George
Washington (Lansdowne portrait)", 1796. Painting, unframed. Oil on canvas.
Unframed: 247.6 × 158.7 cm (97½ × 62½"). National Portrait Gallery,
Smithsonian Institution; acquired through the generosity of the Donald
W. Reynolds Foundation. NPG.2001.13.

The Declaration of Independence, 4 July 1776, 1787 by John Trumbull. This frequently reproduced painting shows Congress receiving the draft of the Declaration from the committee that drafted it. The artist, John Trumbull, son of Connecticut's revolutionary governor, had been a colonel in the Continental Army and an aide to General Washington. A copy of this painting, along with three others portraying signal events in the creation of the republic, hangs today in the rotunda of the Capitol. How did Trumbull envision the Continental Congress and its members? What was the intended effect of his painting on those who viewed it? Source: John Trumbull (American, 1756–1843), "The Declaration of Independence, 4 July 1776", 1786–1820. Oil on canvas, 53 × 78.7 cm (20⅞ × 31 in). Yale University Art Library, Trumbull Collection. 1832.3.

became the task of American educators to design learning environments conducive to the cultivation of socially desirable ideas and attributes. Like most Americans, educational reformers assumed that an informed citizenry—and thus basic literacy—was essential to the survival of popular government. But they also saw schools as social laboratories in which curricular formulae could be applied to produce ideal republicans.

In the 1780s and 1790s, American intellectuals and social critics hotly debated the appropriate content and extent of republican education. Public figures as different as Thomas Jefferson of Virginia—a deist and eventual Republican leader—and Noah Webster of Connecticut—an orthodox Christian and outspoken Federalist—proposed state support for education at all levels, from primary school through college. Jefferson, Washington, and other American leaders also championed the establishment of a publicly funded national university. In his last will and testament, Washington even set aside funds to support such a project, but the plan for a national university never came to fruition.

Benjamin Rush of Philadelphia was probably the foremost advocate for public education in the postrevolutionary era. Rush was a man of science and the country's most influential physician. He also embraced the democratization of politics that accompanied the Revolution but nonetheless averred the necessity of educating newly empowered citizens. Rush concluded that "universal" public education—in other words, schooling for all white males—was especially necessary in states like Pennsylvania, where diverse religious and ethnic traditions complicated the construction of a suitably civic-minded republican political identity. Rush worried that regional loyalties and interests would undermine civic virtue; like Jefferson and Washington, he supported the creation of a national university as a means of diluting local prejudices, at least among the natural aristocracy of prospective leaders of the republic. Rush even contended that republican political culture necessitated improvements in women's education. As mothers of the future citizens of the United States, he suggested, educated women could play an important role in preserving the republic's political and moral character.

As Rush and other educational reformers debated the appropriate course of study for young men—and sometimes women, too—they typically concluded that American education should be practical rather than ornamental. Europe's monarchical political culture dictated that education be accessible only to an aristocratic elite, who relied on ornamental accomplishments to distinguish themselves and thereby enhance their authority. By contrast, the maintenance of a republican polity necessitated that all citizens possess enough skills to be economically self-supporting—and thus politically independent—and that they be sufficiently well informed and civic-minded to participate in political life. Teaching students geography, especially the geography of the United States, therefore was an important part of the nationalists' educational project. So, too, was oratory or eloquence, both because of its roots in classical republicanism and because it remained a critical medium for political discourse in the postrevolutionary era.

No member of the revolutionary generation was more aware of the importance of language than Noah Webster. This Connecticut Federalist recognized that language was a powerful signifier of national identity, both to the nation's citizens and to the outside world. Webster argued that the United States could not be truly independent until it—like England, France, or Spain—had a language of its own. On the one hand, that meant collapsing regional, ethnic, and class dialects into a coherent and unifying national language. On the other hand, it also necessitated the drawing and maintaining of clear distinctions between the American language and its English progenitor.

Webster believed that American English had to mirror the values and attributes of the nation it would create. In *Dissertations on the English*

Language (1789), his most important theoretical work, he argued that in the British Isles language—like politics and society—had in the eighteenth century become increasingly corrupt. In America, by contrast, language had been insulated from the corrupting influence of fashion and frivolity. American grammar and pronunciation, like American political and moral values, retained their original purity and virtue. Enhanced by the addition of native American words and terms from other European languages, the vocabulary of American English was fluid and expansive, as was American society. In the 1780s, Webster argued forcefully in favor of a system of simplified spelling, which he believed would reflect the plain, honest, and unpretentious style of American republicanism, while further distinguishing the language of the United States from its British counterpart. Although most Americans rejected his more radical orthographic reforms, they accepted some modest changes. Webster's spelling book, which first appeared in 1783, was soon selling more than 200,000 copies each year. The book's sales escalated during the nineteenth century, making it the best-selling book ever written by an American.

Through his speller and his famous *American Dictionary of the English Language* (1828), Webster reached a vast audience, but his efforts did not result in the creation of a unified and homogeneous American language. For one thing, Webster's own provincialism, especially his bias in favor of New England pronunciations, made for a peculiarly skewed and exclusive view of what was or should be uniquely American. Conversely, his readers, who increasingly coveted literacy and standardized spelling as tokens of respectability, had no desire to cultivate Webster's New England ways. In the end, Webster's speller and dictionary helped educate generations of Americans, but they did not serve their author's broader purpose of replacing local dialects and usage with a standard national language.

The fate of Webster's more ambitious and controversial undertakings was indicative of that of the nationalists' efforts to shape American culture generally. The neoclassical golden age of learning and culture that nationalist intellectuals anticipated never materialized: their magazines soon folded, Ramsay's histories and Brown's novels found few readers, and most American artists remained itinerants who earned their livings by painting portraits of wealthy clients. Americans founded no national university and no state established a system of universal public education until the middle of the nineteenth century. Both education and literacy improved in the United States after the Revolution, but for most Americans the purposes of education and the books they chose to read differed vastly from the cultural prescriptions of nationalist intellectuals.

Unlike those nationalists who posited a symbiotic relationship between politics and the wider cultural environment, most Americans were increasingly likely to see politics as separate from private life. While revolutionary republicanism presupposed that it was the duty of citizens to serve the public, American political culture increasingly evolved to assert the citizen's right to serve himself. James Madison admitted as much when, in *Federalist, #10*, he argued that political institutions had to be insulated from the corrosive effects of self-interest, which he regarded as the wellspring of human motivation and the inevitable source of factions in a free society. Accordingly, when Americans chose to educate their children, they did so mainly to serve their private needs and interests— whether economic or religious—rather than to implement a political agenda. When they read, they sought information or entertainment that likewise suited their personal needs or tastes. Among postrevolutionary Americans, much to the nationalists' chagrin, the most popular books were sentimental novels.

Although they seem overly pious and moralistic to modern readers, sentimental novels threatened the nationalists' republican project in three important respects. First, national intellectuals and social critics believed that sentimental fiction, which was typically romantic, corrupted the morals of its readers, many of whom were young women. Second, many also worried that because such novels were generally written by, for, and about women, their popularity afforded females too much cultural authority. Because contemporary gender stereotypes associated men with reason and women with passion, critics warned that women's cultural influence would undermine both rationality and virtue in public life. Finally, some critics maintained that sentimental novels subverted the natural superiority of men over women. Sentimental novels often vilified men as predatory seducers and featured heroines who were either virtuous victims of masculine vice or its worthy adversaries. The period's most popular novel, Susanna Rowson's *Charlotte: A Tale of Truth* (1791), which went through more than two hundred editions, exemplified the combination of saccharine sentimentality and latent feminism that critics so despised.

The most popular postrevolutionary narrative that featured a historical figure as its central character was Mason Locke Weems's *Life of George Washington* (1800). Like Rowson, Weems was a literary entrepreneur who sought both to instruct his audience and to make a profit. Like Rowson's *Charlotte*, his *Washington* purported to be truthful, but it was in fact a fanciful account that focused primarily on the great man's private virtues, not his public triumphs. Weems told stories—mostly invented, as it turned out—of Washington as a son, planter, and Christian, but above all as an exemplar of virtues that his readers could emulate in their own lives. Weems hoped his readers would be industrious, frugal, honest, and pious; he did not expect them to lead armies or otherwise devote themselves to the service of the republic. His vision of private citizens prospering through the exercise of private virtue proved both popular and influential. Weems invented the enduring story of young Washington and the cherry tree, and he fabricated the image of the American general kneeling in the snow in prayer at Valley Forge. His stories were hugely popular in part because the values they promoted suited an emerging culture of individualism and self-improvement which construed virtue in primarily private terms.

By 1800, it was clear that the efforts of nationalist intellectuals to pro- mote a shared national identity based on republican values of civic virtue and public service were largely unsuccessful. Although white Americans, indeed, had fashioned a sense of themselves as members of a common national community, the culture of that community, like the environment from which it sprang, was diverse and decentralized. American national identity derived from the political ideals of liberty and independence, which informed a common ethic of individual self-improvement and in- spired a pantheon of mythic heroes, such as Weems's Washington. More democratic than republican, the culture of the new American nation would be driven mainly by the needs and tastes of individuals and the competitive forces of the market economy.

DOCUMENT 1

Notes on the State of Virginia (1782)

Thomas Jefferson

Distinguishing Americans from Europeans—and especially from the British—was the first crucial step in the development of national consciousness. In the course of answer- ing a series of questions posed by a French diplomat, Jefferson described the physical, so- cial, and economic characteristics of Virginia, often pointedly refuting European notions of American backwardness and inferiority. In this famous passage, Jefferson explored the differences between economic life and opportunity in Europe and America.[1]

Questions to consider:

1. What, according to Jefferson, were the chief differences between the European and American economies?

2. Why did Jefferson believe that "those who labour in the earth are the chosen people of God"?
3. Why did he profess to oppose the development of manufacturing in the United States?
4. How did he expect the economy and society of the United States to develop in the decades following the Revolution?

~~◦◦ ◦◦~~

The political economists of Europe have established it as a principle that every state should endeavour to manufacture for itself: and this principle, like many others, we transfer to America, without calculating the difference of circumstance which should often produce a difference of result. In Europe the lands are either cultivated, or locked up against the cultivator. Manufacture must therefore be resorted to of necessity not of choice, to support the surplus of their people. But we have an immensity of land courting the industry of the husbandman. Is it best then that all our citizens should be employed in its improvement, or that one half should be called off from that to exercise manufactures and handicraft arts for the other? Those who labour in the earth are the chosen people of God, if ever he had a chosen people, whose breasts he has made his peculiar deposit for substantial and genuine virtue. It is the focus in which he keeps alive that sacred fire, which otherwise might escape from the face of the earth. Corruption of morals in the mass of cultivators is a phenomenon of which no age nor nation has furnished an example. It is the mark set on those, who not looking up to heaven, to their own soil and industry, as does the husbandman, for their subsistence, depend for it on the casualties and caprice of customers. Dependence begets subservience and venality, suffocates the germ of virtue, and prepares fit tools for the designs of ambition. This, the natural progress and consequence of the arts, has sometimes perhaps been retarded by accidental circumstances: but, generally speaking, the proportion which the aggregate of the other classes of citizens bears in any state to that of its husbandmen, is the proportion of its unsound to its healthy parts, and is a good-enough barometer whereby to measure its degree of corruption. While we have land to labour then, let us never wish to see our citizens occupied at a work-bench, or twirling a distaff. Carpenters, masons, smiths, are wanting in husbandry: but, for the general operations of manufacture, let our work-shops remain in Europe. It is better to carry provisions and materials to workmen there, than bring them to the provisions and materials, and with them their manners and principles. The loss by the transportation of commodities across the Atlantic will be made up in happiness and permanence of government. The mobs of great cities add just so much to the support of pure government, as sores do to the strength of the human body. It is the manners and spirit of a people which preserve a republic in vigour. A degeneracy in these is a canker which soon eats to the heart of its laws and constitution.

DOCUMENT 2

Plan for the Establishment of Public Schools (1786)

Benjamin Rush

Educational opportunities, especially for boys and young men from elite and middling families, expanded dramatically in the postrevolutionary decades. Benjamin Rush of Philadelphia—patriot, physician, educator, and founding member of the country's first antislavery society—was one of the most prominent champions of the idea of a distinctively American system of education. In this essay, Rush specifically advocated the establishment of public schools in his home state of Pennsylvania. He believed that education could mold the state's diverse youth into informed and productive citizens.[2]

Questions to consider:

1. What did Rush believe would be the chief benefits of the improvement of education in Pennsylvania? Whom did he envision as prospective students of the public schools?
2. Was the curriculum he proposed distinctly American?
3. What did Rush mean when he characterized the citizen as "public property"? What did he mean when he said that he hoped to "convert men into republican machines" by virtue of education?

The business of education has acquired a new complexion by the independence of our country. The form of government we have assumed has created a new class of duties to every American. It becomes us, therefore, to examine our former habits upon this subject, and in laying the foundations for nurseries of wise and good men, to adapt our modes of teaching to the peculiar form of our government.

The first remark that I shall make upon this subject is that an education in our own is to be preferred to an education in a foreign country. The principle of patriotism stands in need of the reinforcement of prejudice, and it is well known that our strongest prejudices in favor of our country are formed in the first one and twenty years of our lives. . . .

I conceive the education of our youth in this country to be peculiarly necessary in Pennsylvania while our citizens are composed of natives of so many different kingdoms of Europe. Our schools of learning, by producing one general and uniform system of education, will render the mass of the people more homogeneous and thereby fit them more easily for uniform and peaceable government.

I proceed, in the next place, to inquire what mode of education we shall adopt so as to secure to the state all the advantages that are to be derived from the proper instruction of youth; and here I beg leave to remark that the only foundation for a useful education in a republic is to be laid in RELIGION. Without this, there can be no virtue, and without virtue there can be no liberty, and liberty is the object and life of all republican governments. . . .

Next to the duty which young men owe to their Creator, I wish to see a SUPREME REGARD TO THEIR COUNTRY inculcated upon them . . . Our country includes family, friends, and property, and should be preferred to them all. Let our pupil be taught that he does not belong to himself, but that he is public property. Let him be taught to love his family, but let him be taught at the same time that he must forsake and even forget them when the welfare of his country requires it.

He must watch for the state as if its liberties depended upon his vigilance alone, but he must do this in such a manner as not to defraud his creditors or neglect his family. He must love private life, but he must decline no station, however public or responsible it may be, when called to it by the suffrages of his fellow citizens. He must love popularity, but he must despise it when set in competition with the dictates of his judgment or the real interest of his country. He must love character and have a due sense of injuries, but he must be taught to appeal only to the laws of the state, to defend the one and punish the other. He must love family honor, but he must be taught that neither the rank nor antiquity of his ancestors can command respect without personal merit. He must avoid neutrality in all questions that divide the state, but he must shun the rage and acrimony of party spirit. He must be taught to love his fellow creatures in every part of the world, but he must cherish with a more intense and peculiar affection the citizens of Pennsylvania and of the United States. . . .

From the observations that have been made it is plain that I consider it possible to convert men into republican machines. This must be done if we expect them to perform their parts properly in the great machine of the government of the state. That republic is sophisticated with monarchy or aristocracy that does not revolve upon the wills of the people, and these must be fitted to each other by means of education before they can be made to produce regularity and in unison with government.

Having pointed out those general principles which should be inculcated alike in all the schools of the state, I proceed now to make a few remarks upon the method of conducting what is commonly called a liberal or learned education in a republic. . . .

I do not wish the LEARNED OR DEAD LANGUAGES, as they are commonly called, to be reduced below their present just rank in the universities of Europe, especially as I consider an acquaintance with them as the best foundation for a correct and extensive knowledge of the language of our country. Too much pains cannot be taken to teach our youth to read and write our American language with propriety and elegance. The study of the Greek language constituted a material part of the literature of the Athenians, hence the sublimity, purity, and immortality of so many of their writings. The advantages of a perfect knowledge of our language to young men intended for the professions of law, physic, or divinity are too obvious to be mentioned, but in a state which boasts of the first commercial city in America, I wish to see it cultivated by young men who are intended for the counting house, for many such, I hope, will be educated in our colleges. The time is past when an academical education was thought to be unnecessary to qualify a young man for merchandise. I conceive no profession is capable of receiving more embellishments from it.

Connected with the study of our own language is the study of ELOQUENCE. It is well known how great a part it constituted of the Roman education. It is the first accomplishment in a republic and often sets the whole machine of government in motion. Let our youth, therefore, be instructed in this art. We do not extol it too highly when we attribute as much to the power of eloquence as to the sword in bringing about the American Revolution.

With the usual arts and sciences that are taught in our American colleges, I wish to see a regular course of lectures given upon HISTORY and CHRONOLOGY. The science of government, whether it relates to constitutions or laws, can only be advanced by a careful selection of facts, and these are to be found chiefly in history. Above all, let our youth be instructed in the history of the ancient republics and the progress of liberty and tyranny in the different states of Europe.

I wish likewise to see the numerous facts that relate to the origin and present state of COMMERCE, together with the nature and principles of MONEY, reduced to such a system as to be intelligible and agreeable to a young man. If we consider the commerce of our metropolis only as the avenue of the wealth of the state, the study of it merits a place in a young man's education, but, I consider commerce in a much higher light when I recommend the study of it in republican seminaries. I view it as the best security against the influence of hereditary monopolies of land, and, therefore, the surest protection against aristocracy. I consider its effects as next to those of religion in humanizing mankind, and lastly, I view it as the means of uniting the different nations of the world together by the ties of mutual wants and obligations.

CHEMISTRY, by unfolding to us the effects of heat and mixture, enlarges our acquaintance with the wonders of nature and the mysteries of art; hence it has become in most of the universities of Europe a necessary branch of a gentleman's education. In a young country, where improvements in agriculture and manufactures are so much to be desired, the cultivation of this science, which explains the principles of both of them, should be considered as an object of the utmost importance.

In a state where every citizen is liable to be a soldier and a legislator, it will be necessary to have some regular instruction given upon the ART OF WAR and upon PRACTICAL LEGISLATION . . . But further, considering the nature of our connection with the United States, it will be necessary to make our pupil acquainted with all the prerogatives of the federal government. He must be instructed in the nature and variety of treaties. He must know the difference in the powers and duties of the several species of ambassadors. He must be taught wherein the obligations of individuals and of states are the same and wherein they differ. In short, he must acquire a general knowledge of all those laws and forms which unite the sovereigns of the earth or separate them from each other.

DOCUMENT 3

Thoughts upon Female Education (1787)

Benjamin Rush

Americans also publicly debated improvements in female education in the postrevolutionary era, in large part due to the perceived cultural imperatives of republicanism. Along with Judith Sargent Murray and Noah Webster, Benjamin Rush contended that the education of girls and young women was essential to the future of the United States.

Rush was among the incorporators of the Young Ladies' Academy of Philadelphia in 1787, when he addressed these widely reprinted comments to its Board of Visitors.[3]

Questions to consider:

1. What, according to Rush, should be the objectives of female education in the United States?
2. To what extent was the need for change, in Rush's view, the result of revolutionary republicanism?
3. Did Rush foresee more changes in women's roles and status as a result of the educational improvements he proposed?
4. Did he want or expect all girls and young women to have access to education?

The first remark that I shall make upon this subject, is, that female education should be accommodated to the state of society, manners, and government of the country, in which it is conducted.

This remark leads me at once to add, that the education of young ladies, in this country, should be conducted upon principles very different from what is it in Great Britain, and in some respects different from what it was when we were part of a monarchical empire.

There are several circumstances in the situation, employments, and duties of women, in America, which require a peculiar mode of education.

I.   The early marriages of our women, by contracting the time allowed for education, renders it necessary to contract its plan, and to confine it chiefly to the more useful branches of literature.

II.   The state of property, in America, renders it necessary for the greatest part of our citizens to employ themselves, in different occupations, for the advancement of their fortunes. This cannot be done without the assistance of the female members of the community. They must be the stewards, and guardians of their husbands' property. That education, therefore, will be most proper for our women, which teaches them to discharge the duties of those offices with the most success and reputation.

III.   From the numerous avocations to which a professional life exposes gentlemen in America from their families, a principal share of the instruction of children naturally devolves upon the women. It becomes us therefore to prepare them by a suitable education, for the discharge of this most important duty of mothers.

Frontispiece from *Columbian Magazine, or Monthly Miscellany,*
1787.   Published in Philadelphia, the *Columbian* was one of
several short-lived periodicals whose editors sought to encourage
the growth of a republic of letters among postrevolutionary
Americans. Columbia leads two children to Minerva, who leans
on a pedestal bearing the legend "Independence the reward of
Wisdom, Fortitude and Perseverance." What do the children
signify? Why do a book and a globe rest on Minerva's pedestal?
What figures occupy the background of this scene? Source:
Engraving from Columbian Magazine 1787. Getty Images Inc. Courtesy of
Hulton Archive/Getty Images.

IV. The equal share that every citizen has in the liberty, and the possible share he may have in the government of our country, make it necessary that our ladies should be qualified to a certain degree by a peculiar and suitable education, to concur in instructing their sons in the principles of liberty and government.

V. In Great Britain, the business of servants is a regular occupation; but in America this humble station is the usual retreat of unexpected indigence; hence the servants in this country possess less knowledge and subordination than are required from them; and hence, our ladies are obliged to attend more to the private affairs of their families, than ladies generally do, of the same rank in Great Britain . . . This circumstance should have great influence upon the nature and extent of female education in America. . . .

It should not surprize us that British customs, with respects to female education, have been transplanted into our American schools and families. We see marks of the same incongruity, of time and place, in many other things. We behold our houses accommodated to the climate of Great Britain, by eastern and western directions. We behold our ladies panting in a heat of ninety degrees, under a hat and cushion, which were calculated for the temperature of a British summer. We behold our citizens condemned and punished by a criminal law, which was copied from a country where maturity in corruption renders public executions as a part of the amusements of the nation. It is high time to awake from this servility—to study our own character—to examine the age of our country—and to adopt manners in every thing, that shall be accommodated to our state of society, and to the forms of our government. In particular it is incumbent upon us to make ornamental accomplishments, yield to principles and knowledge, in the education of our women.

DOCUMENT 4

Preface to *The Columbian Magazine, or Monthly Miscellany (1787)*

In the 1780s, nationally minded writers and printers sought to use literature to foster the development and dissemination of a distinctly American public discourse as part of the larger effort to foster national consciousness, especially among elites. The first issue of the Columbian Magazine *included an essay promoting American manufactures, a letter considering the viability of trade with China, an address from a leading agricultural society, a biography of General Nathanael Greene, and an excerpt from David Ramsay's* History of the Revolution in South Carolina. *Its editor described the magazine's objectives in this preface to its premier issue in 1787.*[4]

Questions to consider:

1. Does this preface contain any evidence of self-conscious nationalism? Whom did the editor regard as his magazine's ideal readers?
2. On what grounds did he profess to exclude both religion and politics from the *Columbian*?

The Editor of the Columbian Magazine, has . . . chosen this opportunity to return the humble compensation of thanks for the favour of his correspondents, which has enabled him to furnish novelty, entertainment, and instruction to his readers; and for the approbation of his patrons, which has enabled the proprietors to surmount every consideration of difficulty and expense in prosecuting this work.

Thus, while the historian commemorates the wonderful events of the late revolution, and transmits to [posterity] the long list of illustrious characters that gave wisdom to the councils, and glory to the arms of America, this miscellaneous volume may, perhaps, be regarded as a contemporary evidence of the progress of literature and the arts among her citizens—at least, it will serve to shew, that, the source of all improvement and science, a liberal encouragement, was offered, at this early period of her independency, to every attempt for the advancement of knowledge and virtue.

Regarding it, indeed, as a future criterion of the opinions and characters of the age, the great purpose of the Columbian Magazine has been to communicate essays of entertainment, without sacrificing decency to wit, and to disseminate the works of science, without sacrificing intrinsic utility to a critical consideration of style and composition. Hence, however superior the wisdom of succeeding generations shall prove, posterity might at least be taught to venerate the purity and virtue of their fathers; and, if they find nothing in this work to increase their stock of knowledge, neither will any thing be found to vitiate their taste, or contaminate their manners.

The admission of political and theological controversy, has likewise been studiously declined; for such is the structure of the human mind, that a difference of opinion upon the principles of government or religion, usually generates personal animosity, and the enquiry into these subjects (certainly the most interesting to mankind) has often deviated from reason to reproach—from the discussion of opinions to the defamation of characters. Those disquisitions, however, which cultivate truth without inviting altercation, have found an easy access to the public; for, in closing the source of unprofitable disputation, care was taken not to obstruct the channels of salutary information and rational debate.

Such have been the principles upon which the Columbian Magazine has hitherto proceeded: and, perhaps, the next object entitled to the public consideration, is the encouragement which it has given to native industry, and the useful arts. The labour of the press is performed, the paper and materials for publication are supplied, and the work is embellished, at a monthly expence of one hundred pounds, by the mechanics and manufacturers of the United States. The disbursements, indeed, render it necessary to solicit the punctual payment of the subscriptions in advance, agreeably to the conditions originally proposed; for, however, trifling each sum may appear, it is on the collective amount of the subscriptions, and the regularity of the payments, that the fate of this undertaking must depend. With the fullest confidence, therefore, in the public liberality, the proprietors presume to press this subject upon their attention, which otherwise, from its apparent insignificancy as it affects an individual, might be neglected or forgotten.

DOCUMENT 5

The American Spelling Book (1789)

Noah Webster

Although colonial Americans typically had lamented or ignored inconsistencies between their own language and that of the mother country, many postrevolutionary nationalists accentuated the differences between British and American English and celebrated the virtues of the latter. Noah Webster was the most tireless and forceful champion of American English. His American Dictionary, *begun in the 1780s and completed in 1828, became a standard reference work; generations of schoolchildren studied his* American Spelling Book, *first published in 1783. In this preface to the 1789 edition, Webster explained some of his ideas about the politics of language in postrevolutionary America.*[5]

Questions to consider:

1. What were characteristics of Webster's American English, as compared to the language of the British Isles? How did Webster's construction of the image of American English coincide with his image of American national character?
2. How did Webster hope to enlist language and spelling to promote American patriotism and national self-consciousness?
3. Which English authorities and precedents did he retain? Which did he reject? Why? To what extent did Americans follow his recommendations?

The design of the [Spelling Book] is to furnish schools in this country with an easy, accurate and comprehensive system of rules and lessons for teaching the English language. . . .

As the orthography of our language is not yet settled with precision, I have in this particular followed the most approved authors of the last and present century. . . . The spelling of such words as *publick, favour, neighbour, head, prove, phlegm, his, give, debt, rough, well,* instead of the more natural and easy method, *publik, favor, nabor, hed, proov, flem, hiz, giv, det, ruf, wel,* has the plea of antiquity in its favour; and yet I am convinced that common sense and convenience will sooner or later get the better of the present absurd practice. But when we give new names to places [and] rivers . . . or express Indian sounds by English letters, the orthography should coincide exactly with the true pronunciation. To retain old difficulties may be absurd; but to create them, without the least occasion, is folly in the extreme. It is the work of years to learn the present spelling of our language—a work, which, with a correct orthography, might be performed in a few months.

The advantage of familiarizing children to the spelling and pronunciation of American names is very obvious, and must give this work the preference to foreign Spelling Books. It is of great importance to give our youth early and correct information respecting the geography of this country . . . An explanation of the names and geographical terms . . . will be given in the third part [of the Spelling Book].

The necessity and probable utility of the plan will best appear by examining the execution. Such material alterations of the old system of education, will undoubtedly alarm the rigid friends of antiquity; but in vindication of the work the author assures the public, that it has the approbation and patronage of many of the principal literary characters in America, and that it is framed upon a plan similar to those of the best Lexicographers and Grammarians in the British nation.

To diffuse an uniformity and purity of language in America—to destroy the provincial prejudices that originate in the trifling difference of dialect, and produce reciprocal ridicule—to promote the interest of literature and harmony in the United States—is the most ardent wish of the Author; and it is his highest ambition to deserve the approbation and encouragement of his countrymen.

DOCUMENT 6

"Essay on the City of Washington" (1795)

In 1791, Pierre-Charles L'Enfant drew up plans for a new and permanent national capital on the banks of the Potomac River. Work proceeded slowly on the project during the 1790s. This essay, which appeared in the Federalist Gazette *of the United States in 1795, stressed both the political and cultural significance of the capital-building project.[6] The still-unfinished town of Washington became the official seat of the government of the United States in 1800.*

Questions to consider:

1. What was the purpose of this essay?
2. Why, according to the author, did the United States need a "federal town"? What would it represent? Why did the plan for the American capital seek to "unite true elegance and utility"? Would Americans find this prospect appealing in the 1790s?
3. What did the author mean when he described the capital's architecture as "masculine and bold"?
4. Why did he approve of the planners' preference for allegorical statues over those depicting specific heroes from American history?

In reflecting on the importance of the Union, and on the advantage which it secures to all the inhabitants of the United States, collectively or individually; where is there an American who does not see, in the establishment of a federal town, a natural means of confirming forever the valuable connection, to which the nation is indebted for its liberation from the British yoke—that union which assures to every individual mutual aid against the efforts of any who may care to disturb public order and tranquility—that union, the shield of the wise laws under the protection of which we shall all enjoy a life of peace, a freedom of opinion and moral equality in a degree hitherto unknown to any people on earth—that connection, in short, to which the United States owe the extent and the flourishing condition of their commerce, the respectable station they occupy among the nations of the earth, and which, under such a variety of aspects, ought to be the object of the veneration of every reflecting man.

The Federal City, situated in the center of the United States, is a temple erected to liberty, and towards this edifice will the wishes and expectations of all true friends of their country be incessantly directed.

The City of Washington, considered under such important points of view, could not be calculated on a small scale. Its extent, the disposition of its avenues and public squares, should all correspond with the magnitude of the object for which it was intended, and we need only cast our eyes upon the situation and plan of the city, to recognize in them the comprehensive genius of the President, to whom the direction of the business has been entrusted by Congress. . . .

Washington, as the metropolis of the Union, as a commercial town, and a pleasurable situation, may, in every point of view, present resources that are rarely united; it is sufficient to attend to this establishment under all its aspects to inspire ardent wishes for its success, and to induce one to assign it a distinguished rank among the most celebrated capitals of the world.

When Major L'Enfant conceived the vast and magnificent plan, the execution of which must unite true elegance to utility and agreeableness, his attention was first directed to the situation now occupied by the Capitol. Here he fixed the center of the city, as the city is the center of the American Empire; and he rendered the edifice accessible by more than twenty streets, which terminate at this point. Each street is an emblem of the rays of light, which, issuing from the Capitol, are directed towards every part of America, to enlighten its inhabitants respecting their true interests. Each street is also an emblem of the facility, with which the Capitol may be approached, in every respect, and at all times, by every individual, who shall live under the protection of the Union. This ingenious allusion has been happily favored by the ground. The Capitol has an elevation of 72 feet above the level of high water, and overlooks the city in such a manner, that its horizon will be bounded only by the small mountains at several miles distance.

The situation is well calculated to elevate the mind of the legislator; it will continually remind him, that, if from this Capitol are to proceed the laws, which shall give life and energy to all parts of the dominion; it is towards this central point also that the active vigilance of a nation of free-man will be directed.

The Capitol, which is constructed on the plan drawn by Mr. Hallet, will be one of the most spacious modern edifices. It will comprehend the halls intended for the two branches of the Legislature; the halls of conference; and the different offices attached to them, collectively or separately. The proportions of this magnificent monument correspond with its destination. The architecture is masculine and bold. The details are elegant, and the ornaments are well adjusted. The composition resembles the physical and political situation of the United States; each part has its local advantages; but its true beauty results from the connection of all its parts.

The court of this building is spacious and regular; it enlightens the interior and facilitates the communications. It will be embellished with a colonade of the Doric order; in the center will be placed the altar of Liberty, around which the United States will be represented under the figure of young women, which will be closely joined together. This group will be the emblem of the Union; pedestral statues of all the illustrious men, who by their valor or their writings, have contributed to establish and confirm the Union, may be placed between each portico, in the circumference of the court, and the niches arranged in the interior of the galleries, will be successively filled with the busts of distinguished men, whose life shall have been consecrated to the happiness of their country. . . .

The second principal building is the house intended for the President of the United States. It is constructed on the plan designed by Mr. Hoban, and next to the Capitol, will be the most spacious and splendid monument hitherto erected in America. By its position, it is the point of union for more than fifteen streets. The Capitol and the President's house are so situated, that the President may have continually in his view, the temple where are deposited the laws, the execution of which is committed to him; and it seems, that by the multiplicity of the streets and their diverging direction, it was intended to remind him constantly of the importance of directing his official views to the most distant parts of the Empire; and this ingenious allegory, in an inverted sense, will call to his mind, at the same time, that his actions, are continually and unavoidably open to general inspection.

Upon the square in front of this edifice, may be represented the founder of American liberty, encircled by his companions in arms, governors and ministers, renewing, in the face of heaven, the oath to maintain the union at the hazard of their lives.

These allegorical groups which continually retrace some duties, are doubtless preferable to statues erected by flattery to men, whom impartial history so often strips of their fictitious virtues. America in discharging a duty imposed on her by gratitude to her first magistrate, will at the same time, furnish a useful lesson for his successors, by showing them what she expects from their exertions, and what they have a right to hope from her gratitude.

Every thing around these edifices corresponds perfectly with their grandeur: the streets and the avenues which terminate here, are of a breadth and extent of which one cannot yet form any idea by comparison; indeed no city on earth offers so many points of connection, so spacious and laid out with such regularity.

DOCUMENT 7

Charlotte; A Tale of Truth (1791)

Susanna Rowson

This sentimental novel was the best-selling example of the most popular literary genre of the postrevolutionary era. In this selection, Rowson's protagonist, Charlotte Temple, meets her eventual seducer.[7] Like many tragic heroines in sentimental novels, Charlotte is fated to die abandoned and impoverished shortly after giving birth to an illegitimate child. Her creator, Susanna Haswell Rowson, was born in England and raised in Massachusetts. She was a successful novelist, playwright, and actress, as well as the founder of a Boston academy for young women.

Questions to consider:

1. Why and for whom did Rowson claim to have written her novel?
2. How did she describe her heroine? What did Rowson see as the greatest potential threats to the virtue and welfare of young women?
3. Why was this novel, which was set in England, so popular in the United States?
4. On what grounds might American moralists and social critics condemn Rowson's book? On what grounds might she have defended her work from such criticism?

PREFACE

For the perusal of the young and thoughtless of the fair sex, this Tale of Truth is designed; and I could wish my fair readers to consider it as not merely the effusion of Fancy, but as a reality. The circumstances on which I have founded this novel were related to me some little time since by an old lady who had personally known Charlotte, though she concealed the real names of the characters, and likewise the place where the unfortunate scenes were acted: yet as it was impossible to offer a relation to the public in such an imperfect state, I have thrown over the whole a slight veil of fiction, and substituted names and places according to my own fancy. The principal characters in this little tale are now consigned to the silent tomb: it can therefore hurt the feelings of no one; and may, I flatter myself, be of service to some who are so unfortunate as to have neither friends to advise, or understanding to direct them, through the various and unexpected evils that attend a young and unprotected woman in her first entrance into life.

While the tear of compassion still trembled in my eye for the fate of the unhappy Charlotte, I may have children of my own, said I, to whom this recital may be of use, and if to your own children, said Benevolence, why not to the many daughters of Misfortune who, deprived of natural friends, or spoilt by a mistaken education, are thrown on an unfeeling world without the least power to defend themselves from the snares not only of the other sex, but from the more dangerous arts of the profligate of their own.

Sensible as I am that a novel writer, at a time when such a variety of works are ushered into the world under that name, stands but a poor chance for fame in the annals of literature, but conscious that I wrote with a mind anxious for the happiness of that sex whose morals and conduct have so powerful an influence on mankind in general; and convinced that I have not wrote a line that conveys a wrong idea to the head or a corrupt wish to the heart, I shall rest satisfied in the purity of my own intentions, and if I merit not applause, I feel that I dread not censure.

If the following tale should save one hapless fair one from the errors which ruined poor Charlotte, or rescue from impending misery the heart of one anxious parent, I shall feel a much higher gratification in reflecting on this trifling performance, than could possibly result from the applause which might attend the most elegant finished piece of literature whose tendency might deprave the heart or mislead the understanding.

CHAPTER I

A BOARDING SCHOOL

"Are you for a walk," said Montraville to his companion, as they arose from table; "are you for a walk? or shall we order the chaise and proceed to

Portsmouth?" Belcour preferred the former; and they sauntered out to view the town, and to make remarks on the inhabitants, as they returned from church.

Montraville was a Lieutenant in the army: Belcour was his brother officer: they had been to take leave of their friends previous to their departure for America, and were now returning to Portsmouth, where the troops waited orders for embarkation. They had stopped at Chichester to dine; and knowing they had sufficient time to reach the place of destination before dark, and yet allow them a walk, had resolved, it being Sunday afternoon, to take a survey of the Chichester ladies as they returned from their devotions.

They had gratified their curiosity, and were preparing to return to the inn without honouring any of the belles with particular notice, when Madame Du Pont, at the head of her school, descended from the church. Such an assemblage of youth and innocence naturally attracted the young soldiers: they stopped; and, as the little cavalcade passed, almost involuntarily pulled off their hats. A tall, elegant girl looked at Montraville and blushed: he instantly recollected the features of Charlotte Temple, whom he had once seen and danced with at a ball at Portsmouth. At that time he thought on her only as a very lovely child, she being then only thirteen; but the improvement two years had made in her person, and the blush of recollection which suffused her cheeks as she passed, awakened in his bosom new and pleasing ideas. Vanity led him to think that pleasure at again beholding him might have occasioned the emotion he had witnessed, and the same vanity led him to wish to see her again.

"She is the sweetest girl in the world," said he, as he entered the inn. Belcour stared. "Did you not notice her?" continued Montraville: "she had on a blue bonnet, and with a pair of lovely eyes of the same colour, has contrived to make me feel devilish odd about the heart."

"Pho," said Belcour, "a musket ball from our friends, the Americans, may in less than two months make you feel worse."

"I never think of the future," replied Montraville; "but am determined to make the most of the present, and would willingly compound with any kind Familiar who would inform me who the girl is, and how I might be likely to obtain an interview."

But no kind Familiar at that time appearing, and the chaise which they had ordered, driving up to the door, Montraville and his companion were obliged to take leave of Chichester and its fair inhabitant, and proceed on their journey.

But Charlotte had made too great an impression on his mind to be easily eradicated: having therefore spent three whole days in thinking on her and in endeavouring to form some plan for seeing her, he determined to set off for Chichester, and trust to chance either to favour or frustrate his designs. Arriving at the verge of the town, he dismounted, and sending the servant forward with the horses, proceeded toward the place, where, in the midst of an extensive pleasure ground, stood the mansion which contained the lovely Charlotte Temple. . . .

"'Tis a romantic attempt," said he; "and should I even succeed in seeing and conversing with her, it can be productive of no good: I must of necessity leave England in a few days, and probably may never return; why then should I endeavour to engage the affections of this lovely girl, only to leave her a prey to a thousand inquietudes, of which at present she has no idea? I will return to Portsmouth and think no more about her."

The evening now was closed; a serene stillness reigned; and the chaste Queen of Night with her silver crescent faintly illuminated the hemisphere. The mind of Montraville was hushed into composure by the serenity of the surrounding objects. "I will think on her no more," said he, and turned with an intention to leave the place; but as he turned, he saw the gate which led to the pleasure grounds open, and two women come out, who walked arm-in-arm across the field.

"I will at least see who these are," said he. He overtook them, and giving them the compliments of the evening, begged leave to see them into the more frequented parts of the town: but how was he delighted, when, waiting for an answer, he discovered, under the concealment of a large bonnet, the face of Charlotte Temple. He soon found means to ingratiate himself with her companion, who was a French teacher at the school, and, at parting, slipped a letter he had purposely written, into Charlotte's hand, and five guineas into that of Mademoiselle, who promised she would endeavour to bring her young charge into the field again the next evening.

CHAPTER VI

AN INTRIGUING TEACHER

Madame Du Pont was a woman every way calculated to take the care of young ladies, had that care entirely devolved on herself; but it was impossible to attend the education of a numerous school without proper assistants; and those assistants were not always the kind of people whose conversation and morals were exactly such as parents of delicacy and refinement would wish a daughter to copy.

Among the teachers at Madame Du Pont's school, was Mademoiselle La Rue, who added to a pleasing person and insinuating address, a liberal education and the manners of a gentlewoman. . . . But Mademoiselle possessed too much of the spirit of intrigue to remain long without adventures. At church, where she constantly appeared, her person attracted the attention of a young man who was upon a visit at a gentleman's seat in the neighbourhood: she had met him several times clandestinely; and being invited to come out that evening, and eat some fruit and pastry in a summer-house belonging to the gentleman he was visiting, and requested to bring some of the ladies with her, Charlotte being her favourite, was fixed on to accompany her.

The mind of youth eagerly catches at promised pleasure: pure and innocent by nature, it thinks not of the dangers lurking beneath those pleasures, till too late to avoid them: when Mademoiselle asked Charlotte to go with her, she mentioned the gentleman as a relation, and spoke in such high terms of the elegance of his gardens, the sprightliness of his conversation, and the liberality with which he ever entertained his guests, that Charlotte thought only of the pleasure she should enjoy in the visit. . . .

Madame Du Pont was gone out for the evening, and the rest of the ladies retired to rest, when Charlotte and the teacher stole out at the back gate, and in crossing the field, were accosted by Montraville, as mentioned in the first chapter.

Charlotte was disappointed in the pleasure she had promised herself from this visit. The levity of the gentlemen and the freedom of their conversation disgusted her. She was astonished at the liberties Mademoiselle permitted them to take; grew thoughtful and uneasy, and heartily wished herself at home again in her own chamber.

Perhaps one cause of that wish might be, an earnest desire to see the contents of the letter which had been put into her hand by Montraville.

Any reader who has the least knowledge of the world, will easily imagine the letter was made up of encomiums on her beauty, and vows of everlasting love and constancy; nor will he be surprised that a heart open to every gentle, generous sentiment, should feel itself warmed by gratitude for a man who professed to feel so much for her; nor is it improbable but her mind might revert to the agreeable person and martial appearance of Montraville.

In affairs of love, a young heart is never in more danger than when attempted by a handsome young soldier. A man of an indifferent appearance, will, when arrayed in a military habit, shew to advantage; but when beauty of person, elegance of manner, and an easy method of paying compliments, are united to the scarlet coat, smart cockade, and military sash, ah! well-a-day for the poor girl who gazes on him: she is in imminent danger; but if she listens to him with pleasure, 'tis all over with her, and from that moment she has neither eyes nor ears for any other object.

Now, my dear sober matron, (if a sober matron should deign to turn over these pages, before she trusts them to the eye of a darling daughter,) let me entreat you not to put on a grave face, and throw down the book in a passion and declare 'tis enough to turn the heads of half the girls in England; I do solemnly protest, my dear madam, I mean no more by what I have here advanced, than to ridicule those romantic girls, who foolishly imagine a red coat and silver epaulet constitute the fine gentleman; and should that fine gentleman make half a dozen fine speeches to them, they will imagine themselves so much in love as to fancy it a meritorious action to jump out of a two pair of stairs window, abandon their friends, and trust entirely to the honour of a man, who perhaps hardly knows the meaning of the word, and if he does, will be too much the modern man of refinement, to practice it in their favour.

Gracious heaven! when I think on the miseries that must rend the heart of a doting parent, when he sees the darling of his age at first seduced from his protection, and afterwards abandoned, by the very wretch whose promises of love decoyed her from the paternal roof—when he sees her poor and wretched, her bosom torn between remorse for her crime and love for her vile betrayer—when fancy paints to me the good old man stooping to raise the weeping penitent, while every tear from her eye is numbered by drops from his bleeding heart, my bosom glows with honest indignation, and I wish for power to extirpate those monsters of seduction from the earth.

Oh my dear girls—for to such only am I writing—listen not to the voice of love, unless sanctioned by paternal approbation: be assured, it is now past the days of romance: no woman can be run away with contrary to her own inclination: then kneel down each morning, and request kind heaven to keep you free from temptation, or, should it please to suffer you to be tried, pray for fortitude to resist the impulse of inclination when it runs counter to the precepts of religion and virtue.

DOCUMENT 8

The Life of George Washington (1809)

Mason Locke Weems

As the inventor of the story of George Washington and the cherry tree and several other classic anecdotes, Mason Locke Weems played a vital role in the creation of the mythic Washington and thus in the construction of American national identity. First published as a pamphlet in 1800 but later significantly expanded, Weems's fanciful biography of Washington exaggerated his humble origins, piety, and moral purity to create a role model for ordinary citizens.[8] The book went through twenty-nine printings by 1825, making it by far the most widely read historical work of the postrevolutionary era.

Questions to consider:

1. Why did Weems emphasize Washington's "private" roles, not his public ones?
2. Why did he contend that industry, not bravery or even piety, was his protagonist's chief virtue?
3. Describe the tone and style of Weems's writing. Why do you think his books were so popular?

"Is not [Washington's] history already known? Have not a thousand orators spread his fame abroad, bright as his own Potomac, when he reflects the morning sun, and flames like the sea of liquid gold, the wonder and delight of all the neighbouring shores? Yes, they have indeed spread his fame abroad . . . his fame as Generalissimo of the armies, and first President of the councils of his nation. But this is not half his fame . . . True, he is there seen in greatness, but it is only the greatness of public character, which is no evidence of true greatness; for a public character is often an artificial one. . . .

It is not then in the glare of public, but in the shade of private life, that we are to look for the man. Private life is always *real* life. Behind the curtain, where the eyes of the million are not upon him, and where a man can have no motive but inclination, no excitement but honest nature, there he will always be sure to act himself. Consequently, if he act greatly, he must be great indeed. Hence it has been justly said, that, "our private deeds, if noble, are noblest of our lives."

Of these private deeds of Washington very little has been said. In most of the elegant orations pronounced to his praise, you see nothing of Washington below the clouds—nothing of Washington the dutiful *son*—the affectionate brother—the cheerful school-boy—the diligent surveyor—the neat draftsman—the laborious farmer—the widow's husband—the orphan's father—the poor man's friend. No! this is not the Washington you see; 'tis only Washington the HERO, and the Demigod . . . Washington the sun beam in council, or the storm in war. . . .

These are the drawings usually given of Washington; drawings masterly no doubt, and perhaps justly descriptive of him in some scenes of his life; but scenes they were, which I am sure his soul abhorred, and in which at any rate, you see nothing of his private virtues . . . And yet it was to those old-fashioned virtues that our hero owed everything. For in fact they were the food of the great actions of him, whom men call Washington. . . .

Since then it is the private virtues that lay the foundation of all human excellence . . . be it our first care to present these, in all their lustre, before the admiring eyes of our children. To them his private character is every thing; his public, hardly any thing . . . For who among us can hope that his son shall ever be called, like Washington, to direct the storm of war, or to ravish the ears of deeply listening Senates? To be constantly placing him then, before our children, in this high character, what is it but like springing in the clouds a golden Phoenix, which no mortal calibre can ever hope to reach . . . Oh no! give us his Private Virtues! In these, every youth is interested, because in these every youth may become a Washington—a Washington in piety and patriotism—in industry and honour—and consequently a Washington, in what alone deserves the name, SELF ESTEEM and UNIVERSAL RESPECT. . . .

But of all the virtues that adorned the life of this great man, there is none more worthy of our imitation than his admirable INDUSTRY. It is to this virtue in her Washington, that America stands indebted for services past calculation; and it is from this virtue, that Washington himself snatched a wreath of glory, that will never fade away . . .

What is it that braces the nerves, purifies the blood, and hands down the flame of life, bright and sparkling, to old age? What, but rosy-cheeked industry. See Washington so invigorated by constant exercise, that, though hereditarily subject to the gout, of which all his family died, he entirely escaped it; and, even at the age of 66, continued straight and active as a young grenadier, and ready once more at his country's call, to lead her eager warriors to the field.

What is it that preserves the morals of young men unsoiled, and secures the blessings of unblemished character and unbroken health? What, but snow-robed industry. See Washington under the guardianship of industry, walking the slippery paths of youth, safe and uncorrupted, though born in a country whose fertility and climate furnished both the means and invitation to vice. Early smitten with the love of glory; early engaged in the noble pursuit of knowledge, of independence, and of usefulness, he had no eyes to see bad examples nor ensnaring objects, no ears to hear horrid oaths nor obscene language, no leisure for impure passions nor criminal amours; hence he enjoyed that purity of soul, which is rightly called its *sunshine;* and which impressed a dignity on his character, and gave him a beauty and loveliness in the eyes of men, that contributed more to his rise in the world, that young people are aware of.

And what is it that raises a young man from poverty to wealth, from obscurity to never-dying fame? What, but industry? See Washington, born of humble parents, and in humble circumstances—born in a narrow nook and obscure corner of the British plantations! Yet lo! what great things wonder-working industry can bring out of this unpromising Nazareth. . . .

Since the day that God created man on the earth, none ever displayed the power of industry more signally than did George Washington. Had he, as prince of Wales, or as dauphin of France, rendered such great services, or attained such immortal honours, it would not have seemed so marvelous in our eyes. But that a poor young man with no king, lords, nor commons to back him—with no princes, nor strumpets of princes, to curry favour for him—with no gold but his virtue, no silver but his industry, should, with this old-fashioned coin, have stolen away the hearts of all the American

Israel, and from a sheep-cot have ascended the throne of his country's affections, and gotten himself a name above the mighty ones of the earth! this is marvelous indeed! . . .

Young Reader! go thy way, think of Washington, and HOPE. Though humble thy birth, low thy fortune, and few thy friends, still think of Washington, and HOPE. Like him, honour thy God, and delight in glorious toil; then, like him, "thou shalt stand before kings; thou shalt not stand before common men."

SUGGESTED READING FOR CHAPTER 12

APPLEBY, JOYCE. *Inheriting the Revolution: The First Generation of Americans* (2000).

ALLGOR, CATHERINE. *Parlor Politics: In Which the Ladies of Washington Help Build a City and a Government* (2001).

ANDERSON, BENEDICT. *Imagined Communities: Reflections in the Origins and Spread of Nationalism* (1983).

COHEN, LESTER H. *The Revolutionary Histories: Contemporary Narratives of the American Revolution* (1980).

DAVIDSON, CATHY N. *Revolution and the Word: The Rise of the Novel in America* (1986).

ELLIS, JOSEPH J. *After the Revolution: Profiles of Early American Culture* (1979).

FLIEGELMAN, JAY. *Prodigals and Pilgrims: The American Revolution against Patriarchal Authority, 1750–1800* (1982).

———. *Declaring Independence: Jefferson, Language, and the Culture of Performance* (1993).

JOHN, RICHARD R. *Spreading the News: The American Postal System from Franklin to Morse* (1995).

KORNFELD, EVE. *Creating an American Culture: A Brief History with Documents* (2001).

MONAGHAN, E. JENNIFER. *A Common Heritage: Noah Webster's Blue-Back Speller* (1983).

PURVIS, THOMAS L. "The European Ancestry of the United States Population, 1790." *William and Mary Quarterly*, 3rd ser., 41 (1984): 85–101.

SCHWARTZ, BARRY. *George Washington: The Making of an American Symbol* (1987).

SILVERMAN, KENNETH. *A Cultural History of the American Revolution* (1976).

WOOD, GORDON S. *The Rising Glory of America, 1760–1820*, rev. ed. (1990).

NOTES

[1]Thomas Jefferson, *Notes on the State of Virginia* (Baltimore, 1800), 165–66.

[2] Benjamin Rush, *Plan for the Establishment of Public Schools and the Diffusion of Knowledge in Pennsylvania; to Which Are Added, Thoughts upon the Mode of Education, Proper in a Republic* (Philadelphia, 1786), 13–15, 20–21, 27–30, 32.

[3]Benjamin Rush, *Thoughts upon Female Education* (Philadelphia, 1787), 5–7, 19–20.

[4]"Preface," *The Columbian Magazine, or Monthly Miscellany,* 1 (1787): 1–2.

[5]Noah Webster, *The American Spelling Book* (Boston, 1789), 1–2.

[6]"Essay on the City of Washington," *Gazette of the United States,* 11 Feb. 1795.

[7]Susanna Rowson, *Charlotte: A Tale of Truth* (Philadelphia, 1794), pp. 3–12, 47–54.

[8]M[ason] L[ocke] Weems, *The Life of George Washington . . .* (Philadelphia, 1809), 3–7, 205, 213–14, 216.

CHAPTER THIRTEEN

SECURING THE REVOLUTION

Thomas Jefferson sometimes referred to his election to the presidency as the "revolution of 1800." In so doing, he used the word "revolution" in its most conventional contemporary sense: a circular movement akin to the orbits of celestial bodies. Just as colonial Whigs had maintained that they sought to secure their traditional liberties by resisting Parliamentary taxation, Jefferson and his adherents believed that Americans rescued and reaffirmed the principles of 1776 by ousting the Federalists in 1800. When the Republicans took office, they intended to safeguard the liberties of citizens and to limit the powers of government.

Republicans sought to secure the ideals of the Revolution by reversing the Federalists' centralizing policies. James Madison succeeded Jefferson as president and then James Monroe followed Madison, giving Republicans twenty-four years of uninterrupted political dominance in which to implement their policies. Some changes were immediately apparent. For example, Jefferson introduced a more relaxed style of etiquette and entertaining, one he believed was less regal and more appropriate for a republic. While Federalist administrations valued pomp and ceremony, the new president walked, wigless and plainly dressed, to his inauguration and rode on horseback through the streets of Washington. In his first term, Jefferson allowed the Alien and Sedition Acts to lapse, and he oversaw the acquisition of the Louisiana Territory. In his second term, however, foreign policy posed continual problems, which came to a head during Madison's presidency.

Despite the best efforts of both Jefferson and Madison to avoid involvement in the war in Europe, by 1812 the United States was embroiled with Britain in what many Americans considered a second war of independence. This war was even more divisive than the first, as New Englanders contemplated secession to make a separate peace. In the War of 1812, the United States suffered many military embarrassments and pitifully few triumphs. In 1815, the war ended in a stalemate; no territory changed hands and no issues were resolved as a result of it. Nevertheless, many Americans believed that the ability of the United States to survive a second war with Britain ensured the durability of the republic. The Revolution and its legacy appeared to be secure.

The election of 1800 was a nasty affair. Federalists portrayed Thomas Jefferson as a lawless atheist, while Republicans lampooned his opponent, John Adams, as a tyrant and a closet monarchist. When it was over, Jefferson and Aaron Burr, the Republican candidate for vice-president, each had seventy-three electoral votes to Adams's sixty-five and sixty-four for Charles C. Pinckney, the Federalist vice-presidential candidate. Because the Constitution neither required nor allowed electors to differentiate their votes for president and vice-president, Jefferson and Burr had, in effect, tied for the presidency. With no candidate winning a majority of electoral votes, the contest was thrown into the House of Representatives, where the Federalists refused to vote for Jefferson, though he was clearly most voters' choice for the presidency. Finally, on the thirty-sixth ballot some Federalists defected, after receiving assurances that Jefferson would not dismantle Hamilton's fiscal system. On 4 March 1801, Jefferson and the Republicans thus assumed control of the national government.

Although Jefferson struck a conciliatory pose in his inaugural address, the years following his election were characterized by strident partisanship. While the Federalists, to their credit, left office peacefully, they remained bitter in defeat. The Federalist press featured increasingly salacious stories about the new president—including, most famously, revelations about his sexual relationship with Sally Hemings, an enslaved woman at Monticello. The Republicans, for their part, effusively celebrated their electoral triumph. The fourth of March, the date of Jefferson's inauguration, became a partisan holiday second only to the Fourth of July in some communities. Republican partisans regaled Jefferson as a man of the people, and their civic rituals had a decidedly popular flavor. Victory at the national level, moreover, inspired Republicans to push for reform of the suffrage laws in the individual states. Beginning in 1801, state after state eliminated property qualifications for voting; by 1840, all but four states had enfranchised all white men, though most simultaneously curtailed the voting rights of free blacks.

Jefferson was the first president who was both party leader and chief executive, and he enjoyed remarkable success in both roles during his first term in office. For both political and ideological reasons, Jefferson jettisoned only the most offensive of the Federalists' policies, most notably the Alien and Sedition Acts and the excise tax on whiskey that had sparked the western uprising. Although cheap government was the cornerstone of the Republicans' domestic policy, for the most part they pursued retrenchment within the basic fiscal and institutional frameworks the Federalists had established. For example, Secretary of the Treasury Albert Gallatin convinced Jefferson to retain the Bank of the United States, which Gallatin considered critical to the financial stability of the republic. Both Gallatin and Jefferson also recognized that the new administration could not renege on Hamilton's arrangements with government creditors, but they were nonetheless determined to prevent the perpetuation of a system they found financially costly and politically objectionable. To that end, Gallatin curtailed government expenses, cutting the army to 3,000 men, the navy to six frigates and some small defensive gunboats, and reducing the diplomatic corps from six to three European posts. Gallatin's measures decreased the national debt from $83 million to $57 million by 1809; the government would have retired its debt completely by 1817 had the United States not gone to war in 1812.

As president, Jefferson also used his powers of appointment to alter the political composition of government functionaries. Republicans denounced patronage, asserting that merit, not personal connections, should be the chief prerequisite for attaining political office. When Jefferson assumed the presidency, however, he dismissed the most partisan Federalist officials who he believed—with some justification—could not be trusted to implement his policies. Jefferson's supporters supplanted the displaced Federalists and, as other Federalists died or otherwise departed, Republicans also assumed their posts. In 1801, Jefferson estimated that Federalists had held all but six of some six hundred appointive federal offices, nearly all of which were in Republican hands by the end of his second term in office.

Jefferson's efforts to make the government more Republican were less successful when he turned to the federal judiciary. The Constitution stipulated that federal judges would hold office during "good behavior," which typically meant life tenure. All of the judges Washington and Adams appointed were Federalists, and in 1800 the outgoing Federalist majority in Congress boldly moved to ensure their party's continuing dominance of the judiciary. Just days before the Republicans took office, the Federalists passed the Judiciary Act of 1801, which created sixteen new circuit courts and added some two hundred federal marshals, attorneys, and clerks; this measure also reduced the size of the Supreme Court from six to five, thereby delaying Jefferson's opportunity to appoint a Republican justice. Adams chose Federalist appointees for all the new posts. This transparently political maneuver outraged Republicans, who immediately repealed the law on taking office. The Federalists fought back, taking their case to the Supreme Court.

Although Federalist leaders wanted the court to declare that the Republican Congress exceeded its authority by repealing the Judiciary Act of 1801, Chief Justice John Marshall wanted to avoid an open confrontation with the Jefferson administration. The Constitution gave both the president and Congress specific and substantial powers, while vaguely defining those of the judiciary. In addition, both Jefferson and the congressional Republicans could claim to represent the will of the people, but many Americans remained wary of the appointed federal judiciary. Consequently, when William Marbury, whom Adams had appointed justice of the peace for the District of Columbia under the Judiciary Act of 1801, sued Secretary of State James Madison to obtain his commission, the court responded carefully. In one of his most famous decisions, Marshall argued that though Marbury was legally entitled to the commission, the Supreme Court had no jurisdiction in the case—despite the fact that the Judiciary Act of 1789 said it did. In effect, Marshall declared unconstitutional one section of the Judiciary Act of 1789, thereby establishing the precedent of judicial review.

Marshall strove to elevate the stature of the Supreme Court and make it a full partner in the national government. In *Marbury v. Madison* (1803), he asserted the Court's authority to interpret and enforce the Constitution, if need be, by invalidating congressional legislation. In other cases, the Marshall Court claimed the power to strike down state laws, to hear appeals from state courts, and to promote economic development by assiduously protecting the property rights of private corporations. As chief justice, Marshall consistently upheld a Hamiltonian broad construction of the powers of the national government in relation to those of the states. Thus, while Jefferson and his supporters could take comfort in the short-term political consequences of *Marbury v. Madison*—the recent Federalist appointees lost their commissions—Marshall's ruling in this case and others smacked of judicial tyranny in the eyes of many Republicans.

Indeed, some Republicans demanded that federal judges be popularly elected, as judges were in some states. While Jefferson resisted such a radical change, he nonetheless believed that judicial rulings should reflect public opinion, and he supported congressional efforts to impeach some of the most unabashedly partisan Federalist judges. The Republicans' first target was John Pickering, an alcoholic and probably insane New

Hampshire district court judge. The Senate decided that Pickering's drunken outbursts on the bench counted as criminal offenses and accordingly voted to remove him from office. Then, the House impeached Supreme Court Justice Samuel Chase, who was especially hateful to the Republicans for his outspoken support of the Alien and Sedition Acts. Although Jefferson himself hoped for Chase's removal, enough Senate Republicans believed that he was not guilty of the "high crimes and misdemeanors" the Constitution required to warrant Chase's conviction. This important precedent meant that federal judgeships would not change hands automatically when a new political party came to power.

The acquittal of Samuel Chase in 1805 was the first setback for what had been until then a remarkably successful Jefferson administration. Carefully calculated to reverse what Republicans deemed the worst excesses of Federalism without creating instability or strife, Jefferson's domestic policies sailed through Congress and both he and his congressional supporters won reelection in 1804 by large majorities. For both Jefferson and his successor, however, foreign policy proved far more complicated. The Republican administrations had both their greatest triumph and their worst defeats in the arena of foreign policy.

The continuing war in Europe profoundly affected the United States, notwithstanding repeated assertions of neutrality on the part of its government. In 1803, the United States profited by the resumption of the war in Europe when Napoleon accepted \$15 million for the Louisiana Territory—roughly $3\frac{1}{2}$¢ an acre—in an effort to mobilize all of France's resources for an all-out offensive against Great Britain. The Louisiana Purchase more than doubled the size of the United States. Between 1807 and 1812, however, Jefferson and Madison's efforts to preserve American neutrality led to economic depression, civil unrest, and an unwanted and expensive war.

The Louisiana Purchase was the single most important achievement of Jefferson's presidency. In 1800, France's acquisition of New Orleans and the land west of the Mississippi River had presented the United States with the alarming possibility of having Napoleon as their neighbor in the West. In 1803, the Louisiana Purchase not only removed the potentially troublesome French from the North American mainland, it also opened up vast acreage to settlement, seemingly assuring the liberty and prosperity of Americans for the foreseeable future. Like many of his countrymen, Jefferson saw the preservation of American liberty as dependent on the continual expansion of agriculture because he regarded independent, hard-working, and largely self-sufficient farmers as the ideal citizens of the American republic. The Louisiana Purchase expanded Jefferson's so-called empire of liberty, a project that of course presupposed the dispossession of native Americans.

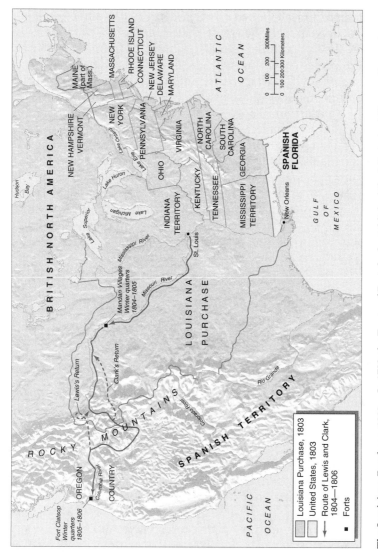

The Louisiana Purchase, 1803. In 1783, the Treaty of Paris had established the Mississippi River as the western boundary of the United States. Twenty years later, the republic more than doubled in size as a result of the purchase and annexation of the Louisiana Territory. President Thomas Jefferson commissioned Meriwether Lewis and George Rogers Clark to explore that territory shortly after the United States acquired it.

While the Louisiana Purchase was a happy by-product of renewed hostilities between France and Britain, the European war soon posed problems for the United States, as it had during the 1790s. After 1803, British naval vessels blockaded continental Europe to deprive Napoleon of much-needed supplies; the French retaliated by seizing ships that respected the British blockade. American shippers often evaded the blockades and profited from European demand for their cargoes, but as the world's largest neutral shipper, the United States resented interference with its freedom on the seas. Commercial freedom, along with westward expansion, was, moreover, integral to Jefferson's vision of a free, prosperous, and largely agricultural America. Farmers, after all, had to be able to sell their surplus safely and profitably in foreign markets. Accordingly, Jefferson repeatedly proclaimed the rights of neutral powers to sail the seas and engage in trade unmolested.

The *Chesapeake* affair forced the United States to act decisively in defense of neutral rights. In June 1807, the British ship *Leopard* approached the *Chesapeake*, an American frigate, off the coast of Virginia. The commander of the *Leopard* demanded to come aboard the *Chesapeake* to search for sailors who were alleged deserters from the Royal Navy. When the commander of the *Chesapeake* refused to submit his vessel to such a search, the *Leopard* fired on the American ship, killing three and wounding eight. The British then boarded the *Chesapeake* and impressed four of its sailors into the Royal Navy. An outraged Jefferson resisted popular calls for revenge, seeking to avoid war. Instead, he barred British warships from American ports and unsuccessfully demanded monetary compensation and an end to impressment. Then, in December 1807, the president prevailed on Congress to pass the Embargo Act, the first in a series of economic sanctions designed to force Europeans to respect American neutrality.

The Republicans' policy of "peaceable coercion" was based on faulty assumptions about European needs and priorities. Jefferson had long believed that Americans could forgo European manufactured goods far more readily than Europeans could do without the foodstuffs and raw materials they imported from the United States. While that might have been true under ordinary circumstances, the ongoing war made placating the United States at best a secondary consideration for Britain and France alike.

Consequently, though the Republicans sought both to avoid war and to protect Americans' rights as neutrals, their policies failed on both counts. The Embargo Act of 1807, which stopped all American exports and prohibited American ships from clearing foreign ports, had less impact in Europe than in the United States, where it angered northern merchants and devastated the economy. In 1809, the Embargo was supplanted by the Nonintercourse Act, which prohibited American trade

Look on This Picture, and on This, 1807. Even before Jefferson's election to the presidency in 1801, Federalists condemned him as an infidel and demagogue. Partisan invective reached new heights, especially in northern commercial centers, after the passage of the Embargo Act. This New York cartoon shows Washington as the champion of religion, law, and order, and Jefferson as his unworthy successor. What are the chief characteristics the artist attributed to Jefferson? Why did the Federalists choose Washington—instead of Adams, Hamilton, or some current party leader—to represent Jefferson's antithesis? How would Jefferson's Republican supporters have responded to this characterization? Source: Collection of The New York Historical Society.

with Britain and France only and allowed the president to reopen trade with whichever belligerent ended restrictions on American shipping. In 1810, Macon's Bill No. 2 opened American trade to all nations, but provided that if either Britain or France reversed its restrictions on neutral shippers, the United States would cease trading with the other. Between 1807 and 1810, then, the Republicans increasingly watered down their economic sanctions in hopes of extracting concessions from one or both of the warring powers. In August 1810, Napoleon promised to stop harassing American shippers. As it turned out, he was bluffing, but in November 1810, President James Madison ordered Americans to stop trading with Britain. From then on, Anglo-American relations deteriorated precipitously.

Although Madison emphasized British intransigence on the issues of neutral rights and impressment when he asked Congress to declare war, other issues contributed to the decision to take on Britain again in 1812. Young members of Congress from the South and the West blamed the British for supporting or even instigating the Indians' continual opposition to white westward expansion, which had culminated in a pan-Indian resistance movement under the leadership of Tecumseh. Known as the War Hawks, these congressmen were adamant in their demands to rid the West of Indians. Ardent expansionists, they also promoted war as a possible means to annex both Canada and Florida.

In June 1812, a divided and unprepared United States officially declared war on Britain. The House of Representatives voted for war by a margin of seventy-nine to forty-nine; nineteen senators supported the declaration of war, while thirteen opposed it. Support for war was strongest in the South and the West, while opposition to it was greatest in New England. Nine-tenths of the Republican members of Congress voted for war, while not one Federalist did so. Federalists regarded France, not Britain, as the chief foe of the United States. Many Federalist merchants, moreover, profited handsomely by the British trade.

Opposition to the war was so vehement among northern Federalists that twenty-two delegates from the five New England states convened in Hartford, Connecticut, in December 1814 to discuss the possibility of secession from the Union in order to make a separate peace. Instead, cooler heads prevailed, and the Hartford Convention merely proposed a series of constitutional amendments—abolishing the three-fifths compromise, prohibiting embargoes of more than sixty days, and requiring a two-thirds majority for declaring war or the admission of new states—all of which aimed to curtail the growing influence of southerners and westerners in the national government. Many Americans regarded the Hartford Convention as treasonous. Outside New England, the proceedings at Hartford utterly discredited the Federalist party.

The actions of the New England Federalists seemed especially outrageous because, after two years of military setbacks, by 1814 the United States was finally winning some major battles. The war began disastrously for the United States with three unsuccessful offensives against British Canada, the loss of Detroit to combined British and Indian forces, and enemy occupation of roughly half of the Northwest Territory. In 1813, the United States regained some of its western territory and raided York (now Toronto), the capital of Upper Canada. But in August 1814, the British retaliated by occupying and burning Washington, the still-unfinished American capital. By late 1814, however, the tide was turning in favor of the United States. In September, at the Battle of Plattsburgh, Commodore Thomas Macdonough thwarted a major offensive by demolishing a British fleet on Lake Champlain in northern New York. On

8 January 1815, General Andrew Jackson, who had annihilated the Creek Indians at the Battle of Horseshoe the preceding March, attained an equally decisive victory against the British at New Orleans.

Jackson's great triumph, in which the British suffered some two thousand casualties to the Americans' twenty-one, gave Americans something to celebrate and set the stage for the exuberant nationalism of the postwar era. Diplomats representing the United States and Great Britain had signed the Treaty of Ghent to end the war on 24 December 1814, more than two weeks before the Battle of New Orleans. That treaty simply reinstated the prewar status quo: no territory changed hands, and no attempts were made to resolve the issues of impressment and neutral rights. In December, the United States accepted these terms gratefully and worried that Britain might renege on the agreement. Jackson's victory ensured that the British would formally ratify the treaty and that they would abandon their claims to New Orleans and any other western territories. After the war, a more confident United States would turn inward to promote westward expansion and economic development.

The War of 1812 convinced Americans that their independence was secure, even as it exposed the republic's potential vulnerability. After 1815, Republicans vowed to insulate the United States from disruptive external forces—such as European wars and commercial entanglements—that had led to war in 1812. To that end, they espoused measures to promote domestic economic development, including the Second Bank of the United States, chartered in 1816, and a protective tariff to promote American manufactures. In foreign policy, the United States resolved to stay aloof from Europe's recurrent conflicts, asserted its leadership in the affairs of the Western Hemisphere, and anticipated the annexation of still more western territory.

In 1800, the Jeffersonians had hoped to secure the future of the American republic by rescinding the policies of the Federalists, which they considered contrary to the revolutionary ideas of popular liberty and limited government. Once in office, they reversed the worst excesses of the Federalist administrations, cultivated a more populist political style, and acquired Louisiana to secure the political and economic aspirations of future generations. Yet, the Republicans' commitment to economy in government, coupled with their persistent fear of military power, left the United States woefully unprepared for war in 1812. When the war was over, the triumphant but nonetheless chastened Republicans adopted some of the policies they had scorned during the Federalist administrations. After 1815, a rising generation of American leaders would seek to use a more activist style of government to promote a Jeffersonian agenda of westward expansion and economic opportunity.

A Federalist Views the Election of 1800 (1801)

Archibald Henderson of North Carolina was a Federalist member of the House of Representatives that decided the outcome of the presidential election of 1800. In this letter to his constituents, dated 28 February 1801, he described the House's deliberations. Although some Federalists eventually voted for Jefferson—who was clearly the voters' choice for president—many, like Henderson, resisted to the bitter end.[1] His constituents must have approved of his conduct because in 1802 they reelected him to Congress.

Questions to consider:

1. What did Archibald Henderson consider the chief achievements of the Federalist administrations?
2. What changes did he fear would occur as a result of the Republican victory?
3. How did he expect the Federalists to behave in opposition? What, according to Henderson, motivated the Federalists? How did they supposedly differ from Jefferson and the Republicans?

On the 11th [of February] the votes for President and Vice President of the United States were counted in the Senate Chamber, when it appeared that Mr. Jefferson and Colonel Burr had each 73 votes, Mr. Adams 65, General Pinckney 64, and Mr. Jay one. The House of Representatives immediately proceeded to choose, by states, a President from the two highest on the list; on the first ballot eight states voted for Jefferson, six for Burr, and two were divided. The states that voted for Jefferson, are New York, New Jersey, Pennsylvania, Virginia, North Carolina, Georgia, Tennessee, Kentucky; those for Burr, New Hampshire, Massachusetts, Rhode Island, Connecticut, Delaware, South Carolina; Maryland and Vermont were divided.

We continued to vote without separating until 9 o'clock of the next morning; the result was uniformly the same; the house then suspended further balloting until 12 o'clock, when, on trying it again, there appeared no variation in the votes; we continued voting from day to day, without doing any other business until the 17th [of February] instant, when on the 36th balloting, ten states voted for Jefferson, four for Burr, and two put blank tickets into the box; Mr. Jefferson was then declared President of the United States, from the 4th of March next. The federalists supported Col. Burr, and the democrats [Republicans] Mr. Jefferson; it is known that neither of those gentlemen are acceptable to the federalists; but of the two they prefer Col. Burr.

The supporters of Jefferson declared they would continue to vote for him until the 4th of March, and risque the consequence of having no President, or in other words, that they would dissolve the government if the man of their choice were not chosen. The federalists think that a weak and inefficient government is better than no government at all, and preferred having Mr. Jefferson President, exceptionable as he is, to anarchy and confusion. It is certainly my duty to inform you, and from it I shall not shrink, that through the whole of this transaction, I uniformly voted for Col. Burr. I did so under a conviction that he was the best qualified of the two candidates to promote the honor, peace and happiness of the nation. I shall forbear to say what I think of Mr. Jefferson; he is now on the eve of being chief magistrate of the nation; respect for the office he is to fill, and not for the man, forbids me to make any comments on his character. . . .

It is now twelve years since the present government was established, during which period we have been engaged in a bloody and expensive Indian war to protect and defend our frontiers, we have suppressed two insurrections, our commerce has been continually interrupted by one or the other of the great powers of Europe; with all these difficulties to encounter, our national debt has actually been diminished at least 3,972,878 dollars, our commerce is extending to every part of the world, our agriculture and manufactures are rapidly increasing, and we have peace and personal security at home. It is proper to observe, in order to shew the rapidity with which the public debt was diminishing, at the time when the hostility of France compelled the government to incur those great and extraordinary expences which appear in the Treasury statements, and to enter upon an expensive system of defence which has resulted in the security of our commerce, that on the first of January 1798, our debt had decreased 7,558,258 dollars. This proves in the most satisfactory manner the case with which the national debt may be extinguished, whenever the government shall be left unembarrassed by internal disorder or foreign hostility.

The government of the nation is about to pass into the hands of those who have never ceased to oppose that system of measures which has been heretofore pursued. If they should trample the constitution under feet, and despise its provisions; if they should reverse the wise maxims of Washington, whose administration they constantly complained of; destroy public credit, and involve us in war; the federalists will certainly oppose them. But if on the contrary the change should be a change of men and not of measures; if all this clamor we have heard is merely to gratify the ambition of designing and ambitious men, who when in power will preserve the constitution, protect the rights of persons and property, maintain the dignity and honor of the nation at home and abroad; the federalists will be their firmest supporters. It is perfectly immaterial to them who are in power, provided that these great objects are attained. I firmly believe that they have been guided by the purest motives and the most enlightened policy; and when that phrenzy which now distracts our country shall cease to exist; when the turbulence of faction shall subside and calm reason once more resume her seat, those men who have been at the head of our affairs will be held in grateful remembrance by the American people, and their names pronounced with pleasure by every friend to his country. I sincerely wish that this period may arrive, without our witnessing those calamities and experiencing those evils, which I fear there is too good reason to dread.

I cannot close this letter without endeavouring to impress on your mind the necessity of resisting the influence of that spirit of reform, which continually aims at the subversion of established order and the settled course of things, which is ever uneasy under present circumstances, and forever promising its deluded votaries some distant good. It is this spirit . . . which has hurled from their thrones, law, religion, and liberty, and placed in their seats, anarchy, infidelity and confusion; which has overturned the best governments and desolated the fairest regions of the earth, which has loosened the social compact, and weakened the obligations of morality.

DOCUMENT 2

Jefferson's First Inaugural Address (1801)

Thomas Jefferson's first inaugural address is widely regarded as one of the best of the best of that genre. In this relatively brief address, delivered on 4 March 1801, the newly elected president sought both to cultivate the goodwill of the Federalists, who were bitter in defeat, and to state succinctly the main tenets of his own political philosophy.[2] Despite the conciliatory and nonpartisan tone of Jefferson's address, the anniversary of his inauguration became an occasion for partisan celebration—second only to the Fourth of July—within his own Republican party.

Questions to consider:

1. What did Jefferson consider to be the chief strengths of the United States and its government?

2. What, if any, changes did he envision as a result of his election, to which he referred elsewhere as the "revolution of 1800"?
3. What did Jefferson mean when he said, "every difference of opinion is not a difference of principle"?
4. How do you think Federalists responded to Jefferson's address? What do you think was the reaction of Republicans?

Friends and Fellow-Citizens:

Called upon to undertake the duties of the first executive office of our country, I avail myself of the presence of that portion of my fellow-citizens which is here assembled to express my grateful thanks for the favor with which they have been pleased to look toward me, to declare a sincere consciousness that the task is above my talents, and that I approach it with those anxious and awful presentiments which the greatness of the charge and the weakness of my powers so justly inspire. A rising nation, spread over a wide and fruitful land, traversing all the seas with the rich productions of their industry, engaged in commerce with nations who feel power and forget right, advancing rapidly to destinies beyond the reach of mortal eye—when I contemplate these transcendent objects, and see the honor, the happiness, and the hopes of this beloved country committed to the issue, and the auspices of this day, I shrink from the contemplation, and humble myself before the magnitude of the undertaking. Utterly, indeed, should I despair did not the presence of many whom I here see remind me that in the other high authorities provided by our Constitution I shall find resources of wisdom, of virtue, and of zeal on which to rely under all difficulties. To you, then, gentlemen, who are charged with the sovereign functions of legislation, and to those associated with you, I look with encouragement for that guidance and support which may enable us to steer with safety the vessel in which we are all embarked amidst the conflicting elements of a troubled world.

During the contest of opinion through which we have passed the animation of discussions and of exertions has sometimes worn an aspect which might impose on strangers unused to think freely and to speak and to write what they think; but this being now decided by the voice of the nation, announced according to the rules of the Constitution, all will, of course, arrange themselves under the will of the law, and unite in common efforts for the common good. All, too, will bear in mind this sacred principle, that though the will of the majority is in all cases to prevail, that will to be rightful must be reasonable; that the minority possess their equal rights, which equal law must protect, and to violate would be oppression. Let us, then, fellow-citizens, unite with one heart and one mind. Let us restore to social intercourse that harmony and affection without which liberty and even life itself are but dreary things. And let us reflect that, having banished from our land that religious intolerance under which mankind so long bled and suffered, we have yet gained little if we countenance a political intolerance as despotic, as wicked, and capable of as bitter and bloody persecutions. During the throes and convulsions of the ancient world, during the agonizing spasms of infuriated man, seeking through blood and slaughter his long-lost liberty, it was not wonderful that the agitation of the billows should reach even this distant and peaceful shore; that this should be more felt and feared by some and less by others, and should divide opinions as to measures of safety. But every difference of opinion is not a difference of principle. We have called by different names brethren of the same principle. We are all Republicans, we are all Federalists.

If there be any among us who would wish to dissolve this Union or to change its republican form, let them stand undisturbed as monuments of the safety with which error of opinion may be tolerated where reason is left free to combat it. I know, indeed, that some honest men fear that a republican government can not be strong, that this Government is not strong enough; but would the honest patriot, in the full tide of successful experiment, abandon a government which has so far kept us free and firm on the theoretic and visionary fear that this Government, the world's best hope, may by possibility want energy to preserve itself? I trust not. I believe this, on the contrary, the strongest Government on earth. I believe it the only one where every man, at the call of the law, would fly to the standard of the law, and would meet invasions of the public order as his own personal concern. Sometimes it is said that man can not be trusted with the government of himself. Can he, then, be trusted with the government of others? Or have we found angels in the forms of kings to govern him? Let history answer this question.

Let us, then, with courage and confidence pursue our own Federal and Republican principles, our attachment to union and representative government. Kindly separated by nature and a wide ocean from the exterminating havoc of one quarter of the globe; too high-minded to endure the degradations of the others; possessing a chosen country, with room enough for our descendants to the thousandth and thousandth generation; entertaining a due sense of our equal right to the use of our own faculties, to the acquisitions of our own industry, to honor and confidence from our fellow-citizens, resulting not from birth, but from our actions and their sense of them; enlightened by a benign religion, professed, indeed, and practiced in various forms, yet all of them inculcating honesty, truth, temperance, gratitude, and the love of man; acknowledging and adoring an overruling Providence, which by all its dispensations proves that it delights in the happiness of man here and his greater happiness hereafter—with all these blessings, what more is necessary to make us a happy and a prosperous people? Still one thing more, fellow-citizens—a wise and frugal Government, which shall restrain men from injuring one another, shall leave them otherwise free to regulate their own pursuits of industry and improvement, and shall not take from the mouth of labor the bread it has earned. This is the sum of good government, and this is necessary to close the circle of our felicities.

About to enter, fellow-citizens, on the exercise of duties which comprehend everything dear and valuable to you, it is proper you should understand what I deem the essential principles of our Government, and consequently those which ought to shape its Administration. I will compress them within the narrowest compass they will bear, stating the general principle, but not all its limitations. Equal and exact justice to all men, of whatever state or persuasion, religious or political; peace, commerce, and honest friendship with all nations, entangling alliances with none; the support of the State governments in all their rights, as the most competent administrations for our domestic concerns and the surest bulwarks against antirepublican tendencies; the preservation of the General Government in its whole constitutional vigor, as the sheet anchor of our peace at home and safety abroad; a jealous care of the right of election by the people—a mild and safe corrective of abuses which are lopped by the sword of revolution where peaceable remedies are unprovided; absolute acquiescence in the decisions of the majority, the vital principle of republics, from which is no appeal but to force, the vital principle and immediate parent of despotism; a well disciplined militia, our best reliance in peace and for the first moments of war, till regulars may relieve them; the supremacy of the civil over the military authority; economy in the public expense, that labor may be lightly burthened; the honest payment of our debts and sacred preservation of the public faith; encouragement of agriculture, and of commerce as its handmaid; the diffusion of information and arraignment of all abuses at the bar of the public reason; freedom of religion; freedom of the press, and freedom of person under the protection of the habeas corpus, and trial by juries impartially selected. These principles form the bright constellation which has gone before us and guided our steps through an age of revolution and reformation. The wisdom of our sages and blood of our heroes have been devoted to their attainment. They should be the creed of our political faith, the text of civic instruction, the touchstone by which to try the services of those we trust; and should we wander from them in moments of error or of alarm, let us hasten to retrace our steps and to regain the road which alone leads to peace, liberty, and safety.

"The Greatest Cheese in America for the Greatest Man in America" (1802)

On 20 July 1801, the "inhabitants" of Cheshire, Massachusetts, made a 1,235-pound cheese as a gift for President Thomas Jefferson. Although women probably made the cheese—dairying was women's work—the town's leading men traveled to Washington to present it to the new president. The purveyors of the mammoth cheese were Baptists, who opposed their state's Congregational establishment and applauded the Jeffersonian ideal of separation of Church and State. The president graciously accepted "this mark of esteem from freeborn farmers, employed personally in the most useful labors of life."[3] He proudly displayed the cheese in the White House, where Federalists ridiculed it as a symbol of Republican vulgarity and impropriety.

Questions to consider:

1. How did the purveyors of the cheese interpret the significance of the election of 1800?
2. Why did they choose to present Jefferson with a cheese, rather than some other token of their esteem?
3. Was it significant that they described their gift as the result of "the personal labour of free-born farmers (without a single slave to assist)" them?

Notwithstanding we live remote from the seat of the national government, and in an extreme part of our own state; yet we claim the right of judging for ourselves.

Our attachment to the national constitution is strong & indissoluable. We consider it a description of those powers, which the people have submitted to their magistrates, to be exercised for definitive purposes, and not a charter of favors, granted by a sovereign to his subjects. Among its beautiful features, the right of free suffrage, to correct all abuses—The prohibition of religious tests, to prevent all hierarchy—The means of amendment, which it contains within itself, to remove defects as fast as they are discovered, appear the most prominent. But for several years past, our apprehension has been, that the genius of the government was not attended to in sundry cases;

and that the administration bordered upon monarchy. Our joy, of course, must have been great, on your election to the first office of the nation; having good evidence, from your announced sentiments and uniform conduct that it would be your strife and glory to turn back the government to its virgin purity. The trust is great! The task is arduous! But we console ourselves, that the Supreme Ruler of the universe, who raises up men to achieve great events, has raised up a Jefferson for this critical day, to defend republicanism and baffle all the arts of aristocracy.

Sir, we have attempted to prove our love to this President, not in words alone, but in deeds and truth. With this address, we send you a cheese, by the hands of Messrs. John Leland and Darius Brown, as a pepper-corn of the esteem which we bear to our chief magistrate, and as a sacrifice to republicanism. It is not the last stone in the Bastille, nor is it of any great consequence as an article of worth; but as a free-will offering, we hope it will be received. The cheese was not made by his lordship, for his sacred majesty; nor with a view to gain dignified titles or lucrative offices; but by the personal labour of free-born farmers (without a single slave to assist) for an elective President of a free people—with the only view of casting a mite into the scale of democracy.

The late triumphant return of republicanism has more animated the inhabitants of Cheshire, to bear the burthens of government, and treat the characters and persons of those in authority with all due respect, than the long list of alien, sedition, naval, and provisional army laws ever did.

Sir, we had some thoughts of impressing some significant inscription on the cheese; but we . . . rather chose to send it in plain republican form.

DOCUMENT 4

Peopling the West (1803)

Jefferson believed that westward expansion—and the economic opportunities it represented—was an essential precondition for the survival of American liberty. As president, he continued the Indian policies of earlier administrations, which aimed to convert native Americans to sedentary agriculture to facilitate white settlement of the western territories. In this letter to William Henry Harrison, governor of the Indiana Territory, however, Jefferson explained that the United States government had other plans for dealing with recalcitrant Indians.[4] Harrison, who made his reputation both before and during his governorship fighting the Indians of the Old Northwest, rode that reputation to the presidency in 1840.

Questions to consider:

1. What was the purpose of Jefferson's letter to William Henry Harrison?
2. What, according to Jefferson, were the short- and long-term objectives of United States policy toward native Americans? What weapons did the president consider using to advance his Indian policy? What were some of the variables that might affect the government's treatment of different Indian nations?
3. Was Jefferson respectful toward the Indians and their cultures?

You will receive . . . from the Secretary of War . . . from time to time information and instructions as to our Indian affairs. These communications being for the public records, are restrained always to particular objects and occasions; but this letter being unofficial and private, I may with safety give you a more extensive view of our policy respecting the Indians, that you may better comprehend the parts dealt out to you in detail through the official channel, and observing the system of which they make a part, conduct yourself in unison with it in cases where you are obliged to act without instruction.

Our system is to live in perpetual peace with the Indians, to cultivate an affectionate attachment from them, by everything just and liberal which we can do for them within the bounds of reason, and by giving them effectual protection against wrongs from our own people. The decrease of game rendering their subsistence by hunting insufficient, we wish to draw them to agriculture, to spinning and weaving. The latter branches they take up with great readiness, because they fall to women, who gain by quitting the labors of the field for those which are exercised within doors. When they withdraw themselves to the culture of a small piece of land, they will perceive how useless to them are their extensive forests, and will be willing to pare them off from time to time in exchange for necessaries for their farms and families.

To promote this disposition to exchange lands, which they have to spare and we want, for necessaries, which we have to spare and they want, we shall push our trading uses, and be glad to see the good and influential individuals among them run in debt, because we observe that when these debts get beyond what the individuals can pay, they become willing to lop them off by a cession of lands. At our trading houses, too, we mean to sell so low as merely to repay us cost and charges, so as neither to lessen nor enlarge our capital. This is what private traders cannot do, for they must gain; they will consequently retire from the competition, and we shall thus get clear of this pest without giving offence or umbrage to the Indians.

In this way our settlements will gradually circumscribe and approach the Indians, and they will in time either incorporate with us as citizens of the United States, or remove beyond the Mississippi. The former is certainly the termination of their history most happy for themselves; but, in the whole course of this, it is essential to cultivate their love. As to their fear, we presume that our strength and their weakness is now so visible that they must see we have only to shut our hand to crush them, and that all our liberalities to them proceed from motives of pure humanity only. Should any tribe be foolhardy enough to take up the hatchet at any time, the seizing the whole country of that tribe, and driving them across the Mississippi, as the only condition of peace, would be an example to others, and a furtherance of our final consolidation.

Combined with these views, and to be prepared against the occupation of Louisiana, by a powerful and enterprising people, it is important that, setting less value on interior extension of purchases from the Indians, we bend our whole views to the purchase and settlement of the country on the Mississippi, from its mouth to its northern regions, that we may be able to present as strong a front on our western as on our eastern border, and plant on the Mississippi itself the means of its own defence . . . I have given you this view of the system which we suppose will best promote the interests of the Indians and ourselves, and finally consolidate our whole country to one nation only; that you may be enabled the better to adapt your means to the object, for this purpose we have given you a general commission for treating. The crisis is pressing; whatever can now be obtained must be obtained quickly. The occupation of New Orleans, hourly expected, by the French, is already felt like a light breeze by the Indians. You know the sentiments they entertain of that nation; under the hope of their protection they will immediately stiffen against cessions of lands to us. We had better, therefore, do at once what can now be done.

I must repeat that this letter is to be considered as private and friendly, and is not to control any particular instructions which you may receive through official channel. You will also perceive how sacredly it must be kept within your own breast, and especially how improper to be understood by the Indians. For their interests and their tranquillity it is best they should see only the present age of their history.

Oration on the Cession of Louisiana to the United States (1804)

David Ramsay

The Louisiana Purchase more than doubled the territory of the United States and laid the foundations for westward expansion in the coming century. Many contemporaries, including South Carolinian David Ramsay, regarded the acquisition of Louisiana as the most significant event in American history since the adoption of the Constitution. In this oration, Ramsay stressed the political, economic, and social benefits of the Louisiana Purchase for all white Americans.[5] Although he wildly overestimated what the population of the United States would be in 2003, his demographic predictions were remarkably accurate for the nineteenth century.

Questions to consider:

1. Why did Ramsay deem the Louisiana Purchase the "greatest political blessing ever conferred on these states," after independence and the adoption of the federal constitution? What did he mean when he spoke of the "new duties" Americans undertook as a result of the acquisition of Louisiana?
2. How did Ramsay define "happiness"? What did he believe were preconditions to the attainment of happiness?
3. How, according to Ramsay, would the Louisiana Purchase affect even those Americans who never ventured westward? Why did he feel obliged to emphasize its potential benefits for his "eastern brethren"?

Louisiana is ours! If we rightly improve the heaven sent boon, we may be as great and happy a nation as any on which the sun has ever shone. The establishment of independence and of our present constitution are prior, both in time and importance; but with these two exceptions, the acquisition of Louisiana is the greatest political blessing ever conferred on these states. Considering it in its most inferior point of view, merely as property, it is of incalculable value. It gives us two to three hundred additional miles of sea coast, with several excellent harbours. The land on both sides of the Mississippi, for two or three hundred miles, below our southern limits, together with the exclusive possession of this noble river, from its source to its mouth, and an extension of our western territory, for its whole length, stretching indefinitely across the continent, till it touches the Pacific ocean. . . .

All this immense country is ours in trust for posterity. With such an ample reversion, what reason has any single man, to be afraid of matrimony? Or what ground is there for any married man to be alarmed at the prospects of a numerous family? Here are plantations enough, and enough, for our children and our children's children, for centuries to come. . . .

The inhabitants of Louisiana will be chiefly agriculturalists and purchase their farming utensils and most other domestic articles. What a field of enterprise will this open to our eastern brethren, whose cheapness of navigation, whose skill in handicraft trades, will entitle them to a decided preference in trading with their new fellow-citizens? Here will be a great and growing demand for the manufactures and shipping of New England, to supply the wants, and carry off the produce of this extensive territory.

Of all branches of trade, that which is carried on between different parts of the same nation is most beneficial. Agriculture, commerce, shipbuilding, and manufactures support, and are supported by, each other. They are separate links of one great chain, which binds all together, and each of which adds to the strength of the whole. Too long has this country been commercially dependent on Europe. Notwithstanding our perfect neutrality, do we not all, at this moment, suffer in consequence of the war between France and England? It is high time we had a commerce of our own, as independent as possible of the ever-changing politics of the old world. This independence will be greatly promoted by the reciprocal wants and capacities of different portions of our now widely extended empire. One extreme of the union abounds in shipping, overflows with inhabitants, and is ripe for manufactures; while the other engaged in the cultivation of a more fertile soil, finds its interest in purchasing manufactures, brought to their doors. A domestic commerce of this kind will cement our union, and make us really independent. . . .

Judging of the future, by the past, what may an infant, born this day, expect to see, in case of his surviving to the age of four-score? . . . A new born infant may live to see the population of the United States, increased to fifty millions, which is more than three times the number of persons which now inhabit Great Britain and Ireland. Proceeding to calculate on the data, which former numerations of our people have sanctioned, our population, in twenty-five years, will amount to ten millions; in fifty years to twenty millions; in seventy years to forty millions; in one century to eighty millions; and, by the same rule, in two centuries to twelve hundred and eighty millions of inhabitants. The great grandsons of our present children, without any extraordinary series of longevity, may live to see this amazing increase of our numbers. What territory can be too large for a people, who multiply with such unequalled rapidity? . . .

On all the citizens of the United States, this day imposes new duties. For the last twenty-eight years we have demonstrated to the world that man is capable of self-government—that the representative system is fully adequate to secure and promote the happiness of its members. It still remains to be proved, that it is equal to the happy government of an extensive country. What a reproach it would be to us all, if our future political condition should be less happy than the past . . . The reputation which the cause of liberty has gained, by our past successful experiment in building a government on reason and the rights of man would, in a great measure be lost.

The happiness enjoyed under our new system, in this new world, has a direct tendency to regenerate the governments of the old, without the horrors and bloodshed of revolutions. If this happiness increases, and extends with the increase and extent of our territory, the advantages to the distressed will be incalculable. The rulers of [Europe], who hold a great part of their fellow-men in bondage, and who are perpetually involving them in wars, will relax in their oppressions, curb their ambition, and study the things that make for the peace and happiness of their subjects. This will be their obvious interest when they know that our now extended limits afford an ample asylum for the poor of all nations, where they may become independent citizens on their own lands and in the peaceable enjoyment of every earthly comfort. The success of the noblest experiment ever made for meliorating the condition of man, in great measure, depends on us. . . .

DOCUMENT 6

Madison's War Message (1812)

On 1 June 1812, James Madison became the first president to ask Congress to issue a formal declaration of war.[6] The resulting votes in both houses of Congress revealed divisions along both regional and party lines: support for war with Britain was strong among southerners and westerners and among Republicans, while Federalists universally opposed the war, as did most New Englanders. Madison led a divided and unprepared nation into war in 1812.

Questions to consider:

1. What was the tone of Madison's war message to Congress?
2. What, according to Madison, were the causes of the as yet undeclared war with Britain? What factors did he stress in asking for a formal declaration of war?
3. Why did many Americans regard the War of 1812 as a second war for independence?

Without going back beyond the renewal in 1803 of the war in which Great Britain is engaged, and omitting unrepaired wrongs of inferior magnitude, the conduct of her Government presents a series of acts hostile to the United States as an independent and neutral nation.

British cruisers have been in the continued practice of violating the American flag on the great highway of nations, and of seizing and carrying off persons sailing under it, not in the exercise of a belligerent right founded on the law of nations against an enemy, but on a municipal prerogative over British subjects. British jurisdiction is thus extended to neutral vessels in a situation where no laws can operate but the law of nations and the laws of the country to which the vessels belong, and a self-redress is assumed which, if British subjects were wrongfully detained and alone concerned, is that substitutions of force for a resort to the responsible sovereign which falls within the definition of war. Could the seizure of British subjects in such cases be regarded as within the exercise of a belligerent right, the acknowledged laws of war, which forbid an article of captured property to be adjudged without a regular investigation before a competent tribunal, would imperiously demand the fairest trial where the sacred rights of persons were at issue. In place of such a trial these rights are subjected to the will of every petty commander. . . .

The practice, hence, is so far from affecting British subjects alone that, under the pretext of searching for these, thousands of American citizens, under the safeguard of public law and of their national flag, have been torn from their country and from everything dear to them; have been dragged in board ships of war of a foreign nation and exposed, under the severities of their discipline, to be exiled to the most distant and deadly climes, to risk their lives in the battles of their oppressors, and to be the melancholy instruments of taking away those of their own brethren.

Against this crying enormity, which Great Britain would be so prompt to avenge if committed against herself, the United States have in vain exhausted remonstrances and expostulations, and that no proof might be wanting of their conciliatory dispositions, and no pretext left for a continuance of the practice, the British Government was formally assured of the readiness of the United States to enter into arrangements such as could not be rejected if the recovery of British subjects were the real and sole object. The communication passed without effect.

British cruisers have been in the practice also of violating the rights and the peace of our coasts. They hover over and harass our entering and departing commerce. To the most insulting pretensions they have added the most lawless proceedings in our very harbors, and have wantonly spilt American blood within the sanctuary of our territorial jurisdiction. . . .

Under pretended blockages, without the presence of an adequate force and sometimes without the practicability of applying one, our commerce has been plundered in every sea, the great staples of our country have been cut off from their legitimate markets, and a destructive blow aimed at our agricultural and maritime interests. . . . Not content with these occasional expedients for laying waste our neutral trade, the cabinet of Britain resorted at length to the sweeping system of blockades, under the name of orders in council, which has been molded and managed as might best suit its political views, its commercial jealousies, or the avidity of British cruisers. . . .

In reviewing the conduct of Great Britain toward the United States our attention is necessarily drawn to the warfare just renewed by the savages on one of our extensive frontiers—a warfare which is known to spare neither age nor sex and to be distinguished by features peculiarly shocking to humanity. It is difficult to account for the activity and combinations which have for some time been developing themselves among tribes in constant intercourse with British traders and garrisons without connecting their hostility with that influence and without recollecting the authenticated examples of such interpositions heretofore furnished by the officers and agents of that Government.

Such is the spectacle of injuries and indignities which have been heaped on our country, and such the crisis which its unexampled forbearance and conciliatory efforts have not been able to avert. . . .

Our moderation and conciliation have had no other effect than to encourage perseverance and to enlarge pretensions. We behold our seafaring citizens still the daily victims of lawless violence, committed on the great common and highway of nations, even within sight of the country which owes them protection. We behold our vessels, freighted with the products of our soil and industry, or returning with the honest proceeds of them, wrested from their lawful destinations, confiscated by prize courts no longer the organs of public law but the instruments of arbitrary edicts, and their unfortunate crews dispersed and lost, or forced or inveigled in British ports into British fleets, whilst arguments are employed in support of these aggressions which have no foundation but in a principle equally supporting a claim to regulate our external commerce in all cases whatsoever.

We behold, in fine, on the side of Great Britain a state of war against the United States, and on the side of the United States a state of peace toward Great Britain.

Whether the United States shall continue passive under these progressive usurpations and these accumulating wrongs, or, opposing force to force in defense of their national rights, shall commit a just cause into the hands of the Almighty Disposer of Events, avoiding all connections which might entangle it in the contest or views of other powers, and preserving a constant readiness to concur in an honorable reestablishment of peace and friendship, is a solemn question which the Constitution wisely confides to the legislative department of the Government. In recommending it to their early deliberations I am happy in the assurance that the decision will be worthy the enlightened and patriotic councils of a virtuous, a free, and a powerful nation.

A Boxing Match, or Another Bloody Nose for John Bull, 1813. Published in Philadelphia, this print commemorates—and gloats over—early British naval losses in the War of 1812. The artist plays on the name of the British warship *Boxer*, which fell to the American frigate *Enterprize* in September 1813. King George III bleeds heavily from his nose, having sustained heavy blows from the fists of President James Madison. Significantly, at this time, the nose was a symbol of virility. Compare the physique, clothing, and demeanor of the two combatants. Why did the artist forgo the customary use of allegory to represent the war as a conflict between two real public figures? Source: Etching with watercolor on wove paper; 25 × 34.8 cm. Courtesy of the Library of Congress, Washington, D.C.

DOCUMENT 7

Margaret Bayard Smith's Account of the Burning of Washington (1814)

In April 1813, American troops destroyed York (now Toronto), the capital of British Upper Canada. In retaliation, in August 1814, British forces occupied and burned Washington. Margaret Bayard Smith was a friend of James and Dolley Madison, the wife of a Republican newspaper editor, a writer in her own right, and a leading figure in Washington society. She wrote this letter to her sister, describing her family's flight from Washington in advance of the British invasion.[7] The Smiths later returned to their home in the nation's capital.

Questions to consider:

1. How did Smith describe the morale of civilians before and after the arrival of the British?
2. How did civilians get information about troop movements and military engagements?
3. To what factors did Smith attribute the utter inability of Americans to defend their capital? What, in her opinion, would be the consequences of the British occupation of Washington?

On Sunday we received information that the British had debarked at Benedict. They seemed in no haste to approach the city, but gave us time to collect our troops. The alarm was such that on Monday a general removal from the city and George Town took place. Very few women and children remained in the city on Tuesday evening, although the accounts then received were that the enemy was retreating. Our troops were eager for an attack and such was the cheerful alacrity they displayed, that a universal confidence reigned among the citizens and people. Few doubted our conquering.

On Tuesday we sent off to a private farm house all our linen, clothing and other movable property; in the afternoon Dr. Bradley's family came from the city and took tea with us . . . We were roused on Tuesday night by a loud knocking, [and] on the opening of the door, Willie Bradley called to us, "The enemy are advancing, our own troops are giving way on all sides and are retreating to the city. Go, for God's sake, go." He spoke in a voice of agony, and then flew to his horse and was out of sight in a moment. We immediately rose, the carriage and horses were soon ready, we loaded a wagon with what goods remained and about 3 o'clock left our house with all our servants, the women we sent to some private farm houses at a safe distance, while we pursued our course. I felt no alarm or agitation, as I knew the danger was not near. I even felt no distress at the idea of forsaking our home. I could not realize the possibility of the B[ritish] gaining possession of the city, or of our army being defeated. . . .

Thursday morning. This morning on awakening we were greeted with the sad news, that our city was taken, the bridges and public buildings burnt, our troops flying in every direction. Our little army totally dispersed. Good God, what will be the event! . . . The President who was on the ground, escaped and has gone into Virginia. . . .

Oh how changed are my feelings, my confidence in our troops is gone, they may again be rallied, but it will require a long apprenticeship to make them good soldiers. Oh my sister how gloomy is the scene. I do not suppose government will ever return to Washington. All those whose property was invested in that place, will be reduced to poverty. Mr. Smith had invested a large portion of his in bridge stock—both the bridges are destroyed. . . .

Thursday evening. Our anxiety has been kept alive the whole day. Our poor men are coming in some two or three, sometimes a dozen at a time, just now another troop of horse have come in, they have not been in the engagement, as they did not arrive until a retreat had been ordered. Mr. Carr, one of the clerks of the Bank, was here just now and has given us the most correct account we have yet had . . . [The enemy] never left the turnpike but entered the city after our retreating army. They first marched to the navy yard which is wholly consumed; then to Capitol Hill. They had great difficulty in firing the Capitol, several houses on the hill were burnt by cinders from the Capitol, but none by design, the President's house, the Potomac bridge, and all the other public buildings. . . .

I am afraid the consequence of leaving the house empty will be its destruction. Our house in the city too is unprotected and contains our most valuable furniture. In a week more and we may be penniless! For I count little on the continuance of Mr. S[mith]'s salary. God only knows when the executive government will again be organized. But I can say with truth, the individual loss of property, has not given me a moment's uneasiness. But the state of our country, has wrung tears of anguish from me. I trust it will only be momentary. We are naturally a brave people and it was not so much fear, as prudence, which caused our retreat. Too late they discovered the dispreparation of our troops. The enemy were 3 to 1. Their army composed of conquering veterans, ours of young mechanics and farmers, many of whom had never before carried a musket. But we shall learn the dreadful, horrid trade of war. And they will make us a martial people, for never, never will Americans give up their liberty. But before that time comes, what sufferings, what reverses, what distress must be suffered.

DOCUMENT 8

"Our Heroes Died Not in Vain." (1815)

In 1811, Hezekiah Niles of Baltimore founded Niles' Weekly Register, *a newspaper that focused on political news and commentary. As an editor and publisher, Niles sought to include diverse opinions in his newspaper, but he was also an ardent nationalist, who had been a member of the Baltimore militia that helped defend Fort McHenry against the British in September 1814. The War of 1812 was fought to a military stalemate, and the Treaty of Ghent that ended the war settled none of the issues that caused it. Nevertheless, like many Americans, Niles believed that the second war with Britain had secured the independence of the United States and thus the objectives of the Revolution.[8]*

Questions to consider:

1. Why did Niles write this celebratory piece?
2. Who were the "heroes" he celebrated? What were their chief virtues? Why was he so optimistic about the future of the American republic?
3. What evidence did Niles furnish in support of his claim that the United States was "in the first rank of nations" in 1815? Do you think his readers found this view persuasive?

Success has crowned our arms in a wonderful manner. The eagle banner, sustained by the Hand of God, through hosts of heroes, triumphantly waved over Champlain, at Plattsburg, at Baltimore, at Mobile, and New Orleans; and some signal victories were gained at sea—so that the war was finished in a blaze of glory, as though the Great Arbiter of all things, had decreed that the wisdom and fortitude of our government, and the desperately daring courage, invincible patience and ingenious qualities of our people, should be tried in a short contest, to secure the future peace and establish our mild and benevolent institutions. Hail, holy freedom! What though traitors within, and barbarians without, assailed thy banner—they have retired before the nervous arm of thy sons, and left thy stars unsullied!

We had shewn to all the world our love of peace, and astonished all people with our forbearance. We have alike astonished it by a single handed contest with a nation that has aspired to govern it . . . Fresh from the plough, our gallant people rushed to the sea board to meet the invader, and beat and discomfit the best proved veterans of the old world, provided with all the needful requisites for the fight, and led on by the ablest and most experienced generals . . . Whatever may be the share of our disgrace for the capture of Washington, that of our late enemy, at Plattsburg, sponges off the stain, and leaves other victories, and especially the magnificent affairs at [New] Orleans, as clear gain in the account of honor. . . .

But no sooner had we acquired the skill and experience necessary to give the war its full force, than the sword was returned to its scabbard . . . We hail the returned peace with unspeakable joy. It best suits the genius of our people and the spirit of our government. The former have no fat offices to fill, nor can the latter have ambition, except to gain the good opinion of those with whom they must shortly mix, in common life; unpensioned, except by the purity of their own hearts. The war has cost us many valuable lives, and much money. The first is beyond estimation, and irretrievable; but the second, a matter of no consequence; for we can pay all our debts in a few years with ease . . . the resources of our country are immense; and it only wanted a bold and steady hand to bring them forth. The people talk much about the taxes . . . Are we to growl and grumble at this, and not to esteem the countless blessings we enjoy—not calculating that the cause that made these slight impositions necessary, redeemed the independence of the United States? If we had not resisted—if we had longer tamely borne with the lusts and ambition of England—we should have been the victim of her despotism, and have become her slave . . . This victory—this rescue from perdition—was worth the war, and our heroes died not in vain. They sealed the safety of their country by their glorious deeds. . . .

However great the sufferings of the war, we have great countervailing advantages, such as the acquirement of knowledge, renown, internal wealth and strength, and security; of which we design to take a future opportunity to speak—proud in the belief that America now stands in the first rank of nations; a rank that, granted at present by courtesy, to her gallantry, she will command a little while hence, through her increased population and multiplied resources of wealth and power.

SUGGESTED READING FOR CHAPTER 13

BANNER, JAMES M., JR. *To the Hartford Convention: The Federalists and the Origins of Party Politics in Massachusetts, 1789–1815* (1970).

BANNING, LANCE. *The Jeffersonian Persuasion: Evolution of a Party Ideology* (1978).

BROWN, ROGER H. *The Republic in Peril: 1812* (1964).

BUEL, RICHARD, JR. *Securing the Revolution: Ideology in American Politics, 1789–1815* (1972).

DeCONDE, ALEXANDER. *This Affair of Louisiana* (1976).

FISCHER, DAVID HACKETT. *The Revolution of American Conservatism: The Federalist Party in the Era of Jeffersonian Democracy* (1965).

FREEMAN, JOANNE B. *Affairs of Honor: National Politics in the New Republic* (2001).

HICKEY, DONALD R. *The War of 1812: A Forgotten Conflict* (1989).
KERBER, LINDA K. *Federalists in Dissent: Imagery and Ideology in Jeffersonian America* (1970).
OWSLEY, FRANK LAWRENCE, JR.; and GENE H. SMITH. *Filibusters and Expansionists: Jeffersonian Manifest Destiny* (1997).
PERKINS, BRADFORD. *Prologue to War: England and the United States, 1805–1812* (1965).
SHEEHAN, BERNARD W. *Seeds of Extinction: Jeffersonian Philanthropy and the American Indian* (1973).
SISSON, DANIEL. *The American Revolution of 1800* (1974).
SMELSER, MARSHALL. *The Democratic-Republic, 1801–1815* (1968).
STAGG, J. C. A. *Mr. Madison's War: Politics, Diplomacy, and Warfare in the Early American Republic, 1783–1830* (1983).
WATTS, STEVEN. *The Republic Reborn: War and the Making of Liberal America, 1790–1820* (1987).
WEISBERGER, BERNARD. *America Afire: Jefferson, Adams, and the Revolutionary Election of 1800* (2001).

NOTES

[1]Archibald Henderson to his constitutents, 28 Feb. 1801, in [Raleigh] *North Carolina Minerva*, 7 Apr. 1801.

[2]James D. Richardson, ed., *A Compilation of the Messages and Papers of the Presidents, 1789–1902*, 10 vols. (Washington, 1897–1904), 1: 309–12.

[3]*National Intelligencer, and Washington Advertiser*, 20 Jan. 1802.

[4]Thomas Jefferson to William Henry Harrison, 27 Feb. 1803, in Andrew A. Lipscomb, ed., *The Writings of Thomas Jefferson*, 20 vols. (Washington, 1904), 10: 368–73.

[5]David Ramsay, *Oration on the Cession of Louisiana* (Charleston, 1804), 4–5, 7, 10–11, 16–17, 23–26.

[6]James D. Richardson, ed., *A Compilation of the Messages and Papers of the Presidents, 1789–1902*, 10 vols. (Washington, 1897–1904), 1: 500–5.

[7]Margaret Bayard Smith to Mrs. Kirkpatrick, Aug. 1814, in Smith, *The First Forty Years of Washington Society*, ed. Gaillard Hunt (New York, 1906), 98–105.

[8]"Retrospect and Remarks," in *Niles' Weekly Register*, 8 (Mar. 1815): 417–19.

CHAPTER FOURTEEN

REMEMBERING THE
REVOLUTION

A major military triumph and the seedtime of the republic, the Revolution understandably dominates Americans' public memory. While other key episodes in our history—westward expansion, the Civil War, the dropping of the atomic bomb—might be painfully embarrassing or bitterly divisive, most Americans today would probably agree that the Revolution was, overall, a positive achievement. At the same, time, however, most Americans today have little substantive knowledge of the revolutionary era, which we imagine chiefly through a variety of elastic symbols or concepts—the flag, the eagle, independence, liberty, equality—that we define and invoke to suit ourselves. In this way, the Revolution can be a source of fictive unity and identity for a diverse people. In modern America, liberals and conservatives, civil rights leaders and tax rebels, can all claim legitimacy by professing affinity with the revolutionary generation. The fact that they do so suggests both a widespread awareness of America's revolutionary past and a deeply contested understanding of it.

So, too, did earlier generations publicly invoke the legacy of the Revolution variously to foster unity and legitimate dissent. While the private or personal memories of those who participated in the Revolution were specific, even idiosyncratic, public memory was both collective and contested, even in the immediate postwar era. Scholars have described public memory as a system of beliefs that uses the past to understand and to shape the present; as such, competitions over the construction of public memory always involve issues of power. In the postrevolutionary era, the Revolution and its principles became the core of America's public memory and the touchstone of political and social legitimacy. But then as now patriotic Americans disagreed about the fundamental nature and significance of the Revolution, just as they had different agendas for the present and aspirations for the future.

As early as the 1780s, Americans competed to define the public memory of the Revolution and thereby chart the future of the republic. Partisan rivalries between Federalists and Antifederalists, and later Federalists and Republicans, shaped the discourse of public memory until the demise of the Federalists after the War of 1812. Triumph in a second war with Britain informed an exuberant nationalism that imagined the Revolution as a simple narrative of heroism and self-sacrifice in pursuit of popular liberty. But dissenting voices soon challenged this nationalist euphoria, as workingmen, African Americans, and women tried in various ways to shape and lay claim to the Revolution's legacy. Sectional differences, too, gave rise to competing versions of the nation's founding and its significance. In 1861, when Americans divided in civil war, each side claimed to represent the true principles of the Revolution and the republic's founders.

In 1776, Americans had used two lines of reasoning to explain how and why the king and Parliament had violated their rights, which in turn explained and justified their assertion of independence. The more conservative view, which derived colonial rights from specific legal and constitutional arrangements—such as the English common law or colonial charters and statutes—implied that the colonists' actions were unique and that the objectives of the Revolution were backward-looking and limited to regaining those historic rights. The more radical view saw colonial rights as a subset of the natural rights all men in theory shared by virtue of their humanity. This view suggested that other peoples could aspire to the same sorts of rights and liberties that Americans asserted; it implied that the Revolution was an ongoing phenomenon whose logical conclusion was or should be the utmost expansion of these natural rights.

These divergent views of the origins and objectives of the Revolution continued to shape political discourse in the 1780s and 1790s, as American political leaders cited revolutionary ideals and principles to legitimate their programs and policies. When nationalists in the Confederation era emphasized the need to create balance in government, they invoked the ideal of stability and protection that the British constitution supposedly afforded in its uncorrupted form. Antifederalists, in response, stressed the Revolution's origins in resisting the tyranny of a remote central government to warn that all centralized power was potentially despotic. In the 1790s, Federalists saw no kinship between the French Revolution and its American counterpart, while Republicans hailed the establishment of the French republic as a sequel to their own defense of natural rights. Significantly, when slaves and free blacks in Santo Domingo revolted in 1790s and established the republic of Haiti in 1804, Republicans did not interpret their revolution in the same light.

The earliest published histories of the Revolution reflected the divided political sensibilities of the postrevolutionary years. Most of these early histories were narratives of the Revolution in a particular state or locality, reflecting the continuing primacy of state and local identities. Historians who created revolutionary narratives that included all the states conversely aimed to use their narratives to equate the Revolution with the founding of a new nation, though the two earliest presented strikingly different perspectives on the nation's origins and ideal character. Reflecting the Federalist sensibilities of its author, David Ramsay's *History of the American Revolution* (1789) described the revolutionary era as one of courage and creativity threatened by chaos and instability, culminating logically and fortuitously with the ratification of the Constitution and the installation of the patriarchal and patrician Washington as the first president of the republic. By contrast, *The History of the Rise, Progress, and Termination of the American Revolution* (1805), by Antifederalist-turned-Republican Mercy Otis Warren, stressed the ongoing contest between liberty and tyranny, first British and later American. For Warren, the ratification of the Constitution and the subsequent Federalist administrations were ominous episodes in a revolution that had gone awry, but then took a turn for the better with the election of 1800.

Although relatively few Americans read Ramsay's and Warren's ponderous multivolume works, the competing memories of the Revolution they promoted were central to the partisan civic rituals of the early republican era. American political leaders orchestrated civic rituals to convince their compatriots that they shared a common national identity. Carefully scripted commemorations of the Revolution could provide common memories for a varied and dispersed population and stimulate the development of a sense of national community. Civic rituals aimed to mask divisions and contradictions in American society to promote shared identity and allegiance, especially among those white men who counted as members of the polity. They rarely succeeded, however, because competing commemorations of the Revolution laid bare the very divisions and contradictions their organizers attempted to deny.

Before 1815, party politics inspired civic commemorations as Federalists and Republicans celebrated rival versions of the Revolution to legitimate their respective views on such fundamental issues as the rights and obligations of republican citizenship and the practical meaning of abstract concepts like liberty and equality. While Federalists held genteel balls on Washington's birthday to commemorate the quasi-regal ideal of leadership he embodied and the policies he pursued, Republicans orchestrated parades and feasts to honor the French Revolution and the anniversary of Jefferson's inauguration on 4 March 1801. Although Federalists and Republicans alike came to agree that the Fourth of July would be the most important date on America's civic calendar, the rituals they chose to celebrate the anniversary of American independence differed significantly. The more populist Republicans emphasized both the natural rights interpretation of the Revolution's origins and the leading role of Jefferson, their leader, by making a public reading of the Declaration of Independence the focal point of the day's festivities, which also featured a militia parade to glorify the past and future achievements of America's citizen-soldiers. When the Federalists observed the Fourth of July—and they were reluctant to do so initially—for both partisan and ideological reasons, they celebrated the Constitution instead of the Declaration and often incorporated the constraining influence of religion into their patriotic observances.

The transformation of political culture in the aftermath of the War of 1812 occasioned major changes in how Americans remembered the Revolution. After 1815, the Federalists were severely weakened and widely discredited as a result of their opposition to the war, while most Republicans adopted a more nationalistic approach to governance. This blurring of party lines, which betokened at least a temporary resolution of many of the old political issues, was reflected in more consensual and assertively nationalistic commemorations of the Revolution and its heroes. Chief among those heroes was George Washington, whose home at Mount Vernon became an increasingly popular destination for patriotic pilgrimages. Courageous, wise, self-sacrificing, and patriotic, an idealized Washington personified both the Revolution and American national character.

American military success in the second war with Britain, especially the great victory at New Orleans, stimulated new interest in and appreciation for the military origins of the republic. After 1815, Americans embraced not only Washington—whose achievements and attributes many lauded even while he lived—but also other previously neglected veterans of the War of Independence. Changes in both civic rituals and public policy reflected this trend. On the one hand, aging war veterans increasingly assumed center stage as icons of patriotism at civic celebrations, most dramatically when the Marquis de Lafayette toured the United States to commemorate the fiftieth anniversary of American independence. On the other hand, civil authorities were more appreciative of the military in 1815 than in 1783, when Congress had disbanded the Continental Army. Congress maintained a peacetime force after 1815, and in 1818 it passed the first general pension act to benefit destitute veterans of

George Washington Crossing the Delaware, 1851, by Emanuel Gottlieb Leutze. This monumental painting, which measures more than twelve feet high and twenty-one feet long, portrays a heroic Washington leading his troops boldly across the Delaware River to surprise the enemy at Trenton, New Jersey, in 1776. What elements of this image are historically inaccurate? Why has this image, despite its vast inaccuracy, become so deeply engrained in the American historical imagination? Source: Emanuel Leutze (American, 1816–1868). Oil on canvas, 149 × 255 inches; signed and dated (lower right): E. Leutze/Dusseldorf 1851. The Metropolitan Museum of Art, Gift of John Stewart Kennedy, 1897. (97.34) Negative No. 340B.

the Continental Army. During this period, some Americans also began to consider building monuments to commemorate revolutionary battles and soldiers, an undertaking previously deemed too authoritarian and too expensive for a republican society. In 1825, Lafayette laid the cornerstone for the first of the genre, Boston's Bunker Hill monument, which opened to the public in 1842.

Such nationalist commemorations of the Revolution, despite their frequent celebration of common soldiers, typically were overseen by conservative political and religious leaders. Patriotic orations at such observances hailed the Revolution and the establishment of the American nation as achievements of great men whose patriotism could be admired, though probably not equaled, by future generations. Revolutionary hero-worship reached its apogee when both Thomas Jefferson and John Adams died on 4 July 1826, the fiftieth anniversary the Declaration of Independence. Contemporary orators mused that the virtues and achievements of these revolutionary heroes, along with their symbolic demise on the day of America's great jubilee, attested to both the uniqueness of the American nation and to the passing of its founding generation. By 1826, many believed, a new generation might admire Adams

Julia Brickers's Sampler, 1846. This North Carolina girl's sampler, which shows Washington "cros[s]ing the delaware bay" on horseback, suggests that improbably heroic images of that event antedated Leutze's famous painting. By including both Washington and the "american war bird," Brickers suggested a historical linkage between the Revolution and the controversial Mexican War of 1846, which was extremely popular among white southerners. What does Julia Brickers's sampler reveal about how Americans of her generation understood the Revolution and its legacy?
Source: Julia Brickers, "Sampler", 1846. Wool on linen, 25⅜" × 16¼". Courtesy of the Museum of Early Southern Decorative Arts; Winston-Salem, North Carolina. Old Salem, Inc./MESDA Neg. No.: S-13194.

and Jefferson, but they were more likely to try to imitate a more recent American hero, the virile, self-asserting, and self-made Andrew Jackson.

Dissenting voices challenged the nationalistic and typically elitist commemorations of the Revolution that were typical after 1815, especially at Independence Day celebrations. Workingmen, either newly enfranchised or on the verge of getting the vote, remembered the Revolution as a popular movement and celebrated the agency of ordinary citizens. White women and African Americans emphasized the revolutionaries' egalitarian ideals, which they appropriated and invoked to condemn the most egregious inequalities of their own times. Other Americans questioned the nationalistic premises that lay at the core of many revolutionary commemorations. While most Americans agreed that the Revolution was worth celebrating, they disagreed profoundly about how Americans should remember the revolutionary era and interpret its significance.

Paradoxically, as the nation created as a result of the Revolution became well established, state and local loyalties inspired claims for revolutionary glory that undermined or at least competed with those of the nation. Politicians and boosters from Massachusetts or Virginia, for example, asserted that their state was the true birthplace of the republic because its citizens had been foremost in the drive for independence. In 1819, some North Carolinians embellished their own revolutionary history, claiming not only that the Scots-Irish Presbyterians of their own Mecklenburg County had formally declared their independence from Great Britain on 20 May 1775 but that Jefferson later plagiarized whole passages from the so-called Mecklenburg Declaration. While the Mecklenburg Resolves of 31 May 1775 were genuine, scholars have long since discredited the invented tradition of the Mecklenburg Declaration of Independence, which expressed state and ethnic pride and touted the sturdy Carolina yeomen as equal to or even surpassing in patriotism the much-lauded gentlemen of Virginia.

Other early nineteenth-century Americans also criticized the patrician bias of most military commemorations. Particularly instructive is the case of John Paulding, Isaac Van Wart, and David Williams, three young New York militiamen from families of modest means, who in 1780 had captured Major John André, a British spy in league with the traitor Benedict Arnold. An officer and a gentleman, André had been romanticized by his American counterparts and their descendants as a tragic hero, an honorable man whose regrettable execution was an unavoidable necessity of war. In 1817, one of André's captors petitioned Congress for a supplemental pension, only to be dismissed as a mercenary rogue by the major's patrician admirers. The incident set off a heated debate on the nature of revolutionary patriotism: who deserved to be honored as patriots and heroes of the Revolution? Did humble men, such as André's captors, deserve commemoration?

One answer to these questions, popularized by a new generation of historians, imagined the great and undifferentiated people of America following exemplary leaders intrepidly along the road to independence and democracy. George Bancroft's popular and intensely nationalistic ten-volume *History of the United States* (1834–74) told the story of American nationhood as the fulfillment of a providential plan. Americans, Bancroft asserted, were divinely destined for independence and democracy, and their history was best understood as progress toward those objectives. Bancroft was a Jacksonian Democrat from Massachusetts, and his own political philosophy shaped his interpretation of the Revolution. For Bancroft, ordinary people were the driving force behind the Revolution, but they became so by following leaders whose honor, courage, and vigor enabled them to do great deeds and to personify the character of incipient American democracy. In Bancroft's *History*, all real Americans were patriots and all patriots were white men who had enough agency to oppose tyranny but enough wisdom to defer to the natural aristocracy.

Bancroft's romantic nationalism belied not only the conflicts of the revolutionary era but also contemporary contests over public memory of the Revolution and hence the meaning and purpose of the American republic. Often abetted by politicians seeking the votes of newly enfranchised masses, efforts to reformulate the Revolution as a popular movement soon challenged the consensual narratives of historians and patrician Fourth of July orators. In New York, workingmen and yeomen farmers pressed for recognition of Major André's captors as patriotic exemplars. In so doing, they sought to make ordinary citizens admirable and active participants in the story of American nationhood and independence. In Boston, an assertive labor movement revived public memory of the destruction of the tea in Boston harbor in 1773, an incident then known as the "Boston Tea Party" only in the oral culture of the city's lower orders. Local elites had excised the tea incident from public memory in their efforts to tell the story of an orderly and respectable revolution that could legitimate order, respectability, and patrician rule in the postrevolutionary era. In the 1830s, workingmen reclaimed and publicly promoted the story of the Tea Party to demonstrate both the radicalism of the Revolution and the agency of ordinary citizens. Although elite Bostonians eventually appropriated the Tea Party and adapted it to their purposes, urban workers increasingly infused the Fourth of July with a class-specific message of liberation and equality.

Focusing on the unfulfilled ideals of the Declaration of Independence, disenfranchised Americans also interpreted the Revolution as a struggle for liberty and equality as they pursued their agendas for egalitarian reform in the early nineteenth century. Excluded from white Fourth of July celebrations and suffering countless other forms of discrimination, free African Americans devised their own civic calendar, celebrating the anniversaries of the abolition of the slave trade, Haitian independence, and, after 1834, the end of slavery in the British West Indies. But black and white abolitionists also invoked the egalitarian legacy of the Revolution to argue that slavery was illegitimate in the world the revolutionaries made. Citing the Declaration of Independence and using the language of natural rights, they challenged those who were complicit in slavery to confront their hypocrisy and be true to the supposedly noble ideals of those who had toppled British tyranny and founded the republic. Abolitionists also promoted the escaped slave Crispus Attucks as a legitimate American hero, urging the erection of a monument to commemorate him and the other victims of the Boston Massacre and decrying the hypocrisy of those who doggedly opposed them until the 1880s.

White women's involvement in the construction of public memory was more complicated, in part because they occupied a more ambiguous position in relation to the nation and the polity than did African Americans. At civic celebrations, white ladies typically were spectators, present but nonetheless relegated to the sidelines as admirers of parading militia. Similarly, if public memory of the Revolution included the participation of women at all, it mainly featured stereotypes of frail ladies being victimized by crude enemies or tearfully sending valiant soldiers off to battle. By the 1840s, the first historians of American women—most notably Elizabeth Ellet—were inserting white women into the historical narrative of the Revolution as patriotic mothers, wives, and daughters. Reflecting prevailing gender conventions of the times, these characterizations could afford white women indirect influence in public life but not agency in the world beyond their households. Around the same time, however, the first American feminists asserted such agency and invoked the rhetoric and ideals of the Revolution to support their demands for rights. In 1848, Elizabeth Cady Stanton's "Declaration of Sentiments," modeled on Jefferson's Declaration of Independence, asserted the equality of all men and women and chastised American men as tyrants who violated women's unalienable rights.

Most Americans, of course, probably did not regard equality as the Revolution's chief objective, and, if they did, they interpreted it as applicable only to white men. As proslavery southerners became an increasingly alienated minority in national politics, they commemorated the Revolution as an assertion of independence from a tyrannous central power, an interpretation they used to justify secession from the Union in 1861. Some antebellum southerners deemed the Declaration of Independence an expression of fuzzy-headed metaphysics that were extraneous to the Revolution's real meaning. Northerners were more receptive to the Declaration's ideals, but most who supported the Union during the Civil War did so less to oppose slavery than to defend majoritarian democracy, which had been subverted by the determination of the southern minority to expand slave labor into the western territories. While some white northerners disliked slavery, nearly all feared and dreaded the political clout of southern slaveholding interests— ominously known as the "Slave Power"—which sought to nationalize slavery to the detriment of free white labor. Abraham Lincoln concluded that chattel slavery was ultimately incompatible with any definition of human equality and that the Declaration of Independence stated the egalitarian ideals of a still-unfinished revolution. He subtly tried to convince Americans to accept his understanding of the Revolution and of America's unfolding destiny in some of his most famous and compelling orations.

In 1776, most Americans rejected their inherited status as subjects of King George III, but they did not immediately assume a new identity. With most of their colonial history irrelevant or extraneous to the process of identity formation, Americans looked to the Revolution for a usable past, an interpretation of their origins and ideals that could serve their programmatic ends in the present and the future. Although nearly all Americans could admire and cherish the attributes and achievements of revolutionary icons such as Washington, remembering the Revolution was a contested process once they went beyond such simple and self-congratulatory formulations. The stakes were high. For, as both Lincoln and his critics well understood, how Americans remembered the Revolution could affect the most fundamental features of their political and social lives.

DOCUMENT 1

"Adams and Jefferson Are No More" (1826)

Daniel Webster was born in 1782, too late to have witnessed or participated in the American Revolution. As an orator, however, Webster played a major role in constructing public memory of the Revolution and the great and famous men who led it. In 1800, at the age of eighteen, Webster gave his first public address, a Fourth of July oration that celebrated the achievements of the Revolution and the virtues of Washington, who had died a few months earlier. By 1826, as a member of Congress from Massachusetts, Webster had become famous for his fine oratory, and he was chosen to give a combined eulogy in Boston for Adams and Jefferson, both of whom had died on the fiftieth anniversary of American independence.[1]

Questions to consider:

1. What was the purpose of this oration? What lesson did Webster hope his listeners would learn from the lives and deaths of Adams and Jefferson?
2. Why did Webster deem the American Revolution "one of the greatest events in human history"?

Adams and Jefferson are no more . . . On our fiftieth anniversary, the great day of national jubilee, in the very hour of public rejoicing, in the midst of echoing and reechoing voices of thanksgiving, while their own names were on all tongues, they took their flight together to the world of spirits. . . .

Adams and Jefferson, I have said, are no more. As human beings, indeed, they are no more. They are no more, as in 1776, bold and fearless advocates of independence; no more, as at subsequent periods, the head of the government; no more, as we have recently seen them, aged and venerable objects of admiration and regard. They are no more. They are dead. But how little is there of the great and good which can die! To their country they yet live, and live forever. They live in all that perpetuates the remembrance of men on earth; in the recorded proofs of their own great actions, in the offspring of their intellect, in the deep-engraved lines of public gratitude, and in the respect and homage of mankind. They live in their example; and they live, emphatically, and will live, in the influence which their lives and efforts, their principles and opinions, now exercise, and will continue to exercise, on the affairs of men, not only in their own country but throughout the civilized world. . . .

And now, fellow-citizens, let us not retire from this occasion without a deep and solemn conviction of the duties which have developed upon us. This lovely land, this glorious liberty, these benign institutions, the dear purchase of our fathers, are ours; ours to enjoy, ours to preserve, ours to transmit. Generations past and generations to come hold us responsible for this sacred trust. Our fathers, from behind, admonish us, with their anxious paternal voices; posterity calls out to us, from the bosom of the future; the world turns hither its solicitous eyes; all, conjure us to act wisely, and faithfully, in the relation which we sustain.

We can never, indeed, pay the debt which is upon us; but by virtue, by morality, by religion, by the cultivation of every good principle and every good habit, we may hope to enjoy the blessing, through our day, and to leave it unimpaired to our children. Let us feel deeply how much of what we are and of what we possess we owe to this liberty, and to these institutions of government. Nature has, indeed, given us a soil which yields boun-teously to the hand of industry, the mighty and fruitful ocean is before us, and the skies over our heads shed health and vigor. But what are lands, and seas, and skies, to civilized man, without society, without knowledge, with-out morals, without religious culture; and how can these be enjoyed, in all their extent and all their excellence, but under the protection of wise institu-tions and a free government? Fellow-citizens, there is not one of us, there is not one of us here present, who does not, at this moment, and at every mo-ment, experience, in his own condition, and in the condition of those most near and dear to him, the influence and the benefits, of this liberty and these institutions. Let us then acknowledge the blessing, let us feel it deeply and powerfully, let us cherish a strong affection for it, and resolve to maintain and perpetuate it. The blood of our fathers, let it not have been shed in vain; the great hope of posterity, let it not be blasted.

DOCUMENT 2

"All Men and Women Are Created Equal" (1848)

In July 1848, the first American women's rights convention met in Seneca Falls, New York. About 300 people, including forty men, attended the convention, which opened with a reading of Elizabeth Cady Stanton's "Declaration of Sentiments," a document modeled on the Declaration of Independence.[2] Stanton, a veteran of both the temper-ance and antislavery movements, also drafted eleven resolutions, claiming various eco-nomic, social, and political rights for women, including the right to vote. Although widely opposed and ridiculed, women's rights advocates held conventions each year thereafter until the Civil War.

Questions to consider:

1. How did Stanton attempt to shape the public memory of the Revolu-tion? Why did she choose to parody the Declaration of Independence?
2. Which of her criticisms of American men were the most radical?

3. How did Stanton define "life, liberty, and the pursuit of happiness"? How do you think her definitions compared to those of the revolutionary generation?

When, in the course of human events, it becomes necessary for one portion of the family of man to assume among the people of the earth a position different from that which they have hitherto occupied, but one to which the laws of nature and of nature's God entitle them, a decent respect to the opinions of mankind requires that they should declare the causes that impel them to such a course.

We hold these truths to be self-evident: that all men and women are created equal; that they are endowed by their Creator with certain inalienable rights; that among these are life, liberty, and the pursuit of happiness; that to secure these rights governments are instituted, deriving their just powers from the consent of the governed. Whenever any form of government becomes destructive of these ends, it is the right of those who suffer from it to refuse allegiance to it, and to insist upon the institution of a new government, laying its foundation on such principles, and organizing its powers in such form, as to them shall seem most likely to effect their safety and happiness. Prudence, indeed, will dictate that governments long established should not be changed for light and transient causes; and, accordingly, all experience has shown that mankind are more disposed to suffer, while evils are sufferable, than to right themselves by abolishing the forms to which they were accustomed. But when a long train of abuses and usurpations, pursuing invariably the same object, evinces a design to reduce them under absolute despotism, it is their duty to throw off such government and to provide new guards for their future security. Such has been the patient sufferance of the women under this government, and such is now the necessity which constrains them to demand the equal station to which they are entitled.

The history of mankind is a history of repeated injuries and usurpations on the part of man toward woman, having in direct object the establishment of an absolute tyranny over her. To prove this, let facts be submitted to a candid world.

He has never permitted her to exercise her inalienable right to the elective franchise.

He has compelled her to submit to law in the formation of which she had no voice.

He has withheld from her rights which are given to the most ignorant and degraded men, both natives and foreigners.

Having deprived her of this first right as a citizen, the elective franchise, thereby leaving her without representation in the halls of legislation, he has oppressed her on all sides.

He has made her, if married, in the eye of the law, civilly dead.

He has taken from her all right in property, even to the wages she earns.

He has made her morally, an irresponsible being, as she can commit many crimes with impunity, provided they be done in the presence of her husband. In the covenant of marriage, she is compelled to promise obedience to her husband, he becoming, to all intents and purposes, her master—the law giving him power to deprive her of her liberty and to administer chastisement.

He has so framed the laws of divorce, as to what shall be the proper causes and, in case of separation, to whom the guardianship of the children shall be given, as to be wholly regardless of the happiness of the women—the law, in all cases, going upon a false supposition of the supremacy of man and giving all power into his hands.

After depriving her of all rights as a married woman, if single and the owner of property, he has taxed her to support a government which recognizes her only when her property can be made profitable to it.

He has monopolized nearly all the profitable employments, and from those she is permitted to follow, she receives but a scanty remuneration. He closes against her all the avenues to wealth and distinction which he considers most honorable to himself. As a teacher of theology, medicine, or law, she is not known.

He has denied her the facilities for obtaining a thorough education, all colleges being closed against her.

He allows her in church, as well as state, but a subordinate position, claiming apostolic authority for her exclusion from the ministry, and, with some exceptions, from any public participation in the affairs of the church.

He has created a false public sentiment by giving to the world a different code of morals for men and women, by which moral delinquencies which exclude women from society are not only tolerated but deemed of little account in man.

He has usurped the prerogative of Jehovah himself, claiming it as his right to assign for her a sphere of action, when that belongs to her conscience and to her God.

He has endeavored, in every way that he could, to destroy her confidence in her own powers, to lessen her self-respect, and to make her willing to lead a dependent and abject life.

Now, in view of this entire disfranchisement of one-half the people of this country, their social and religious degradation, in view of the unjust laws above mentioned, and because women do feel themselves aggrieved, oppressed, and fraudulently deprived of their most sacred rights, we insist that they have immediate admission to all the rights and privileges which belong to them as citizens of the United States.

DOCUMENT 3

The Domestication of Deborah Sampson (1848)

Elizabeth Ellet's The Women of the American Revolution *recounted the stories of 168 women, most of whom were wives or daughters of famous men. To her credit, Ellet also included a biographical sketch of Deborah Sampson, a cross-dressing Continental soldier, despite the fact that Sampson clearly did not fit her own ideal of American womanhood.[3] The first two of three volumes of Ellet's pioneering work appeared in 1848, the same year the women's rights convention met in Seneca Falls. A native of New England, Ellet lived most of her adult life in South Carolina. She never seems to have criticized slavery, and she opposed the movement for women's rights.*

Questions to consider:

1. Why do you think Ellet wrote *The Women of the American Revolution* ? How did she envision women's ideal role, even in times of crisis?
2. Why did Ellet include a sketch of Deborah Sampson in a work over-whlemingly dominated by stories of more conventional women? What moral lesson did Ellet expect readers to draw from Sampson's story?

Deborah Samson was the youngest child of poor parents, who lived in the county of Plymouth, Massachusetts. Their poverty, rendered hopeless by pernicious habits, was the least of the evils suffered by the unfortunate children. Charity interposed to rescue them from the effects of evil example; they were removed from their parents, and placed in different families, where a prospect was afforded of their receiving proper care and instruction to fit them for maintaining themselves when arrived at a suitable age. . . .

Meantime, the Revolutionary struggle had commenced . . . [and] the zeal which had urged the men to quit their homes for the battle-field, found its way to a female bosom; Deborah felt as if she would shrink from no effort or sacrifice in the cause which awakened all her enthusiasm. She entered with the most lively interest into every plan for the relief of the army, and bitterly regretted that as a woman she could do no more, and that she had not the privilege of a man, of shedding her blood for her country.

There is no reason to believe that any consideration foreign to the purest patriotism, impelled her to the resolution of assuming male attire, and enlisting in the army. She could have been actuated by no desire of gaining applause; for the private manner in which she quitted her home and associates, entrusting no one with her design, subjected her to surmises of a painful nature; and the careful preservation of her secret during the period of her military service, exonerates her from the least suspicion of having been urged to the step by an imprudent attachment. It is very likely that her youthful imagination was kindled by the rumor of brave deeds . . . It must be borne in mind, too, that she was restrained by no consideration that could interfere with the project. Alone in the world, there were few to inquire what had become of her, and still fewer to care for her fate. She felt herself accountable to no human being. . . .

She now pursued her way to the American army, where she presented herself, in October 1778, as a young country man anxious to join his efforts to those of his countrymen in their endeavors to oppose the common enemy . . . Distrusting her own constancy, and resolute to continue in the service, notwithstanding any change of her inclination, she enlisted for the whole term of the war. She was received and enrolled in the army by the name of Robert Shirtliffe. She was one of the first volunteers in the company of Captain Nathan Thayer of Medway, Massachusetts; and as the young recruit appeared to have no home or connections, the Captain gave her a home in his family until his company should be full, when they were to join the main army. . . .

For three years our heroine appeared in the character of a soldier, being part of the time employed as a waiter in the family of Colonel Patterson. During this time, and in both situations, her exemplary conduct, and the fidelity with which her duties were performed, gained the approbation and confidence of the officers. She was a volunteer in several hazardous enterprizes, and was twice wounded, the first time by a sword cut on the left side of the head. Many were the adventures she passed through; as she herself would often say volumes might be filled with them. Sometimes placed unavoidably in circumstances in which she feared detection, she nevertheless escaped without the least suspicion being awakened among her comrades. The soldiers were in the habit of calling her "Molly," in playful allusion to her want of a beard; but not one of them ever dreamed that the gallant youth fighting by their side was in reality a female.

About four months after her first wound she received another severe one, being shot through the shoulder. Her first emotion when the ball entered she described to be a sickening terror at the probability that her sex would be discovered. She felt that death on the battlefield were preferable to the shame that would overwhelm her, and ardently prayed that the wound might close her earthly campaign. But, strange as it may seem, she escaped this time also unsuspected; and soon recovering her strength, was able again to take her place at the post of duty, and in the deadly conflict. Her immunity was not, however, destined long to continue—she was seized with a brain fever, then prevalent among the soldiers. For the few days that reason struggled against the disease, her sufferings were indescribable; and most terrible of all was the dread lest consciousness should desert her, and the secret she had guarded so carefully be revealed to those around her. She was carried to the hospital, and there could only ascribe her escape to the number of patients, and the negligent manner in which they were attended. Her case was considered a hopeless one, and she perhaps received less attention on this account. One day the physician of the hospital, inquiring "How is Robert?" received from the nurse in attendance the answer "Poor Bob is gone." The doctor went to the bed, and taking the hand of the youth supposed dead, found that the pulse was still feebly beating; attempting to place his hand on the heart, he perceived that a bandage was fastened tightly round the breast. This was removed, and to his utter astonishment he discovered a female patient where he had least expected one! . . .

After the termination of the war, [Deborah Sampson] married Benjamin Gannett, of Sharon. When Washington was President, she received a letter inviting Robert Shirtliffe, or rather Mrs. Gannett, to visit the seat of government. Congress was then in session, and during her stay at the capital, a bill was passed granting her a pension in addition to certain lands, which she was to receive as an acknowledgement for her services to the country in a military capacity. She was invited to the houses several of the officers, and to parties given in the city; attentions which manifested the high estimation in which she was there held.

In 1805 she was living in comfortable circumstances, the wife of a respectable farmer, and the mother of three fine, intelligent children, the eldest of whom was a youth of nineteen . . . It is but a few years since she passed from the stage of human life. The career to which her patriotism urged her, cannot be commended as an example; but her exemplary conduct after the first step will go far to plead her excuse.

DOCUMENT 4

Crispus Attucks and the Quest for African-American Citizenship (1851)

While Boston's elite preferred to remember the Revolution as a decorous and legalistic defense of traditional rights and liberties, others celebrated its egalitarian legacy. In 1851, black and white opponents of slavery began lobbying for the erection of a monument to honor Crispus Attucks, the escaped slave who was the first casualty of the Boston Massacre. William Cooper Nell, a black abolitionist and historian, penned this response to the state legislature's rejection of the proposed monument.[4] Finally, in 1888, a monument honoring Attucks and the Massacre's four other victims was erected on Boston Common, despite the protests of both the Massachusetts Historical Society and the New England Genealogical Society.

Questions to consider:

1. How was the memory of Crispus Attucks and the other victims of the Boston Massacre perpetuated, despite the elite's best efforts to suppress it?
2. Why did state legislators prefer to commemorate the death of Christopher Snyder (or Sneider)? Did other issues besides race influence this debate?
3. Describe the tone of William Cooper Nell's essay. Why did he equate opponents of the Attucks monument with the Tories of the Revolutionary era?

On the fifth of March, 1851, a petition was presented to the Massachusetts Legislature, asking an appropriation of $1,500 for erecting a monument to the memory of Crispus Attucks, the first martyr in the Boston Massacre, of March 5th, 1770. The matter was referred to the Committee on Military Affairs, who granted a hearing of the petitioners, but finally submitted an adverse report, on the ground that a boy, Christopher Snyder, was previously killed. Admitting this fact, (which was the result of a very different scene from that in which Attucks fell) does not offset the claims of Attucks, and those who made the fifth of March famous in our annals—the day which history selects as the dawn of the American Revolution. . . .

Attucks was killed by [Private] Montgomery, one of Captain Preston's soldiers. He had been foremost in resisting, and was first slain; as proof of front and close engagement, received two balls, one in each breast.

John Adams, counsel for the soldiers, admitted that Attucks appeared to have undertaken to be the hero of the night, and to lead the army with banners. Him and Caldwell, not being residents of Boston, were both buried in Faneuil Hall. The citizens generally participated in the funeral solemnities.

The *Boston Transcript*, of March 7, 1851, published an anonymous correspondence disparaging the whole affair, denouncing Crispus Attucks as a

The Boston Massacre Monument.   Commissioned in 1887 after decades of lobbying, this monument was unveiled just one year later. What message did the erection of such a monument on Boston Common convey about the Revolution and its significance? Why do you suppose this monument to the Boston Massacre became known almost universally as the "Crispus Attucks Monument"? Source: Courtesy of the Library of Congress, Washington, D.C.

very firebrand of disorder and sedition the most conspicuous, inflammatory, and uproarious of the misguided populace, and who, if he had not fallen a martyr, would richly have deserved hanging as an incendiary. If the leader Attucks deserved the epithets above applied, is it not a legitimate inference that the citizens who followed on are included, and hence, should swing in his company on the gallows? If the leader and his patriot band were misguided, the distinguished orators who, in after days, commemorated the fifth of March, must, indeed, have been misguided, and with them the masses who were inspired by their eloquence. For John Hancock in 1774, invoked the injured shades of Maverick, Gray, Caldwell, *Attucks*, and Carr. . . .

In judging, then, the morals of those who launched the American Revolution, we should not take counsel from the Tories of that or the present day, but rather the approving eulogy of . . . Hancock. . . .

Welcome, then be every taunt that such correspondents have flung at Attucks and his company, as the best evidence of their merits and strongest claim on our gratitude. Envy and the foe do not labor to abuse any but prominent champions of a cause.

The rejection of this petition was to be expected, if we accept the axiom that a colored man never gets justice done him in the United States, except by mistake. The petitioners only asked for that justice, and that the name of Crispus Attucks be surrounded with the same emblems constantly appropriated by a grateful country to other gallant Americans.

During the Revolutionary War, public opinion was so strongly in favor of the abolition of slavery, that in some of the country towns, votes were passed in town meetings that they would have no slaves among them; and that they would not exact, of masters any bonds, for the maintenance of liberated blacks, should they become incapable of supporting themselves.

DOCUMENT 5

"What, to the American Slave, Is Your 4th of July?" (1852)

Frederick Douglass was born a slave in Maryland in 1818. Twenty years later, he escaped slavery, settling first in New York and then in Massachusetts. Douglass soon became a rising star in the abolitionist movement, and in 1845 he published his Narrative of the Life of Frederick Douglass, *which chronicled the horrors of slavery and his dramatic flight to freedom. An influential editor, writer, and public speaker, Douglass persistently challenged white Americans to live up to the ideals of their*

Revolution.[5] In this Fourth of July oration, which he delivered in 1852 in Rochester, New York, he appropriated the Revolution and used it powerfully to promote the abolitionist cause.

Questions to consider:

1. To whom did Douglass address this speech? Why do you suppose he was invited to address this Independence Day gathering?
2. What was the main argument of Douglass's oration? Was his interpretation of the causes and objectives of the Revolution accurate or invented? What techniques or evidence did he use to persuade his audience of the validity of his views?
3. Why do you suppose that Douglass was the most influential of the black abolitionists among northern whites?

Fellow-citizens, pardon me, allow me to ask, why am I called upon to speak here today? What have I, or those I represent, to do with your national independence? Are the great principles of political freedom and of natural justice, embodied in that Declaration of Independence, extended to us? And am I, therefore, called upon to bring our humble offering to the national altar, and to confess the benefits and express devout gratitude for the blessings resulting from your independence to us?

Would to God, both for your sakes and ours, that an affirmative answer could be truthfully returned to these questions! Then would my task be light, and my burden easy and delightful . . . But, such is not the state of the case. I say it with a sad sense of the disparity between us. I am not included within the pale of this glorious anniversary! Your high independence only reveals the immeasurable distance between us. The blessings in which you, this day, rejoice, are not enjoyed in common. The rich inheritance of justice, liberty, prosperity and independence, bequeathed by your fathers, is shared by you, not by me. The sunlight that brought life and healing to you, has brought stripes and death to me. This Fourth of July is yours, not mine. You may rejoice, I must mourn. . . .

Fellow-citizens; above your national, tumultuous joy, I hear the mournful wail of millions whose chains, heavy and grievous yesterday, are, today, rendered more intolerable by the jubilee shouts that reach them . . . To forget them, to pass lightly over their wrongs, and to chime in with the popular theme, would be treason most scandalous and shocking, and would make me a reproach before God and the world. My subject, then fellow-citizens, is AMERICAN SLAVERY. I shall see, this day, and its popular characteristics, from the slave's point of view. Standing, there, identified with the American bondman, making his wrongs mine, I do not hesitate to declare, with all my soul, that the character and conduct of this nation never looked blacker to me than on this 4th of July! Whether we turn to the declarations of the past, or to the professions of the present, the conduct of the nation seems equally hideous and revolting. America is false to the past, false to the present, and solemnly binds herself to be false to the future. . . .

What, to the American slave, is your 4th of July? I answer: a day that reveals to him, more than all other days in the year, the gross injustice and cruelty to which he is the constant victim. To him, your celebration is a sham; your boasted liberty, an unholy license; your national greatness, swelling vanity; your sounds of rejoicing are empty and heartless; your denunciations of tyrants, brass fronted impudence; your shouts of liberty and equality, hollow mockery; your prayers and hymns, your sermons and thanksgivings, with all your religious parade, and solemnity, are, to him, mere bombast, fraud, deception, impiety, and hypocrisy—a thin veil to cover up crimes which would disgrace a nation of savages. There is not a nation on the earth guilty of practices, more shocking and bloody, than are the people of these United States, at this very hour.

DOCUMENT 6

The Age of Romantic Nationalism (c.1860)

George Bancroft, like David Ramsay and Mercy Otis Warren, believed that history served a didactic purpose. The lessons Bancroft hoped to teach his readers, however, differed from those offered by earlier historians of the Revolution and the founding of the American republic. Writing in an age of exuberant nationalism complicated by sectional, class, and party divisions, Bancroft sought to explain the significance of the American nation and its place in the unfolding providential design of human history.[6] Trained in Germany in the latest techniques of historical scholarship, Bancroft did extensive research in primary sources, and he believed that his History of the United States *was an objective historical narrative. Bancroft published eight of ten volumes of his* History *before the Civil War.*

Questions to consider:

1. What, according to Bancroft were the causes of the Revolution?
2. Who were the actors in his story and what were their respective roles? Did Bancroft's account include all the inhabitants of revolutionary America? Who did he exclude? Why?

3. What portions of Bancroft's narrative seem reasonably accurate? What parts are less persuasive? How could Bancroft insist that he was writing objective history?

The hour of the American revolution was come. The people of the continent obeyed one general impulse, as the earth in spring listens to the command of nature and without the appearance of effort bursts into life. The movement was quickened, even when it was most resisted; and its fiercest adversaries worked with the most effect for its fulfillment. Standing in manifold relations with the governments, the culture, and the experience of the past, the Americans seized as their peculiar inheritance the traditions of liberty. Beyond any other nation, they had made trial of the possible forms of popular representation, and respected individual conscience and thought. The resources of the country in agriculture and commerce, forests and fisheries, mines and materials for manufactures, were so diversified and complete that their development could neither be guided nor circumscribed by a government beyond the ocean. The numbers, purity, culture, industry, and daring of its inhabitants proclaimed the existence of a people rich in creative energy, and ripe for institutions of their own.

They refused to acknowledge even to themselves the hope that was swelling within them, and yet in their political aspirations they deduced from universal principles a bill of rights, as old as creation and as wide as humanity. The idea of freedom had always revealed itself at least to a few of the wise whose prophetic instincts were quickened by love of their kind, and its growth can be traced in the tendency of the ages. In America, it was the breath of life to the people. For the first time it found a region and a race where it could be professed with the earnestness of an indwelling conviction, and be defended with the enthusiasm that had marked no wars but those for religion. When all Europe slumbered over questions of liberty, a band of exiles, keeping watch by night, heard the glad tidings which promised the political regeneration of the world. A revolution, unexpected in the moment of its coming, but prepared by glorious forerunners, grew naturally and necessarily out of the series of past events by the formative principle of a living belief. . . .

The heart of Jefferson in writing the declaration [of independence], and of congress in adopting it, beat for all humanity; the assertion of right was made for the entire world of mankind and all coming generations, without any exception whatever; for the proposition which admits of exceptions can never be self-evident. As it was put forth in the name of the ascendant people of that time, it was sure to make the circuit of the world, passing everywhere through the despotic countries of Europe; and the astonished nations, as they read that all men are created equal, started out of their lethargy, like those who have been exiles from childhood, when they suddenly hear the dimly remembered accents of their mother tongue. . . .

The declaration was not only the announcement of the birth of a people, but the establishment of a national government; a most imperfect one, it is true, but still a government, in conformity with the limited constituent powers which each colony had conferred upon its delegates in congress. The war was no longer a civil war; Britain was become to the United States a foreign country. Every former subject of the British king in the thirteen colonies now owed primary allegiance to the dynasty of the people, and became a citizen of the new republic; except in this, everything remained as before; every man retained his rights; the colonies did not dissolve into a state of nature, nor did the new people undertake a social revolution. The management of the internal police and government was carefully reserved to the separate states, which could, each for itself, enter upon the career of domestic reforms. But the states which were henceforth independent of Britain were not independent of one another: the United States of America, presenting themselves to mankind as one people, assumed powers over war, peace, foreign alliances, and commerce.

DOCUMENT 7

The Fourth of July:
A Confederate Holiday? (1861)

Most southerners went to war in 1861 believing that they, not Lincoln and the Unionists, were the true heirs of the spirit of the Revolution. On 20 May 1861, the eighty-fifth anniversary of the mythic Mecklenburg Declaration of Independence, North Carolina seceded from the Union. About six weeks later, the pro-secession Raleigh Register *argued that citizens of the southern Confederacy should still celebrate the Fourth of July and the ideals for which it stood.*[7]

Questions to consider:

1. How did this North Carolina Confederate explain the meaning and purpose of the American Revolution?
2. What were the "principles of 1776" he wished to honor?

3. Why did this North Carolinian claim George Washington as a southern hero, instead of some other revolutionary worthy? In your opinion, which side more fully represented "Washington's Principles" in 1861, the Union or the Confederacy?

※◎ ◎※

Tomorrow will be the Fourth of July, and as yet we have heard of no note of preparation made for its celebration in any southern community. A difference of opinion exists among some of the editors of the country as to whether the anniversary of the Declaration of American Independence should in future be celebrated in the Confederate States. We cannot see any reason why the birth day of liberty should be permitted to pass unheeded wherever liberty has its votaries. The principles asserted on the Fourth Day of July, 1776, were those of man's competency for self-government, and the South in her late act of separation from the North has but re-asserted those principles. The conduct of the North in trampling the principles of 1776 underfoot, and throwing ashes on the memory of its forefathers, is no sufficient reason for a failure by the South to recognize and celebrate the Fourth of July as the anniversary of the most glorious human event in the history of mankind.

It is too late now to make arrangements for a celebration, but we hope in future that proper respect will be paid to the day. The accursed Yankees are welcome to the exclusive use of their "Doodle," but let the South hold on tenaciously to Washington's March and Washington's Principles, and on every recurring anniversary of their promulgation, reassert the great principles of Human Liberty.

DOCUMENT 8

"The Revolutions of 1776 and 1861 Contrasted" (1863)

George Fitzhugh

Not all secessionists emphasized the similarities between the colonists' withdrawal from the British Empire and the South's secession from the Union, nor did they all deny or ignore the implicit challenge that the egalitarian language of the Declaration of Independence posed for the legitimacy of chattel slavery. George Fitzhugh of Virginia was an

insightful but eccentric proslavery extremist, who believed that all labor should be en-
slaved to promote social stability. He bemoaned the modern values of capitalist competi-
tion and individualism, which destroyed organic social relations and undermined social
harmony. In 1863, Fitzhugh published this essay, in which he argued that the "Southern
Revolution of 1861" was better than—and not similar to—that of 1776.[8]

Questions to consider:

1. What was Fitzhugh's opinion of human nature? What was his assessment of the character and achievements of the revolutionary generation?
2. What did he believe were the causes and significance of the American Revolution?
3. What did he believe were the causes and significance of the "Southern Revolution of 1861"? What did he believe would be the Civil War's final outcome?

The Revolution of '76 had nothing dramatic, nothing novel, nothing grand about it. Every child and every chicken, that, getting old enough and strong enough to take care or itself, quits its parents and sets up for itself, is quite as singular and admirable a spectacle, as that of the thirteen adult states of America solemnly resolving to cut loose from the state of pupilage and dependence on their parent, England, and ever thereafter to assert and enjoy the rights of independent manhood. It was an exceedingly vulgar, commonplace affair; it had nothing poetic or dramatic about it . . . All the artillery in the world, fired simultaneously, could not make the birth or the weaning of a baby or a nation a grand or imposing event. Either occurrence is decidedly vulgar and common-place, and . . . fourth of July orations . . . endeavoring to celebrate and dramatise them, only serve to render them more ridiculous.

All the bombastic absurdities in our Declaration of Independence about the inalienable rights of man, had about as much to do with the occasion, as would a sermon or an oration on the teething of a child or the kittening of a cat. . . It would have been well for us, if the seemingly pompous inanities of the Declaration of Independence, of the Virginia Bill of Rights and the [Statute for Religious Freedom] had remained dead letters. But they had a strength, a vitality and a meaning in them, utterly uncomprehended by their charlatanic, half-learned, pedantic authors, which rendered them most potent engines of destruction. Our institutions, state and federal, imported from England, where they had grown up naturally and imperceptibly, and adapted to our peculiar circumstances by like natural growth and accretion, might, and would, have lasted for very many ages, had not silly, thoughtless, half-informed, speculative charlatans, like Jefferson, succeeded in basing them on such inflammable and explosive [doctrines]. . . .

The Revolution of '76 was, in its action, an exceedingly natural and conservative affair; it was only the false and unnecessary theories invoked to justify it that were radical, agrarian and anarchical. The Fathers of the Republic most officiously and unwisely rested the splendid political edifice which they erected, on powder-cask abstractions . . . The North is still following out most vigorously, and to their ultimate conclusions, the doctrines of Locke, Adam Smith, and the Republican sages of the Revolution of 1776. They are demonstrating, in their every-day practice, that the tendency of that Revolution was towards dislocation, disruption, infidelity, sensuality, agrarianism, and anarchy.

We now come to the Southern Revolution of 1861, which we maintain was reactionary and conservative . . . a solemn protest against the doctrines of natural liberty, human equality and the social contract, as taught by Locke and the American sages of 1776, and an equally solemn protest against the doctrines of Adam Smith, Franklin, . . . Tom Paine, and the rest of the infidel political economists who maintain that the world is too much governed . . . The reason of this new departure is that it was perceived that the doctrines of Jefferson and of the other illustrious Fathers of the Republic were being successfully employed to justify [the] abolition [of slavery] and to upset the whole social system of the South—besides, excluding her from equal or any participation in the public lands, most of which she had acquired against the protests of the North, that was now greedily and rapaciously seeking to monopolize them. . . .

Viewed in this aspect, and it is the only true one in which to view it, the Revolution of '61 is the grandest, most momentous event since the days of Luther and Calvin. The grandest in conception, and the grandest in action; for never did a people of the same numbers display such heroic courage and giant strength as have the people of the South in this revolutionary struggle . . . For we fight to vindicate the ways of God against the profane doctrines and schemes of charlatanic man.

DOCUMENT 9

Abraham Lincoln Interprets the Revolution (1863)

On 4 July 1863, the tide of the Civil War turned decisively against the Confederacy, as Union forces won major victories at Gettysburg, Pennsylvania, and Vicksburg, Mississippi. Three days later, in this brief impromptu speech, President Abraham Lincoln situated these military triumphs in the broader history of the republic, meditating on the meaning of the Revolution, the Fourth of July, and the principles they represented to Americans in the midst of civil war.[9]

Questions to consider:

1. What was the "glorious theme" of Lincoln's speech? What message did he seek to convey to his listeners?
2. Why did Lincoln not mention the word "slavery" in this speech, which he delivered six months after the enactment of the Emancipation Proclamation?
3. What did Lincoln see as the meaning of the Revolution? What did he see as the significance of the efforts to defeat the "gigantic rebellion"?

Fellow-Citizens:

I am very glad indeed to see you to-night, and yet I will not say I thank you for this call; but I do most sincerely thank Almighty God for the occasion on which you have called. How long ago is it?—eighty-odd years since, on the Fourth of July, for the first time in the history of the world, a nation, by its representatives, assembled and declared, as a self-evident truth, "that all men are created equal." That was the birthday of the United States of America. Since then the Fourth of July has had several very peculiar recognitions. The two men most distinguished in the framing and support of the Declaration were Thomas Jefferson and John Adams—the one having penned it, and the other sustained it the most forcibly in debate—the only two of the fifty-five who signed it that were elected Presidents of the United States. Precisely fifty years after they put their hands to the paper, it pleased Almighty God to take both from this stage of action. This was indeed an extraordinary and remarkable event in our history. Another President [James Monroe], five years after, was called from this stage of existence on the same day and month of the year; and now on this last Fourth of July just passed, when we have a gigantic rebellion, at the bottom of which is an effort to overthrow the principle that all men are created equal, we have the surrender of a most powerful position and army on that very day. And not only so, but in a succession of battles in Pennsylvania, near to us, through three days, so rapidly fought that they might be called one great battle, on the first, second, and third of the month of July; and on the fourth the cohorts of those who opposed the Declaration that all men are created equal "turned tail" and run. Gentlemen, this is a glorious theme, and the occasion for a speech, but I am not prepared to make one worthy of the occasion. I would like to speak in terms of praise due to the many brave officers and soldiers who have fought in the cause of the Union and liberties of their country from the beginning of the war. These are trying occasions, not only in success, but for the want of success. I dislike to mention the name of one single officer, lest I might do wrong to those I might forget. Recent events bring up glorious names, and particularly prominent ones; but these I will not mention. Having said this much, I will now take the music.

SUGGESTED READING FOR CHAPTER 14

BODNAR, JOHN. *Remaking America: Public Memory, Commemoration, and Patriotism in the Twentieth Century* (1992).

CRAY, ROBERT E., JR. "Major John André and the Three Captors: Class Dynamics and Revolutionary Memory Wars in the Early Republic, 1780–1831." *Journal of the Early Republic*, 17 (1997): 371–97.

DAVIS, SUSAN G. *Parades and Power: Street Theatre in Nineteenth-Century Philadelphia* (1986).

GILLIS, JOHN R., ed., *Commemorations: The Politics of National Identity* (1994).

KAMMEN, MICHAEL. *Mystic Chords of Memory: The Transformation of Tradition in American Culture* (1991).

———. *A Season of Youth: The American Revolution and the Historical Imagination* (1978).

LEE, JEAN B. "Historical Memory, Sectional Strife, and the American Mecca: Mount Vernon, 1785–1853." *Virginia Magazine of History and Biography*, 109 (2001): 255–300.

LOWENTHAL, DAVID. *The Past Is a Foreign Country* (1985).

MORGAN, EDMUND S. *The Meaning of Independence: George Washington, John Adams, Thomas Jefferson* (1978).

NEWMAN, SIMON P. *Parades and the Politics of the Street: Festive Culture in the Early American Republic* (1997).

TRAVERS, LEN. *Celebrating the Fourth: Independence Day and the Rites of Nationalism in the Early Republic* (1997).

WILLS, GARRY. *Lincoln at Gettysburg: The Words that Remade America* (1992).

YOUNG, ALFRED F. *The Shoemaker and the Tea Party: Memory and the American Revolution* (1999).

NOTES

[1]"Eulogy on Adams and Jefferson," 2 Aug. 1826, in B. F. Tefft, comp., *The Speeches of Daniel Webster* (New York, n.d.), 193–97, 208, 210, 214, 235–36.

[2]"Declaration of Sentiments," in Elizabeth Cady Stanton, et al., *History of Woman Suffrage*, 2 vols. (New York, 1881), 1: 70–73.

[3]"Deborah Samson," in Elizabeth F. Ellet, *The Women of the American Revolution*, 3 vols. (New York, 1848), 2: 124–31, 134–35.

[4]William C. Nell, *Services of Colored Americans, in the Wars of 1776 and 1812* (Boston, 1851), 5–7.

[5]Frederick Douglass, *Oration* (Rochester, N.Y., 1852), 14–16, 20.

[6]George Bancroft, *History of the United States of America, from the Discovery of the Continent*, 6 vols. (New York, 1883–85), 4: 3–4, 450, 452.

[7]"Fourth of July," *Raleigh Register*, 3 July 1861.

[8]George Fitzhugh, "The Revolutions of 1776 and 1861 Contrasted," *Southern Literary Messenger*, 37 (1863): 718–19, 722–23.

[9]"Response to a Serenade," 7 July 1863, in John G. Nicolay and John Hay, eds., *Complete Works of Abraham Lincoln*, 12 vols. (n.p., 1894), 9: 20–21.